FINDING THE RIGHT CHURCH

A Guide to Denomination Beliefs

FINDING THE RIGHT CHURCH

A Guide to Denomination Beliefs

by Shelly Steig

Finding the Right Church: A Guide to Denomination Beliefs
Copyright © 1997 by Shelly Steig
Published by World Bible Publishers, Inc.
Iowa Falls, IA 50126

Material from pp. 213–215 copyright 1994 by Concordia Publishing House. Used with permission.

Material from pp. 296–298 adapted from The Book of Discipline of the United Methodist Church, 1996. Copyright © 1996 by The United Methodist Publishing House. Adapted by permission.

"What Kind of Church Is This?" Copyright 1993 by Leroy Lawson. Standard Publishing Company. Used by permission.

Cover design by Barfuss Creative Services, Grand Rapids, MI.
Interior design by David C. Den Boer.
Typesetting by The Composing Room of Michigan, Inc., Grand Rapids, MI.
Edited by Heidi Venlet and Carol Ochs.

ISBN 0-529-10770-8

Library of Congress Catalog Card Number 97-060495

Printed in the United States of America.
2 3 4 5 6 7   01 00

Table of Contents

Table of Contents

Introduction

The "Smith" family, consisting of Dad, Mom, two children, a dog, and a hamster, packed up their U-Haul truck and moved from the deep south to the east coast. When they arrived, they began to look for a church, but their previous denomination was exclusive to the south. The Smiths searched for three months before they found a church whose doctrine they agreed with.

At 29 years of age, Mr. "Jones," a single, upwardly mobile stock broker, began to feel an emptiness in his life. Jones thought if he started going to church, he could fill this void. But he had no idea what church to attend.

The "Doe" family were members of the same church for seven years, but were disappointed with some decisions made by the main headquarters. They felt the need to find a new church body, but didn't know where to begin.

This book is for all the Smiths, Jones, and Does who are seeking to find the right group to worship with. It is also for those who are doing research or for those who are simply curious about what different denominations believe.

There are other books on the market, including the *Encyclopedia of American Religions*, the *Handbook of Denominations in the United States*, and the *Yearbook of American and Canadian Churches*, that are excellent resources for the pastor or layperson. However, these do not deal with some of the "hot button" issues (such as abortion and homosexuality) that are being faced by congregations and church members today.

My hope is that this book will be used by individuals to find a congregation that "fits" their needs, a place where they feel they belong. My intent is not to cause dissension or division, for truly all Christians are one in the body of Christ. Therefore, I have made no judgments and no comparisons. I have simply chronicled information.

The wording in the text is as close to the original wording of the separate denominations as possible, with some changes for style, readability, and consistency. Notes at the end of the book indicate exactly where the information came from. If there are no end notes for a particular section, the answers were provided directly from the headquarters or by a spokesperson.

I have attempted to include every possible group that could be contacted. Additional denominations that did not respond to my contacts are included in the Appendix at the back of the book.

Inclusion in this work should not be construed as an endorsement of any denomination. It is the readers' responsibility to judge for themselves what they believe regarding the doctrines of the different bodies. Readers are encouraged to obtain additional information before making the important decision of joining a church.

Advent Christian General Conference

The Advent Christian General Conference grew out of the Advent Awakening led by William Miller.[1] Officially founded in 1860, the Advent Christian Church stressed the importance of bodily resurrection. This church merged with Life and Advent Union in 1964. In 1986, the Advent Christian General Conference joined the National Association of Evangelicals. Churches uphold the doctrine of conditional immortality, which means that only believers will receive immortality at their bodily resurrection.[2] In 1997 there were 324 churches with 20,000 members.

Abortion: The Conference supports a constitutional amendment defining life as beginning at conception.

Baptism: Only believers are baptized by immersion.

Birth Control: No statement.

Capital Punishment: No position.

Christ's Return: (Central to the doctrine of Advent Christians.) Jesus Christ will come again to this earth to reign here forever. This coming is the hope of the church, inasmuch as upon that coming depend the resurrection and reward of the righteous, the abolition of sin and its consequences, and the renewal of the earth to become the eternal home of the redeemed. After this event the earth will be forever free from sin and death.[3]

Communion: Communion is a memorial remembrance of Christ's death, reserved for believers.

Creation vs. Evolution: Advent Christians take a conservative and evangelical position.

Deity of Jesus: Jesus Christ, the Lord, the only begotten Son of God, was conceived of the Holy Spirit and born of the Virgin Mary. He came into the world to seek and save that which was lost. He died for sins, he was raised bodily from the dead for the justification of sinners, and he ascended into heaven as the High Priest and mediator.[4]

Divorce and Remarriage: No position.

Government: Congregational.

Heaven/Hell: When a person dies, they enter an intermediate state of sleep or unconsciousness. At Christ's second coming, Christians will be resurrected to spend eternity with Christ on the renewed and sinless earth. Those who rejected Christ during their lifetimes will suffer for a period of time as they are destroyed, but then will completely cease to exist. Their suffering is not eternal.[5]

Homosexuality: Homosexual practice is sinful, but no worse than any other sinful behavior.

Inspiration of Scripture: The Bible is the inspired Word of God, being in its entirety a revelation given to man under divine inspiration and providence. Its historic statements are correct and it is the only divine and infallible standard of faith and practice.[6]

Miracles: No official position.

Restrictions: None.

Security of Salvation: No one who truly believes will fail to receive immortality.[7]

Speaking in Tongues and Other Gifts of the Spirit: No official position.

Trinity: Advent Christians believe in the oneness or unity of God, and reject belief in a plurality of gods, including any view that there are three separate gods.[8]

Women in Ministry: The church allows women to minister.

For more information contact: P.O. Box 23152, Charlotte, NC 28227; Phone: (704) 545-6161; Fax: (704) 573-0712; E-mail: mayerpub@aol.com

---

African Methodist Episcopal Church

In 1787, Rev. Richard Allen and Rev. Absalom Jones founded the Free African Society, which was the beginning of the African Methodist Episcopal Church. The motto of the church is "God Our Father, Christ Our Redeemer, and Man Our Brother." African Methodists hold rites and rituals in high esteem.[9] In 1997 there were more than two million members.[10]

Abortion: Members are encouraged to reject abortion except in the cases of rape, incest, health of the unborn child, or danger to the health of the mother.

Baptism: Baptism is one of two sacraments in the church. Infants as well as adults are baptized by pouring, sprinkling, or immersion. The church does not sanction re-baptism.[11]

Birth Control: No statement.

Capital Punishment: The church opposes capital punishment and feels that it is applied disproportionately to minorities.

Christ's Return: Christ will come again to judge the living and the dead.

Communion: The Lord's Supper is the other sacrament of the A.M.E. Church. All members are encouraged to attend this service at every opportunity.[12]

Creation vs. Evolution: The church believes God is responsible for the creation of the world, without necessarily believing in a literal time frame. Thus, no matter how it evolved, God is the prime creative force.

Deity of Jesus: Jesus Christ is Lord and Savior.[13]

Divorce and Remarriage: Divorce is a viable option in cases of adultery or life-threatening situations provoked by either marital partner. Attempts for reconciliation should be made before divorce is sought. Divorced persons may remarry.

Government: Episcopal in form, conference in practice. The church is governed by bishops who are elected every four years by the General Conference. The General Conference also makes laws and elects general officers to various departments that make up the operation of the church. The Annual Conference is the primary conference. It sends delegates to constitute the General Conference. The District Conference, the Quarterly Conference, and the Local Church Conference also have governance responsibility. A bishop's cabinet, made up of presiding elders who are appointed by the Presiding Bishop, supervises the work of the church by presiding over sub-districts of each annual conference. Pastors, who appoint stewards in the local church, are appointed by the Presiding Bishop. Trustees are elected by the local church. The *A.M.E. Discipline* provides rules and regulations which are applied to all persons in the church.[14]

Heaven/Hell: Heaven is eternal fellowship with God. Hell is alienation or absence of God.

Homosexuality: Homosexuality violates both biological design and God's intent. The union of two persons of the same sex cannot constitute marriage and is contrary to biblical teachings.

Inspiration of Scripture: The Scriptures contain everything necessary for salvation and are the Word of God. The Holy Spirit will guide interpretation.

Miracles: The A.M.E. Church believes in the divine manifestation of God and the revelation of his Spirit through the actual visualization of his actions in one's life.

Restrictions: None stated. However, the church opposes any activity that would keep one out of God's Kingdom.

Security of Salvation: Salvation is an on-going process, and one can fall from grace. However, once forgiveness is sought, the seeker can be reaffirmed as a member of the family of God.

Speaking in Tongues and Other Gifts of the Spirit: No answer.

Trinity: The A.M.E. Church is trinitarian and the Trinity is invoked in many of their rituals.

Women in Ministry: Women are capable of serving God through any official position in the denomination.

For more information contact: 500 Eighth Ave. S., Nashville, TN 37203. Phone: (803) 691-0771; Fax: (803) 691-0674; Web site: http://www. voicenet.com/~jfisher/ame.html

Allegheny Wesleyan Methodist Connection (Original Allegheny Conference), The

The parenthetical name refers to the original conference formed by the Wesleyan Methodist Church when it split with the Methodist Episcopal Church in 1843. The Allegheny Wesleyan Methodist Connection began in 1968 when church leaders could not support the merger of the Wesleyan Methodist Church of America with the Pilgrim Holiness Church.[15] The Connection believes sanctification is the removal of the carnal nature which makes a person sin, and holiness is the second definite work of grace. In 1996 there were 120 churches with 2,050 members.

Abortion: The Connection traditionally believes that every unborn baby has a right to life.

Baptism: Baptism is a condition of membership, performed in any mode, at any age.

Birth Control: No statement.

Capital Punishment: No official stand.

Christ's Return: Members believe in Christ's imminent, bodily return. This will include a triumph over all evil. They take no official position on his coming before or after the millennium.

Communion: The Lord's Supper is commemorated every quarter and is an open communion.

Creation vs. Evolution: The Connection believes that God created the universe.

Deity of Jesus: The church believes in the deity of Christ.

Divorce and Remarriage: No official stance.

Government: Republican.

Heaven/Hell: Heaven is the final home of every righteous person. Hell is the final doom of ungodly believers.

Homosexuality: It is a sin.

Inspiration of Scripture: The Scriptures are the inspired and infallibly written Word of God, fully inerrant in their original manuscript.

Miracles: No statement.

Restrictions: None.

Security of Salvation: A believer is conditionally, eternally secure.

Speaking in Tongues and Other Gifts of the Spirit: They are not an evidence of the fullness of the Spirit.

Trinity: There are three persons of one substance in the unity of the Godhead—God the Father, God the Son, and God the Holy Spirit.

Women in Ministry: Women are ordained.

For more information contact: P.O. Box 357; Salem, OH 44460; Phone: (330) 337-9376; Fax: (330) 337-9700: E-mail: awmc@juno.com

---

Amended Christadelphians (Brethren in Christ)

When a young doctor, John Thomas, found himself in the midst of a storm aboard a ship that seemed doomed to sink, he promised God that if he survived he would seek for religious truth. When the ship made it safely to shore, Thomas began examining religious thought. After rejecting several beliefs, he joined a small group of people who emphasized the merit of the sacrifice of Christ, his coming again to transform the world into a Kingdom of God, and the importance of baptism (being buried in water) so that sins were covered. However, he later differed with the group over the issues of immortality and heaven and hell. He and several of his followers then separated into their own group and took on the name Christadelphian.[16] The original group split in 1898 over an amendment to the statement of faith which stated that some who were not Christians would be resurrected and judged at Christ's return.[17] Amended Christadelphians are the largest of the two bodies. Congregations are small and preachers are all laymen who are unpaid. They refuse to take part in secular affairs.[18]

Abortion: No answer.

Baptism: This is tremendously important to Christadelphians, as the coverage by water in obedience to Christ is a symbolic imitation of the death and resurrection of Jesus.[19]

Birth Control: No statement.

Capital Punishment: No answer.

Christ's Return: Christ will one day return from heaven in power and glory to rid the earth of evil and to bring a Kingdom of righteousness and peace. This will happen in the very near future. At his return, Christians will be resurrected from the dead and will be refashioned by divine power into an immortal being who will live forever with Christ in a perfect world.[20]

Communion: No answer.

Creation vs. Evolution: No answer.

Deity of Jesus: Jesus Christ is the divine Son of the eternal God. He was born of the Virgin Mary. Through the death and resurrection of Christ, sinners experience forgiveness of sin.[21]

Divorce and Remarriage: No answer.

Government: No answer.

Heaven/Hell: Death—the wages of sin really is death: a state of sleep and utter unconsciousness.[22]

Homosexuality: No answer.

Inspiration of Scripture: The Bible is the Word of God and the only rule of life.[23]

Miracles: No answer.

Restrictions: No answer.

Security of Salvation: No answer.

Speaking in Tongues and Other Gifts of the Spirit: No answer.

Trinity: The Christadelphians believe there is an eternal God, the Father, and Jesus Christ, his divine Son.[24]

Women in Ministry: No answer.

For more information contact: Christadelphian Book Supply, 36516 Parkdale, Livonia, MI 48150; Phone: (313) 425-5058.

American Association of Lutheran Churches

The American Association of Lutheran Churches was organized in 1987 as a continuation of the former American Lutheran Church with specific emphasis on: the full authority, inerrancy, and infallibility of Scripture; the veracity of the Lutheran Confessions; the primacy of evangelism and world missions; and the authority of the local congregation. In 1995 there were 93 churches with 17,918 members.

Abortion: The AALC is a pro-life church body and is opposed to elective abortions.

Baptism: God acts in baptism to forgive original sin, to begin a new relationship with the baptized person, and to give the Holy Spirit. Infants and young children are baptized. The method may be sprinkling, pouring, or immersion.

Birth Control: No statement.

Capital Punishment: There is no official statement. However, many associated with the church support capital punishment as used biblically.

Christ's Return: Christ will return in glory on the last day to judge the living and the dead.

Communion: Those who partake of the Lord's Supper receive the true body and blood of Jesus Christ. Through Holy Communion, the repentant believer receives the forgiveness of sins which renews life and gives assurance of salvation.

Creation vs. Evolution: God created all things according to their kinds. Therefore, the AALC rejects the hypothesis of evolution, including the notion of theistic evolution.

Deity of Jesus: Jesus Christ is true God and true man.

Divorce and Remarriage: Divorce is sinful and contrary to God's intention. Divorce can be justified only when adultery is involved.

Government: Congregational. The AALC authorizes local congregations to manage their own property, make local decisions, and call their own pastor. The congregations hold primary authority through the annual General Convention to which each congregation sends delegates. A joint council with representation from each region carries out the legislative and judicial functions between general conventions. All constitution and bylaw changes, as well as major policy decisions approved by the General Convention, must be referred to a congregational referendum for final approval.

Heaven/Hell: Heaven is the reality of eternal life in the presence of God. Hell is the reality of eternal separation from the presence of God.

Homosexuality: Homosexual desires and behavior are sinful and contrary to God's pattern for his children. Homosexual desires, behavior, and/or lifestyle are not another form of sexuality equal with the God-given male and female pattern.

Inspiration of Scripture: The canonical Scriptures of the Old and New Testament as a whole and in all their parts are the divinely inspired, revealed, and inerrant Word of God. They are the only infallible authority in all matters of faith and life.

Miracles: The AALC accepts the historic reality of miracles recounted in both the Old and New Testaments.

Restrictions: Pastors are not allowed to be members of any secret society which teaches salvation by works or salvation in any other name than Jesus Christ. Also, no participation to any degree is allowed in the World Council of Churches or National Council of Churches.

Security of Salvation: Salvation is by grace through faith in Jesus Christ and is assured to those who believe in Christ and are baptized. However, the AALC church body does not teach "once baptized, always saved," or "once saved always saved." Believers can fall away.

Speaking in Tongues and Other Gifts of the Spirit: God, the Holy Spirit, gives his gifts today to individuals as he wills. However, the AALC rejects the notion that speaking in tongues should ever be equated with justification before God. Furthermore, they reject the concept that the fullness of the Spirit for an individual Christian requires speaking in tongues.

Trinity: God is triune: three persons in one God. God the Father is truly God, God the Son is truly God, and God the Holy Spirit is truly God.

Women in Ministry: God calls and uses both men and women in different areas of ministry. However, the church ordains only men who have experienced the call of the Lord and have been prepared for the office of holy ministry.

For more information contact: 10800 Lyndale Ave. S., Ste. 120, Minneapolis, MN 55420; Phone: (612) 884-7784; Fax: (612) 884-7894; E-mail: gloriaalc@aol.com; Web site: http://www.taalc.org

---

American Baptist Association

The American Baptist Association does not claim to be "Protestant." Instead, the group believes they continue a succession of churches that began with Jesus and the Apostles. The group was originally named the Baptist General Conference but changed to American Baptist Association in 1925. In 1996 there were approximately 1,600 churches.[25]

Abortion: There is no official position, but abortion is generally opposed.

Baptism: Scriptural baptism is the immersion of penitent believers in water, administered by the authority of a New Testament church in the name of the Father, Son, and Holy Spirit.[26]

Birth Control: No official stand.

Capital Punishment: No official stand.

Christ's Return: American Baptists believe in the premillennial, personal, bodily return of Christ as the crowning event of the Gentile age.[27]

Communion: The Lord's Supper is a memorial ordinance, restricted to the members of the church observing the ordinance.[28]

Creation vs. Evolution: The church believes in the Genesis account of creation.[29]

Deity of Jesus: American Baptists believe in the deity of Jesus Christ.[30]

Divorce and Remarriage: The act of divorce and remarriage does not please God, but there are specific situations where God will permit such an act.

Government: Congregational. All associations, fellowships, and committees are servants and under control of the churches.[31]

Heaven/Hell: The bodily return of Christ will include the resurrection of the righteous to eternal heaven. The millennium will be followed by the resurrection of the unrighteous into eternal punishment in the lake of fire and then the righteous shall enter into the heaven age.[32]

Homosexuality: This life-style is opposed.

Inspiration of Scripture: American Baptists believe in the infallible, verbal inspiration of the whole Bible and that the Bible is the all-sufficient rule of faith and practice.[33]

Miracles: Miraculous spiritual manifestation gifts were done away with when the Bible was completed. Faith, hope, and love are the abiding spiritual gifts.[34]

Restrictions: None.

Security of Salvation: All who trust Jesus Christ for salvation are eternally secure in him and shall not perish.[35]

Speaking in Tongues and Other Gifts of the Spirit: See Miracles.

Trinity: The triune God: Father, Son, and Holy Spirit are equal in divine perfection.[36]

Women in Ministry: There are two divinely appointed offices in a church, pastors and deacons, to be filled by men whose qualifications are set forth in Titus and 1 Timothy.[37]

For more information contact: 4605 N. State Line, Texarkana, TX 75503-2928; Phone: (903) 792-2783; Fax: (903) 792-8128; E-mail: 103353.457@compuserve.com; Web site: http://www.abaptist.org

---

American Baptist Churches U.S.A.

Northern and Southern Baptists split in 1845 over the question of slavery. The Northern Baptist Convention was officially organized in 1907 to coordinate the work of its various societies. The name was changed to American Baptist Convention in 1950, then to the current title in 1972. The

American Baptist organization continues the Baptist tradition of autonomy, "soul liberty," and the priesthood of believers. The organization does not dictate policy to its approximately 5,800 local churches. Instead, the denomination exists as a resource to support church missions. The denomination has tended to avoid embracing prepared creeds or other statements that might compromise their obligation to interpret Scripture as individuals within the community of faith under the guidance of the Holy Spirit.[38]

Abortion: No position.

Baptism: Baptism by full immersion is administered only to those who have the maturity to understand its profound significance: resurrection to new life in Christ.[39]

Birth Control: No statement.

Capital Punishment: No statement.

Christ's Return: Church tradition holds that Christ will return in glory.

Communion: Communion commemorates the sacrifice of the Lord.[40] Many churches practice open communion.

Creation vs. Evolution: Beliefs vary within the denomination.

Deity of Jesus: American Baptists affirm that God is sovereign over all and that this sovereignty is expressed and realized through Jesus Christ. Therefore, they affirm the lordship of Christ over the world and the church.[41]

Divorce and Remarriage: No position.

Government: Individual churches are autonomous. Regional organizations and national boards lend support to local churches. The office of the general secretary coordinates these efforts. The general board, made up of a diverse group of ordained and lay leaders, speaks to issues of importance within the denomination through policy statements, resolutions, and other declarations. While its decisions give direction to national staff, it does not obligate any congregation or region to any position or course of action.[42]

Heaven/Hell: Beliefs vary, but most believe in a literal heaven and hell.

Homosexuality: The general board resolution is not binding on churches, but it states that the practice of homosexuality is incompatible with Christian teaching.

Inspiration of Scripture: Holy Scripture always has been the most authoritative guide to knowing and serving God. As the divinely inspired

Word of God, the Bible reveals a person's faith and its mandated practice.[43]

Miracles: Beliefs vary by church.

Restrictions: None.

Security of Salvation: There are a variety of beliefs on this topic.

Speaking in Tongues and Other Gifts of the Spirit: There is no denominational statement. Some churches affirm a charismatic lifestyle.

Trinity: There is a triune God: Father, Son, and Holy Spirit (creator, redeemer, sustainer).[44]

Women in Ministry: The American Baptist Churches have ordained women for more than a century, and approximately eight percent of professional church leaders are women.

For more information contact: P.O. Box 851, Valley Forge, PA 19482-0851; Phone: (800) 222-3872 or (610) 768-2000; Fax: (610) 768-2320; E-mail: richard.schramm@abc-usa.org; Web site: http://www.abc-usa.org

---

American Evangelical Christian Churches

American Evangelical Christian Churches began in 1944 as an interdoctrinal church body.[45] Although its churches are generally known as American Evangelical Christian, member clergy may serve other denominational or independent churches.[46]

Abortion: The church opposes abortion.

Baptism: No answer.

Birth Control: No answer.

Capital Punishment: American Evangelical Christian Churches support capital punishment.

Christ's Return: The next great event in the fulfillment of prophecy will be the imminent, personal return of the Lord in the air to receive into heaven those who are alive and remain on earth at his coming, and those who have fallen asleep in him. He will return to earth in person on the clouds of heaven, with great power and great glory, to establish the millennial age, to bind Satan and place him in the abyss, to lift the curse which now rests on the whole creation, to restore Israel to her own land and to give her the realization of God's covenant promise, and to bring the whole world to the knowledge of God.[47]

Communion: No answer.

Creation vs. Evolution: The AECC believes in creation.

Deity of Jesus: The Lord Jesus Christ, eternal Son of God, became man without ceasing to be God.[48]

Divorce and Remarriage: No answer.

Government: The church is governed by a board of directors.

Heaven/Hell: No answer.

Homosexuality: Homosexuality is a sin.

Inspiration of Scripture: The AECC believes in the plenary verbal inspiration of the original writing of the 66 books of the Bible. The Bible is the full and complete revelation of God's will for man, and it is the supreme and final authority in all matters of faith and practice.[49]

Miracles: The church believes in miracles.

Restrictions: No answer.

Security of Salvation: No answer.

Speaking in Tongues and Other Gifts of the Spirit: No answer.

Trinity: American Evangelical Christian Churches believe in the Trinity.

Women in Ministry: The church approves of having women in ministry.

For more information contact: 1421 Roseland Ave., Sebring, FL 33870; Phone: (941) 314-9370; Fax: (941) 314-9570; Web site: http://www.rhesys.mb.ca/rhema/aecc/

American Rescue Workers

Incorporated in 1884 as The Salvation Army and in 1896 as The American Salvation Army, the American Rescue Workers' name was amended to the organizational charter in 1913. The denominational motto, Saved to Serve, reflects the churches' commitment to social service. Programs provide food, clothing, halfway houses, homeless shelters, and rehabilitation centers. In 1996 there were 15 churches in the United States.

Abortion: It depends on the condition of the mother—whether rape has occurred, etc. The decision is left to the woman.

Baptism: Christian baptism is a sacrament signifying acceptance of the benefits of the atonement of Jesus Christ. It is to be administered to believers and is declarative of their faith in Jesus Christ as their Savior, and demonstrates their full purpose to obey him in holiness and righteousness.

Birth Control: No statement.

Capital Punishment: Each individual person must decide for themselves. Capital punishment of any kind pertaining to correction of children is not acceptable.

Christ's Return: The Lord Jesus will come again. Those alive at his coming shall not precede those that are asleep in Christ Jesus. Those abiding with him will be caught up with the risen saints to meet with the Lord in the air and will be with him forever.

Communion: The memorial and communion instituted by the Lord and Savior Jesus Christ is essentially a New Testament sacrament, declarative of his sacrificial death, through the merits of which believers have life and salvation and promise of all spiritual blessings in Christ. It is distinctively for those who are prepared for reverent appreciation of its significance, and by it they show forth the Lord's death until he comes again.

Creation vs. Evolution: The American Rescue Workers believe in creation as outlined in the Bible.

Deity of Jesus: Jesus Christ is the second person of the triune Godhead. He was eternally one with the Father. That is to say, the Godhead and manhood are united in one person—very God and very man. The God-man Jesus Christ died for sins and arose from the dead. He ascended into heaven and there engaged in intercession.

Distinguishing Beliefs/Practices: The social service part of the American Rescue Workers provides lodgings, clothing, food, halfway houses, shelters for the homeless, and rehabilitation centers for alcoholics and drug addicts.

Divorce and Remarriage: Divorce should be obtained only when adultery is involved. However, in this day and age, any type of abuse is not acceptable. The clergy makes decisions with each case on remarriage.

Government: A general and a commander-in-chief lead the organization, which is part of the universal Christian church. A board of managers oversees the affairs of workers.

Heaven/Hell: Glorious and everlasting life are assured to all who believe in, and obediently follow, Jesus Christ. The impenitent shall suffer eternally in hell.

Homosexuality: Although homosexuality is not an acceptable lifestyle, the church accepts the sinner and not the sin.

Inspiration of Scripture: The 66 books of the Old and New Testaments were given by divine inspiration and inerrantly reveal the will of God concerning man in all things necessary to salvation, so that whatever is not contained therein is not to be enjoined as an article of faith.

Miracles: American Rescue Workers believe in the biblical doctrine of divine healing and urge their people to offer the prayer of faith for the healing of the sick.

Restrictions: No games of chance.

Security of Salvation: Man, though in possession of the experience of regeneration and entire sanctification, may fall from grace and apostatize. Unless he repents of this sin, he will be hopelessly and eternally lost.

Speaking in Tongues and Other Gifts of the Spirit: The evidence of a spirit-filled life is a life lived out of love, not speaking in an unknown tongue.

Trinity: There is one eternally existent, infinite God, Sovereign of the universe. He only is God, creative and administrative, holy in nature, attributes, and purpose. He, as God, is triune in essential being, revealed as Father, Son, and Holy Spirit.

Women in Ministry: Women are ordained into the ministry and they have equal standing with men in rank and position.

For more information contact: Rev. Col. Robert N. Coles, 1209 Hamilton Blvd., Hagerstown, MD 21742-3340; Phone: (301) 797-0061; Fax: (301) 797-1480; E-mail: chiefcoles@aol.com; Web site: http://www.arwus.com

Anglican Orthodox Church

The Most Right Reverend James P. Dees founded the Anglican Orthodox Church on November 16, 1963, after resigning from the Protestant Episcopal Church.[50].The Anglican Orthodox Church is a low liturgical church in the Reformation tradition, having apostolic succession and using the

1928 Book of Common Prayer in its worship. The church is Bible-based while also being apostolic and liturgical. In 1997, there were 50,000 members.

Abortion: Believing that abortion (the killing of an unborn baby) is murder, the church opposes abortion except in cases of rape, incest, or when the life of the mother is threatened. This must be supported by a physician's recommendation.

Baptism: One of two sacraments recognized by the Anglican Orthodox Church. A sacrament is an outward and visible sign of an inward and spiritual grace. The outward act of baptism does not procure one's regeneration and justification. It is an outward evidence of the faith residing in the inner man, which is acceptable to God and which God is pleased to bless with his Spirit, bringing regeneration. In infant baptism, this is effected by the faith resident in the sponsors or godparents and the minister.

Birth Control: No statement.

Capital Punishment: Laws exist for the protection and well-being of society. In extreme cases where the rights and/or life of another have been violated (such as aggravated rape or murder), capital punishment may be warranted, though not in the spirit of vengeance or retaliation, but of justice.

Christ's Return: Christ is now seated at the right hand of the Father in heaven and he shall one day return in glory to claim those who have trusted in him. Regarding the time of his return, no one knows either the day or the hour.

Communion: Holy Communion is the other sacrament of the church. For those who receive it worthily in faith, communion is a great blessing as Christ is spiritually present. This church believes in the real, spiritual presence of Christ in Holy Communion, but not in the doctrine of transubstantiation (which means that after consecration of the elements, the substance of Christ's body and blood is present in communion[51]).

Creation vs. Evolution: God created the world out of nothingness. It did not happen by chance or evolve as secular humanists believe.

Deity of Jesus: Jesus Christ is the only begotten Son of the Father, and he is very God as well as very Man.

Divorce and Remarriage: Marriage is a physical, spiritual, and mystical union of a man and woman created by their mutual consent of heart, mind, and will. It is a holy estate instituted of God in which God dwells and is in intention lifelong. When marital unity is imperiled by dissension, it shall be the duty of either or both parties, before contemplating legal action, to lay the matter before a minister of the church. It is the minister's duty to labor so that the parties may be reconciled. If a person who has been divorced desires to remarry, and if the bishop or ecclesiastical authority is satisfied that the parties intend a true Christian marriage, he shall take what action he deems advisable in the interest of the promotion of a Christian home and the Kingdom of God.

Government: Episcopal, with a presiding bishop and bishops, priests, and deacons. The Anglican Orthodox Church believes it is in, and believes it has, apostolic succession.

Heaven/Hell: God has created a heavenly home for those who love him and who come to him by faith in Christ. God also made people with free will, so they may choose to accept or reject him. Those who do not accept Christ as their Savior must pay the penalty for their own sins in a place of eternal torment known as hell.

Homosexuality: This is an immoral lifestyle contrary to the will of God as revealed in Holy Scripture. The church stands opposed to this sin, as to all others. But God will forgive anyone who forsakes his sin and turns to him in penitence.

Inspiration of Scripture: The Bible is the divinely inspired, infallible Word of God, without error. It contains all things necessary to salvation.

Miracles: With God, nothing is impossible. The miracles contained in Scripture happened as they are recorded.

Restrictions: None.

Security of Salvation: People have freedom to accept and freedom to reject Christ. Becoming a Christian does not remove free will. God will never lose us or cast us away, but neither will he force us to remain against our will.

Speaking in Tongues and Other Gifts of the Spirit: Tongues and such when used in the church often tend toward confusion and dissension. Worship should be reverent and in order. Thus, the Anglican Orthodox Church is not what would commonly be referred to as charismatic.

Trinity: There is one living and true God—everlasting, without body, parts, or passions and of infinite power, wisdom, and goodness. He is the maker and preserver of all things both visible and invisible. And in unity of this Godhead there are three persons of one substance, power, and eternity: the Father, the Son, and the Holy Spirit.

Women in Ministry: Only men are ordained to Holy Orders.

For more information contact: The Most Rev. Robert J. Godfrey, P.O. Box 128, 323 Walnut St., Statesville, NC 28687; Phone: (704) 873-8365; Fax: (704) 873-8948.

Apostolic Christian Church of America

Under persecution in 1832, Swiss state church minister Samuel Froehlich turned away from the practices of his church (including the baptizing of infants) and formed The Evangelical Baptists. The Apostolic Christian Church was started in America by one of Froehlich's elders. The doctrines are built upon the teachings of Christ and the Apostles and are similar to those of the Anabaptist heritage. In 1997, there were 80 churches with 12,000 members.

Abortion: This denomination is fully committed to the sanctity of human life.

Baptism: By immersion, following a testimony of faith and conversion, and a covenant of faithfulness to God.

Birth Control: No statement.

Capital Punishment: No position.

Christ's Return: At the return of Christ, his bride, the glorious church (which includes the saints of all ages), will become fully manifested.

Communion: The bread and fruit of the vine in Holy Communion symbolizes the body and blood of Christ. A closed communion is observed following members' self-examination.

Creation vs. Evolution: The eternal God is the creator of all things.

Deity of Jesus: Jesus Christ is the Son of God, begotten of the Holy Spirit, and a member of the Trinity.

Divorce and Remarriage: Marriage is a lifelong union ordained of God in which a man and woman of like mind, faith, and fellowship are united in the Lord in holy matrimony. Divorce is only acceptable if unfaithfulness is involved. Remarriage after divorce of converted persons is not supported.

Government: Elders and ministers are selected from the brothers of the congregation. They are not formally trained and work without salary. The elder administers the spiritual duties in the church. The national government is made up of elders from all churches in the U.S. and overseas.

Heaven/Hell: Both the saved and the lost will be resurrected—the saved unto eternal life in heaven and the lost unto eternal damnation in hell.

Homosexuality: Homosexual acts are grievous sins.

Inspiration of Scripture: The Bible is the inspired and infallible Word of God to man.

Miracles: No position.

Restrictions: No theater or organized sports. Television use is strongly discouraged. Members live separated lives. Discipline procedures are established based on the Word of God and relate to the seriousness of the sin and the circumstances.

Security of Salvation: Although the gift of eternal life is the present possession of every true believer, it is possible for a believer to forsake his faith, willfully return to a life of sin, and consequently forfeit eternal life with Christ.

Speaking in Tongues and Other Gifts of the Spirit: Speaking in tongues is not practiced in the Apostolic Christian Church.

Trinity: There is one eternal God, the creator of all things, who exists in three persons: the Father, the Son, and the Holy Spirit.

Women in Ministry: Men serve in all leadership, ministry, and teaching positions with the exception of the teaching of children, which is done by both men and women.

For more information contact: 6913 Wilmette Ave., Darien, IL 60561; Phone: (630) 969-7021; Fax: (630) 969-7086; E-mail: eisenman@uic.edu

Apostolic Faith Church

The Apostolic Faith Church, whose motto is "Jesus is the light of the world," began in Los Angeles in 1906 as revivalists waited for the promise of a "Latter Rain" prophesied in the Old Testament book of Joel and the New Testament book of Acts. The church upholds the doctrine of entire sanctification and was incorporated in 1907. It began publication of the Apostolic Faith paper that same year. In 1997, there were 50 churches with no formal membership.

Abortion: Abortion is killing a child.

Baptism: Baptism is by immersion only.

Birth Control: Birth control is left to the discretion and conscience of the individual.

Capital Punishment: The church backs the law of the land.

Christ's Return: The first stage will be the rapture of the church. The second stage will be the revelation of Christ after the seven-year tribulation period.

Communion: The emblems used—the grape juice and the unleavened wafer—are symbols of Christ's blood and body. Taken by faith in the power of Christ they can bring great blessing.

Creation vs. Evolution: The Apostolic Faith Church believes the biblical account of creation as recorded in the first two chapters of Genesis. Evolution is man's theory only.

Deity of Jesus: Jesus is the divine Son of God, the mighty God, and God with us.

Divorce and Remarriage: Divorce and remarriage are not allowed.

Government: Church government is made up of a five-man board of trustees, one of which is the overseer or president. It includes a board of elders made up of ministers and lay persons according to the bylaws of the corporation.

Heaven/Hell: These are literal places to be occupied by the redeemed or the damned.

Homosexuality: This sinful act is an abomination to the creator God.

Inspiration of Scripture: The Apostolic Faith Church believes in the absolute inspiration of the Scriptures.

Miracles: God, through Jesus Christ, performs miracles today as he did in the past.

Restrictions: None stated.

Security of Salvation: There is conditional security of salvation due to the free will of man.

Speaking in Tongues and Other Gifts of the Spirit: The witness of receiving the baptism of the Holy Ghost is the speaking in tongues as the Spirit gives utterance.

Trinity: The Apostolic Faith Church believes in the divine Trinity as verified by the Scriptures: God the Father, God the Son, and God the Holy Ghost—omnipotent, omnipresent, and omniscient.

Women in Ministry: Women are included in the preaching of the gospel.

For more information contact: P.O. Box 86128, Portland, OR 97286-0128; Phone: (503) 777-1741; Fax: (503) 777-1743.

Apostolic Lutheran Church of America

The Apostolic Lutheran Church of America began during the Scandinavian revival, which was started by Lars Levi Laestadius and lasted during the years 1844–1861. The church was established in America by immigrants in 1870. In 1997, there were 61 churches with 7,000 baptized members.

Abortion: The Apostolic Lutheran Church of America is against abortion.

Baptism: Water baptism is the seal or token of the New Testament covenant of faith for the believer. It is an outward sign of grace that has been instituted in the place of circumcision. Little children are baptized because they are God's children and are of the Kingdom of God. Nothing can invalidate a baptism that has been administered in the name of the Father, Son, and Holy Ghost.[52]

Birth Control: The church is against the use of birth control.

Capital Punishment: The Apostolic Lutheran Church supports capital punishment.

Christ's Return: The church awaits the fulfillment of Christ's return.

Communion: Communion is a sacrament instituted by the Lord in remembrance of his suffering and death. It was instituted in place of the Feast of Passover.[53] It is for believers.

Creation vs. Evolution: The Apostolic Lutheran Church believes in the biblical account of creation.

Deity of Jesus: Jesus is divine.

Divorce and Remarriage: The church allows divorce, but is against remarriage.

Government: There is an elected central board which carries out decisions of the congregations and upholds bylaws which are determined at the annual meeting.

Heaven/Hell: There is a literal heaven and hell. After eternal judgment at the throne of God, each person will find themselves in one of two groups: those blessed by God who will go to heaven, and those cursed who will be cast into the lake of fire.[54]

Homosexuality: The church is opposed to homosexuality.

Inspiration of Scripture: The Scriptures, both Old and New Testament, are the inspired Word of God.

Miracles: Miracles still occur.

Restrictions: None stated except those taught by the Word of God.

Security of Salvation: There is security in Christ.

Speaking in Tongues and Other Gifts of the Spirit: Speaking in unknown tongues has ceased, but God gives the gifts of the Spirit according to his power.

Trinity: There is a triune God who is unified in God the Father, the Son, and the Holy Ghost.[55]

Women in Ministry: Women are not allowed to be ordained.

For more information contact: Rt. 1, Box 462, Houghton, MI 49931; Phone: (906) 482-8269; Fax: (906) 482-6392.

Armenian Church, The

According to tradition, the Church of Armenia was established by the apostles Thaddeus and Bartholomew. The works of fourth and fifth century historians contain references to the existence of Christian communities in Armenia during the course of the second and third centuries. At the beginning of the fourth century, the kingdom of Armenia under King Tiridates III converted to Christianity through the efforts of St. Gregory the Illuminator, becoming the first Christian state in the world. (In 2001, the Armenians will celebrate the 1700th anniversary of this event.) Christianity became an integral part of the identity of the Armenian people, spawning the creation of a distinctive Armenian written language, as well as a rich literary, intellectual, and artistic tradition. The first Armenian church in America was established in Worcester, MA in 1891. An American diocesan jurisdiction was created in 1898. The Armenian Church accepts only the canons of the first three ecumenical councils and the local councils associated with them, rejecting all the subsequent councils (4–22). It is a liturgical church, accepting seven sacraments. Its major worship service, the Divine Liturgy, is recited in the medieval poetic dialect of the Armenian language. The church has married clergymen as well as celibate clergymen. There are currently 123 Armenian churches in the U.S., with approximately one million members.

Abortion: The church is opposed to abortion, provided there are no valid medical reasons.

Baptism: Baptism and Chrismation (anointing with blessed oil) are prerequisites for all who wish to be members of the Armenian Church. Baptism is a sacrament that cannot be repeated, so Christians baptized into a trinitarian confession who wish to join the church are not obliged to be immersed again.

Birth Control: The church leaves this matter up to the conscience of the individual.

Capital Punishment: The Armenian Church is not opposed to capital punishment. According to medieval Armenian law (which was prepared by Armenian clergyman), capital punishment may be enforced by civil authorities.

Christ's Return: The church believes in the second coming of Jesus Christ as specified in the Nicene Creed, which states, "He is to come with the same body and with the glory of the Father to judge the living and the dead; of His kingdom there is no end."

Communion: Communion is one of the sacraments of the church, administered to the faithful during the Divine Liturgy, or upon request. The church considers it to be the body and blood of Christ.

Creation vs. Evolution: The church has no specific position on this matter, although the creation story is accepted as a part of the general Scripture. The church affirms God as the prime cause of the universe.

Deity of Jesus: Jesus Christ is the Logos (the Word of God), the second person of the Holy Trinity, and God the Son.

Divorce and Remarriage: In principle, the church does not grant divorce to a married couple unless there are valid reasons given for the annulment or an account of mental illness. Other causes for divorce could be seven years absence due to war, slavery, physical separation, or other adversity. The church does grant divorce for moral causes (which are adultery, prostitution, etc.). In theory and in liturgical practice only one re-marriage is allowed, although the church has been more lenient in this regard recently.

Government: The church has an episcopal foundation and is hierarchical in structure, with the Catholicos of All Armenians (historically the chief bishop of Greater Armenia) serving as the head of the church structure. The Catholicos of the Great House of Cilicia, the patriarchs (of Constantinople and Jerusalem), archbishops, and bishops administer jurisdictions of various sizes and have under their immediate command parish priests. The parish priests as well as the prelates of the church are elected by the lay and clerical members of the church. Delegates from each parish form the assembly of an episcopal jurisdiction (referred to as a diocese). Representatives from all dioceses elect the Catholicos of All Armenians.

Heaven/Hell: The Kingdom of heaven is specified in the Armenian version of the Nicene Creed. The church also believes in the existence of hell and in the concept of eternal damnation for sinners.

Homosexuality: Church canons based on Old Testament law and the Pauline epistles forbid any kind of sexual activity other than that between a man and a woman whose marriage has been sanctioned by the church.

Inspiration of Scripture: Armenians use the adjectival form "inspired by God" as a noun and refer to the Bible as God-inspired books in their language. However, the Scriptures are not the only source of knowledge and inspiration by the divine. The church considers the Scriptures to be a part and parcel of the Holy Tradition and divine inspiration can also be experienced in the church during worship and in church councils, where laity and clergy gather to discuss religious matters.

Miracles: The church believes in miracles.

Restrictions: The church does not impose restrictions on social practices, other than the seven deadly sins: pride, envy, wrath, sloth, avarice, gluttony, and lechery.

Security of Salvation: Salvation is possible only through Jesus Christ and his church.

Speaking in Tongues and Other Gifts of the Spirit: Speaking in tongues in the colloquial sense is not a definitive characteristic of the Armenian worship services.

Trinity: Each of the three persons of the Trinity are affirmed, and the term Trinity appears in several contexts in the Armenian Divine Liturgy.

Women in Ministry: The priestly orders are reserved exclusively for men. The church has a tradition of convents and nuns and a feminine diaconate in monastic institutions. The church's understanding of the scope of ministry is not confined to the ordained orders. Women play other important roles in Sunday School and other non-liturgical capacities.

For more information contact: 630 Second Ave., New York, NY 10016-4885; Phone: (212) 686-0710; Fax: (212) 779-3558; E-mail: armenianch@aol.com; Web site: http://www.stleon.org

---

Assemblies of Yahweh

Assemblies of Yahweh were founded in 1966 through Elder Jacob O. Meyer's "The Sacred Name Broadcast" radio ministry. The church is distinguished by its use of the sacred names. In 1996, there were 30 churches with approximately 2,000 members.

Abortion: Abortion is murder.

Baptism: Baptism is a necessary act following repentance. Baptism is by immersion, once backward in Yahshua's name. It represents an inner cleansing.

Birth Control: Birth control is not prohibited. Some methods are discouraged, such as the pill and implants, due to hormonal and health problems and unclean substances that are used.

Capital Punishment: The church favors capital punishment.

Christ's Return: Although the date of Yahshua the Messiah's return is unknown, it will be soon. He will establish his millennial Kingdom on earth.

Communion: The Passover memorial supper in the New Testament era is the annual observance of the Savior's death. The memorial will be held on the evening of Abib 14 (which is scriptural dating) using unleavened bread and grape juice. Passover is the day before the seven-day Feast of Unleavened Bread. Foot washing precedes the communion.

Creation vs. Evolution: Evolution is speculation. The earth was created in six days with Yahweh Elohim resting on the seventh (or the Sabbath).

Deity of Jesus: Yahshua the Messiah has come in human form and has pre-existed with the Father. He was born of a virgin and lived a sinless life.

Divorce and Remarriage: Divorce and remarriage is allowed in the case of sexual sin only.

Government: The church government is a "system of judges," with a presiding bishop who makes final decisions and selects teaching elders and deacons. Teaching elders, deacons, and senior missionaries make up the rest of government structure. A bishop is selected for life. A new bishop is chosen by a vote of the teaching elders.

Heaven/Hell: At Yahshua's return, this earth will be rebuilt into a paradise like that of Eden, which man lost originally through sin. The wicked will be punished in the lake of fire (Gehenna) by complete destruction. The church disavows an eternal torment in an ever-burning hell.

Homosexuality: It is an abomination to Yahweh. To be saved, homosexuals must repent and change their behavior.

Inspiration of Scripture: The Scriptures are inspired in their original autographs.

Miracles: The power of heaven set aside certain physical laws to allow for miracles. The Scriptures teach anointing with oil in the name of Yahweh and in the name of Yahshua the Messiah for healing of illness.

Restrictions: Alcoholic beverages are acceptable in moderation.

Security of Salvation: Those who endure to the end shall be saved when Yahshua returns.

Speaking in Tongues and Other Gifts of the Spirit: The Holy Spirit is manifested within an individual by the fruits listed in Galatians. In Acts, tongues are actual languages. Corinthians discusses a foreign language liturgy, not a confusion of sounds. Although all gifts apply, some are restricted (such as healing to elderships).

Trinity: The trinitarian doctrine is foreign to the inspired Scriptures.

Women in Ministry: The Scriptures exclude women from preaching.

For more information contact: 190 Frantz Rd. P.O. Box C, Bethel, PA 19507; Phone: (717) 933-4518.

Associate Reformed
Presbyterian Church

The Associate Reformed Presbyterian Church traces its roots to the preaching of Scotsman John Knox and the formation of the official Church of Scotland in 1560. King William III reorganized the church into the Established Presbyterian Church of Scotland in 1688. However, controversy over the close alliance of church and state continued, resulting in the formation of a separate Associate Presbytery in 1733. Ten years later another group formed the Reformed Presbytery. Both churches spread to northern Ireland and then to America as the Scots were forced to emigrate.[56] The organization, whose motto is, "In Thy light shall we see light," shifted several times before officially forming the Associate Reformed Presbyterian Church. In 1996 there were 205 churches with 38,782 members.

Abortion: The Scriptures clearly and plainly testify to the infinite worth of human life by virtue of man having been created in the image and likeness of God. Decisions about life and death are God's prerogatives and not man's. Even in the case of the rare exceptions such as judgments by medical personnel about highly technical medical problems, human judgment should always stand in submission to the divine judgment and wisdom of God. The Scriptures point out a unique relationship between God the Creator and the unborn child. Regarding the divine mysteries of the conception and development of human life, it is not for men to be determiners of life and death, even for the unborn child. Therefore, in all instances, one should seek to preserve the life of the unborn child.[57]

Baptism: Infants and adults are baptized by sprinkling, pouring, or immersion.

Birth Control: No official stance.

Capital Punishment: No statement.

Christ's Return: The Associate Reformed Presbyterian Church confirms that Christ will surely return, although they do not take a millennial stance.

Communion: All members of all evangelical denominations are invited to the Lord's table.

Creation vs. Evolution: No official stance.

Deity of Jesus: Jesus is the Son of God and is fully God.

Divorce and Remarriage: Remarriage of the innocent party is allowed.

Government: Presbyterian or representative in form. Each church is represented at all levels. The presbytery is the most powerful and authoritative level.

Heaven/Hell: The Associate Reformed Presbyterian Church believes in both a literal heaven and a literal hell.

Homosexuality: God's Word clearly forbids homosexual practice as a sin against God. The church affirms their obligation to show Christian love and concern for homosexuals and to call them to repentance, cleansing, and deliverance in the saving power of Jesus Christ.[58]

Inspiration of Scripture: The Scriptures of the Old and New Testament are the Word of God, without error in all that it teaches.[59]

Miracles: Miracles are affirmed both in biblical times and at this present time.

Restrictions: None.

Security of Salvation: No official stance.

Speaking in Tongues and Other Gifts of the Spirit: No official stance.

Trinity: The Associate Reformed Presbyterian Church holds an absolute belief in the Triune God.

Women in Ministry: Women are allowed to serve in the office of deacon, but not elder.

For more information contact: One Cleveland St., Ste 110, Greenville, SC 29601-3696; Phone: (864) 232-8297; Fax: (864) 271-3729; E-mail: dragondraw@aol.com; Web site: http://www.arpsynod.org

---

Association of Free Lutheran Congregations, The

The Association of Free Lutheran Congregations was organized in 1962 when approximately 40 congregations opposed the merger of the Lutheran Free Church with the American Lutheran Church. Organizers dissented on two main points: they wanted to maintain a conservative theology and not join the World Council of Churches.[60] There are currently 31,474 members in 235 congregations.

Abortion: Unborn children stand under the protection of God's command against murder.

Baptism: Baptism is one of two sacraments and a means of grace. It is most often done by pouring, but the method is not prescribed and individual churches may vary the practice.

Birth Control: No position.

Capital Punishment: No position.

Christ's Return: He shall come again to judge the living and the dead.[61]

Communion: The second sacrament, communion, is celebrated monthly in most congregations. It is open for those who confess Jesus Christ as their personal savior. As with baptism, communion practices may vary from church to church.

Creation vs. Evolution: A creationist viewpoint is taught in the Association of Free Lutheran Congregations' Bible school and seminary.

Deity of Jesus: Jesus Christ, true God and also true man, born of the Virgin Mary, is Lord.[62]

Divorce and Remarriage: No position.

Government: Congregational polity.

Heaven/Hell: Both are literal places.

Homosexuality: Homosexuality is a sinful life choice for which there is forgiveness and cleansing in Christ.

Inspiration of Scripture: The Bible is the infallible, inerrant Word of God.

Miracles: The miracles of the Bible are literally true. God performs miracles today in answer to prayer and in accordance with his sovereign will.

Restrictions: None stated.

Security of Salvation: Free Lutherans believe in the possibility of apostasy as well as the Christian's security in Christ.

Speaking in Tongues and Other Gifts of the Spirit: Not charismatic in the usual sense of the term, the church affirms the gifts of the Spirit for today in their Fundamental Principles.

Trinity: The church's faith in the triune God is expressed in the Apostles', Athanasian, and Nicene Creeds.

Women in Ministry: The Association of Free Lutheran Congregations does not ordain women.

For more information contact: 3110 E. Medicine Lake Blvd., Minneapolis, MN 55441; Phone: (612) 545-5631; Fax: (612) 545-0079; E-mail: hqmail@aflc.org; Web site: http://www.aflc.org

---

Association of Independent Methodists

The Association of Independent Methodists separated from the Methodist Episcopal Church in 1965 over the issue of polity. The Association rejected the episcopal form of government of the parent organization in favor of a congregational polity. It is orthodox Methodist, Wesleyan, and Arminian in doctrine. In 1997, there were 38 churches with 2,500 members.

Abortion: Independent Methodists are anti-abortion.

Baptism: The church practices three modes: sprinkling, pouring, and immersion.

Birth Control: This is a personal issue.

Capital Punishment: Independent Methodists are in favor of capital punishment.

Christ's Return: Christ's return will be premillennial and pretribulation.

Communion: Communion is a sign or symbol of an inward work of grace and is open to all believers.

Creation vs. Evolution: The church holds a creationist view.

Deity of Jesus: Both God and man, Jesus is of the same essence as the Father.

Divorce and Remarriage: The church does not prohibit divorce or remarriage. However, members are encouraged to try to prevent divorce if possible.

Government: Congregational.

Heaven/Hell: Both are scriptural.

Homosexuality: The Association of Independent Methodists is against homosexual practice just as they are against the sin of adultery. However, they are not against the individual in either case. The church believes that homosexuality is not biological.

Inspiration of Scripture: The Scriptures are both inspired and inerrant in the original manuscript.

Miracles: The church believes in miracles.

Restrictions: The Association of Independent Methodists discourages gambling and the use of alcohol.

Security of Salvation: A person can lose their salvation after they believe if they choose to willfully sin and continue in that sin.

Speaking in Tongues and Other Gifts of the Spirit: The Association of Independent Methodists believes in the gifts of the Holy Spirit, but not in a prayer language or tongues as an indication of being filled with the Holy Spirit.

Trinity: The church is trinitarian with a belief in God the Father, God the Son, and God the Holy Spirit.

Women in Ministry: At the present, the church does not ordain women.

For more information contact: Box 4274, 5201 Cedar Park, Ste. J, Jackson, MS 39296-4274; Phone: (601) 362-1301; Fax: (601) 362-1328; E-mail: rjmill100@aol.com

---

Association of Seventh Day Pentecostal Assemblies

The Association of Seventh Day Pentecostal Assemblies was officially incorporated in 1964, although it existed as an informal fellowship for more than 30 years prior. Because each church is locally autonomous, there are no membership figures. The church prefers to be called a fellowship as opposed to a denomination.

Abortion: The church does not support abortion.

Baptism: Baptism is by immersion.

Birth Control: The church does not support its use.

Capital Punishment: The Association of Pentecostal Assemblies supports capital punishment.

Christ's Return: His second coming is personal, imminent, and the blessed hope of the church. The millennium is rest for both soul and body.[63]

Communion: Communion is practiced once a year in conjunction with foot washing.

Creation vs. Evolution: God created all things.

Deity of Jesus: Jesus Christ is the Son of God.

Distinguishing Beliefs/Practices: Each of the Ten Commandments are equal. No one commandment is subordinate to another.[64]

Divorce and Remarriage: No official position.

Government: Congregationally organized with each church autonomous.

Heaven/Hell: Seventh Day Pentecostal Assemblies believe in a literal heaven, hell, and a lake of fire.

Homosexuality: The church opposes homosexuality.

Inspiration of Scripture: The Scriptures were inspired by God.

Miracles: The church believes in the healing of all sickness and disease.[65]

Restrictions: Restrictions are decided autonomously.

Security of Salvation: No answer.

Speaking in Tongues and Other Gifts of the Spirit: The Assembly is Pentecostal and believes the baptism of the Holy Spirit is rest for the soul and endows with power for service.[66]

Trinity: Seventh Day Pentecostal Assemblies believe that there are three distinct entities, but do not hold to a trinitarian doctrine. Instead, the Holy Ghost is believed to be a personality of both the Father and Son, but not a person.

Women in Ministry: Women are given credentials to serve as missionaries, but not preachers.

For more information contact: 4700 N.E. 119th St., Vancouver, WA 98686; Phone: (360) 573-0121.

Association of Vineyard Churches

In 1978, John Wimber started a Bible study group in Yorba Linda, CA. Four years later he became associated with Kenn Gullikson, who headed a congregation that had a similar beginning and beliefs. Wimber named his group the Vineyard Christian Fellowship of Yorba Linda and the next year the group moved to Anaheim, CA, where they eventually merged with several other congregations.[67] The church values being culture current. The church reflects this value through music that is of a popular style, and through dressing, acting, and speaking in ways in which the current culture can respond positively.[68] In 1986, the Association of Vineyard Churches was officially formed.

Abortion: No statement.

Baptism: One of two sacraments. Water baptism is open to all believers.[69]

Birth Control: No statement.

Capital Punishment: No statement.

Christ's Return: God's Kingdom will be consummated in the glorious, visible, and triumphant appearing of Christ—his return to earth as King. After Christ returns to reign, he will bring about the final defeat of Satan and all of his minions and works, the resurrection of the dead, the final judgment, and the eternal blessing of the righteous and eternal conscious punishment of the wicked. Finally, God will be all in all and his Kingdom, his rule, and his reign will be fulfilled in the new heavens and the new earth, recreated by his mighty power in which righteousness dwells and in which he will forever be worshipped.[70]

Communion: The second ordinance. Performed regularly, communion is open and is informal.[71]

Creation vs. Evolution: God created, upholds, and governs all that exists: the heavenly places, the angelic hosts, the universe, the earth, every living thing, and human beings. God created all things very good.[72]

Deity of Jesus: Conceived by the Holy Spirit and born of the Virgin Mary, God's only Son, Jesus, is fully God and fully human in one person. After dying for the sins of the world, Jesus was raised from the dead on the third day. In his atoning death on the cross, he took God's judgment for sin.[73]

Divorce and Remarriage: No policy.

Government: Includes an international and national director. Regional overseers and area pastoral coordinators are selected from ministers of Vineyard churches.[74]

Heaven/Hell: No answer.

Homosexuality: No answer.

Inspiration of Scripture: The Holy Spirit inspired the human authors of Holy Scripture so that the Bible is without error in the original manuscripts. The 66 books of the Old and New Testaments are the final, absolute authority and the only infallible rule of faith and practice.[75]

Miracles: The Spirit's powerful presence is invoked, which allows ministering through the Spirit's gifts and seeing God heal and work wonders.[76]

Restrictions: None.

Security of Salvation: No answer.

Speaking in Tongues and Other Gifts of the Spirit: The filling or empowering of the Holy Spirit is often a conscious experience. Vineyard churches believe in the present ministry of the Spirit and in the exercise of all the biblical gifts of the Spirit. They practice the laying on of hands for the empowering of the Spirit, for healing, and for recognition and empowering of those whom God has ordained to lead and serve the church. They also encourage prayer of the tongues and prayer of faith in healing and in expulsion of demons.[77]

Trinity: God exists as the one living true God in three persons of one substance: the Father, the Son, and the Holy Spirit, equal in power and glory.[78]

Women in Ministry: Women are encouraged to minister, but not as senior pastors.

For more information contact: P.O. Box 17580, Anaheim, CA 92817; Phone: (800) 852-8463 or (714) 777-1433; Fax: (714) 777-8841; Web site: http://www.avc.vineyard.org/avc-home.html

Baptist Bible Fellowship, International

Baptist Bible Fellowship began in 1950 as an offshoot of the World Fundamental Baptist Missionary Fellowship. Nearly 100 pastors and a handful of missionaries formed the nucleus of the movement. The number of adult missionaries has now grown to more than 800 in 97 fields. The Baptist Bible College in Springfield, MO is the teaching arm. In 1996, there were 4,500 churches with more than one million members.

Abortion: The church traditionally opposes abortion.

Baptism: Christian baptism is the immersion in water of a believer in the name of the Father, of the Son, and of the Holy Ghost. With the authority of the local church, baptism demonstrates in a solemn and beautiful emblem faith in the crucified, buried, and risen Savior. It is prerequisite to the privileges of a church relation and to the Lord's Supper.[1]

Birth Control: No official stance.

Capital Punishment: No statement.

Christ's Return: Jesus shall return bodily, personally, and visibly. The dead in Christ shall rise first. The living saints shall be changed in a moment at the last trump. God shall give Jesus Christ the throne of his father David, and Christ shall reign a thousand years in righteousness until he puts all enemies under his feet.[2]

Communion: During the Lord's Supper, members of the church, by the sacred use of bread and the fruit of the vine, commemorate together the dying love of Christ. This should always be preceded by solemn self-examination.[3]

Creation vs. Evolution: The Genesis account of creation is to be accepted literally, not allegorically or figuratively. Man was created in God's own image and after his own likeness. Man's creation was not a matter of evolution or evolutionary change of species, or development through interminable periods of time from lower to higher forms. All animal and vegetable life was made directly, and God's established law was that they should bring forth after their kind.[4]

Deity of Jesus: Jesus Christ was begotten of the Holy Ghost in a miraculous manner. He was born of the Virgin Mary, as no other man was ever born or can ever be born of woman. He is both the Son of God, and God the Son.[5]

Divorce and Remarriage: Each church makes its own decision regarding this issue.

Government: There are two national fellowship meetings each year. Representatives from each state attend monthly state meetings. If something is to be voted on or discussed at the national meeting, these issues are dealt with first at the state level. Local churches are autonomous.

Heaven/Hell: The Baptist Bible Fellowship believes in the everlasting felicity of the saved and the everlasting conscious suffering of the lost.[6]

Homosexuality: The church traditionally opposes homosexuality.

Inspiration of Scripture: The Holy Bible (the collection of 66 books, from Genesis to Revelation) was written by men supernaturally inspired. These holy men of old were moved by the Holy Spirit in such a definite way that their writings were supernaturally and verbally inspired and free from error as no other writings have ever been or ever will be inspired. It has truth without any admixture of error for its matter. Therefore it is, and shall remain to the end of the age, the only complete and final revelation of the will of God to man; the true center of Christian union and the supreme standard by which all human conduct, creeds, and opinions should be tried.[7]

Miracles: The church holds traditional beliefs in biblical miracles.

Restrictions: Decided by individual churches.

Security of Salvation: In the new birth, the one dead in trespasses and sins is made a partaker of the divine nature and receives eternal life.[8]

Speaking in Tongues and Other Gifts of the Spirit: Churches in the Baptist Bible Fellowship are not involved with speaking in tongues.

Trinity: In the unity of the Godhead there are three persons: the Father, the Son, and the Holy Ghost, equal in every divine perfection and executing distinct but harmonious offices in the great work of Redemption.[9]

Women in Ministry: Women are not ordained.

For more information contact: 720 E. Kearney, P.O. Box 191, Springfield, MO 65801; Phone: (417) 862-5001; Fax: (417) 865-0794; E-mail: 76043.2702@compuserve.com

---

Baptist General Conference

On August 13, 1852, Swedish immigrant Gustaf Palmquist, along with two men and a woman he had baptized five days earlier, organized the first Swedish Baptist Church in America. With roots in the pietistic movement of Sweden, the small group marked the beginning of the Baptist General Conference.[10] There are now 875 churches with 136,120 members.

Abortion: The BGC opposes abortion on demand and encourages its members to influence public opinion in this regard.

Baptism: The church requires immersion for membership.

Birth Control: No statement.

Capital Punishment: No statement.

Christ's Return: The church believes in the personal and visible return of Jesus to earth and the establishment of his Kingdom.

Communion: Communion should be observed and administered until the return of Jesus. Frequency and style is determined by individual churches.

Creation vs. Evolution: The BGC believes God created all things.

Deity of Jesus: The BGC believes in Jesus Christ, God's only Son, his conception by the Holy Spirit, his virgin birth, sinless life, miracles, and teachings. The BGC believes in his substitutionary atoning death, bodily resurrection, ascension into heaven, perpetual intercession for his people, and personal visible return to earth.[11]

Divorce and Remarriage: Christian marriage is a sacred institution ordained of God for the happiness of mankind and the propagation of the race. It is a spiritual and physical union into which one man and one woman may enter for the glory of God and, according to the scriptural ideal, is to be broken only by death. Churches should deal with people involved in divorce and remarriage with firmness, love, forgiveness, patience, and prayer.[12]

Government: Churches are autonomous.

Heaven and Hell: The BGC believes in the resurrection of the body, the final judgment, the felicity of the righteous, and the endless suffering of the wicked.[13]

Homosexuality: Heterosexuality is God's revealed will for humankind. A homosexual orientation is a result of the fall of humanity into a sinful condition. Hateful, fearful, unconcerned harassment of persons with a homosexual orientation should be repudiated. Those who believe that homosexual behavior is a biblically acceptable lifestyle are not qualified to serve in the leadership of the conference, to teach in its educational institutions, or to serve as pastors of Baptist General Conference churches or as missionaries of the Baptist General Conference.[14]

Inspiration of Scripture: The Bible is the Word of God, fully inspired, and without error in the original manuscripts, written under the inspiration of the Holy Spirit. It has supreme authority in all matters of faith and conduct.[15]

Miracles: No answer.

Restrictions: No statement.

Security of Salvation: The BGC believes in the security of true salvation.

Speaking in Tongues and Other Gifts of the Spirit: Some individual churches allow the private use of tongues.

Trinity: There is one living and true God, eternally existing in three persons. These are equal in every divine perfection, and they execute distinct but harmonious offices in the work of creation, providence, and redemption.[16]

Women in Ministry: Ordination is granted by the local church. If a local church chooses to ordain a woman they may.

For more information contact: 2002 S. Arlington Heights Rd., Arlington Heights, IL 60005; Phone: (800) 323-4215 or (847) 228-0200; Fax: (847) 228-5376; Web site: http://www.bgc.bethel.edu

---

Baptist Missionary Association of America

Formerly the North American Baptist Association, the Baptist Missionary Association of America is a group of regular Baptist churches, with common ties of faith and practice, who formed an association in 1950. The name was changed from the original in 1969, since the term "North" was misunderstood by many, especially in the South. The BMA prefers not to be called a denomination since at the time of the reorganization no new principles or practices were instituted.[17]

Abortion: The Baptist Missionary Association of America strongly stands in opposition to the continued murdering of unborn children and to the attempt by congress or the President to enact a litmus test for federal judges insisting they be pro-abortion. The church calls upon all committed Christians to renew commitment to support and work for legislation and/or a constitutional amendment which will prohibit abortion. The BMA calls upon the President to sign into law the Partial-birth Abortion Ban and they ask God to convict the hearts of the justices of the Supreme Court to overturn Roe vs. Wade.[18]

Baptism: One of two ordinances. Believers are immersed in water as a confession of faith in Jesus Christ. Baptism is a prerequisite of church membership and participation in communion.[19]

Birth Control: No statement.

Capital Punishment: No statement.

Christ's Return: Jesus Christ will return personally in bodily form to receive his redeemed unto himself. His return is imminent. After Jesus returns, all of the dead will be raised bodily, each to his own order: the righteous dead in the resurrection of life and the wicked dead in the resurrection of damnation. Prior to the eternal state, God will judge everyone to confer rewards or to consign punishment. Most BMA churches believe that Christ's return will be premillenial, after which he will reign in peace upon the earth for 1,000 years. Most also believe that the Scriptures teach two resurrections: the first of the righteous at Christ's coming, the second of the wicked at the close of the thousand-year reign.[20]

Communion: The second ordinance is the sacred sharing of the bread of communion and the cup of blessing by the assembled church as a memorial to the crucified body and shed blood of Christ.[21]

Creation vs. Evolution: God created all things for his own pleasure and glory. God created an innumerable host of spirit beings called angels. God created man in his own image. As the crowning work of creation, every person is of dignity and worth and merits the respect of all other persons.[22]

Deity of Jesus: God the Son is the Savior of the world. Born of the Virgin Mary, he declared his deity among men, died on the cross as the only sacrifice for sin, rose bodily from the grave, and ascended back to the Father. He is at the right hand of the Father, interceding for believers until he returns to rapture them from the world.[23]

Divorce and Remarriage: Although some divorced pastors have remarried, the BMA frowns upon divorce and remarriage unless the divorce was based on biblical grounds such as infidelity.

Government: Pastors and deacons are the permanent offices. Each church may select men of its choice, who meet biblical qualifications, to fill those offices. Pastors oversee and teach the church, while the church provides for them financially. Deacons are servants of the church and assistants to the pastors. A president and two vice-presidents, elected at the annual meeting, oversee the association along with three recording secretaries and the various department officers.[24]

Heaven/Hell: After Jesus returns, all of the dead will be raised bodily, each in his own order: the righteous dead in the resurrection of life, and the wicked dead in the resurrection of damnation.[25]

Homosexuality: The BMA deplores the proliferation of all homosexual practices and reaffirms the biblical position that all such practices are sin and are condemned by the Bible. The church also opposes the identification of homosexuality as a minority with attendant benefits or advantages. The BMA affirms that while the Bible condemns such practice as sin, it also teaches forgiveness and transformation, upon repentance, through Jesus Christ.[26]

Inspiration of Scripture: The Scriptures are God's inerrant revelation, complete in the Old and New Testaments, written by divinely inspired men as they were moved by the Holy Spirit. Those men wrote not in their own words of human wisdom but in words taught by the Holy Spirit. The Scriptures provide the standard for the believer's faith and practice, reveal the promises by which God will judge all, and express the true basis of Christian fellowship.[27]

Miracles: The church believes God still performs miracles today.

Restrictions: The BMA opposes the spread of legalized gambling.[28]

Security of Salvation: All believers are eternally secure in Jesus Christ. They are born again, made new creatures in Christ, and indwelt by the Holy Spirit, enabling their perseverance in good work. A special providence watches over them, and they are kept by the power of God.[29]

Speaking in Tongues and Other Gifts of the Spirit: Gifts ceased with the first century church, therefore the church does not practice speaking in tongues.

Trinity: There is one living and true God, the creator of the universe. He is revealed in the unity of the Godhead as God the Father, God the Son, and God the Holy Spirit. These are equal in every divine perfection.[30]

Women in Ministry: The BMA does not endorse women in the ministry.

For more information contact: 1530 E. Pine St., Jacksonville, TX 75766; Phone: (903) 586-2501; Fax: (903) 586-0378; E-mail: bmaam@aol.com

Berean Fundamental Church

Dr. Ivan E. Olsen, a graduate of Denver Bible Institute, founded the first Berean Fundamental Church in North Platte, NE in 1936. Eleven years later, his church, along with other planted churches, formed the Berean Fundamental Church Council, Inc.[31,32]

Abortion: The Berean Fundamental Church is opposed to abortion in all circumstances.

Baptism: One of two ordinances, baptism is performed by immersion in water after salvation.[33]

Birth Control: No answer.

Capital Punishment: No answer.

Christ's Return: The world is fast ripening for the tribulation judgments which all believers will escape by the rapture of the church prior to the tribulation. Jesus Christ will come in power, majesty, and glory to close the tribulation period and establish his millennial reign. He shall reign as King with resurrected saints of all ages in the last dispensation known as the millennium.[34]

Communion: The second ordinance is for all believers present in fellowship.[35]

Creation vs. Evolution: The Berean Fundamental Church believes that God divinely created the universe in six days.

Deity of Jesus: The Lord Jesus Christ was begotten in the flesh by the Holy Spirit, born of the Virgin Mary, and is both true God and true man. He was resurrected in bodily form.[36]

Divorce and Remarriage: No answer.

Government: Berean churches are autonomous and interdependent. Policy is determined on the local level.

Heaven/Hell: All believers at death enter eternal bliss and all unbelievers at death enter eternal misery.[37]

Homosexuality: No answer.

Inspiration of Scripture: All Scripture is equally and fully inspired in all its parts and inerrant in the original manuscripts. The Bible should be interpreted literally, grammatically, contextually, and historically, with God progressively revealing himself in dispensations.[38]

Miracles: No answer.

Restrictions: No answer.

Security of Salvation: It is the privilege of all who are born again to be assured of their eternal salvation on the authority of the Word of God.[39]

Speaking in Tongues and Other Gifts of the Spirit: The Berean Fundamental Church is non-Pentecostal.

Trinity: The Godhead eternally exists in three persons: the Father, the Son, and the Holy Spirit.[40]

Women in Ministry: It is God's plan and purpose for only men to be elders, deacons, and pastors.[41]

For more information contact: P.O. Box 6103, Lincoln, NE 68506; Phone and Fax: (402) 489-8056.

Bible Fellowship Church

The Bible Fellowship Church originated in 1858 as a Mennonite body but has evolved so that it no longer considers itself as Mennonite. The church places a strong emphasis on evangelism and world missions (missionaries serve around the world under faith mission boards, supported through the Bible Fellowship Church board of missions). In 1997 there were 59 churches with a membership of 7,200.

Abortion: The Bible Fellowship Church is opposed to abortion except where the mother's life is seriously threatened.

Baptism: Believers are baptized by immersion. This is a pre-requisite to church membership.

Birth Control: The Bible Fellowship Church has no stated position on birth control except that it is opposed to forms that are abortifacient.

Capital Punishment: There is no stated position on capital punishment.

Christ's Return: Christ's return will be personal and premillennial.

Communion: The church has an ordinance regarding communion that states: "Those who worthily partake in this remembrance of him feed upon him to their spiritual nourishment and growth in grace."

Creation vs. Evolution: The Bible Fellowship Church is creationist.

Deity of Christ: Christ is truly God and truly man.

Divorce and Remarriage: Divorce is permissible only on the grounds of adultery. Men who have been divorced may not serve as pastors or elders. However, divorce does not bar one from membership.

Government: Local churches are governed by a plurality of elders. They are autonomous and interdependent, submitting to mutual decisions by the annual conference in matters which the churches have agreed to take care of together.

Heaven/Hell: Heaven and hell are both eternal places and states.

Homosexuality: God's Word declares that the expression of sexual relations is authorized only in the union of male and female within the bond of marriage. Homosexual lust and practice are sinful in God's sight.

Inspiration of Scripture: The inspiration of all 66 books in the original manuscript is verbal and plenary.

Miracles: The church prays for and expects supernatural acts of God.

Restrictions: Members are not allowed to belong to secret oath-bound societies such as Free Masons.

Security of Salvation: Those regenerated by the work of God are preserved by the power of God so that they will never totally or finally fall away. They will persevere until the end.

Speaking in Tongues and Other Gifts of the Spirit: Sign gifts are not promoted, but they are also not forbidden. Other gifts of the Spirit are looked for. Believers are encouraged and helped to discover and use their spiritual gifts.

Trinity: The Bible Fellowship Church is trinitarian.

Women in Ministry: Ministry by women is desired and encouraged. However, women are not permitted to serve as elders or ordained ministers based on 1 Timothy 2:12.

For more information contact: P.O. Box 2628, Plainfield, NJ 07060; Phone and Fax: (908) 753-6978; Web Site: http://www.bfc.org

---

Bible Holiness Church

The Bible Holiness Church left the Methodist Church in the late 1800s to found a congregation that centered on "Holiness Unto the Lord." The church was initially called the Southeast Fire Baptized Holiness Association. Later the name was changed to The Fire Baptized Holiness Church, then in 1995 to Bible Holiness Church. The Bible Holiness Church does not practice ordinances. In 1997 there were 46 churches with 600 members.

Abortion: The Bible Holiness Church opposes abortion.

Baptism: Baptism is not practiced in the church.

Birth Control: The method is up to the individual.

Capital Punishment: The church does not have a law against it.

Christ's Return: The church is looking for Christ's return anytime.

Communion: The church does not take communion, since Paul said the ordinances were "nailed to the tree."

Creation vs. Evolution: The Bible Holiness Church believes the biblical account of creation.

Deity of Jesus: Jesus is divine. This is part of the church's creed.

Divorce and Remarriage: Sometimes a divorce cannot be helped. However, the church does not believe in remarriage. If a person is remarried, God can still save that person, but remarried people are not used in offices or teaching.

Government: Made up of a general board, the government consists of the general superintendent, first and second assistant, and six district superintendents. Each church has a church board.

Heaven/Hell: There is a literal heaven and hell.

Homosexuality: The church will have no part of homosexuality.

Inspiration of Scripture: The Bible Holiness Church believes the Scriptures were divinely inspired.

Miracles: The church believes in miracles.

Restrictions: The church is very strict in its actions and living. Ladies wear dresses and do not cut their hair. Men do not wear neck ties.

Security of Salvation: Christians are justified to the will of God. They are ready without question for heaven.

Speaking in Tongues and Other Gifts of the Spirit: God has many gifts. The Bible Holiness Church does not believe in speaking in an unknown tongue as evidence of the Holy Spirit. The Holy Ghost is its own witness.

Trinity: God is three in one: Father, Son, and Holy Spirit.

Women in Ministry: Women are allowed to be ministers.

For more information contact: 600 College Ave., Independence, KS 67301; Phone: (316) 331-3049 or (316) 331-3901.

Bible Methodist Connection of Churches

The Bible Methodist Connection of Churches was formed in 1970 when the Bible Methodists of Alabama and Ohio merged. The church's stated purpose is to spread scriptural (second blessing) holiness over the lands in order to build up a holy and separated people for the first resurrection. It is a proponent of the doctrine of two works of grace. The first work is the initial sanctification of the new birth which is characterized by repentance, regeneration by the Holy Spirit, adoption into the family of God, the forsaking of all known sin and the dedication to live a life based on the Holy Scriptures. The second work of grace is entire sanctification, which is subsequent to the new birth. In the second work of grace the heart is purified by the Holy Ghost, appropriated by faith, and effected by the shed blood of Jesus Christ. In 1997, there were three conferences with a total of 67 churches.

Abortion: Biblical teaching strongly sets forth the value of life. Therefore, the church regards the slaughter of millions of unborn children as a tragic national sin. The church urges all of its members to get actively involved in right-to-life organizations.[42]

Baptism: Baptism is not only a sign of profession and mark of difference whereby Christians are distinguished from others who are not baptized; it is also a sign of regeneration or new birth. Young children are baptized.[43]

Birth Control: No stand.

Capital Punishment: Although most of the churches in the denomination favor capital punishment, there is no official statement.

Christ's Return: The doctrine of the second coming is a very precious truth and this good hope is a powerful inspiration to holy living and godly effort for the evangelization of the world. The imminent coming of Christ will be a bodily return to the earth and he will cause the fulfillment of all evil.[44]

Communion: The Supper of the Lord is not only a sign of love that Christians ought to have among themselves, but rather it is a sacrament of redemption by Christ's death. For those that rightly, worthily, and with faith receive communion, it is made a medium through which God communicates grace to the heart.[45]

Creation vs. Evolution: The Bible Methodist Connection of Churches believes in the biblical account of creation.

Deity of Jesus: The only begotten Son of God was conceived by the Holy Ghost, born of the Virgin Mary, suffered under Pontius Pilate, was crucified, dead, and buried—to be a sacrifice, not only for original guilt, but also for the actual sins of men and to reconcile them to God.[46]

Divorce and Remarriage: Adultery is the only scriptural grounds for divorce. The guilty party has by his or her act forfeited membership in the church. In the case of divorce for other cause, neither party shall be permitted to marry again during the lifetime of the other; the violation of this law shall be punished by expulsion from the church.[47]

Government: The quadrennial General Conference may designate local Bible Methodist Churches as an annual conference. These annual conferences operate under the jurisdiction of the General Conference and promote the interests of the Connection whose voting membership include elders, conference preachers, and lay delegates. The ministry and the laity are equally represented at annual conference sessions.[48]

Heaven/Hell: The righteous dead will be resurrected at Christ's second coming and the resurrection of the wicked will occur at a later time. Resurrection will be the reuniting of soul and body preparatory to final reward or punishment.[49] There is a literal heaven and hell.

Homosexuality: Bible Methodists are opposed to the concept of gay rights and hold that all homosexual acts are an abomination to God and an offense to the dignity of man. They also favor the adoption of children only by traditional families. They are opposed to the protection under the Civil Rights Act of those afflicted with the AIDS virus because of a perverted lifestyle. However, they also believe homosexuals can be redeemed.[50]

Inspiration of Scripture: The Old and New Testaments are the inspired and infallibly written Word of God, fully inerrant in their original manuscripts and superior to all human authority.[51]

Miracles: God still performs miracles today, such as the gift of divine healing.

Restrictions: Members are exhorted to avoid evil. This includes: doing ordinary work; buying or selling on the Lord's Day; manufacturing, buying, or selling of alcohol; wearing gold jewelry (including rings); joining secret societies; using tobacco; theater-going; dancing; card-playing; skating rinks; games that could be interpreted as gambling; mixed swimming; attending organized sports; and possessing television sets.[52]

Security of Salvation: Salvation is conditional.

Speaking in Tongues and Other Gifts of the Spirit: Members of the BMC do not believe in the charismatic type of speaking in tongues. However, they do believe that God may call a person to a mission field and enable them to learn the actual language instantaneously for the spreading of the gospel.

Trinity: There is but one living and true God, everlasting, of infinite power, wisdom, and goodness, and the maker and preserver of all things visible and invisible. And in the unity of this Godhead there are three persons of one substance, power, and eternity—the Father, the Son (the Word), and the Holy Ghost.[53]

Women in Ministry: Women are allowed in ministry.

For more information contact: The Alabama Conference, P.O. Box 523, Pell City, AL 35125; Phone: (205) 338-2743; Fax: (205) 338-7964.

Bible Missionary Church

The Bible Missionary Church began as the Bible Missionary Union in 1955 under the leadership of Rev. Glen Griffith, who was elected its first general moderator. He was joined in 1956 by the Rev. Elbert Dodd, who was elected the second general moderator. At that time the name was changed to the present one. The impetus for pioneering is expressed in the church's motto: "In order to preserve scriptural holiness with a standard." The church is a proponent of the doctrine of two works of grace. The first is initial sanctification of the new birth, which is characterized by repentance, being regenerated by the Holy Spirit and adopted into the family of God, the forsaking of all known sin, and living a life in accordance with the Holy Scriptures. The second is entire sanctification, which is subsequent to the new birth whereby the heart is purified by the Holy Ghost, appropriated by faith, and effected by the shed blood of Jesus Christ. The BMC has expanded into thirty-seven states and two Canadian provinces.

Abortion: The church takes a pro-life position.

Baptism: The church allows the candidate to choose his own mode: sprinkling, pouring, or immersion.

Birth Control: No answer.

Capital Punishment: The Bible Missionary Church favors capital punishment for certain crimes.

Christ's Return: The church believes the Rapture is pre-tribulation and the second coming pre-millennial.

Communion: The church practices an open communion for all who are born again believers whether members or not. Communion is observed quarterly.

Creation vs. Evolution: The church denies the claims of Darwinism and believes the biblical account of creation.

Deity of Jesus: The Bible Missionary Church believes Jesus Christ is the only begotten Son of God, God incarnate in the flesh. He is truly and verily man. He is the unoriginated God. Substantial deity and real humanity are combined in the person of Jesus Christ.

Divorce and Remarriage: The church believes there is only one scriptural ground for divorce and remarriage—the act of adultery (fornication) after the marriage vow is taken.

Government: It is primarily congregational, believing in the autonomy of the local church which elects representatives to a general conference each quadrennium where church policy is established. The church is divided into fourteen geographical districts in the U.S. with an elected district moderator as overseer.

Heaven/Hell: The church believes in a literal heaven, the eternal abode of all redeemed and purified believers, and a literal hell for all who would reject Christ as a personal Savior, the final punishment for all who are disobedient to God's Word.

Homosexuality: The church opposes the homosexual lifestyle and considers it as an abomination to God.

Inspiration of Scripture: The church believes in the inerrancy of Scriptures and the plenary inspiration of the Bible. It is the only safe rule for conduct and faith. The membership adheres to and uses the authorized King James Version of the Bible.

Miracles: The Bible Missionary Church believes in divine miracles as revealed by the Scriptures and in answer to believing faith.

Restrictions: For those seeking membership in the church, certain requirements must be met: showing the fruits of grace evidenced in the life and agreeing with the general, special, and governmental rules of the church. Members are required to follow a scriptural standard of modesty and an absence of worldliness in dress and behavior, abstinence from the use of tobacco and alcohol, a prohibition on television, moral-destroying videos (including movies), jewelry, card-playing, and other entertainments not consistent with Scripture and Christian ideals which glorify God.

Security of Salvation: The church believes in a conditional security which is dependent upon a continual obedience to the revealed will of God, walking in the light of the Holy Scriptures, and appropriating faith in the power of God and divine grace.

Speaking in Tongues and Other Gifts of the Spirit: The church does not recognize the speaking in unknown tongues as evidence of the Holy Ghost, but gives credence to a gift of a known language (glossia) for service.

Trinity: The Bible Missionary Church believes the Trinity is the union of three persons in one Godhead: the Father, the Son, and the Holy Ghost.

Women in Ministry: The church licenses and ordains women into the ministry when there is a conviction or a call from God, bestowed graces necessary for such calling, and the evidence of the Spirit's seal upon the claim.

For more information contact: 3501 46th Ave., P.O. Box 6070, Rock Island, IL 61204; Phone: (309) 788-0491; Fax: (309) 788-0493.

Brethren Church (Ashland, OH), The

In 1708, after the Reformation, a group of Pietists organized in Germany under the leadership of Alexander Mack. Initially known simply as Brethren, this young organization suffered severe persecution and fled

Germany for the new world in the early 1700s. Known as the German Baptist Brethren or Dunkers in America, the Brethren continued to increase in number. Differences of opinion resulted in the division of the German Baptist Brethren into five separate denominations, one of which is The Brethren Church.[54] In 1997 there were 120 Brethren congregations in the United States.

Abortion: The moral issue of abortion is more than a question of the freedom of a woman to control the reproductive functions of her own body. It is rather a question of those circumstances under which a human being may be permitted to take the life of another. All human life has value, is a creative act of God, and begins at conception. Therefore, the church opposes the use of abortion for personal or sociological purposes. Therapeutic abortions may be necessary when the pregnancy endangers the life of the mother, as in tubal pregnancies.[55]

Baptism: The Brethren Church practices the trine immersion of believers (immersion three times forward).[56]

Birth Control: No statement.

Capital Punishment: The Brethren Church has not taken a position on this issue. There are members who are opposed and members who are not opposed.

Christ's Return: Prior to the return of Christ, the human body at death returns to dust. The soul of the Christian goes immediately to be with the Lord, while the souls of the unsaved enter into torment. The climax of God's plan will include the personal, visible return of Jesus Christ from heaven as King of kings and Lord of lords.[57]

Communion: The Brethren Church observes a threefold communion derived from three actions that Jesus observed with his disciples during the last meal he shared with them before his crucifixion. First comes the washing of the saints' feet which is a symbolic cleansing, then supper which is a love feast, and then the Eucharist which is the communion of the bread and the wine.[58]

Creation vs. Evolution: Brethren affirm that the world and specifically humanity exist because of God's direct creative work.

Deity of Jesus: Jesus is the living Word, the revelation and revealer of the unseen Father. Although he possessed the divine nature from eternity, the Word became flesh. He was born of a virgin and lived the perfect human life upon earth. As man and God, Jesus lovingly gave himself for others in a ministry of service and reconciliation. His obedient life led to his sacrificial death in fulfillment of prophecy. Upon the cross he bore sin and its penalty in man's place. He was raised and glorified in the body in which he suffered and died. He ascended into heaven where he intercedes for those who are his.[59]

Divorce and Remarriage: Marriage is an ordinance of God. It is for life and divorce is only justifiable on the grounds of adultery and, possibly, if an unbelieving spouse leaves. Even then, divorced persons should remain unmarried or be reconciled. While this is the ideal, Brethren recognize that people fall short of this standard. Therefore forgiveness, acceptance, and church membership are extended to those who are divorced and to those who divorce and remarry.[60]

Government: There are three levels of church government: local congregations which are semi-autonomous, district conferences which are composed of delegates from local congregations, and the denominational level General Conference which is composed of delegates from local congregations and from the districts. The district conferences and the General Conference have no authority to interfere directly in the affairs of local congregations, but local congregations tend to abide by the decisions of these conferences since those decisions are made by local delegates. New congregations must be recognized by both a district conference and the General Conference to become member churches in the denomination. If a church strays from the beliefs and practices of the denomination, its district conference and the General Conference could refuse to accept delegates from that congregation. At the denominational level, an executive board headed by an executive director sets the vision for the organization, proposes priorities, and cares for other executive level matters. Two councils, the Congregational Ministries Council and the Missionary Ministries Council, each headed by a director, are responsible for implementing the vision of the church by carrying out the priorities and functions assigned to it.

Heaven/Hell: After Christ's return, there will be a bodily resurrection and judgment of believers unto eternal life. The wicked will be resurrected unto eternal punishment. The saved will live eternally with the Lord in a new heaven and a new earth in which righteousness dwells.[61]

Homosexuality: Homosexual activity, like adulterous relationships, is condemned in Scripture. Homosexuality is not an inherited condition in the same category as race, gender, or national origin, all of which are free from moral implication. Homosexuality is a deviation from the creator's plan for human sexuality. While homosexuals as individuals are entitled to civil rights, including free protection of the law, the Brethren Church opposes legislation which would extend special consideration to such individuals based upon their sexual orientation. The good news of forgiveness should compassionately be preached to homosexuals, and they should be accepted into fellowship upon confession of faith and repentance.[62]

Inspiration of Scripture: The nature of Scripture is both human and divine. It is inspired or breathed out by God. God guided human writers to such an extent that what they wrote could be considered God's Word written. It is the only reliable source of knowledge about the mind and will of God. The Bible records God's revelation, witnesses to its truth, and explains it.[63]

Miracles: The Brethren strongly believe in the miracles recorded in the Bible. Many Brethren believe in miraculous healing in answer to prayer. While the Brethren tend to be open to God's miraculous working, they also believe that such divine activity will always be consistent with the witness of Scripture.

Restrictions: Members are encouraged to avoid gambling and pornography. Historically, the Brethren have also encouraged the practice of non-conformity (following the way of Christ rather than the way of the world), non-resistance (renouncing violence and seeking reconciliation), and non-swearing (being trustworthy so that oath-taking becomes unnecessary).[64]

Security of Salvation: Scripture uses various terms to describe aspects of salvation, but ultimately it means Christlikeness—conformity to the image of God's Son by the work of his Spirit within. To that end believers are kept by the power of God, which operates through faith.[65]

Speaking in Tongues and Other Gifts of the Spirit: Some members speak in tongues, while other members think it is a gift that was limited to New Testament times. Most Brethren fall somewhere in between, not speaking in tongues themselves, but also not denying that the gift continues to be practiced today. Brethren emphasize the ministry gifts rather than the sign gifts.

Trinity: The Bible reveals one true and living God as three equal persons: the Father, the Son, and the Holy Spirit. This one God is eternal, infinite, personal, and perfect.[66]

Women in Ministry: The National Ordination Council considers for ordination all qualified candidates (including females) who give evidence of God's call to ordained Christian service and who have met the
educational and procedural requirements. The National Ordination
Council has ordained two women elders in the past 20 years, but neither is currently serving as a pastor. This issue continues to be discussed
among the Brethren. There are differing viewpoints among individuals, congregations, and districts. Some extend the same privileges to
women as to men with regard to preaching and ordination, while others believe that women should neither be ordained nor preach.

For more information contact: 524 College Ave., Ashland, OH 44805;
Phone: (419) 289-1708; Fax: (419) 281-0450; E-mail: brethren@
bright.net

Brethren in Christ Church

The Brethren in Christ Church emerged out of the pietistic revival movement of the late eighteenth century near Harrisburg, PA. From its beginnings in 1778, it was largely an ethnic church which spread by migration
to Canada, California, and Florida. Beginning in 1950, the church began
to diversify so that now the majority of members are non-ethnic. The
Brethren in Christ Church's *Manual of Doctrine and Government* reflects
the group's evangelical, pietistic, Anabaptist, and Wesleyan understanding of Scripture. In 1997 there were 190 churches with 35,000 members
and adherents.

Abortion: Abortion is considered a form of violence which the church
believes is incompatible with the teachings of the New Testament and
the modeling of people like Jesus, Stephen, and Paul. Only when the
life of the mother is endangered should abortion be considered.

Baptism: Applicants shall be baptized as a witness of faith and discipleship. The church affirms the practice of believer's baptism in which
the candidate kneels in humble submission to the Christ and the
church, and is immersed three times forward in the name of the Father,
Son, and Holy Spirit. Re-baptism is not required for those who have
been baptized by another mode of believer's baptism subsequent to
their rebirth.

Birth Control: No stated policy. Methods practiced are those that hold a high view of the sanctity of life.

Capital Punishment: The Brethren in Christ Church rejects all acts of violence which devalue human life. The church believes capital punishment is inconsistent with the teachings of Christ.

Christ's Return: The return of Christ in power and glory is certain and may occur at any time. No one knows when he will come. The conflict between God and Satan, and good and evil, will intensify at the approach of the end of this age. At Christ's return the enemies of God will be conquered and the reign of God will be established forever.

Communion: Communion is open to all who have come to salvation through the sacrificial death and resurrection of Jesus Christ and have thus become a part of the Lord's body and the community of believers.

Creation vs. Evolution: The Bible opens with the words, "In the beginning God created." God is the eternal source and foundation of all that is. God created all things, visible and invisible, including all spiritual beings. All creation is finite and dependent upon the Creator, who was before all things and will continue forever. God's work of creation was good, both physically and morally.

Deity of Jesus: Jesus Christ is truly divine and truly human. He is a distinct person of the Trinity, in perfect equality and unity with God the Father and God the Holy Spirit. He is eternally existent and is fully God. He created all things and is the source and sustainer of life. In the fullness of time, God the Son took on human likeness, conceived by the Holy Spirit, born of the Virgin Mary. He was God incarnate (God in the flesh) and lived on earth as a man, truly human, yet without sin.

Divorce and Remarriage: The Brethren in Christ Church acknowledges the reality of divorce and remarriage but teaches that it is not God's will. There may be occasions when separation or divorce is necessary due·to abuse, etc. When divorce occurs, counseling is done to work through the issues leading to the divorce, especially at the point of remarriage—which may be permitted.

Government: The church is connectional. The highest authority in faith and policy is the biennial General Conference. Congregations are largely autonomous but work within the guidance of a regional bishop (so polity is between episcopal and independent).

Heaven/Hell: Both are realities: the former for those who have trusted

Christ and obediently follow him, the latter for those who have rejected Christ and his offer of salvation. Those who reject Christ will be
punished with everlasting destruction in hell, eternally shut out from
the presence of God.

Homosexuality: There is a difference between practice and orientation.
Practicing homosexuality is sin and has no place in God's Kingdom
since it is an aberration of God's creation and relationships. God has
given standards for expression of sexuality that are necessary for
proper relationships among people. Human sexuality is affirmed within the chaste single life or a life-long marriage between a man and a
woman.

Inspiration of Scripture: The Scriptures are God's message, written by
people in their own language and settings, as inspired by the Holy Spirit. This same Spirit guided the processes of selection and transcription
through which the Scriptures were passed on. Therefore the Bible is
the authoritative and reliable Word of God.

Miracles: God works miracles according to his sovereign will. They are
not the norm of life, but God can intervene in marvelous ways. On occasion the church will pray for and anoint the sick and leave the results
to God.

Restrictions: None required by constitution.

Security of Salvation: Saints are eternally secure as long as they walk
in obedience to the Lordship of Christ. Persistent rebellion results in
the loss of salvation.

Speaking in Tongues and Other Gifts of the Spirit: The Holy Spirit
gives spiritual gifts to all believers according to his sovereign will and
purpose. There are a variety of gifts, given for the building up of the
church and for ministry in the church. Love, the greatest gift of all, is
emphasized. Although no gifts are denied, tongues are seldom heard.

Trinity: There is one triune God—Father, Son, and Holy Spirit.

Women in Ministry: Any person may exercise their gifts, hence women
have been ordained. However, practically speaking, most churches
prefer men as senior pastors. Therefore, women are solo pastors in
smaller churches and hold staff positions of larger churches.

For more information contact: 431 Grantham Rd., Box 290, Grantham,
PA 17027; Phone: (717) 697-2634; Fax: (717) 697-7714; E-mail:
bicgc@messiah.edu

Bruderhof Communities, Inc.

Roots of the Bruderhof can be found in Anabaptism and the Radical Reformation of the early 1500s. Thousands left institutional churches to live a life of sharing and non-violence in Christian communities called Bruderhofs. In 1920, German writer and theologian Eberhard Arnold, his wife Emmy, and a circle of fellow seekers left middle-class Berlin and founded a rural settlement in the spirit of these original Bruderhofs. After expulsion from Germany by the Nazis in 1937, members moved to England, Paraguay, and later to the United States. Bruderhof Communities believe in communal living, sharing all things in common as the early Christians. They are also pacifist. In 1997 there were 2,000 members in six communities.

Abortion: Abortion destroys life and mocks God in whose image every unborn baby is created. Abortion is murder. There are no exceptions.

Baptism: Baptism is the declaration of a good conscience before God, which is possible only through confession and repentance of sins and through the gracious help and cleansing power of Christ's blood. Only adults are baptized.

Birth Control: To indulge in sexual pleasure as an end in itself, without regard for the gift of life, is wrong. To close the door to children for any but the gravest consideration is to despise both the gift and the giver. When used selfishly, all contraceptive measures, especially permanent surgical methods, are objectionable. This is true even of natural family planning, unless there is good reason not to have a child.

Capital Punishment: Bruderhof Communities believe that death is life's most powerful enemy. Therefore, they are against killing anyone. Death is so tremendous and irreversible that they leave the power over life and death to God alone.

Christ's Return: No one knows the date and hour when the end will be. Only the Father knows.

Communion: The Lord's Supper is an outward symbol, a sign of giving of ourselves in brokenness to Jesus, whose body was broken and crucified, whose death made it possible for believers to find forgiveness of sins, love, and unity with one another. Partakers must be in unity and have a clear conscience.

Creation vs. Evolution: God created the heavens and the earth—everything in the universe. Evolution is man's attempt to explain creation without God.

Deity of Jesus: In the beginning there was Christ with God. He has always been alive and is himself God. He created everything there is, nothing exists that he didn't make. Eternal life is in him, and this life gives life to all mankind. His life is the light that shines through the darkness and the darkness can never extinguish it.

Divorce and Remarriage: Bruderhof Communities follow the words of the Apostle Paul when he said that a wife must not leave her husband, but if she is separated from him, let her remain single or else go back to him. And the husband must not divorce his wife. The Communities allow no remarriage for a divorced person.

Government: The governing body, the Brotherhood, consists of all committed members. Responsibilities are delegated to various individual members or married couples with the united agreement of the Brotherhood. This is often done for a trial period in order to ascertain the wisdom of the decision. Each member is accountable to the Brotherhood.

Heaven/Hell: Heaven and hell are realities.

Homosexuality: Homosexuality is an abomination in God's eyes. It is a sin, and it must be repented of and completely rejected to become free.

Inspiration of Scripture: The Scriptures are inspired by God. However, they will be valueless unless hearts are so moved by them that the fruits become obvious.

Miracles: The Bible gives a true account of how God has worked among men. Both the judgments and miracles are true.

Restrictions: None.

Security of Salvation: Christ's cross opened the door to salvation, but it must be embraced. If a person continues to sin and refuses to recognize their guilt and repent, the door of grace is closed. The choice is an individual's.

Speaking in Tongues and Other Gifts of the Spirit: The gifts of the Spirit are great and wonderful, but can easily be misused. The fruits of the Spirit must be sought first. If the fruits are present, the gifts will follow.

Trinity: Bruderhof Communities believe in the Father, the Son, and the Holy Spirit.

Women in Ministry: Women are not appointed to the ministry. However, this service needs the help of a wife.

For more information contact: 207 West Side Rd., Norfolk, CT 06058-1225; Phone: (860) 542-5545; Fax: (860) 542-5548; Web Site: http://www.bruderhof.org

---

Charismatic Episcopal Church

Although the Charismatic Episcopal Church has roots that go back to the third century Anglican tradition, the church is actually a new phenomena whose seeds were planted in a 1977 meeting of evangelical leaders known as the Chicago Call. The CEC officially began on June 26, 1992 when three churches formed the CEC and consecrated the Most Rev. A. Randolph Adler as Bishop.[1] The church holds to historical doctrinal statements including the Apostle's and Nicene Creeds and the Creed of St. Athanasius. It seeks to adhere to the ancient stream of catholicity while also adhering to the ancient evangelical and charismatic streams of the faith. This church also places tremendous importance on the liturgy. In 1997, there were more than 200 churches with 40,000 members worldwide.[2]

Abortion: No answer.

Baptism: Children as well as adults are baptized by sprinkling or pouring. There is one baptism for the remission of sins.[3]

Birth Control: No answer.

Capital Punishment: No answer.

Christ's Return: Christ will come again in glory to judge the living and the dead.[4]

Communion: The Charismatic Episcopal Church takes a high view of the sacraments and believes in the real presence of Christ at the Eucharist.[5]

Creation vs. Evolution: The church believes God is the maker of all things.[6]

Deity of Jesus: The church believes in one Lord, Jesus Christ, the only Son of God, eternally begotten of the Father (not made of one being with the Father), God from God, Light from Light, true God from true God. He came down from heaven, became incarnate by the Virgin Mary and was made man. He was crucified, suffered death, and was buried. On the third day he arose again, ascended into heaven, and sits at the right hand of the Father.[7]

Divorce and Remarriage: No answer.

Government: Episcopal. In the parish, diocesan, and provincial spheres of governance, bishops shepherd the church by consensus along with the priests. The laity participate in ministry at all levels. There is no house of deputies.[8]

Heaven/Hell: No answer.

Homosexuality: No answer.

Inspiration of Scripture: No answer.

Miracles: The church believes that God still performs miracles today, such as healing.[9]

Restrictions: No answer.

Security of Salvation: No answer.

Speaking in Tongues and Other Gifts of the Spirit: The church seeks to restore the ongoing power of the Holy Spirit to the church. They are charismatic.[10]

Trinity: The church believes in the one God, His Son Jesus Christ, and the Holy Spirit who proceeds from the Father and Son as stated in the Nicene Creed.[11]

Women in Ministry: No answer.

For more information contact: 107 W. Marquita, San Clemente, CA 92672; Phone: (714) 366-9480; Fax: (714) 492-7238; E-mail: plsharp@iiccec.org; Web site: http://www.iccec.org/

Christian and Missionary Alliance

The C&MA traces it roots to the vision of Dr. Albert B. Simpson, a Presbyterian clergyman who was motivated by the spiritual needs of the unevangelized. Simpson launched a ministry of evangelism and Bible teaching that was joined by others from a variety of denominations. This mission society soon became a major evangelical movement.[12] The denomination focuses on essentials, such as the deity of Jesus. Non-essential decisions are left up to individual churches. It considers itself a "Great Commission" or missionary church. There were 1,957 churches with an inclusive membership of 307,300 in 1996.

Abortion: Abortion on demand is morally wrong.

Baptism: Most churches prefer baptism by immersion, however this is up to the individual church.

Birth Control: No official stand.

Capital Punishment: No official stand.

Christ's Return: The second coming of the Lord Jesus Christ is imminent and will be personal, visible, and premillennial. This is the believer's blessed hope, and it is a vital truth which is an incentive to holy living and faithful service.[13]

Communion: Churches practice open communion, but the frequency varies.

Creation vs. Evolution: The general consensus is that God created all things.

Deity of Jesus: Jesus Christ is true God and true man. He was conceived by the Holy Spirit and born of the Virgin Mary. He died on the cross, the just for the unjust, as a substitutionary sacrifice. All who believe in him are justified on the ground of his shed blood. He arose from the dead according to the Scriptures. He is now at the right hand of the majesty on high as the great high priest. He will come again to establish his Kingdom of righteousness and peace.[14]

Divorce and Remarriage: This issue is evolving. Credentialled workers are restricted if they have divorced and been remarried. However, there is a less stringent viewpoint taken for layworkers.

Government: The international headquarter's administrative staff includes the president, five vice presidents who oversee church ministries, overseas ministries, general services and finance, an executive administration, and a number of directors who give leadership to the Alliance work. Each year pastors, administrators, and lay delegates from local churches gather for the general council to formulate policies. The program is given oversight by a 28-member board of managers and is carried out by the staff of headquarters and the district offices. Each local church has a voice in national and district policy by sending its pastor and lay delegates to the council and district conference.[15]

Heaven/Hell: There shall be a bodily resurrection of the just and the unjust. For the former there will be a resurrection to life; for the latter, a resurrection to judgment. The prospect for the impenitent and unbelieving person is existence forever in conscious torment. That of the believer in Christ is to have everlasting joy and bliss.[16]

Homosexuality: Homosexuality is an aberration of normal relations and its practice is inconsistent with the Word of God. However, the church does not isolate or reject the individual.

Inspiration of Scripture: The Old and New Testaments, inerrant as originally given, were verbally inspired by God, and are a complete revelation of his will for the salvation of men. They constitute the divine and only rule of Christian faith and practice.[17]

Miracles: Provision is made in the redemptive work of the Lord Jesus Christ for the healing of the mortal body. Prayer for the sick and anointing with oil are taught in the Scriptures and are privileges for the church in this present age.[18]

Restrictions: None.

Security of Salvation: Salvation has been provided through Jesus Christ for all men. Those who repent and believe in him are born again of the Holy Spirit, receive the gift of eternal life, and become the children of God.[19]

Speaking in Tongues and Other Gifts of the Spirit: There is no official stand, but all the gifts are still considered operative in the church.

Trinity: There is one God, who is infinitely perfect, existing in three persons: Father, Son, and Holy Spirit.[20]

Women in Ministry: Women are credentialled, but not ordained.

For more information contact: 8595 Explorer Dr., Colorado Springs, CO 80920; Phone: (719) 599-5999; Fax: (719) 599-3817.

Christian Church (Disciples of Christ)

The Christian Church (Disciples of Christ) is the largest Protestant denomination founded on American soil. In the early 1800s, Barton Stone of Kentucky led the "Christians." Thomas Campbell and his son, Alexander, led the "Disciples" in Pennsylvania. The two movements joined with a formal handshake in 1832 at Lexington, KY. The movement functioned as a brotherhood and matured until 1968, when it took a denominational design and their current name. In 1997 there were 933,011 members in 3,929 congregations.

Abortion: The church is on record as abhorring abortion, but they are also on record as recognizing that civil law gives a person choice in this matter.

Baptism: Disciples baptize by immersion, because it mirrors New Testament practice. Disciples are typically baptized when they can express, as a choice, their desire to become part of the body of Christ. Disciples call this "believer's baptism." However, they recognize the validity of other forms of baptism and welcome those baptized in other customary ways into Christian fellowship and congregational membership.

Birth Control: The Disciples support responsible family planning, but the method is up to the individual.

Capital Punishment: The General Assembly has spoken out against capital punishment.

Christ's Return: There is freedom for each individual to choose their own belief in this area.

Communion: Disciples celebrate the Lord's Supper each Sunday, and invite all believers to the table. The open table is a reminder of the Disciple's commitment to Christian unity.

Creation vs. Evolution: Individuals may believe what they choose.

Deity of Jesus: As members of the Christian Church, Disciples confess that Jesus is the Christ, the Son of the living God, and proclaim him Lord and Savior of the world.

Divorce and Remarriage: The General Assembly has recognized that divorce is traumatic for all involved.

Government: The church government is expressed in three manifestations: congregations, regions, and the general church. Disciples recognize no hierarchy among the three manifestations, but describe the relationship among them as covenantal.

Heaven/Hell: Each individual may choose what they believe.

Homosexuality: The Christian Church (Disciples of Christ) is on record as supporting civil rights, regardless of sexual orientation. Homosexuality and the ordination of homosexuals have been studied in the past.

Inspiration of Scripture: Within the universal church, Disciples receive the gift of ministry and the light of Scripture.

Miracles: Each individual must decide their own beliefs in this area.

Restrictions: None.

Security of Salvation: The confession of faith and baptism secure salvation.

Speaking in Tongues and Other Gifts of the Spirit: Speaking in tongues is not ordinarily part of the Disciples' tradition.

Trinity: Disciples baptize in the name of the holy Trinity.

Women in Ministry: Approximately 11 percent of pastors of Disciples congregations are women. In 1995, for the first time, Disciples ordained more women than men.

For more information contact: 130 E. Washington St., Indianapolis, IN 46204-3645; Phone: (317) 635-3100; Fax: (317) 635-3700; E-mail: cmm@disciples.org; Web site: http://www.disciples.org/

Christian Churches and churches of Christ

Christian Churches and churches of Christ were founded by nineteenth century Christians who rejected denominationalism in favor of unity in the body of Christ. Groups in New England, Kentucky (led by Barton W. Stone), and Pennsylvania (led by Thomas Campbell and his son, Alexander) broke away from their current denominations with the intention of following the Bible only. These early leaders, of what was later called the Restoration Movement, emphasized the unity of all Christians. They believed that to achieve this they must let go of human traditions and loyalties to Christian leaders. Two slogans of the church, "In essentials, unity; in non-essentials, liberty; in all things, love," and "No creed but Christ, no book but the Bible, no law but love," wrap up the basic stance of the churches. A wide variety of differences are tolerated as long as they do not contradict biblical teaching, are not made a test of fellowship or church membership, nor made essential to the church's teaching.[21]

Abortion: No official stance, although traditionally it is opposed.

Baptism: Baptism is by immersion.[22]

Birth Control: No official stance.

Capital Punishment: No statement.

Christ's Return: Christian Churches believe in the future punishment of the wicked and the future reward of the righteous.[23]

Communion: Communion is practiced every Lord's day.[24]

Creation vs. Evolution: No official stance.

Deity of Jesus: Jesus is the Christ, the Son of the living God, and the Savior. The divinity of Christ is the fundamental truth of the Christian system.[25]

Divorce and Remarriage: No official stance.

Government: There are no bishops, superintendents, or national headquarters to determine local church policy. Individual Christian Churches and Churches of Christ elect their own leaders, call and support their own ministers, and decide where mission money will go.[26]

Heaven/Hell: Christian Churches believe in the future punishment of the wicked and the future reward of the righteous.[27]

Homosexuality: No official stance, although it is traditionally opposed.

Inspiration of Scripture: Christian Churches accept both the Old and New Testament Scriptures as the inspired Word of God.[28]

Miracles: No official stance.

Restrictions: None.

Security of Salvation: No statement.

Speaking in Tongues and Other Gifts of the Spirit: No official stance.

Trinity: Christian Churches believe in God the Father. They believe that Jesus is the Christ, the Son of the living God. They believe in the Holy Spirit, both as to his agency in conversion and as indwelling in the heart of the Christian.[29]

Women in Ministry: No statement.

For more information contact: Standard Publishing Co., 8121 Hamilton Ave., Cincinnati, OH 45231; Phone: (513) 931-4050.

Christian Church of North America, The General Council

The Pentecostal revival that swept through America at the turn of the 20th century resulted in an Italian Pentecostal movement that produced several groups of Italian Christian leaders who joined together to evangelize Canada, South America, and Italy. In 1927, this leadership met in Niagara Falls, NY, to formally unite under the name General Council, Christian Church of North America. These leaders established a code of doctrine known as the Articles of Faith.[30] The church believes the nine gifts of the Spirit should be manifested in the church today. In 1997, there were 113 congregations associated with the CCNA.

Abortion: The church opposes abortion.

Baptism: Believers are baptized in water by single immersion in the name of the Father, the Son, and the Holy Spirit. Water baptism is a public declaration of faith in Jesus Christ. It is an outward demonstration of an inward act. Immersion fully portrays the death, burial, and resurrection of Jesus and shows the believer's identification with Christ.[31]

Birth Control: The matter of birth control is left up to the individual.

Capital Punishment: Although there is no official position, the general attitude is that capital punishment is scriptural.

Christ's Return: Before the millennium, the Lord will descend from heaven with a shout, with the voice of the archangel, and with the trump of God. The dead in Christ shall rise first. Then, those that are alive and are left shall together with them be caught up in the clouds to meet the Lord in the air. There will be a first and then a final resurrection that will occur at least 1,000 years apart.[32]

Communion: The Articles of Faith states that during the Lord's Supper, the body of Christ is given, received, and eaten in a heavenly and spiritual manner. The means of receiving and partaking is by faith.

Creation vs. Evolution: Nothing was made without the maker, there is no life without the life-giver, and there is no effect without a cause.[33]

Deity of Jesus: Jesus Christ existed before his incarnation, participated in the creation, and has titles that indicate his eternal being and deity. He was conceived of the Holy Spirit.[34]

Divorce and Remarriage: It is the will of God not to divorce. However, there are circumstances where divorce is permissible, such as fornication or adultery.

Government: The Christian Church of North America utilizes a democratic form of government with an Executive Board that meets at least three times a year to discuss matters, and a General Council that meets annually to make final decisions.

Heaven/Hell: There shall be a bodily resurrection of the just and unjust. The righteous will have eternal life but the unjust shall go into everlasting punishment. There they will be thrust out from the presence of God, away from the light, the joy, and everlasting presence of the Savior. There will be weeping and gnashing of teeth with agony, wrath, and despair.[35]

Homosexuality: Homosexuality is opposed.

Inspiration of Scripture: The entire Bible is the infallible Word of God. Inspired by the Holy Spirit, it is the only perfect order of faith and manner of living. Nothing can be added or taken away. It is the power of God unto salvation for believers.[36]

Miracles: The CCNA believes in miracles performed by God, but does not put their approval on any manifestation that does line up with the Word of God. People may be afflicted because of their sin, but it is also possible for someone to suffer ill health simply because they are part of the human race. Therefore, the church encourages anointing with oil, not because the oil can heal, but because calling for the elders and asking for prayer is an act of faith. God heals, but why he does not heal all is left up to his sovereignty.[37]

Restrictions: The church opposes gambling.

Security of Salvation: Scripture teaches that a person can backslide. Therefore, the Christian Church of North America does not believe in eternal security.

Speaking in Tongues and Other Gifts of the Spirit: The baptism of the Holy Spirit is an experience received subsequent to salvation, with the sign of speaking in tongues as the Spirit gives utterance. The Church believes the nine gifts of the Spirit should be manifested in the church today.[38]

Trinity: There is one living and true God. He is eternal with unlimited power and is the creator of all things. In the one God there are three distinct persons: the Father, the Son, and the Holy Spirit.[39]

Women in Ministry: There are three credentials in the church. Women have been credentialled to preach and to minister the gospel, but not to ordination. There is a current resolution before the General Council to allow the ordination of women.

For more information contact: P.O. Box 141-A, 1294 Rutledge Rd., Transfer, PA 16154; Phone: (412) 962-3501; Fax: (412) 962-1766; E-mail: ccna@nauticom.net; Web site: http://www.ccna.org

Christian Methodist
Episcopal Church, The

The church was organized on December 16, 1870 in Jackson, TN, as the Colored Methodist Episcopal Church. Its name was changed to the Christian Methodist Episcopal Church on May 17, 1954. Worship is orderly yet open to the in-breaking of the Holy Spirit, manifested in shouts of praise, amens, and other spontaneous responses. In 1997 there were 2300 churches with 886,000 members.

Abortion: The termination of a pregnancy is a decision a woman makes. She should make it prayerfully in communion with God and professionally in consultation with a competent physician. Abortion should not be used as contraception, for controlling family size, or for economics. While the church prefers that abortion be resorted to only when a mother's life is at risk, or in cases of incest or rape, in all instances of abortion the church reaches out in love, offering grace to the woman.

Baptism: Baptism is one of two sacraments practiced. The other is the Lord's Supper or Holy Communion. As a sacrament, baptism is something done to individuals, infants, children, youth, or adults in one of several modes—sprinkling, pouring, or immersion. It is the initiatory act through which individuals are received into the body of Christ and is at the same time the beginning of a process of growth in faith.

Birth Control: It is acceptable for married couples to engage in sexual relations utilizing contraceptives to avert procreation while enjoying the other blessings of the sexual act.

Capital Punishment: All human life is God's gift. Thus, it is sacred. The Christian Methodist Episcopal Church leaves vengeance up to God. In the final analysis, the taking of one innocent life by the State is one life too many.

Christ's Return: Christ, who ascended into heaven and sits at the right hand of God the Father, will come again to judge the living and the dead. No one knows when.

Communion: Holy Communion is one of two sacraments. Holy Communion celebrates and proclaims, in the present, the past death of Jesus the Christ and looks forward with hope for his coming again.

Creation vs. Evolution: Creation does not oppose evolution. Both are ways and means of understanding the universe and of understanding order in the world. Creation refers to the initial beginning of all things by God. It refers also to a far reaching structural pattern. God's hand remains on creation. And to the extent that evolution enhances human understanding of the unfolding knowledge of creation, it is more than a theory and becomes creation's servant.

Deity of Jesus: Jesus was conceived by the Holy Spirit. He was born of the Virgin Mary. He was indeed the Son of God—very man and very God, the God-man.

Divorce and Remarriage: Marriage is sacred. However, due to certain circumstances that may develop in marriages, maintaining a quality of relationship that does justice to the sacredness of marriage and family becomes impossible. Thus, divorce may be the only viable option. The church counsels those whose marriages are falling in disrepair to seek help in shoring them up. Where this fails, divorce may follow. Should divorce occur, no prohibitions to remarriage exist.

Government: The government of the Christian Methodist Episcopal Church is episcopal, that is, governed or superintended by bishops. It has three branches: legislative (General Conference), executive (College of Bishops), and judicial (Judicial Council).

Heaven/Hell: Heaven and hell are terms that convey everlasting human relationships with God. Heaven is the eternal enjoyment of a perfect relationship with God and others. Hell is to be without a perfect relationship with God here and beyond time.

Homosexuality: While the church does not bless or condone the practice of homosexuality, it does not ex-communicate or curse the human beings involved. God's grace is sufficient for all.

Inspiration of Scripture: All Scriptures are the work of inspired human beings. Through the in-breathing of the Holy Spirit, the words of God were entrusted to fallible men and women.

Miracles: The Christian Methodist Episcopal Church believes in miracles, which are signs of God's immediate power in events upon the external world.

Restrictions: The *General Rules of John Wesley's Societies* prohibit drinking alcohol and taking another Christian to court. The church's social creed prohibits gambling.

Security of Salvation: Salvation is God's gift in Jesus Christ. It is received through the Holy Spirit. Should a believer sin after justification, by the grace of God he may rise again and amend his life.

Speaking in Tongues and Other Gifts of the Spirit: Speaking in tongues is but one gift of the Spirit. God gives gifts for the exercise of ministry and for use for the common good of the church. Where exercising gifts does not enhance the common good of the people of God in Christ or equip the saints of ministry, they are suspect.

Trinity: God is one, living and true, everlasting and without parts. In the unity of the God-head, there are three persons of one substance, power, and eternity—the Father, the Son, and the Holy Ghost.

Women in Ministry: Women have had full clergy rights since 1966. They may be ordained as deacons and elders or serve the church as pastors, presiding elders, or bishops.

For more information contact: 1616 E. Illinois Ave., Dallas, TX 75216; Phone: (214) 372-9073; Fax: (214) 372-2082.

Christian Pilgrim Church

While its deepest roots came out of the ministries of John and Charles Wesley, the Christian Pilgrim Church began in the United States in response to the holiness movement.[40] The church recently joined hands with the Wesleyan Bible Holiness Church. In 1997, there were more than 20 churches.

Abortion: The church is anti-abortion.

Baptism: Water baptism is an outward sign of an inward work.

Birth Control: Birth control methods are left up to the individual.

Capital Punishment: The church supports capital punishment.

Christ's Return: Christ will return again.

Communion: Communion is celebrated in remembrance of Christ's suffering.

Creation vs. Evolution: All things were created by God.

Deity of Jesus: Jesus is the Son of God.

Divorce and Remarriage: While the Christian Pilgrim Church believes marriage is for life, they also recognize that divorce does happen.

Government: Congregational.

Heaven/Hell: There is a literal heaven and hell—heaven to gain, hell to shun.

Homosexuality: Homosexuality is an abomination.

Inspiration of Scripture: The Scriptures are God inspired.

Miracles: Since Jesus is the same yesterday, today, and tomorrow, miracles still occur.

Restrictions: The Christian Pilgrim Church encourages its members to avoid worldliness.

Security of Salvation: Believers must walk in the light day by day and moment by moment. If they turn back, it becomes a great darkness.

Speaking in Tongues and Other Gifts of the Spirit: There is a genuine speaking in tongues as well as a false one.

Trinity: God is three in one—God the Father, Jesus the Son, and God the Holy Spirit.

Women in Ministry: Women are allowed in ministry.

For more information contact: 3797 Chapel Rd., Spring Arbor, MI 49283; Phone: (517) 750-1929.

Christian Reformed Church in North America

The Christian Reformed Church has roots that go back to the 1830s, when members of the Reformed Church of the Netherlands refused to be under control of the Dutch monarchy and formed an independent body. In 1847, members immigrated to the United States. They formed an alliance with the Reformed Church in America. However, some members broke away from the main body. First known as the Dutch Reformed Church in 1859, the Christian Reformed Church was officially named in 1894.[41] In 1996, there were 740 churches in the United States with approximately 285,864 members distributed throughout the U.S. and Canada.

Abortion: Christian Reformed Churches condemn the wanton or arbitrary destruction of any human being at any state of its development from the point of conception to the point of death. An induced abortion is an allowable option only when the life of the mother is genuinely threatened by the continuation of the pregnancy.[42]

Baptism: Infants are baptized.[43]

Birth Control: It is the solemn duty of the church to bear testimony against the growing evil of a selfish birth restriction and to hold up the sacred ordinances of God and the Christian ideal of marriage and parenthood, which are increasingly being ignored and flouted in this day.[44]

Capital Punishment: No statement.

Christ's Return: Christ will return bodily and take to himself all believers. This one-time return will thereby establish his eternal, perfect Kingdom.[45]

Communion: Only those who have professed faith in Christ may participate in communion. It is celebrated at least four times a year. Check with a local church for frequency of practice.[46]

Creation vs. Evolution: The historical character of the revelation in Genesis 1 and 2 must be maintained without compromise.[47] The church believes in the ancient credal confession that God created the heavens and earth.

Deity of Jesus: The church joyfully confesses their faith in Jesus Christ as Savior and Lord.[48]

Divorce and Remarriage: The church recognizes one instance where divorce is biblically approved—in the case of persistent and unrepentant adultery. Regarding remarriage: The basic declaration of Scripture is that divorce and remarriage while one's spouse is still alive constitutes adultery. However, the church also recognizes that Scripture is not always clear on what constitutes a biblical divorce, except in the case stated above.[49]

Government: Synod, made up of pastors and elders from each classis, meet once per year. The Synod has jurisdiction over all ministers and congregations.

Heaven and Hell: Those who have been saved by grace through faith will live with Christ in eternal paradise. Those who reject him will suffer the pains of hell.

Homosexuality: Homosexuality is a condition of disordered sexuality which reflects the brokenness of a sinful world and for which the homosexual may himself bear only minimal responsibility. The homosexual may not, on the sole ground of his sexual disorder, be denied community acceptance. If he is a Christian, he is to be wholeheartedly received by the church as a person for whom Christ died. Explicit homosexual practice must be condemned as incompatible with obedience to the will of God as revealed in Holy Scripture.[50]

Inspiration of Scripture: Holy Scripture in its entirety is the Word of God written. It was given by inspiration of God to be the rule of faith and practice—an inspiration of an organic nature which extends not only to the ideas but also to the words, and is so unique in its effect that Holy Scripture alone is the Word of God. Scripture in its whole extent and in all its parts is infallible and inerrant.[51]

Miracles: The Spirit may guide at times in strange and wonderful ways.[52]

Restrictions: Christian Reformed churches firmly oppose lodge membership.

Security of Salvation: God holds those in his hands whom he has called and regenerated.

Speaking in Tongues and Other Gifts of the Spirit: The church firmly rejects the teaching that baptism with the Holy Spirit is a second blessing distinct from and usually received after conversion. Synod warns the churches to be alert to the many errors and excesses involved in much of today's exercise of charismatic gifts such as tongue-speaking, faith healing, and exorcism.[53]

Trinity: The church believes in the triune God.

Women in Ministry: Synod now allows ordination of women to offices of deacon, elder, minister, and evangelist.

For more information contact: 2850 Kalamazoo Ave. SE, Grand Rapids, MI 49560; Phone: (616) 241-1691; Fax: (616) 224-5895; Web site: http://www.crcna.org/

Christ's Sanctified Holy Church

In 1887, on Chincoteague Island, VA, a group of 51 members of the Methodist Episcopal Church, led by Joseph B. Lynch and Sarah E. Collins, became convinced that one could not be saved without sanctification. When they requested a minister, they were turned out of the Methodist Episcopal Church. They organized themselves into a body on

February 14, 1892. Christ's Holy Sanctified Church believes no ordinances or rituals are necessary to establish a relationship with God, and it believes that the new birth, baptism, communion, circumcision, the second coming, and resurrection are to be interpreted in a spiritual sense. It does not practice tithing and has no paid ministers. The church's motto is, "No Creed But Christ, No Law But Love, No Guide But the Bible," and there were 17 congregations with 1,500 members in 1997.

Abortion: Abortion is not approved of because every person is created in the likeness and image of God. The creation of a human child is a miraculous work of God involving body, soul, mind, and spirit, and is thus the offspring of God. Abortion violates the commandment given to Moses and confirmed by Christ, "Thou shalt not kill."

Baptism: Water baptism is not practiced, but the church believes in the spiritual baptism of the Holy Ghost received instantaneously at sanctification subsequent to the forgiveness of sins. Baptism by water was a valid ordinance under the first covenant. However, with the advent of the new covenant—brought about by Christ's death, burial, and resurrection from the dead—all ordinances, signs, types, and shadows were brought to their spiritual reality in Christ. Therefore, the understanding of a spiritual baptism brings freedom from the bondage of ordinances.

Birth Control: The question of birth control shall be left to the discretion of a man and his wife.

Capital Punishment: The church does not believe in capital punishment. Mortal life and death are in the hands of God and not man. Vengeance belongs to God. Capital punishment is in direct opposition to the commandment, "Thou shalt not kill." Persons who prove themselves incapable of rehabilitation should be permanently incarcerated.

Christ's Return: Christ's Sanctified Holy Church does not believe in the literal return of Christ. Christ's promise, "I will come again," was fulfilled on the day of Pentecost by the pouring out of the Holy Spirit on the believers.

Communion: The Lord's Supper is not practiced. No act or ritual is necessary to establish a relationship between God and mankind. True Communion is a spiritual experience of believers in eating his flesh and drinking his blood. This witness is by prayers, reading his word, meditation, and divine revelation from God by the Holy Spirit.

Creation vs. Evolution: The creation by God is a fact, witnessed by all, and substantiated by numerous circumstantial evidences. The earth, along with the entire universe, mankind, and all other forms of life both physical and spiritual, were created by God.

Deity of Christ: Jesus Christ was the Son of God, born of the Virgin Mary, begotten by the Holy Ghost, and is the second person in the Trinity. Jesus the Christ was God manifested in the flesh. Coming to earth in the form of man was one of the greatest events that has ever happened in the history of mankind. He is the High Priest, intercessor, redeemer, Lord, Savior, and King of kings.

Divorce and Remarriage: God, in his infinite wisdom, from the very beginning, ordained the relationship of man and woman in the context of a sacred marriage. The entire structure of the family, and consequently society at large, rests upon the foundation of the observance of the marriage vow. This is to supersede all human bonds, to be founded upon love, to be understood as a commitment to love each other and also as a commitment to God, and is not to be broken. Man in his fragility sometimes fails to achieve this lofty estate, but God in his mercy does not exclude such from salvation.

Government: Church government is composed of three bodies. The Board is the spiritual and ruling body. The Board of Extension is responsible for the real and chattel properties and all business functions. It is subject to the first board. The General Conference's function is to present matters to the first board. Each church has an ordained minister or leader to oversee that congregation.

Heaven/Hell: There is a reward for righteousness and a penalty for sin. Sinners shall go into everlasting punishment, but the righteous into life eternal.

Homosexuality: The church does not condone homosexuality.

Inspiration of Scripture: All Scripture is given by the inspiration of God and is profitable for doctrine, for reproof, for correction, and for instruction in righteousness. The Old and New Testaments were divinely inspired by holy men of God who spoke as they were moved by the Holy Ghost. Furthermore, only true believers may be inspired by the Spirit in the Holy Scriptures.

Miracles: Jesus and his disciples did many miracles to heal the sick and raise the dead, but the greatest was when Jesus gave believers eternal life. Prayer, communion, divine revelation, and a spiritual resurrection are the wonderful miracles of God.

Restrictions: Members of Christ's Sanctified Holy Church do not wear jewelry, consume alcoholic beverages, use any form of tobacco, gamble, go to worldly forms of entertainment, use foul language, or do anything else that is not consistent with God-fearing disciples of Christ.

Security of Salvation: Believers are saved by hope and have an anchor of the soul both sure and steadfast. God's love and care for his children creates an assurance and confidence that he has given eternal life and this life is in his Son.

Speaking in Tongues and Other Gifts of the Spirit: The disciples spoke in a known tongue. It was a miracle of God in which every man heard them speak in his own language. Paul states his desire to speak five words of understanding rather than ten thousand in an unknown tongue. All the gifts of the Spirit are from God.

Trinity: There is but one uncreated, unoriginated, infinite, and eternal being—the creator, preserver, and governor of all things. There is in this infinite essence a plurality of what is commonly called persons, not separately subsisting, but essentially belonging to the Godhead. These persons are commonly termed the Father, Son, and Holy Ghost and are generally named the Trinity.

Women in Ministry: Women share equal participation in all church functions in the ministry since there is neither male nor female, for all are one in Christ Jesus.

For more information contact: 4632 Lelia Court, Columbia, SC 29206; Phone: (803) 787-4212; Fax: (803) 790-9229.

Church(es) of Christ, The

The Churches of Christ originated in the American Restoration movement (also known as the Stone-Cambell movement) of the early 1900s. The movement emphasized the New Testament and rejected denominational labels.[54] Within the Churches of Christ are several branches that have separated over issues such as the use of one cup to serve communion, Sunday School, the question of when Christ will return, and Pentecostalism. But while interpretations may differ, Churches of Christ are united on one issue and that is their commitment to the New Testament. There are no governing boards, and each church independently and autonomously makes its own decisions regarding social issues and some doctrinal issues. A capella singing is the only music used in worship services.[55] In 1997, there were 20,000 congregations with a total membership of up to three million.

Abortion: No statement. Check your local church.

Baptism: Baptism is not a church ordinance, but a command of Christ. Only adult baptism by immersion is practiced because New Testament baptism is only for sinners who profess belief and penitence. An infant has no sin and cannot qualify as a believer.[56]

Birth Control: No statement. Check your local church.

Capital Punishment: No statement. Check your local church.

Christ's Return: No statement. Check your local church.

Communion: The Lord's Supper is observed on the first day of every week.[57]

Creation vs. Evolution: No statement. Check your local church.

Deity of Jesus: No statement. Check your local church.

Divorce and Remarriage: No statement. Check your local church.

Government: Each congregation is self-ruled and independent from all others. There are no governing boards, no headquarters, no conventions or annual meetings, and no official publications. Each local congregation is governed by a plurality of elders selected from the membership.[58]

Heaven/Hell: No statement. Check your local church.

Homosexuality: No statement. Check your local church.

Inspiration of Scripture: No statement. Check your local church.

Miracles: No statement. Check your local church.

Restrictions: Churches of Christ subscribe to no creed other than the New Testament. Some reject the use of instrumental music in worship because there is no mention of mechanical instruments in the New Testament.

Security of Salvation: No statement. Check your local church.

Speaking in Tongues and Other Gifts of the Spirit: No statement. Check your local church.

Trinity: No statement. Check your local church.

Women in Ministry: No statement. Check your local church.

For more information contact: Gospel Advocate Co., P.O. Box 150, Nashville, TN 37202-9875; Phone: (800) 251-8446 or (615) 254-8781.

Churches of Christ in Christian Union

Churches of Christ in Christian Union were founded in 1909 by a group of ministers who were seeking greater freedom to preach the Wesleyan Holiness message. With beginnings in southern Ohio, the organization had 220 congregations located in 14 states in 1997. It sponsors 40–50 missionaries in six areas of the world in cooperation with the World Gospel Mission and has approximately 110 congregations internationally.

Abortion: The churches are opposed to abortion.

Baptism: Baptism is one of two sacraments recognized by the church. It is viewed as an outward testimony of an inward work of saving grace.

Birth Control: No official position.

Capital Punishment: No official position, although it is generally supported.

Christ's Return: At the end of this age, the coming of Christ will be in two phases: first, to translate the church to heaven or to himself, and second, to judge the existing nations.

Communion: Communion is one of two sacraments recognized by the church. Communion was instituted by Christ as a memorial of his death. Open communion is extended to all persons who have true faith in Christ.

Creation vs. Evolution: Creation as recorded in Genesis is the accurate record of beginnings.

Deity of Jesus: Jesus is the second person of the Trinity. He is one with the Father and the Holy Spirit, and all that has been said of the Father is true of the Son.

Divorce and Remarriage: The churches accept the right of divorce and remarriage for the person whose partner was guilty of fornication or adultery.

Government: Each local church governs itself within the guidelines of the denominational manual.

Heaven/Hell: Heaven and hell are both eternal and literal.

Homosexuality: The churches reject all forms of homosexuality or lesbianism. All such practices are viewed as sinful.

Inspiration of Scripture: The Bible is an infallible guide. It is entirely accurate in every detail, especially in its original Hebrew and Greek texts. It is inspired by the Holy Spirit in a sense that no other book can be said to be inspired. It is a sufficient rule of faith and practice.

Miracles: Miracles are possible and do occur. God primarily intervenes during times of human helplessness and need. Furthermore, miracles are intended to advance God's glory, not human glory.

Restrictions: No member may use or deal in tobacco or alcoholic beverages, use any form of illegal drugs, or be an avowed and/or practicing homosexual or lesbian.

Security of Salvation: Each Christian is a free moral agent who could personally freely choose to come to or reject the invitation to come to Christ. In like manner, each Christian has the freedom to choose to sever the saving relationship existing with Christ.

Speaking in Tongues and Other Gifts of the Spirit: All the gifts of the Spirit are under the sovereign disposition of the Holy Spirit and are granted to individuals as the Spirit wills. The phenomena of speaking in tongues, as best illustrated on the day of Pentecost, was distinctly the miracle of speaking in other languages already in existence. The problem at the Corinthian church regarding the gift of tongues is not the phenomena that occurred on the day of Pentecost but rather the problem of several language groups present for worship within a single congregation.

Trinity: The Godhead is a Trinity of persons: the Father, the Son, and the Holy Spirit.

Women in Ministry: Women are accepted in all forms of ministry and in all levels of licensing.

For more information contact: 1426 Lancaster Pike, Circleville, OH 43113; Phone: (614) 474-8856; Fax: (614) 477-7766.

Church of Christ (Holiness) of the United States of America

The Church of Christ (Holiness) U.S.A. had its beginning in the holiness movement which swept the United States during the last decade of the 19th century. Charles Price Jones, poet, musician and nationally-known preacher, called a holiness convocation which convened on June 6, 1897. The movement which resulted from this convention was originally non-denominational, but various organized bodies eventually formed out of the group. Jones led the assemblage which became the Church of Christ (Holiness) U.S.A. In 1997, there were 170 congregations with between 12,000 and 18,000 members.

Abortion: Human life, at whatever stage of development, is sacred and precious and should be sustained by all reasonable means. At no stage should life be aborted for mere contraceptive or psychological reasons. When, and if, abortion is necessary to preserve the life of the mother, it must be done only as an alternative, after prayerful and specific medical and ministerial advice is rendered.

Baptism: Baptism is commanded by the Lord as an ordinance in the church. It belongs to the believer in the gospel of Jesus Christ (not infants who cannot believe). The biblical means of administering baptism is by immersion.

Birth Control: No official statement.

Capital Punishment: No official statement.

Christ's Return: The Lord Jesus Christ will return to rapture the church and to judge the living and the dead.

Communion: The Lord's Supper is a New Testament ordinance. It was instituted when the Lord celebrated his last Passover with his disciples. It consists of bread and unfermented wine. As often as it is taken it shows forth the Lord's death until he comes again.

Creation vs. Evolution: The Church of Christ (Holiness) believes in one God, and that he is eternal. He is the maker of heaven and earth.

Deity of Jesus: Jesus Christ, the Son of the living God, is the second person in the Godhead, co-equal and co-existent with the Father, and the Holy Ghost. In the fullness of time, he was manifested in the flesh and incarnated by the power of the Holy Ghost in the womb of the Virgin Mary.

Divorce and Remarriage: God hates "putting away." However, Jesus gives one specific grounds for divorce and remarriage, which is adultery. Any member of the Church of Christ (Holiness) U.S.A. must consult with church officials before seeking counsel from a lawyer or marriage counselor. Failing to follow steps in the church manual regarding marriage and divorce subjects members and ministers to disciplinary action.

Government: Representative. Final authority in defining the organizational responsibilities rests with the national convention. The bishops of the church are delegated special powers to act in behalf of or speak for the church. Pastors are ordained ministers, who under the call of God and his people have divine oversight of local churches. The representative form of government gives ministry and laity equal authority in all deliberative bodies.

Heaven /Hell: There is an actual place called heaven (the eternal home of the Christian) and a place called hell (the eternal home of the lost).

Homosexuality: The Church of Christ (Holiness) U.S.A. teaches against homosexuality in the general rules of their manual.

Inspiration of Scripture: The Holy Bible, composed of the Old and New Testaments, contains the eternal, inerrant Word of God and was written by holy men as they were moved by the Holy Ghost.

Miracles: The church believes in divine healing.

Restrictions: The church restricts the use of strong drinks, tobacco, illegal drugs, unwholesome literature, oathbound secret orders or fraternities, lotteries and games of chance, and entertainment that is not to the glory of God. Quarreling, returning evil for evil, gossiping, slandering, spreading false reports, dishonesty, taking advantage in buying and selling, going to extreme in dress (indecorum), sodomy or adultery of any form, impropriety of conduct, rebellion and neglect of duty are also restricted.

Security of Salvation: The church accepts the possibility of one falling from grace, while holding to the strong improbability for those who abide in Jesus.

Speaking in Tongues and Other Gifts of the Spirit: No one gift is the specific sign or evidence of the Holy Spirit's presence. Though these gifts may be of use to edify, they may be counterfeited and are not to be trusted as evidence. The three evidences of a Spirit-filled life are faith, hope and love. The Bible endorses speaking in tongues and a gift of tongues, but in a language understood by man. Speaking with tongues is merely a sign, and if exercised should follow biblical guidelines.

Trinity: God is triune, being revealed as Father, Son, and Holy Ghost. The Holy Spirit is the third person in the triune God head, ever present and active in the church of Christ, which is the body of Christ.

Women in Ministry: Those women who evidence their gift and anointing of God to teach, shall have the privilege to teach and conduct religious services in the churches under the direction of the pastor in charge. The Church of Christ (Holiness), U.S.A. does not license or ordain women to preach, but under the pastor's supervision, women may teach and do general missionary work.

For more information contact: P.O. Box 6182, Pearl, MS 39288; Phone: (601) 353-0222 or (601) 982-4044; Fax: (601) 362-7864 or (601) 939-1950.

Church of Christ (No Sunday School)

The Church of Christ which does not have Sunday School and uses only one cup and one loaf for communion is one of the many branches of the Churches of Christ that have their origination in the American Restoration Movement (see preceding entry). With, "Where the Scriptures Speak, We Speak; Where the Scriptures are Silent We are Silent," as their motto, the church had 500 churches with 25,000 members in 1997. The teaching of the Bible is done in an individual assembly with only men speaking. There are no Sunday school or Bible classes. The Communion (Lord's Supper) is observed with one loaf of unleavened bread and one cup of unfermented grape juice in each congregation. All singing is a capella.

Abortion: The church is against abortion.

Baptism: Baptism is necessary for the remission of sins.

Birth Control: Birth control is an individual matter.

Capital Punishment: Capital punishment is a matter that belongs to the civil government.

Christ's Return: Christ will come again. The time of his return is unknown.

Communion: The Lord's Supper is observed every first day of the week using one loaf of unleavened bread from which each communicant breaks and one cup containing unfermented grape juice from which each communicant drinks.

Creation vs. Evolution: The church believes in the creation of all things by God. They oppose the theory of evolution.

Deity of Jesus: Jesus is the divine Son of God.

Divorce and Remarriage: Anyone who divorces his wife, except in the case of infidelity, and remarries another commits adultery.

Government: Each church is autonomous and is governed by its elders and deacons.

Heaven/Hell: The Church of Christ believes in heaven as the eternal home of the redeemed. Hell is the final abode of the devil and his angels and all those who serve him.

Homosexuality: The Church of Christ considers homosexuality to be an ungodly practice and is opposed to it.

Inspiration of Scripture: All Scriptures are inspired of God.

Miracles: Miracles have ceased. They were a part of and belonged to the period of church history prior to the completion of the New Testament Scriptures.

Restrictions: None.

Security of Salvation: The Church of Christ believes that Christians can fall from grace and be lost.

Speaking in Tongues and Other Gifts of the Spirit: All such gifts have ceased. They belonged to the days prior to the completion of the Scriptures.

Trinity: The church believes in God the Father, God the Son, and God the Holy Spirit.

Women in Ministry: The Church of Christ is opposed to women preachers.

For more information contact: P.O. Box 10811, Springfield, MO 65808; Phone: (417) 883-2315.

Church of God, The

The Church of God was organized after a number of reformations. The first Church of God was started in 1903 by A.J. Tomlinson. In 1922, a second church known as The Church of God of Prophecy branched off. In 1957, The Church of God was formed by Bishop Grady R. Kent. It believes in the Judaic Christian heritage and that Jesus did not start another religion called Christianity even though the term Christian is now used. The church also believes that God is the author of one eternal religion set forth and systematized at Sinai by Moses, reformed and perfected at Calvary by Jesus Christ, believed and practiced by the New Testament Church, and restored and observed among the Gentiles by the last days' church. The church celebrates the feasts of the Lord, including his Sabbath. In 1997 there were 18 churches in the United States with 320 members who hold to the motto, "No Lawbook but the Bible."

Abortion: The Church of God believes that abortion is the taking of a human life. From the time of fertilization, there is no justification for inducing miscarriage by surgical or chemical means.

Baptism: One of the sacraments of the church, water baptism by immersion, is an outward sign of an inward grace. It demonstrates to the world and the person being immersed that through the baptism of repentance they have been brought forth to eternal life through faith in Jesus Christ.

Birth Control: Since there is no independent life in the womb until the time of fertilization, The Church of God recognizes the right of married couples to use contraceptives according to the dictates of their conscience.

Capital Punishment: Capital punishment should be used in the case of murder.

Christ's Return: The blessed hope of the gospel is the second coming of the Lord Jesus Christ and the resurrection and change of the righteous of the earth.

Communion: Communion, or the Lord's Supper, is an important part of the system of worship that the Church of God employs. It is the visible means of worship that Jesus commanded believers to observe in remembrance of his death. While the church's primary observance of communion is at Passover, the communion service may be employed in any worship service.

Creation vs. Evolution: The Church of God does not accept the unproven allegations of the theory of evolution. The Church of God teaches that God created heaven and earth from nothing in the beginning. He subsequently formed everything in heaven (including the angels) and everything in the earth.

Deity of Christ: John 1:1–2, 14 speak clearly of the deity of Christ.

Divorce and Remarriage: God hates divorce. It grieves God for couples to separate after they have been joined by a holy covenant. Though God hates divorce, he has made provision for divorce and remarriage in cases of marital infidelity for the believer. In cases where people have divorced and remarried for whatever reason, they are to remain in the marital state in which they are at the time of conversion. God does forgive the sin of divorce.

Government: The church government is ecclesiastical. Theocratic government is constituted by the leadership of God over the spiritual affairs of his people through an anointed leader and a system of delegated authority, comprised of a pattern of bishops appointed under the anointed leader's supervision.

Heaven/Hell: There is eternal life for the righteous and eternal punishment for the wicked.

Homosexuality: Same-sex relationships are never accepted in the Holy Scriptures and are therefore condemned as sin in all situations. There are no exceptions.

Inspiration of Scripture: The whole Bible is the inspired Word of God and is the true doctrine for faith and practice. Government and discipline must be determined from the New Testament.

Miracles: The Church of God believes in the full restoration of gifts to individuals in the church, both the nine gifts of the Spirit and the five gifts of the ministry, which includes the gift of miracles.

Restrictions: The church has no stated restrictions.

Security of Salvation: Matthew 10:28, 29 says that no man can pluck us out of our Father's hand. If believers continue in his hand, they are eternally secure. However, individuals can leave the hand of God and be lost. So, the promise is in continuance.

Speaking in Tongues and Other Gifts of the Spirit: See entry on miracles.

Trinity: God exists eternally as one God in three persons—namely God the Father (Yahweh), God the Son (Yahshua of Jesus), and God the Spirit (Ruach Hachodesh).

Women in Ministry: The Church of God welcomes women into the ministry. It licenses and ordains women and places women in the role of pastor.

For more information contact: 1826 Dalton Pike SE, Cleveland, TN 37312 or P.O. Box 1207, Cleveland, TN 37364-1207; Phone: (423) 472-1597 or (423) 476-5596; Fax: (423) 478-5572.

Church of God (Anderson, IN), The

While the Church of God (Anderson, IN) was influenced by the holiness movement, the most distinctive attribute of this body is its emphasis on Christian unity and its lack of emphasis on creeds and codes. Organized in 1880, the church does not have a book of discipline or book of order, and doctrinal positions are not set for the entire denomination. Therefore, specific points of doctrine may vary depending on the church and the geographical area. There are, however, some issues that all the churches agree upon. Those issues are listed in this section.[59] The Church of God does not require membership and keeps no registration of members.

Abortion: The Church of God opposes abortion on demand.

Baptism: Baptism is by immersion.

Birth Control: No position.

Capital Punishment: No position.

Christ's Return: Christ will return a second time, but that return is not connected to the millennium. The Kingdom of God is ongoing.[60]

Communion: Communion is open to all believers.[61]

Creation vs. Evolution: No position.

Deity of Jesus: Jesus is divine.[62]

Divorce and Remarriage: No position.

Government: Congregational. There is an annual General Assembly, and state and regional associations.[63]

Heaven/Hell: There will be rewards for the righteous and punishment of the unrighteous.[64]

Homosexuality: The Church of God (Anderson, IN) does not endorse or promote homosexual behavior as an acceptable alternate or Christian lifestyle.

Inspiration of Scripture: The Bible is the Word of God.[65]

Miracles: No position.

Restrictions: None.

Security of Salvation: No answer.

Speaking in Tongues and Other Gifts of the Spirit: No answer.

Trinity: The church holds a traditional view of the Trinity: God the Father, God the Son, and God the Holy Spirit.[66]

Women in Ministry: Women have been accepted in ministry since the beginning.

For more information contact: 1303 E. Fifth St., P.O. Box 2420, Anderson, IN 46018-2420; Phone: (765) 642-0256; Fax: (765) 642-5652.

Church of God by Faith, Inc.

The Church of God by Faith, Inc. was established in 1914 at Jacksonville, FL, by founders Crawford Bright, John Bright, Aaron Matthews, Sr., and Nathaniel Scrippes. A charter was drafted at the Alachua, FL, headquarters in 1922. The Church of God by Faith seeks the experience of sanctification and strives to advance the Kingdom of God. In 1997 there were 200 churches with approximately 16,500 members.

Abortion: Abortion is murder and the church neither sanctions nor approves of anyone engaging in or being a party to abortion.

Baptism: The church believes in one God, one faith, and one baptism— and the baptism by the Holy Ghost is the only baptism essential for complete revelation.

Birth Control: The Church of God by Faith, Inc. does not support the use of birth control since the Bible states, "Be fruitful and multiply."

Capital Punishment: The church does not support capital punishment based on the passage in Exodus which states, "Thou shall not kill."

Christ's Return: Jesus Christ will return again. He will come quickly and his reward is with him.

Communion: The Word of God is the communion of the blood and the body of Christ. Christ is the lamb of God and his broken body is bread and his shed blood is life. This is the true communion.

Creation vs. Evolution: No answer.

Deity of Jesus: Obedience to God is supreme. God is, and should be, recognized as the sovereign ruler of all things.

Divorce and Remarriage: The only biblical grounds for divorce are adultery and fornication. Anyone who obtains a divorce that does not meet these requirements and remarries is living in adultery.

Government: At the national level there is a Board of Elders, including the bishop who oversees the Board. There are two national meetings each year where the national Board of Elders appoints pastors to local congregations and makes decisions that are binding on the local churches.

Heaven/Hell: The saints will be with the Lord forever. Those whose names are not found in the Book of Life will be cast into the lake of fire.

Homosexuality: Homosexuality is the result of man turning from God to believe a lie and not the gospel. For this cause God gave them up to vile affections.

Inspiration of Scripture: All Scripture is given by inspiration of God and is profitable for doctrine, reproof, correction, and instruction in righteousness.

Miracles: The church believes in miracles and divine healing.

Restrictions: Card-playing, ballrooms, lotteries, and games of chance.

Security of Salvation: Salvation is the complete work of God. There is security in Christ by the unmerited favor of grace from God to man.

Speaking in Tongues and Other Gifts of the Spirit: The Church of God by Faith, Inc. believes in receiving the gifts of the Spirit and speaking in tongues as the Spirit gives utterance.

Trinity: There is one eternally existent, infinite God, sovereign of the universe. Jesus Christ, the second person of the Godhead, was eternally one with the Father. The Holy Spirit, the third person of the Godhead, is ever present and efficiently active in and with the Church of Christ.

Women in Ministry: Women have a ministry in the church, but under the authority of men.

For more information contact: P.O. Box 121, Gainesville, FL 32609; Phone: (352) 376-3366; Fax: (352) 372-9444.

Church of God (Cleveland, TN)

The Church of God (Cleveland, TN) has its roots in the holiness movement led by the elder R.G. Spurling and his son. First named The Christian Union, then the Holiness Church,[67] the Church of God celebrated its centennial in 1996. In 1997, there were 4.1 million members worldwide.

Abortion: The General Assembly of the Church of God is committed to the sacredness of human life and stands opposed to the use of abortion as a means of birth control. They also have urged their constituency to actively oppose any liberalization of abortion laws.[68]

Baptism: Baptism is performed by total immersion in the name of the Father, Son, and Holy Spirit. It is done at the age of accountability, when an individual makes a personal commitment to follow Christ.

Birth Control: No stand.

Capital Punishment: No stand.

Christ's Return: Christ's return will be premillennial. At that time all believers will be caught up in the air to be with him.

Communion: Communion is open to all believers. Individual congregations decide the frequency.

Creation vs. Evolution: The church supports the principle that where evolution is taught in the public schools, provision should be made for teaching the biblical alternative of creation.[69]

Deity of Jesus: Jesus Christ is the only begotten Son of the Father, born of the Virgin Mary. He existed with the Father, rose again on the third day, and sits at the right hand of God.

Divorce and Remarriage: The Church of God considers marriage a holy and sacred union between one man and one woman.[70]

Government: The church utilizes a centralized form of government with a five-man Executive Committee made up of a general overseer, first, second, and third assistants, and a general secretary/treasurer. The Executive Committee is accountable to the Executive Council, which is made up of 18 ordained ministers elected by the General Assembly which convenes every two years. Every church member registered at the General Assembly, who is 16 years or older, is eligible to vote and ratify actions taken by the General Council.

Heaven/Hell: There is a literal heaven and hell. All God's children go to heaven. All others go to hell, where they will experience eternal torment.

Homosexuality: The church opposes the legitimizing of homosexual unions.[71]

Inspiration of Scripture: All Scripture is verbally inspired by God.

Miracles: Miracles still occur today.

Restrictions: The church opposes membership in secret societies.

Security of Salvation: A believer may choose to turn their back on God.

Speaking in Tongues and Other Gifts of the Spirit: The Church of God (Cleveland, TN) is classical Pentecostal and believes all gifts are still in effect today.

Trinity: The church is trinitarian and believes in the Father, Son, and Holy Spirit.

Women in Ministry: The Church of God does not ordain women, but they do license women ministers and exhorters.

For more information contact: 2490 Keith St., P.O. Box 2430, Cleveland, TN 37320-2430; Phone: (423) 472-3361; Fax: (423) 478-7066; E-mail: cog@chatt.mindspring.com; Web site: http//www.mindspring.com/%7ecog/cog.html

---

Church of God (Evening Light)

The Church of God (Evening Light) has its roots in the reformation of 1880 led by Daniel S. Warner. It was once connected to the Church of God (Anderson, IN) but split off around the year 1913. Its denominational motto is, "At evening time it shall be light." There were 50 congregations in the United States in 1997. The denomination does not keep any membership rolls as it feels that every person who has accepted Christ is part of the universal church of God.

Abortion: The fetus is a life which God puts great value on. Therefore, it is a sin against God, as well as the child, to abort it.

Baptism: Baptism is one of the ordinances which the church keeps. Christ practiced it and commanded the church to do it also. The Church of God (Evening Light) submerges in the name of the Father, Son, and Holy Ghost.

Birth Control: The church has no official stance on this issue.

Capital Punishment: Those who are redeemed by Christ's blood have accepted the dispensation of grace in which Christ forbade any murder. However, for the purpose of having an orderly society, those who choose not to live under the dispensation of grace would do well to live under the law which teaches capital punishment.

Christ's Return: Someday Christ will return. At that time, every person will be brought forth and awarded with heaven or hell.

Communion: The Church of God (Evening Light) practices foot washing and the Lord's Supper.

Creation vs. Evolution: The church believes the account of God's creation of the world.

Divorce and Remarriage: It is adultery to marry someone who has a living companion.

Government: The Church of God does not have a headquarters. The "Holy Spirit leadership" is depended upon for carrying out the operation of the church.

Heaven/Hell: Heaven is the eternal dwelling place of God, as well as the reward for those who accept the redemption which was purchased on Calvary by Christ. Hell is the dwelling place of the devil and his angels, and the place of punishment for those who reject Christ.

Homosexuality: Homosexuality is an abomination to the Lord and has a recompense even in this life.

Inspiration of Scripture: All Scripture is given by inspiration of God and is profitable for doctrine, for reproof, for correction, and for instruction in righteousness. The Church of God also promotes the use of the King James Version of the Bible as they believe it is a translation that was done with no political agendas.

Miracles: God still works miracles in the present age, as there is no biblical indication of any time that they were to end. This belief is enforced by the church's experience of miracles.

Restrictions: None stated.

Security of Salvation: God's salvation for man enables man to live above sin. He is able to do that as long as his will is yielded to God. The breaking of God's commandments will bring spiritual death.

Speaking in Tongues and Other Gifts of the Spirit: In order to spread the gospel, the early Christian church was endowed by the Holy Ghost to speak other languages. Although it was unknown to themselves, the languages they spoke were the languages of other nationalities.

Trinity: The Trinity consists of God the Father, God the Son, and the Holy Spirit. They all share equally in the Godhead.

Women in Ministry: The Church of God (Evening Light) is a proponent of equality regardless of nationality or sex.

For more information contact: P.O. Box 518, Guthrie, OK 73044; Phone: (800) 767-1479 or (405) 282-1479; Fax: (405) 282-6318; E-mail: faithpub@theshop.net; Web site: http://www.theshop.net/faithpub

---

Church of God (O'Beirn), The

The Church of God (O'Beirn) was born out of a radio broadcast that reached most of the United States and Canada. Its leader, Carl O'Beirn, provided a follow-up for listeners which included literature, personal visitation, and church gatherings. The church was officially formed in the early 1970s. Only Psalms are sung during services, and the seventh-day Sabbath and holy days are observed. There are no membership figures.

Abortion: The church does not accept killing of any kind.

Baptism: Baptism is by immersion.

Birth Control: The use of birth control is encouraged.

Capital Punishment: The Church of God (O'Beirn) does not accept killing of any kind.

Christ's Return: Christ's return will follow a great chaotic period in the future. He will return to save his people and establish his Kingdom.

Communion: The Lord's Supper is served according to the biblical example.

Creation vs. Evolution: The biblical account of creation is taught in the church.

Deity of Jesus: Jesus is the only begotten Son of the Father.

Divorce and Remarriage: Divorce and remarriage is frowned upon and discouraged.

Government: The church employs the New Testament example of governing.

Heaven/Hell: The resurrection will occur according to I Corinthians 15, after which the wicked will receive their retribution.

Homosexuality: Homosexuality is frowned upon and discouraged as sin (of which there are many others) that should be repented of.

Inspiration of Scripture: The Scriptures are the Word of God.

Miracles: The historical supernaturalism of the Bible was real and miracles still occur.

Restrictions: There are no rules other than those contained in the Bible.

Security of Salvation: Security rests only in growing in the grace and knowledge of the Lord.

Speaking in Tongues and Other Gifts of the Spirit: The gifts of the Spirit are apportioned to each one individually as God wills and are manifestations of the Holy Spirit.

Trinity: God the Father is an individual. The Lord Jesus Christ is an individual and the Holy Spirit is a power that emanates from both of them.

Women in Ministry: Women are not ordained into the ministry.

For more information contact: P.O. Box 81224, Cleveland, OH 44181.

Church of God General Conference (Abrahamic Faith)

The earliest record of Church of God believers predates the Great Disappointment of October 12, 1844 (when Christ failed to return as predicted by William Miller). The movement emerged primarily from the Unitarian Christian Connection which was a minority revivalistic movement in New England in the early 1800s. Through the work of evangelists, small groups sprang up around the United States. The association of churches was permanently organized in 1921. The denomination's motto is, "Working Together for Christ and the Kingdom of God." In 1997 there were 89 churches with an inclusive membership of 5,195.

Abortion: Life is a sacred gift from God which should be protected from the time of conception until the occurring of natural death. Therefore, the church opposes the practice of abortion, feeling that it is morally opposed to the Word of God and its practice results in the devaluation of all human life.

Baptism: Baptism is by immersion in the name of Jesus Christ for the remission of sins.

Birth Control: No official position.

Capital Punishment: No official position.

Christ's Return: The Kingdom of God will be established on earth when Christ returns personally and physically to reign as king in Jerusalem over the whole earth, with the church as joint heirs with him. His millennial reign will be followed by the final judgment and destruction of the wicked after which will be established new heavens and a new earth. Then there will be no more death and God will be all in all.

Communion: Communion is commonly observed in churches, although the frequency may differ.

Creation vs. Evolution: The Church of God accepts the account of creation as reported in the book of Genesis.

Deity of Jesus: Jesus Christ, born of the Virgin Mary, is the sinless and only begotten Son of God. He existed only from his birth.

Divorce and Remarriage: A ministerial license will not be granted to applicants who have been divorced and remarried, or to someone whose mate was formerly divorced and is living in a state of matrimony while their former companion is alive.

Government: Churches are independent and generally congregationally governed. Churches have chosen to work together in an association to accomplish things together that would be difficult or impossible to do alone. Local churches elect or appoint elders to oversee spiritual matters and elect or appoint deacons to oversee physical needs.

Heaven/Hell: Man was created innocent, but through disobedience to God fell under condemnation of death (the cessation of all life and consciousness). At death, a person goes to his grave. At the resurrection when Christ returns, the faithful will live throughout eternity on the earth. Sinners will be annihilated in a lake of fire at the end of the 1,000 year reign of Christ.

Homosexuality: Active homosexuality is against God's will and plan for his creation. God loves the homosexual, but declares homosexual activities unnatural and indecent. As with other acts of sexual misconduct, repentance, and repudiation of them opens the way for forgiveness and reconciliation with God, Christ, and Christ's church. Practicing homosexuals will not be given recognition as ministers in the Church of God General Conference.

Inspiration of Scripture: The Bible is the Word of God, given by divine inspiration. It is the only authoritative source of doctrine and practice for Christians.

Miracles: God is free to perform miracles today.

Restrictions: The church will recognize those members who, because of their religious convictions, claim exemption from military service.

Security of Salvation: It is possible for a person to fall away from the faith and lose his hope of salvation.

Speaking in Tongues and Other Gifts of the Spirit: Speaking in tongues is not forbidden. God gives spiritual gifts to each person who is a part of his family.

Trinity: Only one person is God. He is a literal corporeal being—almighty, eternal, immortal, and the creator of all things. Jesus Christ, born of the Virgin Mary, is the sinless and only begotten Son of God. He existed only from birth. The Holy Spirit is God's divine power and influence manifest in God's mighty works and in the lives of his people. It is not a person.

Women in Ministry: Women are licensed for pastoral ministry.

For more information contact: P.O. Box 100,000, Morrow, GA 30260-7000; Phone: (404) 362-0052; Fax: (404) 362-9307; E-mail: atl-bc@mindspring.com

---

Church of God of Prophecy

The Church of God of Prophecy is rooted in the radical reformation, when groups including the Anabaptists, Mennonites, Baptists, and Quakers felt the initial reformation had not gone far enough to restore the true church. Some members of these groups immigrated to America in the sixteenth and seventeenth centuries, where they experienced revivals marked by

Pentecostal manifestations. In 1886, the Christian Union, a church with no man-made creeds or traditions, was organized. Influenced also by the Holiness Movement, the organization officially adopted the name Church of God in 1907. In 1923, the Church of God split and the suffix "of Prophecy" was legally added. In 1997 there were more than 300,000 members worldwide.[72]

Abortion: The church is committed to the sanctity of life.

Baptism: Baptism is by water.[73]

Birth Control: No statement.

Capital Punishment: No statement.

Christ's Return: Christ will personally return in power and glory before the millennium to resurrect the dead saints and to catch away the living saints to meet him in the air.[74]

Communion: One of two sacraments.[75]

Creation vs. Evolution: The church holds a creationist viewpoint.

Deity of Jesus: The Church of God of Prophecy believes in the deity of Christ, in his virgin birth, in his sinless life, in the physical miracles he performed, and in his atoning death on the cross.[76]

Divorce and Remarriage: The church is against the evils of divorce and remarriage, and the constitution states that a member must not be involved in a biblically invalid marriage relationship.[77]

Government: There are three interdependent levels of organization. At the international level, the General Assembly is the highest decision-making body. Convening every two years, the General Assembly is open to all members. At the state/regional/national level, an overseer functions as the presiding bishop in his territory. He selects, equips, and appoints pastors and an administrative staff. At the local level, pastors shepherd the church and select lay leaders.[78]

Heaven/Hell: There is eternal life for the righteous and eternal punishment for the wicked.[79]

Homosexuality: No statement.

Inspiration of Scripture: The Bible is God's holy Word, inspired, inerrant, and infallible. The Bible is God's written revelation to mankind and the guide for all matters of faith. It is the highest authority for doctrine, practice, organization, and discipline.[80]

Miracles: The Church of God of Prophecy looks for the full restoration of all the gifts to the church, including signs following believers, divine healing, and speaking in tongues.[81]

Restrictions: Members cannot belong to a lodge or other secret society and they must not use tobacco, illicit drugs, or alcoholic beverages.[82]

Security of Salvation: Security rests only in growing in the grace and knowledge of the Lord.

Speaking in Tongues and Other Gifts of the Spirit: The Church of God of Prophecy recognizes speaking in tongues as evidence of the baptism with the Holy Spirit.[83]

Trinity: There is one God, eternally existing in three persons: Father, Son, and Holy Spirit.[84]

Women in Ministry: The Church of God of Prophecy recommends that women be acknowledged in the preaching ministry. Those who feel a calling on their lives will be set forth by a local church and after meeting certain requirements within a specified time frame be examined by the state/national and international offices and issued a minister's license. State/national leadership may place temporary restraints relative to their ministerial functions based upon cultural consideration which would hinder the work of the gospel until full implementation can be achieved.

For more information contact: P.O. Box 2910, Cleveland, TN 37320-2910; Phone: (423) 559-5102; Fax: (423) 559-5108; E-mail: wilson@cogop.org; Web site: http://www.cogop.org/

Church of God of the Apostolic Faith

The Church of God of the Apostolic Faith started out during the holiness/Pentecostal movement that began in Topeka, KS. The group held their first conference and ordained their first ministers at the Cross Roads Mission near Ozark, AR, in 1914. In 1996 there were 45 churches in the United States.

Abortion: The church is pro-life.

Baptism: Baptism is by immersion in the name of the Father, Son, and Holy Ghost.

Birth Control: This is a personal choice.

Capital Punishment: The church is against capital punishment.

Christ's Return: Christ will return mid-tribulation.

Communion: The church practices open communion.

Creation vs. Evolution: The Church of God, Apostolic upholds the biblical account of creation.

Deity of Jesus: Jesus is God in the flesh.

Divorce and Remarriage: The church will accept divorced members, but will not ordain or license divorced ministers.

Government: Congregational or episcopal.

Heaven/Hell: Heaven and hell are both eternal. The wicked shall be cast into a burning hell, a lake that burns with fire and brimstone forever.

Homosexuality: It is against God's natural order, therefore it is a sin.

Inspiration of Scripture: The Scriptures are inspired and inerrant in their original text.

Miracles: Miracles occur today.

Restrictions: Gambling is a sin because it is based on greed.

Security of Salvation: The church believes in the freedom of man's will.

Speaking in Tongues and Other Gifts of the Spirit: The Church of God of the Apostolic Faith encourages the baptism of the Holy Ghost with the evidence of speaking in tongues and spiritual gifts.

Trinity: The church believes in the triune Godhead.

Women in Ministry: The church ordains women ministers.

For more information contact: 13334 E. 14th St., P.O. Box 691745, Tulsa, OK 74169-1745; Phone and fax: (918) 437-7652.

Church of God of the Union Assembly, The

Ordained in 1910, C.T. Pratt began to preach in Kentucky, Tennessee, and Georgia. After he gathered a following, he was granted a charter to start a church in 1920. One year later the first assembly meeting was held with like-minded churches. The organized church filed for a corporation charter in 1942 and has subsequently spread to 15 states. It encourages freewill offerings instead of teaching a system of tithing. In 1997 there were 32 churches with 5,000 members.

Abortion: The Church of God of the Union Assembly opposes abortion.

Baptism: Baptism, by full immersion, is performed on request or after a profession of belief in Jesus Christ. Infants are not baptized.

Birth Control: This is a matter left up to the individual.

Capital Punishment: In some cases capital punishment is justified.

Christ's Return: Christ will return, and this second coming will signal the end of time.

Communion: There is no set schedule for communion and it is open to all believers.

Creation vs. Evolution: The Church of God of the Union Assembly believes God created all things.

Deity of Jesus: Jesus Christ was born of the Virgin Mary. He is the Son of God and is one in spirit with God, although he is a distinct personality.

Divorce and Remarriage: Although the church wishes divorce and remarriage did not happen, it does not exclude a person if they have been divorced and remarried.

Government: The president of the corporation is the General Overseer of ecclesiastical work. The Supreme Council, which is the governing body that works under the General Overseer, is made up of a board of 12 ordained ministers. State overseers, pastors, and assistant pastors take care of business on the state and local levels.

Heaven/Hell: There is a literal heaven and hell. Those who profess Christ will go to heaven. Those who reject him will go to hell.

Homosexuality: The Church of God of the Union Assembly opposes homosexual practice.

Inspiration of Scripture: All Scripture is the inspired Word of God.

Miracles: God still performs miracles today.

Restrictions: The church strongly opposes alcohol, illegal drugs, and tobacco.

Security of Salvation: The Christian faces a daily battle and may fall from grace.

Speaking in Tongues and Other Gifts of the Spirit: All the gifts of the Spirit are still in effect.

Trinity: There are three in the Godhead: the Father, Son, and Holy Ghost. These are three distinct personalities.

Women in Ministry: Women are not ordained.

For more information contact: P.O. Box 1323, Dalton, GA 30722-1323; Phone: (706) 275-0510; Fax: (706) 278-4732.

Church of God (7th Day), Salem, WV

The Church of God (7th Day) was officially reorganized in 1933 in Salem, WV. However it had roots in Europe and had been part of the Church of God which was headquartered in Stanberry, MO. There are established churches in Texas, Ohio, Minnesota, and Florida. Congregations also meet in homes throughout the country. The church observes the Sabbath on the seventh day (which begins at sundown on Friday and ends at sundown on Saturday) and practices footwashing in conjunction with communion.[85]

Abortion: No statement.

Baptism: Baptism is by immersion for the remission of sins. It is performed in the name, Lord Jesus Christ, which is the name of the Father, Son, and Holy Spirit. After the immersion, a minister performs the laying on of hands for the reception of the Holy Spirit.[86]

Birth Control: No statement.

Capital Punishment: No statement.

Christ's Return: The return of Jesus will be literal, visible, and personal. The imminent second coming will be in two parts: the reaping phase where Christ comes only as far as the clouds and air to gather his saints, and the warring phase where Jesus returns to punish the unrighteous and destroy the wicked.[87]

Communion: The Lord's Supper is observed annually, at the beginning of the 14th day of the first month Abib. (The 14th day of the first month always falls on the full moon. The new moon nearest the vernal equinox is the first day of the month of Abib.) Footwashing is performed before communion.[88]

Creation vs. Evolution: God is the creator of all things. Jesus was with God at the beginning of the creation.[89]

Deity of Jesus: Jesus of Nazareth is the only begotten Son of God, conceived by the power of God, born of the Virgin Mary, and is the Lord, Christ, and Redeemer. Jesus was with God at the beginning of creation. He is the firstborn of all things created by God.[90]

Divorce and Remarriage: The Church of God stands opposed to divorce and remarriage for any cause except as recorded in Matthew 19:9.[91]

Government: The organization and government of the church is as "God did set." First there are twelve apostles, secondly 70 prophets, then seven deacons who take care of the business of the church. All leaders are selected by lot, in conjunction with fasting and prayer.[92]

Heaven/Hell: The dead are unconscious between death and resurrection. The wicked will be totally destroyed. The righteous will be rewarded and recompensed in the earth, and they will never be permanently removed.[93]

Homosexuality: Homosexuality is biblically wrong.

Inspiration of Scripture: The Bible, the Old and New Testaments, is inspired as no other writing is. It is complete, infallible, and expresses God's complete will to man.[94]

Miracles: There is power to produce in the prayer of the righteous. The laying on of hands, with the prayer of faith, and anointing with oil shall save the sick.[95]

Restrictions: The church stands opposed to participation in carnal warfare. It also restricts eating unclean meats, the use of alcohol, narcotics, tobacco, or any habit-forming drug.[96]

Security of Salvation: On the day of judgment many will be disappointed and rejected who have believed in Christ and performed works in his name. The benefits of God's plan of salvation will be realized only by those who, through faith, accept it as divine, make use of it in accordance with God's purpose and conform their lives to his requirements—to do his will continually.[97]

Speaking in Tongues and Other Gifts of the Spirit: The church stands opposed to speaking in tongues unless it is an understandable and translatable language. God will give the gift of tongues or languages when he deems it necessary, not as evidence of the Holy Spirit, but rather to those who have the Spirit.[98]

Trinity: God, the heavenly Father, and Jesus Christ, his Son, are two separate persons, but are one in agreement. The Holy Spirit is the power from God through his Son Jesus, which abides in the believer.[99]

Women in Ministry: Women are not ordained.

For more information contact: P.O. Box 328, Salem, WV 26426; Phone: (304) 782-1411; Fax: (304) 782-2248; E-mail: cogsd@encode.com; Web site: http://www.encode.com/user/rcain/cogsd.htm

---

Church of the Brethren

The Church of the Brethren began in central Germany in 1708. Its followers drew on Anabaptism and Pietism to form a movement independent from the established churches. Upon emigrating to North America in 1719, the Brethren became known as one of the historic peace churches, along with the Mennonites and Quakers. In 1997, there were 1,083 congregations with 146,713 members. Pacifism is central to the faith of the Brethren. Simple living is also a basic tenet. The church adheres to no creed but the New Testament.

Abortion: Brethren state their opposition to abortion because human life is a sacred creation of God. However, members are encouraged to be non-judgmental and compassionate toward those who choose abortion in difficult circumstances.

Baptism: Only confessing believers are baptized by being immersed three times forward in the name of the Father, Son, and Holy Spirit. Baptism is the symbol of the believer's decision to die with Christ and be raised into the community of saints to do the work of Jesus.

Birth Control: No stance.

Capital Punishment: In the 1970s, the Church of the Brethren Annual Conference studied and called for reform of the American criminal justice system and encouraged the abolition of capital punishment.[100]

Christ's Return: No official statement.

Communion: Celebrated once or twice a year, communion (or the love feast) includes a period of meditation and preparation, the washing of feet, a common meal, then a quiet sharing of the bread and the cup. The love feast closes with a hymn. Congregations may also observe the Eucharist at other times and in other settings.[101]

Creation vs. Evolution: Opinions vary.

Deity of Jesus: A 1991 Annual Conference action affirmed that Jesus Christ is the Son of God, Savior of the world, and head of the church, according to the Scriptures.

Divorce and Remarriage: The Church of the Brethren holds marriage to be sacred and permanent before God. There is no official rule, however, instructing the church how to handle divorce and remarriage. Congregations vary in their acceptance of divorced clergy.

Government: The Church of the Brethren is communitarian and operates with a modified presbyterial polity, emphasizing both connectionalism and autonomy. Delegates from each congregation engage in an annual conference to seek the mind of Christ on issues important to the church. The Annual Conference is the highest authority in the church's polity.

Heaven/Hell: Heaven is a place or condition of bliss in which faithful Christians experience oneness with God in the fullness of time. Hell is the condition, place, or state of final punishment of the wicked. An important element in the history of Brethren thought has been the hope that God may eventually empty hell, restoring souls and uniting all things in heaven and on earth to God.[102]

Homosexuality: The Church of the Brethren upholds the biblical declaration that heterosexuality is the intention of God for creation. However, it also encourages a compassionate redemptive ministry towards those who struggle with their sexuality. This includes: welcoming all believers into fellowship; seeking understanding of how genetic and environmental factors influence sexual orientation; challenging fear, hatred, and harassment of homosexuals; and advocating the rights of homosexuals to jobs, housing, and legal justice.[103]

Inspiration of Scripture: Scripture is a product of divine inspiration. Some view inspiration in terms of the spiritual awareness of biblical writers. Others view the words of scripture as God-breathed as in verbal or plenary (full, complete) inspiration.

Miracles: No official statement.

Restrictions: Service in the military is discouraged, but not forbidden.

Security of Salvation: No official statement.

Speaking in Tongues and Other Gifts of the Spirit: No official statement.

Trinity: The doctrine of the Trinity is implicit in the Scriptures in references to God's working as Father (creator and Lord of history), Son (Redeemer), and Spirit (God's active presence); but it is not developed in a systematic way.[104]

Women in Ministry: Women are ordained into the ministry and considered equal to their male counterparts. Several women have served as moderator of the Annual Conference—the highest elected office in the church. Brethren supported the Equal Rights Amendment in 1970.

For more information contact: 1451 Dundee Ave., Elgin, IL 60120; Phone: (800) 323-8039, (847) 742-5100; Fax: (847) 742-6103; E-mail: cobnews@aol.com

---

Church of the Lutheran Brethren of America

The Church of the Lutheran Brethren was organized by five independent Lutheran congregations in 1900. Facilitating the sending forth of missionaries was a primary factor in this decision. The first missionary couple was called to work in China at the initial convention. World missions in China, Japan, Taiwan, Cameroon, and Chad have been a primary focus throughout the church's history. The church is Lutheran in theology with an emphasis on a personal living faith in Jesus Christ. In 1997 there were 115 congregations with almost 13,000 members.

Abortion: Human life begins at conception. To destroy a developing human fetus is the destruction of a life.

Baptism: Infants and adults are baptized. God, through baptism, receives the child into a saving grace relationship. God's saving action in baptism is parallel to the eight-day old child being brought into the covenant in the Old Testament. As a developing young adult is taught the truth of God's love, Christ's redemption from sin, and his forgiveness, they need to consciously possess for themselves the saving grace offered in Christ.

Birth Control: No official statement.

Capital Punishment: No official statement.

Christ's Return: The most commonly accepted viewpoint has been that Christ will return to earth and establish a millennial reign. The church grants freedom of thought on this issue.

Communion: The Church of the Lutheran Brethren of America believes that communion is a sacrament instituted by Christ for believers. It is open to those who believe in Jesus Christ and confess their need of his forgiving grace. The usual practice is to offer communion to believers after they have been confirmed.

Creation vs. Evolution: God is the creator and preserver of the heavens and the earth. His creative work has design and purpose. Scripture declares God's very personal involvement with the creation but does not give specific details of the creative acts.

Deity of Christ: Jesus Christ is the Son of God, fully God and fully human. He is the second person in the Trinity. He was conceived of the Holy Spirit and born of the Virgin Mary in order that he might accomplish the work of redemption for the human race.

Divorce and Remarriage: Divorce is sin. Persons may remarry if they recognize their failure in marriage as sin, repent, and possess the healing grace of the gospel. A Lutheran Brethren pastor may officiate with approval from the Board of Elders, but only after consultation with the couple ascertains the above stated condition and with approval from the Board of Elders.

Government: The local church is autonomous. Synod serves the local congregation by helping it accomplish its mission locally, nationally, and internationally. In the local church the primary governing board is the Board of Elders, who are spiritually mature men elected by the congregation to serve together with the pastor in providing vision and leadership for the accomplishment of the church's mission.

Heaven/Hell: Scripture teaches the eternal reality of both heaven and hell. Heaven is the eternal destiny, the gift of God, to all those who believe in Jesus Christ as their Savior. Hell is the destiny of all those who do not believe in Jesus Christ as Savior.

Homosexuality: God created humans male and female. Scripture teaches that homosexual practice is a sinful behavior.

Inspiration of Scripture: The Old and New Testaments, as originally given, are the verbally and plenarily inspired Word of God. It is free from error in whole and in part, and is therefore the final authority for faith and life.

Miracles: God and Jesus are all-powerful. The Bible reports Jesus occasionally manifested his divine power by means of miracles. On a few occasions the Holy Spirit gave that power to other individuals. The church accepts those miracles as reported.

Restrictions: The church does not prohibit certain behaviors unless they are stated in Scripture.

Security of Salvation: The Church of the Lutheran Brethren of America believes that a Christian is secure in their faith in Jesus Christ. Scripture exhorts and teaches believers to live the life of faith. Scripture also clearly warns that those who cease to live in the relationship of faith in Christ will perish.

Speaking in Tongues and Other Gifts of the Spirit: The Scriptures teach that the Holy Spirit gives the gifts he chooses to his children. Therefore the church does not recognize the requirement of one particular gift in order to be filled with the Spirit. Many gifts are listed in Scripture and the guidelines stated in the Bible concerning the exercise of gifts were given to be followed.

Trinity: There is one God eternally existent in three distinct persons in one divine essence: Father, Son, and Holy Spirit.

Women in Ministry: The Scriptures teach that women are called and gifted to serve God in many and varied ways. Scripture also teaches that the office of pastor and elder are to be filled by men.

For more information contact: Box 655, Fergus Falls, MN 56538-0655; Phone: (800) 332-9232 or (218) 739-3336; Fax: (218) 739-5514; E-mail: rovergaard@mcimail.com or lularson@mcimail.com

---

Church of the Lutheran Confession

The Church of the Lutheran Confession, officially formed in 1960, descended from the Evangelical Lutheran Synodical Conference which was formed in 1872 and lasted until the early 1960s. The church subscribes without qualification to the Lutheran Confessions as found in the *Book of Concord of 1580*. The CLC emerged from three former member churches of the Synodical Conference—the Wisconsin Evangelical Lutheran Synod, the Lutheran Church Missouri Synod, and the Evangelical Lutheran

Synod—because of long standing differences in doctrine and practice, particularly over the clarity of Scripture and the doctrine of fellowship against erring church bodies. The Church of the Lutheran Confession repudiates unionism.[105] In 1997, there were 75 congregations in the United States.

Abortion: The CLC rejects abortion for the following reasons: God created all human life, God imparts a living soul to babies at the moment of conception, termination of a life rests with God alone, and God prohibits murder.[106]

Baptism: The sacrament of holy baptism is a washing of regeneration, having power by means of the Word connected with it to work faith and confer all the blessings of Christ upon young or old. The church baptizes infants and does not prescribe to a particular mode.[107]

Birth Control: Birth control is a personal issue. Abortion is not an acceptable birth control method.

Capital Punishment: The CLC as a church does not lobby for or against capital punishment or any other social or political cause.

Christ's Return: Christ will return again to judge the quick and the dead as confessed in the Apostolic Creed.

Communion: During the Sacrament of the Altar, the body and blood of Christ is really present in the eating and drinking. This sacrament is a means of grace, like baptism, imparting the forgiveness of sins, life, and salvation. Holy Communion, instituted for the comfort of penitent sinners, is only offered to those who have properly signified their intention to attend and who have publicly identified with the confession of the congregation.[108]

Creation vs. Evolution: Neither the world nor man himself is the product of an evolutionary process. The Father created all things.[109]

Deity of Jesus: The Son is true God and true man. By his coming into human flesh, his life of perfect obedience, and his suffering upon the cross in the place of sinners, he atoned for the sins of the world, removed all guilt, reconciled men to God, and was raised again from the dead for their justification.[110]

Divorce and Remarriage: Divorce is contrary to God's intent for the institution of marriage. The Word of God will be applied to each case individually as it arises.

Government: Each congregation is autonomous with respect to its polity. The presidium and members of boards of the CLC are elected by the convention which meets every two years.

Heaven/Hell: There is a literal heaven and hell. One's personal judgment occurs at death.[111]

Homosexuality: This is a sin to be repented of. The CLC believes patience and love needs to be shown to homosexuals whose intent and desire is to forsake the lifestyle.

Inspiration of Scripture: The Bible is the divinely inspired Word of God.[112]

Miracles: God, with whom nothing is impossible, can do and does things according to his will, through whom he chooses.

Restrictions: None.

Security of Salvation: They who by the power of the Spirit working through the Gospel believe in the Lord Jesus Christ are saved. The security of salvation lies in the Word and the promise of the Lord as recorded in Scripture.

Speaking in Tongues and Other Gifts of the Spirit: The gift of tongues without interpretation does not edify the church. While the Spirit can do what he chooses, there is no evidence for, or need for, this gift in the church since the Spirit works through the spoken and written Word.

Trinity: The Church of the Lutheran Confession confesses and worships the triune God: Father, Son, and Holy Ghost revealed in his Word and in the person of the Son, Jesus Christ. In this triune God the church finds and declares the source and promise of salvation.[113]

Women in Ministry: Women are not ordained.

For more information contact: 460 75th Ave. NE, Minneapolis, MN 55432-3240 or Immanuel Lutheran College, 22 Grover Rd., Eau Claire, WI 54701-7199; Phone: (612) 784-8784; E-mail: djflei@msn.com; Web site: http://www.primenet.com/~mpkelly/clc/clc.html

---

Church of the Nazarene

The church of the Nazarene was a product of the nineteenth century holiness movement in American Methodism. It was created in the early 1900s through the mergers of three regional denominations. The first general assembly united an eastern body, the Association of Pentecostal

Churches of America, with one from the west, the Church of the Nazarene. The new denomination adopted the name, Pentecostal Church of the Nazarene. The second general assembly brought a southern denomination, the Holiness Church of Christ into the united body. The second general assembly was later chosen as the church's official anniversary event. In 1919, the word Pentecostal was dropped from the church name because new meanings had developed since 1900. Various other churches and associations have since united with the Church of the Nazarene. In 1997, there were 611,000 members in the United States. The church emphasizes the doctrines of justification by faith, regeneration, and the adoption of believers as the children of God. It teaches that entire sanctification is a second work of divine grace wrought by the Holy Spirit upon the heart of believers, cleansing the heart from sin and empowering believers for life and service through the indwelling presence of God's Spirit.

Abortion: The Church of the Nazarene affirms the sanctity of human life as established by God the creator and believes that such sanctity extends to the child not yet born. Therefore, the church opposes induced abortion when used for personal convenience or population control. It also opposes laws that allow abortion on demand. A decision to have an abortion when the life of the mother is endangered should be made only on the basis of sound medical and Christian counsel.[114]

Baptism: The majority of Nazarenes affirm believers baptism and choose to dedicate, rather than baptize, their children. But as a sign of the New Covenant, the church will baptize infants upon request of their parents or guardians if assurance of Christian training is given. Baptism may be by sprinkling, pouring, or immersion.[115]

Birth Control: No stance.

Capital Punishment: No statement.

Christ's Return: The Church of the Nazarene affirms that Christ will physically come again, but it takes no official stand on millennial theories.

Communion: The Lord's Supper is a New Testament sacrament distinctively for those who are prepared for reverent application of its significance. Only those who have faith in Christ and love for the saints should participate.[116]

Creation vs. Evolution: The church affirms that God is the creator of the universe and opposes an atheistic interpretation of evolution. However, it accepts as valid all scientifically verifiable discoveries.

Deity of Jesus: Jesus Christ, the second person of the Godhead, is eternally one with the Father. He became incarnate by the Holy Spirit and was born of the Virgin Mary so that the two whole and perfect natures (Godhead and humanity) are united in one person, very God and very man.

Divorce and Remarriage: The marriage covenant is intended by God to be permanent so long as both partners live. The breaking of it is a breach of the divine plan for marriage. Where a marriage has been dissolved and remarriage has followed, the marriage partners may be received into membership upon evidence of their genuine repentance and an awareness of their understanding of the sanctity of marriage.[117]

Government: Nazarene government is a blend of episcopal, presbyterian, and congregational elements. The church is organized at the local, district, and international levels. The General Assembly meets quadrennially. It is the highest legislative body and its decisions are binding on districts and congregations. The six general superintendents are the highest officers in the church and are elected by the General Assembly. Local churches belong to districts supervised by an elected superintendent. Churches call their own pastors subject to the district superintendent's approval. Each church elects delegates to the annual district assembly and district assemblies elect delegates to the quadrennial General Assembly.

Heaven/Hell: The dead will be resurrected to be joined with their spirits. Every person will be judged according to their deeds in life. Glorious and everlasting life is assured to all who savingly believe in, and obediently follow, Jesus Christ. The finally impenitent shall suffer eternally in hell.[118]

Homosexuality: Homosexuality is a perversion of human sexuality. Homosexual acts are sinful and subject to the penalty for sin. The grace of God is sufficient to overcome homosexuality. There is no compatibility between Christian morality and the practice of homosexuality.[119]

Inspiration of Scripture: The church believes in the plenary inspiration of the Bible: the 66 books of the Old and New Testaments, given by divine inspiration, inerrantly reveal the will of God concerning all things necessary for salvation, so that whatever is not in the Bible is not to be enjoined as an article of faith.[120]

Miracles: The Church of the Nazarene believes in the possibility of divine healing and urges its people to offer the prayer of faith for the healing of the sick.[121] The church also teaches that medical assistance, when necessary, should not be refused.

Restrictions: Members are encouraged to avoid entertainments that are subversive of the Christian ethic, lotteries and other forms of gambling, membership in an oath-bound secret order or society, all forms of dancing that detract from spiritual growth and break down proper moral inhibitions and reserve, the use of intoxicating liquors, illicit drugs, or tobacco, and the unprescribed use of hallucinogenics, stimulants, and depressants or the misuse and abuse of regularly prescribed drugs.[122]

Security of Salvation: All persons, though in the possession of the experience of regeneration and entire sanctification, may fall from grace and apostatize. Unless they repent of their sins, they may be hopelessly and eternally lost.

Speaking in Tongues and Other Gifts of the Spirit: To affirm that any special or alleged physical evidence or prayer language is evidence of the baptism with the Spirit is contrary to the biblical and historic position of the church.[123]

Trinity: The Church of the Nazarene believes in one eternally existent, infinite God, sovereign of the universe. He only is God, creative and administrative, holy in nature, attributes, and purpose. He, as God, is triune in essential being, revealed as Father, Son, and Holy Spirit.[124]

Women in Ministry: The church has ordained women to the ministry since its founding in 1908 and supports the right of women to use their God-given spiritual gifts within the church. Nazarenes affirm the right of women to be elected and appointed to places of leadership at all levels of the church.

For more information contact: 6401 The Paseo, Kansas City, MO 64131; Phone: (816) 333-7000; Fax: (816) 361-4983; Web site: http://www.nazarene.org

---

Church of the United Brethren in Christ

The United Brethren Church grew out of a discontent with the formalism of established churches in the 1700s. Philip William Otterbein, a German Reformed minister who came to the United States in 1752, and Martin Boehm, a Mennonite Evangelist, spearheaded a revival movement that swept through Pennsylvania, Maryland, and Virginia. Gradually the movement grew into a denomination which in 1800 adopted the name the Church of the United Brethren in Christ. In 1889, a controversy over changes in the church's constitution led to division. The smaller of the two groups (the larger eventually became the United Methodist Church) reorganized.[125] The church avoids taking sides on issues. In 1997, there were 400 churches with 37,000 members worldwide.

Abortion: Human life is sacred from the moment of conception and abortion must not occur anytime after conception. Abortion cannot be recognized morally and scripturally as a means of birth control, as a solution to a pregnancy resulting from rape or incest, or as a way to prevent or eliminate congenital or hereditary defects. The church recognizes the possibility of therapeutic abortion. However, it can be performed in Christian conscience only when the mother's life is in imminent danger, as determined by two competent physicians, one of whom has been or would be attending her pregnancy.[126]

Baptism: Baptism is to be used and practiced, but the means is up to the individual.[127]

Birth Control: Members should carefully consider the responsibilities of family planning, using methods medically and psychologically suited to their needs. They must not use methods which conflict with the church's stand on abortion.[128]

Capital Punishment: No official stand.

Christ's Return: Jesus Christ will come again on the last day to judge the living and the dead.[129]

Communion: The sufferings of Jesus Christ are to be remembered, but the manner of remembrance is left up to the individual. Whether or not to practice foot washing is also left up to the individual.[130]

Creation vs. Evolution: There is no official stand. However, the prevailing view is that God created all things.

Deity of Jesus: Jesus Christ is both God and man. He became a man by the power of the Holy Ghost in the Virgin Mary and was born of her. He is the Savior and mediator of the whole human race, if accepted with full faith the grace offered in him.[131]

Divorce and Remarriage: Divorce should not occur. However, the Bible recognizes that because of hard-heartedness, this ideal isn't always maintained. The Bible allows a Christian to remarry in these situations: when the spouse dies, when the marriage and divorce occurred prior to salvation, when the spouse has been unfaithful, when an unbeliever deserts a believer, and when the spouse assumes the position of an unbeliever by choosing to divorce the believing partner. (In this case the believing partner may remarry another believer.) When the spouse or children suffer severe physical or emotional abuse, a divorce may be obtained. However, the spouses must remain unmarried or reconcile.[132]

Government: The United Brethren is connectional, which means that ministers are assigned to congregations by the bishop and Conference Stationing Committee. It also has a modified episcopal form of governing. Bishops are elected by the General Conference and serve four-year terms. Each annual conference elects superintendents to help the bishop oversee the churches.[133]

Heaven/Hell: The Church of the United Brethren in Christ believes in a literal heaven and hell.

Homosexuality: The biblical view of sex firmly establishes it within the framework of marriage and family life. Therefore, the church cannot condone homosexual behavior.[134]

Inspiration of Scripture: The Bible, Old and New Testaments, is the Word of God. It contains the only true way of salvation. Every true Christian is bound to acknowledge and receive it, with the influence of the Spirit of God, as the only rule and guide.[135]

Miracles: God still performs miracles today.

Restrictions: The church prohibits members from drinking alcohol and joining lodges. They also encourage their members to avoid the use of: tobacco; hallucinogenic, narcotic and mind-altering drugs; gambling; pornography; and the occult, which includes fortune-telling and astrology.[136]

Security of Salvation: Historically, the Church of the United Brethren in Christ has not taught eternal security, but that view is accepted in many churches.

Speaking in Tongues and Other Gifts of the Spirit: All the spiritual gifts mentioned in the Bible are available today. However, a person may have the Spirit's fullness and power without ever speaking in tongues.

Trinity: The United Brethren believe in the only true God—the Father, the Son, and the Holy Ghost. These three are one—the Father in the

Son, the Son in the Father, and the Holy Ghost equal in essence or being with both.[137]

Women in Ministry: There shall be no discrimination between men and women in granting ministerial credentials.[138]

For more information contact: 302 Lake St., Huntington, IN 46750; Phone: (219) 356-2312; Fax: (219) 356-4730.

Congregational Holiness Church

The Congregational Holiness Church was organized in 1921 and officially chartered on August 25, 1925. It has historically been placed in the Wesleyan Holiness wing of the Pentecostal movement and its doctrines are based on the Wesleyan tradition. In 1997 there were 182 churches with approximately 10,000 members.

Abortion: The Congregational Holiness Church believes in protecting the sanctity of life. Since the Bible teaches that life begins in the womb, then abortion must be opposed.

Baptism: All Christians should be baptized in water by immersion. It is performed by an ordained minister or pastor in the name of the Father, and of the Son, and of the Holy Ghost.

Birth Control: The individual has the right of choice.

Capital Punishment: In the dispensation of human government, God established capital punishment when He said, "Whoso sheddeth man's blood, by man shall his blood be shed; for in the image of God made he man."

Christ's Return: The church believes in the imminent, personal, and premillennial second coming of Jesus Christ.

Communion: The church recognizes the sacrament of the Lord's Supper. All Christians are invited to partake of the Lord's Supper and foot washing.

Creation vs. Evolution: The church teaches and preaches that God created all things. Therefore it rejects the validity of the theory of evolution.

Deity of Jesus: Jesus Christ is the eternal Son of God. The Scriptures declare his virgin birth, his sinless life, his miracles, his substitutionary work on the cross, his bodily resurrection from the dead, and his exaltation to the right hand of God.

Divorce and Remarriage: Anyone involved in a double marriage who applies for license must qualify according to Matthew 19:9.

Government: Congregational. The Articles of Faith, form of government, and condition of membership cannot be changed except by a majority vote of the local churches.

Heaven/Hell: All who die out of Christ will be punished eternally, but those who die in him shall share in his glory forever.

Homosexuality: A homosexual does not qualify for membership in the church.

Inspiration of Scripture: The Bible is the inspired Word of God.

Miracles: The working of miracles is included as one of the nine gifts of the Spirit. Christ performed miracles and the Apostles worked miracles. Therefore, miracles are a present day ministry of the Holy Spirit.

Restrictions: Members cannot use tobacco of any form, belong to a secret oath society, or be a homosexual.

Security of Salvation: There is eternal redemption for all saints who are faithful to the end. The church rejects the theory of "once in grace, always in grace," regardless of conduct.

Speaking in Tongues and Other Gifts of the Spirit: Speaking in tongues as the Spirit gives utterance is the initiatory evidence of the baptism with the Holy Ghost. The church believes in the nine gifts of the Spirit and encourages its members to live so that these gifts may be manifest in their lives. Since the Spirit gives the utterance when one is baptized in the Holy Ghost, the church rejects the teaching that one who has received the baptism can speak in tongues at will without the Spirit prompting the utterance.

Trinity: There is but one live and true God, the great creator, and there are three persons in the Godhead: the Father, the Son, and the Holy Ghost.

Women in Ministry: Woman shall be ordained to preach and are encouraged to exercise all gifts imparted by the Holy Ghost.

For more information contact: 3888 Fayetteville Highway, Griffin, GA 30223; Phone: (800) 633-0877 or (770) 228-4833/34; Fax: (770) 228-1177.

Congregational Methodist Church

In 1729, Englishmen John and Charles Wesley began a spiritual journey that started the revival that led to the formation of the Methodist church. The Methodist church came to America and then took several forms, including the Methodist Episcopal Church. The Congregational Methodist Church split off from that group on May 8, 1852, over the issues of congregationalism and church government.[139] In 1997, there were 190 churches with 22,000 members.

Abortion: The Congregational Methodist Church opposes abortion except in cases where the mother's life is endangered.[140]

Baptism: Baptism does not save, but serves as a badge of one's Christian profession. It strengthens and confirms a person's faith in Christ. Baptism is performed with water in the name of the holy Trinity by sprinkling, pouring, or immersion.[141]

Birth Control: No statement.

Capital Punishment: The Congregational Methodist Church supports capital punishment.

Christ's Return: At the last day Christ will return in bodily form to judge all men. The first resurrection of the dead shall occur at his premillennial second coming in which the saved dead shall be resurrected and living saints raptured. The second resurrection shall be after the millennium when the unsaved dead shall be resurrected at the great white throne judgment.[142]

Communion: *What Congregational Methodists Believe* states that the second sacrament is open to all Christians, but an unworthy participant will bring condemnation on himself. The church does not believe that the consecrated bread and wine become the literal body and blood of Christ during communion.

Creation vs. Evolution: God is the maker and preserver of all things.[143] The Congregational Methodist Church supports the teaching of creationism and opposes the teaching of humanism in public schools.[144]

Deity of Jesus: Jesus Christ was God in human flesh. He is the Son, the Word of the Father who took man's nature in the womb of the Virgin Mary bringing two whole perfect natures, God and man, together in one person. Through this virgin birth the invisible God was made man-

ifest to mankind. Christ arose from the dead on the third day following his crucifixion, took again his human, yet glorified, body and ascended into heaven.[145]

Divorce and Remarriage: Marriage was designed to be a lifelong commitment. Divorce is permitted under the conditions of adultery, desertion, or apostasy of the spouse. Only when a marriage is unalterably
broken by those conditions may the offended party in a divorce consider remarriage, and then only after receiving competent Christian
counseling.[146]

Government: The church uses a representative form of government.
Each church elects delegates to the General Conference which convenes every two years. Boards made up of church members elected by
the General Conference oversee missions, education, and publications.
The General Conference president, vice president, secretary, and assistant secretary coordinate the efforts of the boards.

Heaven/Hell: The wicked suffer forever in the lake of fire. There is no
purgatory where a sinner gets a second chance to redeem himself.[147]

Homosexuality: The Congregational Methodist Church believes that a
homosexual lifestyle is incompatible with Christian living and they oppose the employment of practicing homosexuals.[148]

Inspiration of Scripture: The 66 books of the Old and New Testament
which compose the Holy Scriptures, God's written Word, are authoritative. God directed those human authors to compose and record, without error, God's Word to man.

Miracles: Miracles still happen today.

Restrictions: The church opposes pornography, the use of alcohol, tobacco, illegal drugs, and the abuse of other drugs.[149]

Security of Salvation: Because conversion does not destroy a person's
moral freedom, it is possible for one who has been justified to fall into
sin and depart from grace. But with God's help, the backslider who truly repents may rise again and amend his life.[150]

Speaking in Tongues and Other Gifts of the Spirit: The Congregational Methodist Church does not endorse speaking in tongues as evidence of the baptism of the Holy Spirit. They also do not believe
tongues are given as a special prayer language.[151]

Trinity: There is but one living and true God—everlasting, without body
or parts, of infinite power, wisdom, and goodness. This triune God has

chosen to manifest himself in three persons of one substance, power, and eternity—the Father, Son, and Holy Ghost. Each of the three is distinguished from the others; each possesses all the divine attributes, yet the three are one.[152]

Women in Ministry: The Congregational Methodist Church ordains women.

For more information contact: P.O. Box 9, Florence, MS 39073; Phone: (601) 845-8787; Fax: (601) 845-8788; E-mail: cmchdq@aol.com

---

Conservative Baptist of America (CBAmerica)

Conservative evangelical pastors within the Northern Baptist Convention sought to establish biblical standards for missionary candidates. In 1943, they formed the Conservative Baptist Foreign Mission Society. Four years later, the National Association of Churches was launched. With its commitment to evangelism through church planting in the United States and abroad, the organization grew rapidly. There are now three sister agencies: CBInternational, Mission to the Americas and CBAmerica, which in 1997 included 1,250 churches with 250,000 members in the United States. Conservative Baptists believe in the separation of church and state, and the separation from all theological liberalism. The active, voting membership has the final authority in the church, although they may voluntarily delegate it to a ruling board of the church.

Abortion: Any form of abortion, for any reason, is murder according to the Bible.

Baptism: Believers are baptized by immersion. Being baptized displays a personal allegiance to Jesus Christ and a personal identification with the death, burial, and resurrection of Jesus Christ. Baptism is usually a requirement for church membership.

Birth Control: Biblical birth control is always to prevent a pregnancy from occurring, not eliminating one which has already occurred. Any form of prevention should be mutually agreed upon by both husband and wife.

Capital Punishment: The Bible teaches an eye for an eye, a tooth for a tooth, and a life for a life. Though there are several degrees of murder, it seems biblically reasonable that in the case of a premeditated murder, the life of the murderer should be taken in exchange. It is always appropriate to seek to lead that murderer to a personal relationship with Jesus Christ before their execution so they may have eternal life in heaven.

Christ's Return: Jesus Christ will return to take his bride, the church, out from the wrath promised for this world into heaven (this is called the rapture or relocation of the body of Christ). This second coming occurs when Jesus Christ returns from heaven, with his church to this earth, to victoriously conclude the battle of Armageddon and begin the millennial reign.

Communion: Communion is the remembrance of the suffering and death of Christ. The bread is a symbol of the physical body of Christ which Jesus took upon himself in order to be able to suffer and die for the sins of the world. The cup or grape juice is a symbol of Christ's blood, which provides for the forgiveness of all sin. Communion is usually celebrated once a month. All born-again believers, not living in open sin, are invited to partake.

Creation vs. Evolution: The origin of life and the universe is clearly taught in the Bible as life created by a voluntary act of the almighty triune God. Man is created in the image of God. Evolution is a theory proposed by those desirous of excluding God as the absolute authority in their life.

Deity of Jesus: Jesus Christ is God's eternal Son and has precisely the same nature, attributes, and perfections as God the Father and God the Holy Spirit. He was conceived by the Holy Spirit and born of the Virgin Mary. He was born without sin and lived a sinless life. Thus, he is able to be the substitutionary atonement for sin.

Divorce and Remarriage: The Bible permits divorce for at least two reasons, thereby permitting remarriage for the same reasons. If there has been repeated sexual misconduct, the spouse is permitted to initiate a divorce. Also, if one of the partners is an unbeliever, he or she is permitted to initiate the divorce. Other reasons for dissolution of a marriage would have been sins punishable by death in Bible times. Biblically permitted divorce therefore permits a genuine biblical remarriage if both are born-again believers.

Government: The voting membership of the local church has final authority in CBAmerica in areas such as election of officers, approval of budgets, purchase and sale of property, and approval and amendments of the constitution and by-laws. The membership can constitutionally relegate its voting privilege to many of the issues of the church, but needs to retain the rights to have them returned at any time.

Heaven/Hell: There is a very literal heaven and hell, as the permanent dwelling place of all living creatures. Heaven is for God's righteous chosen people, born-again believers in Jesus Christ, and unfallen angels. Hell, or the lake of fire, is for all unrepentant sinners, unbelievers in Jesus Christ, and fallen angels. Heaven and hell are everlasting and permanent for their inhabitants.

Homosexuality: The Bible condemns all homosexual activities, but does not condemn the individual themselves. All born-again, baptized, repentant, nonpracticing homosexuals may be accepted into local church fellowship, since God accepts them through the cleansing power of the cross of Christ and the powerful grace of God.

Inspiration of Scripture: The Scriptures of the 66 Old and New Testament books are the inspired work of God, inerrant in the original writings, complete as the revelation of God's will for salvation. They are the supreme and final authority in all matters to which they speak.

Miracles: Miracles still happen today to display God's sovereign power and bring him ultimate glory. CBAmerica believes in the grace of faith healing, but does not endorse faith healers.

Restrictions: The only biblical restrictions given to the local church involve three areas: Shun those who participate in repeated sexually immoral activities, those who promote and teach false doctrine, and those who are divisive in their attitudes and actions toward the elected leadership of the church.

Security of Salvation: God the Father, God the Son, and God the Holy Spirit all work, all of the time, to keep each and every truly born-again believer safe and secure in the family of God. Since Jesus Christ paid the incredible price to provide salvation, man at his immature whim is unable to walk away from such a precious gift. God's power to keep salvation is much stronger than man's desire to get rid of it.

Speaking in Tongues and Other Gifts of the Spirit: With the completion of the New Testament Scripture, there appears to be no valid need for the display of the gift of tongues today, unless it might again be as a sign of judgment upon the Jewish nation for their continued rejection of Jesus Christ as the Messiah.

Trinity: There is one God, the creator and sustainer of all things, who eternally exists in three persons: Father, Son, and Holy Spirit. These are equal in every divine perfection. They execute distinct but harmonious offices in the work of creation, providence, and redemption.

Women in Ministry: Women are gifted by the Holy Spirit for effective service in the body of Christ. The office of pastor or elder is always stated biblically in the masculine gender, and especially when accompanied by ordination, is limited to men. Women may serve as leaders to women and children in the local church, in missions, education, and the home.

For more information contact: P.O. Box 66, Wheaton, IL 60189-0066; Phone: (630) 260-3800; Fax: (630) 653-5387; E-mail: cba@cb. usa.com

---

Conservative Congregational Christian Conference

In 1935, Rev. Hilmer B. Sandine began publishing the Congregational Beacon, a conservative monthly which challenged the theology of existing Congregationalists. Ten years later, the Conservative Congregational Christian Fellowship was formed. This eventually became the current conference.[153] In 1996, the Conservative Congregational Christian Conference had 224 churches with 39,069 members.

Abortion: Abortion on demand for reasons such as personal convenience, social adjustment, economic advantage, genetic defect, or physical malformation is morally wrong. While the church agrees that a woman has a right to do with her own body as she sees fit, they cannot conclude that she therefore has the right to take the life of her child. However, in the rare situation when the life of the unborn child mortally threatens the equal life of the mother, the mother is not required to sacrifice her life.[154]

Baptism: Both children and adults are baptized upon request.

Birth Control: No statement.

Capital Punishment: No statement.

Christ's Return: The church expects Christ's personal return in power and glory, but individuals differ as to the sequence of events associated with his return.[155]

Communion: No statement.

Creation vs. Evolution: No statement.

Deity of Jesus: The CCCC believes in the deity of Jesus, in his virgin birth, in his sinless life, in his miracles, in his vicarious and atoning death through his shed blood, in his bodily resurrection, in his ascension to the right hand of the Father, and in his personal return in power and glory.[156]

Divorce and Remarriage: While the church recognizes that God designed marriage to be a permanent union of a man and a woman, it also recognizes that not everyone interprets the Bible's teachings concerning divorce in the same way. Every church decides for itself what its practice shall be regarding divorce. However, ordained ministers who experience divorce are required to be reviewed by the Credentials Committee.[157]

Government: Congregational.

Heaven/Hell: Both the saved and the lost will be resurrected: the saved unto the resurrection of life and they that are lost unto the resurrection of damnation.[158]

Homosexuality: God condemns the practice of homosexuality in the Bible. Therefore, individual Christians, ministers, or congregations should not urge or concede that the State should give special protection or approval to this practice, or promote it as a matter of personal taste, free choice, or sexual orientation. The CCCC renounces any unbiblical prejudice against homosexuals because of their orientation and they proclaim forgiveness, cleansing, restoration, and power for godly living for all who repent and believe in the Gospel. A non-practicing homosexual may be admitted into fellowship after a confession of faith and evidence of repentance. The church counsels homosexuals who do not experience full healing to remain celebate.[159]

Inspiration of Scripture: The Bible, consisting of the Old and New Testaments, is the only inspired, inerrant, infallible, and authoritative Word of God.[160]

Miracles: No statement.

Restrictions: The CCCC abhors the use of pornography. Churches are encouraged to insist on legislation and firm enforcement of laws which prohibit pornography.[161]

Security of Salvation: For salvation of lost and sinful man, regeneration by the Holy Spirit is absolutely essential.

Speaking in Tongues and Other Gifts of the Spirit: The apostle Paul taught that the more spectacular gifts were secondary to those that instructed believers in faith and morals and that evangelized non-Christians. Tongue speaking was not forbidden, but intelligent exposition of the Bible, along with instruction in faith and duty, was definitely superior. Messages received by means of these gifts are not equal to the revelation of God in Holy Scripture.[162]

Trinity: There is one God, eternally existent in three persons: Father, Son, and Holy Ghost.[163]

Women in Ministry: Each congregation ordains whomever it freely chooses. Whoever is duly ordained in the local church, whether male or female, may apply to the CCCC Credentials Committee, and if qualified, be recognized as ordained. This should not be understood as conference approval nor disapproval of the ordination of women.[164]

For more information contact: 7582 Currell Blvd., #108, St. Paul, MN 55125; Phone: (612) 739-1474; Fax: (612) 739-0750.

Conservative Lutheran Association

The Conservative Lutheran Association was formed in 1980 by Lutheran pastors and laymen who were concerned with the growing liberalism in several of the major Lutheran synods. They first came together under the organization of Lutherans Alert Nation, which had started Faith Evangelical Lutheran Seminary in Tacoma, WA. The churches who formed the CLA either left the American Lutheran Church or the Lutheran Church of America, or were graduates of the seminary before the Evangelical Lutheran Church of America was formed in the mid-1980s. The churches which remain today in the Conservative Lutheran Association are closely allied to Faith Evangelical Seminary. In 1997 there were eight churches in the United States with a membership of 1,200.

Abortion: The Conservative Lutheran Association is against abortion.

Baptism: The church baptizes infants, and the mode of baptism is optional.

Birth Control: The church does not encourage teenagers to use birth control because they prefer teens to abstain from sexual relations. The use of birth control is optional for married couples.

Capital Punishment: Capital punishment is appropriate in certain circumstances if a proper judicial process has proven guilt.

Christ's Return: Jesus will return when he chooses one more time. At his coming there will be a simultaneous resurrection of the dead and the living.

Communion: Participation in Holy Communion is open to confirmed members of Lutheran congregations. Worthy participation requires sincere repentance, faith in Jesus Christ as Savior and the scriptural teaching regarding the real presence of Christ with his body and blood in the sacrament.

Creation vs. Evolution: The church teaches a literal six day creation, with God resting on the seventh day.

Deity of Jesus: Jesus is divine. He is both God and man, the God-man.

Divorce and Remarriage: Divorce and remarriage is appropriate in limited circumstances. Remarriages should be done judiciously and with proper counsel.

Government: Congregations are autonomous. The voting membership is anyone over age 21.

Heaven/Hell: At the second coming of Christ all will be judged. There is a literal heaven and hell.

Homosexuality: Homosexuality is not an acceptable lifestyle. The church does not believe that a person is born a homosexual.

Inspiration of Scripture: The Scriptures, which were inspired by God, are inerrant and infallible.

Miracles: Miracles still occur today.

Restrictions: No answer.

Security of Salvation: One can fall from grace.

Speaking in Tongues and Other Gifts of the Spirit: While speaking in tongues is not encouraged or allowed publicly in worship, the use of a personal prayer language is left up to the individual.

Trinity: God is triune. The Father, Son, and Holy Spirit are three equal persons who comprise the one God.

Women in Ministry: Women are important to the ministry of the church. However, they are not ordained into the clergy.

For more information contact: 4101 E. Nohl Ranch Rd., Anaheim, CA 92807; Phone: (714) 637-8370; Fax: (714) 637-6534; E-mail: pastor-pj@ix.netcom.com

---

Conservative Mennonite Conference

While the Conservative Mennonite Conference has roots that go back to the sixteenth century Anabaptist movement in Switzerland and the influence of Menno Simons (1496–1561) of Holland, the group traces its more recent development to a 1910 meeting. Attended by five Amish Mennonite ministers, the meeting focused on concerns about the intense conservatism and influence of the Old Order Amish Mennonites and the progressive cultural adaptations of other Mennonite groups. The church is pacifistic and practices the washing of feet. Some congregations expect females to cover their heads and simplicity of attire is encouraged. In 1997, there were approximately 10,000 members in 101 churches.

Abortion: Conception is the beginning of life. Taking a life through abortion is wrong.

Baptism: Baptism is symbolic of the cleansing of the blood of Christ in regeneration and new birth. Both pouring and immersion are acceptable modes.

Birth Control: The prevention of pregnancy by birth control with pre-fertilization methods is acceptable.

Capital Punishment: The State is ordained of God to maintain law and order and is expected to use the sword for enforcement. Capital punishment should never be advocated by a Christian, but can be recognized as a legitimate function of government.

Christ's Return: The return of Christ is personal, certain, and imminent.

Communion: Communion is an ordinance instituted by Jesus Christ to symbolize the New Covenant. The bread and the cup are symbols which commemorate Christ's broken body and shed blood, our spiritual life in him, and the spiritual unity and fellowship of the body of Christ.

Creation vs. Evolution: Creation is the explanation of the origin and existence of all things including the material universe, the spiritual cosmos, and those beings which by freewill rebelled against God and chose an attitude and condition of evil. The origin of the universe was not a process of natural or theistic evolution.

Deity of Jesus: Jesus Christ is one with the Father and the Holy Spirit in the triune Godhead. He is the eternal Word and the divine Son of God. Before his incarnation, he was eternally with God the Father and was God. In his incarnation he was fully God and fully man.

Divorce and Remarriage: There is no rightful provision for divorce, although in dire cases separation may be feasible or required. Divorce and remarriage after divorce are regarded as violating God's plan, forgivable with repentance, but not to be repeated by the believer.

Government: A combination of the congregational and presbyterial forms of government prevails, with an emphasis on the first. Major decisions are subject to congregational approval. Most congregations include a church council or board of elders consisting of laymen and ordained clergy. Other committees and officers are constituted by local congregational decision and provision.

Heaven/Hell: Heaven is the place of everlasting glory and bliss to which the regenerated and cleansed children of God are ushered. The unjust are cast into everlasting punishment and torment in hell. Satan, death, and hell will be cast into the lake of fire and the glorious reign of the Kingdom of God will be eternally fulfilled.

Homosexuality: Homosexuality is a condition outside of God's creational intent. Homosexual orientation is a condition short of the plan of God, calling for reorientation through transformation. Through prayer, God's grace, therapy, and the love and support of brothers and sisters in the body of Christ, this transformation can occur.

Inspiration of Scripture: The Scriptures, both Old and New Testament, are the Word of God, a supernatural revelation from God to mankind, verbally inspired by the Holy Spirit through human instrumentality, and without error in the original writings in all that they affirm. The Scriptures are the final authority for faith and practice, with the New Testament being the fulfillment of the Old Testament and the perfected rule for the Christian church.

Miracles: Miracles are works of God in which he intervenes in the natural and usual order of his creation. Accounts of miracles in the Scriptures are to be accepted. God does miracles today as he chooses. However, the occurrence of a miracle is not necessarily a test of faith, since God may choose to do or not to do a miracle in the presence of faith.

Restrictions: The church expects its members to refrain from gambling, drinking alcohol, smoking or chewing tobacco, immodest attire, taking oaths, and premarital or extra-marital sexual activity.

Security of Salvation: The believer is secure in an ongoing faith expressed and fostered by obedience to Christ. The believer's security is conditional rather than unconditional. The condition for ongoing salvation is a continuing trusting, living faith in Christ.

Speaking in Tongues and Other Gifts of the Spirit: The gifts of the Holy Spirit are meant for the church from Pentecost until his return. The gifts are distributed as the Holy Spirit wills in various times and places. Speaking in tongues is recognized and permitted today, but is not required.

Trinity: God is three divine persons—Father, Son, and Holy Spirit—who are distinct in function, but equal in power and glory. The triune nature of God is both ontological and expressive. The more definitive New Testament teaching on the divine Trinity, in comparison to the less definitive teaching of the Old Testament, is not a matter of development of human thought or of God rearranging himself in order to reveal himself, but of progression of revelation. The perfect God is triune.

Women in Ministry: It is appropriate for women to be engaged in a large range of ministries. Leadership and governance through authority in administration, teaching, and discernment of the prophetic word are assigned to men. Ordination is restricted to men.

For more information contact: 9910 Rosedale-Milford Center Rd., Irwin, OH 43025-9506; Phone: (614) 857-1234; Fax: (614) 857-1605.

Cumberland Presbyterian Church and Cumberland Presbyterian Church in America

Three Presbyterian ministers, Finis Ewing, Samuel King and Samuel McAdow, started the Cumberland Presbytery on February 4, 1810 in Dickson County, TN. At that time, there were a large number of people who needed ministers to lead them. However, the Presbyterian church's rigid requirements for education left many congregations without leadership. The Cumberland Presbytery separated over this issue and an objection to the doctrine of predestination in the Westminster Confession of Faith. In 1874, black congregations formed a separate church known as the Second Cumberland Presbyterian Church.[165] That group is now known as the Cumberland Presbyterian Church in America. The Cumberland Presbyterian Church in America has its headquarters in Huntsville, AL. The central headquarters of the Cumberland Presbyterian Church is located in Memphis, TN.

Abortion: No answer.

Baptism: Baptism symbolizes the baptism of the Holy Spirit and is the external sign of the covenant which marks membership in the community of faith. The sacrament of baptism, in the name of the Father, and of the Son, and of the Holy Spirit, is administered to infants, one or both of whose parents or guardians affirm faith in Jesus Christ and assume the responsibilities of the covenant, and to all persons who affirm personal faith in Jesus Christ and have not received the sacrament. It is administered by sprinkling or pouring. The validity of the sacrament is not dependent upon its mode of administration.[166]

Birth Control: No answer.

Capital Punishment: No answer.

Christ's Return: In the consummation of history, at the coming of Jesus Christ, the kingdoms of the world shall become the Kingdom of the Lord and of the Christ, and he shall reign forever and ever.[167]

Communion: The Lord's Supper is a means by which the church remembers and shows forth Christ's passion and death on the cross. It is a perpetual means given to the church to celebrate and experience the continuing presence of the risen Lord and the church's expectation of the Lord's return. The elements used are bread and the fruit of the vine, which represent the body and blood of Christ. The elements themselves are never to be worshipped, for they are never anything other than bread and fruit of the vine. The sacrament should not be received without due self-examination, reverence, humility, and grateful awareness of Christ's presence. Communion is open to all who are part of the covenant community and are committed to the Christian life.[168]

Creation vs. Evolution: God is the creator of all that is known and unknown. All creation discloses God's glory, power, wisdom, beauty, goodness, and love. Among all forms of life, only human beings are created in God's own image. In the sight of God, male and female are created equal and complementary.[169]

Deity of Jesus: Jesus Christ, being truly human and truly divine, was tempted in every respect as every person, yet he did not sin. While fully sharing human life, Christ continued to be holy, blameless, undefiled, and thoroughly fitted to be the Savior of the world. On the third day after being crucified, Christ was raised from the dead, ascended to God, and makes intercession for all persons.[170]

Divorce and Remarriage: Marriage is a covenant relationship under God. As such it symbolizes the relationship of Jesus Christ and the church. Marriage is a lifetime commitment. It is morally wrong and unlawful for any person to have more than one living partner. If a marriage is dissolved by divorce, the covenant community is responsible to minister to the victims, including any children of the marriage and to counsel divorced persons who are considering remarriage.[171]

Government: Cumberland Presbyterian churches are governed by representative bodies: session, presbytery, Synod, and General Assembly. Each of these church bodies in its special areas of responsibility has legislative, judicial, and executive authority. Yet all are to be conducted in recognition of their interdependence and Christian mission. These bodies determine matters of faith, practice, and government, propose forms of worship and witness, exercise discipline, and resolve appeals.[172]

Heaven/Hell: Those who have been regenerated in Christ live with joyful and confident expectation that after death their redemption will be complete in the resurrection of the body. As in regeneration the whole person is resurrected to new life in Christ, so in the resurrection of the dead the whole person is raised to live in and enjoy the presence of God forever. Those who reject God's salvation in Jesus Christ remain alienated from God and in hopeless bondage to sin and death, which is hell.[173]

Homosexuality: No answer.

Inspiration of Scripture: God inspired persons of the covenant community to write the Scriptures, in and through which God speaks about creation, sin, judgment, salvation, the church, and the growth of believers. The Scriptures are the infallible rule of faith and practice, the authoritative guide for Christian living.[174]

Miracles: No answer.

Restrictions: No answer.

Security of Salvation: The transformation of believers begun in regeneration and justification will be brought to completion. Although believers sin and thereby displease God, the covenant relationship is maintained by God, who will preserve them in eternal life.[175]

Speaking in Tongues and Other Gifts of the Spirit: No answer.

Trinity: Cumberland Presbyterian churches believe in the only true and living God, Father, Son, and Holy Spirit, the Holy Trinity, who is holy love, eternal, unchangeable in being, wisdom, power, holiness, justice, goodness, and truth.[176]

Women in Ministry: Women are allowed to serve as minister, elders, and deacons.[177]

For more information contact: 1978 Union Ave., Memphis, TN 38104; Phone: (901) 276-4572; Fax: (901) 272-3913; E-mail: assembly@cumberland.org; Web site: http://people.delphi.com:8080/gorematt/

Deliverance Evangelistic Centers, Inc.

Deliverance Evangelistic Centers had their beginning in Brooklyn, NY in 1950 when a young man named Arturo Skinner heard the call of God as he was planning to commit suicide. After fasting and prayer he started the first church.

Abortion: Abortion is frowned upon because it is an act of murder. A fetus is a human being in development.

Baptism: Everyone should be baptized as a public announcement of their decision to turn away from sin. It is also a confirmation of their belief that Jesus, the Son of God, died and rose from the grave.

Birth Control: No official position.

Capital Punishment: Capital punishment is the law and has the support of the Scriptures. If one refuses to obey the laws of the land, punishment will follow.

Christ's Return: This is a prominent theme in Acts, the epistles, and Revelation. The return of Christ is an event, not a process, and is personal and corporeal. His return has a threefold relation: to the church, to raise the believers who have died and to change the living Christians; to Israel, to accomplish yet unfulfilled prophecies of Israeli nations re-gathering, converting, and being established in peace; and to the nations, to bring destruction of the present political world system, followed by worldwide conversion and participation in the blessings of the kingdom.

Communion: The Lord's Supper is a sacrament which calls Christ to mind. Every time someone eats the bread and drinks from the cup in this ceremony, they are retelling the message of the Lord's death. This is to be done until Jesus returns.

Creation vs. Evolution: There are only three creative acts of God recorded in Genesis—the heavens and earth, animal life, and human life. There is also the implication that some things were already in existence or were visible. However, Deliverance Evangelistic Centers believe man did not evolve, he was created. Man has a God consciousness. The highest or most intellectual of beasts, which may have derived from a lineage of evolution, have no God consciousness.

Deity of Jesus: Jesus, spoken of as the Son of God, shares in deity with his Father. He has a title greater than that of an angel, yet in his earthly form he was made a little lower than the angels. He is now crowned by God with glory and honor because he suffered death in the place of sinners. For this he holds the highest honor and sits beside the great God of heaven in his deity.

Divorce and Remarriage: In the Old Testament Moses was not instituting divorce, but regulating the ancient practice, first by insisting on a grievance and second by issuing a formal paper. In the New Testament, Jesus went back to the fundamental meaning and purpose of marriage. The bond made when two become one flesh is indissoluble. Thus, divorce is unthinkable, except where someone has broken the bond already.

Government: No answer.

Heaven/Hell: Heaven is the dwelling place of God and his angels. It has several heights or levels where other powers and elements abide. It is the proposed resting place for the saints. It is the highest attainable goal of the believer. Hell is the opposite of heaven. It is the holding abode for sinners who die unregenerated. It is considered by, and believed to be in, the bowels or inner of the earth's core. Because of its concept of horror, it is the suggested abode of Satan and his host of demons.

Homosexuality: Paul warns his readers in Corinth of vices that will disqualify them from inheriting the Kingdom of God. Homosexuality is one of these vices. The word homosexuality renders two Greek terms, which may refer to potential and actual homosexuals. In the Greco-Roman world homosexuality was not greatly condemned; but Paul, in company with Jewish teachers and Christians, attacks it as a grave evil.

Inspiration of Scripture: The whole Bible is given by inspiration of God and is useful for teaching doctrine, giving instructions in Christian living, and illuminating sin. It is God's way of making believers well prepared at every point, fully equipped to do good to everyone.

Miracles: Miracles, supernatural occurrences in the sphere of every day life, are divine interventions of God—not magic. Miracles are accompanied by signs and wonders. They are activated by faith.

Restrictions: No answer.

Security of Salvation: Salvation offers security from the terrors of the apocalyptic events, including hell. Security means being regenerated and at union with God, and having believers' names written in the lamb's Book of Life.

Speaking in Tongues and Other Gifts of the Spirit: Deliverance Evangelistic Centers believe in the full manifestation of the Holy Spirit as evidenced in the days of the Pentecostal outpouring as recorded in Acts. It is a believer's privilege to be baptized in the Holy Spirit. It is even better to be filled with the Holy Spirit with the evidence of speaking in other tongues, as the Spirit of God gives the ability to speak. The gifts of the Spirit, as recorded in Scripture, come with the maturity of a believer in constant fellowship and manifestation of the indwelling Holy Spirit.

Trinity: God is a triune being; he is God in all three aspects: God the Father, God the Son, and God the Holy Spirit. The fundamentals of this belief lie in the operation of the triune God as one being, having different administrations of the Godhead to function or intervene in universal matters.

Women in Ministry: The Scripture invites men to help, respect, and support women who are in ministry.

For more information contact: 621 Clinton Ave., Newark, NJ 07108; Phone: (201) 824-7300; Fax: (201) 242-1902.

Elim Fellowship

Elim Fellowship began in 1933 as an informal group of churches, ministers, and missionaries who trained at Elim Bible Institute. In 1947, the fellowship was incorporated as Elim Missionary Assemblies. The title was changed to the current name in 1972. The church is Pentecostal in conviction and charismatic in orientation.[1] In 1997, there were 190 churches either officially affiliated or informally related. Total inclusive membership was 21,500.

Abortion: Elim Fellowship strongly opposes abortion.

Baptism: Baptism is for believers in the Lord Jesus Christ and is to be administered by immersion which bears witness to the gospel of Christ's death, burial, and resurrection, and indicates new life in him.[2]

Birth Control: No statement.

Capital Punishment: No statement.

Christ's Return: Elim Fellowship believes in Christ's imminent personal return in power and great glory and in his present and everlasting dominion.[3]

Communion: Communion, when shared by believers, witnesses to the saving power of the gospel and to Christ's presence in his church, and it looks forward to his victorious return.[4]

Creation vs. Evolution: Although there is no stated position, the church takes a creationist orientation.

Deity of Jesus: Elim Fellowship believes in the deity of Jesus Christ, his virgin birth, his sinless life, his miracles, his vicarious death and atonement through his shed blood, his bodily resurrection, his ascension to the right hand of the Father, and his present priestly ministry.[5]

Divorce and Remarriage: For ministerial credentials, each person's circumstances are considered. Elim does credential people with a history of divorce. Church membership for divorced persons is a local matter.

Government: Churches are autonomous.

Heaven/Hell: Both the saved and the lost will be resurrected: they that are saved to the resurrection of eternal life, and they that are lost to the resurrection of eternal punishment.[6]

Homosexuality: Homosexuality is a sin that needs to be repented. Elim believes in ministering to the individual with this problem.

Inspiration of Scripture: The Bible is the inspired and only infallible, authoritative Word of God.[7]

Miracles: Miracles still happen. Divine healing is obtained on the basis of the atonement.

Restrictions: None.

Security of Salvation: Most of the churches associated with Elim Fellowship believe in the keeping power of Christ. However, there are those in the fellowship who do not hold to the "once saved always saved" philosophy.

Speaking in Tongues and Other Gifts of the Spirit: Elim Fellowship believes in the baptism of the Holy Spirit as on the day of Pentecost, in the continuing ministry of the Holy Spirit as evidenced in charismatic gifts and ministries, and in the fruit of the Holy Spirit in the life of the believer.

Trinity: The triune Godhead is eternally existent in three persons: Father, Son, and Holy Spirit.

Women in Ministry: Although women are credentialled, there is not unanimity on this subject.

For more information contact: 7245 College St., Lima, NY 14485; Phone: (716) 582-2790; Fax: (716) 624-1229; E-mail: 75551. 743@compuserve.com; Web site: http://www.frontiernet.net/~elim/ efexec.htm

---

Episcopal Church, The

The Episcopal Church has a long history that dates back hundreds of years to the Church of England. With roots in the Catholic Church (the Anglican Communion separated at the time of Henry the VIII's reign), the Episcopal church is the American branch of the Anglican Communion. When the Church of England spread throughout the United States, sister churches sprang up. The Episcopal Church became an independent denomination after the American revolution. It grants great latitude in interpretation of doctrinal issues, emphasizes liturgy, and observes the traditional Christian calendar.[8] In 1997, there were between two and three million members in the United States, Mexico, and Central America.[9]

Abortion: The Episcopal Church supports a woman's right to choose.

Baptism: Baptism is one of two sacraments. Infants, children, and adults are baptized by sprinkling.

Birth Control: The church supports family planning.

Capital Punishment: At the 1991 General Convention, the Episcopal Church stated its opposition to capital punishment.

Christ's Return: Christ will come again in glory to judge the quick and the dead.[10]

Communion: The other of the two sacraments, communion is a central act of Christian worship.[11]

Creation vs. Evolution: The Episcopal Church accepts the Nicene Creed, which states that God created all things.[12] There are differences of opinion on how exactly this was done.

Deity of Jesus: There is one Lord, Jesus Christ.[13]

Divorce and Remarriage: The church ordains ministers who have been divorced.

Government: Episcopal.

Heaven/Hell: By heaven, the church means eternal life in enjoyment of God; by hell, it means eternal death in rejection of God.

Homosexuality: The Standing Commission on Human Affairs has encouraged the Episcopal Church to welcome homosexuals into all areas of church life and for members to take public stands against local initiatives that deprive homosexuals of civil rights. They support the ordination of practicing homosexuals. However, the issue is unresolved since the 1976 General Convention admonition, which still stands, opposes the ordination of practicing homosexuals.[14]

Inspiration of Scripture: The Episcopalian church believes the Bible is divinely inspired.[15]

Miracles: No answer.

Restrictions: None.

Security of Salvation: As Christians, nothing, not even death, can separate a believer from the love of God which is in Christ Jesus.

Speaking in Tongues and Other Gifts of the Spirit: Although the practice is not encouraged, there are some members who speak in tongues.

Trinity: The church upholds the traditional view that God is manifested in three persons: Father, Son, and Holy Spirit.[16]

Women in Ministry: The Episcopal church in America has ordained women for more than two decades.[17]

For more information contact: 815 2nd Ave., New York, NY 10017; Phone: (800) 334-7626 or (212) 867-8400; Fax: (212) 949-8059; Web site: http://www. ai.mit.edu/people/mib/anglican/anglican.html and http://www. dfms.org

---

Estonian Evangelical Lutheran Church

The Estonian Evangelical Lutheran Church was formally established in 1917. Forced into exile after World War II by Communist aggression, congregations formed into deaneries in Europe, Canada, the United States, Australia, and South America. Under overall leadership by the Archbishop and Consistory in Toronto, Ontario, the church is now in close relationship with the Estonian Evangelical Lutheran Church in Estonia. In 1997, there were 33 congregations with approximately 4,000 members.

Abortion: Abortion is favored only in extreme medical cases as determined by medical experts, but never as a means of birth control.

Baptism: Baptism is a full sacrament. Infants are baptized, according to original Lutheran traditions.

Birth Control: The Estonian Evangelical Lutheran Church is not opposed to family planning.

Capital Punishment: Capital punishment is not fully opposed in clearcut, extreme cases.

Christ's Return: The church believes in the return of Christ as stated in the Nicene and Apostles' Creeds.

Communion: Communion is a full sacrament according to original Lutheran tradition. It is not a communal meal.

Creation vs. Evolution: There are marked parallels in creation and evolution.

Deity of Jesus: Jesus is the true son of God.

Divorce and Remarriage: Divorce and remarriage are accepted according to the laws of the state.

Government: The government consists of a hierarchy which includes the Archbishop and Consistory, districts (deaneries), congregations with congregational councils, pastors, special service groups, and auxiliaries.

Heaven/Hell: Heaven and hell are accepted as defined spiritually by the Holy Scriptures.

Homosexuality: No answer.

Inspiration of Scripture: The Scriptures are the true source of faith.

Miracles: No statement.

Restrictions: None.

Security of Salvation: Salvation is by faith and faith alone.

Speaking in Tongues and Other Gifts of the Spirit: The Estonian Evangelical Lutheran Church does not deny the gifts of the Spirit, however speaking in tongues is not recognized as one of these gifts.

Trinity: There is one God existing in three persons: Father, Son, and Holy Spirit.

Women in Ministry: Several practicing pastors are women.

For more information contact: 383 Jarvis St., Toronto, Ontario, Canada M5B 2C7; Phone: (416) 923-5172 or (905) 624-6128; Fax: (416) 925-5688.

Evangelical Congregational Church

Itinerant preacher and follower of John Wesley's philosophies, Jacob Albright preached the gospel throughout Pennsylvania, Maryland, and Virginia in the late 1700s. When coerced by his many converts to found a new denomination, Albright, who was of German descent, started the Evangelical Association in 1800. After he died in 1808, his co-laborers continued to evangelize German-speaking people throughout the east. Differences of opinion and practice divided the group in 1891, which resulted in the formation of the East Pennsylvania Conference of the United Evangelical Church. After rejecting a merger with the Evangelical Church in 1922, the conference in 1928 adopted the current name. The church believes that entire sanctification or Christian perfection is a state of righteousness and true holiness, which every regenerate believer may attain. This gracious state of perfect love is attainable in this life by faith, both gradually and instantaneously, and should be earnestly sought by every child of God; but it does not deliver from the infirmities, ignorance, and mistakes which are common to man.[18]

Abortion: It is neither right nor proper to terminate a pregnancy solely on the basis of personal convenience or sociological considerations. Abortion on demand for social adjustment or to solve economic problems is morally wrong. On those rare occasions when abortion may seem morally justified, the decision should be made only after there has been thorough and sensitive medical, psychological, and religious consultation and counseling.[19]

Baptism: The sacrament of baptism is the formal application of water to an infant or to an adult believer, in the name of the Father, the Son, and the Holy Spirit. It is a visible sign and seal that the person so consecrated stands in a holy covenant relationship to God and his people.[20]

Birth Control: No statement.

Capital Punishment: No official position.

Christ's Return: The Evangelical Congregational Church believes in the personal and certain return of the Lord Jesus Christ in power and glory. He will return in the same way as the disciples saw him go.[21]

Communion: The sacrament is instituted in memory of the sufferings and death of Christ, whereby those who rightly and worthily receive the same partake of the body and blood of Christ by faith, not in a bodily but in a spiritual manner, in eating the broken bread and in drinking the blessed cup.[22]

Creation vs. Evolution: God is the creator and preserver of all things visible and invisible.[23]

Deity of Jesus: The Lord Jesus Christ, who is the only begotten Son of God, was born of the Virgin Mary, grew into perfect manhood, and became acquainted with all the infirmities, temptations, and sorrows of men. In him dwelt all the fullness of the Godhead, so that, uniting deity and humanity in one Christ, he is sole mediator between God and man.[24]

Divorce and Remarriage: Marriage is a life-long monogamous commitment between a man and a woman. The Lord Jesus declared this union to be indissoluble. Extreme caution must be exercised by pastors in solemnizing a marriage in which either party has been divorced. Clear evidence of biblical grounds shall be present, and adequate counseling shall be given to guard against the recurrence of a broken relationship. As long as reconciliation with the previous spouse is a viable option, marriage to another person should not be considered.[25]

Government: Local conferences, which are the highest judicial or legislative body, meet at least once during the conference year. They are made up of the official board (the administrative body of a particular congregation) plus all itinerant and licensed ministers and an elected lay delegate. Annual conferences meet once a year. The General Conference meets every four years. The highest legislative body, the General Conference, is made up of one ministerial and one lay delegate for every 1,500 church members in the Annual Conference. The Administrative Council of the General Conference coordinates and implements the general church program of the denomination between sessions of the General Conference. The council consists of the bishop, the district or conference superintendents of the Annual Conference, the General Conference treasurer, the director of church ministries, the director of missions, and elected itinerant elders.[26]

Homosexuality: Homosexual relationships are not acceptable as an alternative life-style, and any homosexual act, even between consenting adults, is a violation of the biblical ethic.[27]

Heaven/Hell: No statement.

Inspiration of Scripture: The Holy Scriptures of the Old and New Testaments, which are given by divine inspiration, contain the will of God concerning us in all things necessary to our salvation. Whatever is not contained therein, nor can be proven thereby, is not to be enjoined on any as an article of faith.[28]

Miracles: No official position.

Restrictions: The Evangelical Congregational Church discourages the use of mind-altering drugs, over-dependence on prescription and over-the-counter drugs, smoking and other personal use of tobacco. They affirm abstinence from the use of, and traffic in, alcoholic beverages as the only truly responsible position for members of the church.[29]

Security of Salvation: The gracious help of God is pledged to all those who continue steadfast in faith. But, on account of man's free will, which no power may coerce, apostasy from God is possible so long as someone continues in the flesh. Therefore, constant watchfulness, prayer, and holy living are necessary on the part of man, lest he fall away from the grace of God, grieve and quench the Holy Spirit, and lose his soul at last.[30]

Speaking in Tongues and Other Gifts of the Spirit: No official answer.

Trinity: The Trinity, namely the Father, the Son, and the Holy Ghost, is of one substance and power, and is co-eternal.[31]

Women in Ministry: No official position.

For more information contact: 100 W. Park Ave., Myerstown, PA 17067; Phone: (717) 866-7581; Fax: (717) 866-7383; E-mail: webmaster@ eccenter.com; Web site: http://www.eccenter.com/church/homepage.htm

---

Evangelical Covenant Church

The Evangelical Covenant Church has its roots in the Scandinavian revival movements of the 1800s, particularly as it found expression in the home Bible study movement within the Lutheran State Church of Sweden. Upon immigrating, members formed a new denomination in the United States in 1885. The church takes a high view of the sacraments, practices freedom in baptism, has a confirmation program, loves celebrative traditions, and values the church year.[32] In 1997, there were 621 churches with an aggregate attendance of 107,000.

Abortion: Abortion as an alternative to abstinence or other contraceptive measures is not an acceptable practice. Women are encouraged to continue their pregnancies and place their newborn infants for adoption, preferably through Christian placement agencies. In some tragic instances, abortion may need to be considered to safeguard the life of the mother or in cases of rape or incest.[33]

Baptism: Baptism testifies to three biblical truths of Christ's grace: cleansing from sin, identification with Christ, and incorporation into the church. The Covenant affirms the sacrament of baptism for either infants or new believers. For the infant, baptism looks forward to the realization of those truths in a person's life at the point of personal faith in Christ. For the new believer, it looks back to the fulfillment of those three truths at the time of personal faith. The mode of baptism can be either immersion or pouring.[34]

Birth Control: Birth control is a matter of personal conscience.

Capital Punishment: Capital punishment is a matter of personal conscience.

Christ's Return: Christ shall come in glory to judge those still alive and those who are dead.[35] The Covenant affirms the return of Christ as a clear teaching of Scripture. However, it recognizes that Scripture is less clear on a specific scenario and therefore allows freedom of interpretation as to the details.

Communion: One of the two sacraments (the other being baptism) expressly commanded by the Lord.[36] Communion is given to the church to commemorate the Lord's death until he returns.

Creation vs. Evolution: According to the Nicene Creed, God made heaven and earth and things both visible and invisible. The emphasis is more "who" than "how."

Deity of Jesus: According to the Apostles' and Nicene Creeds, Jesus is the only begotten Son of God. The Covenant affirms the deity of Christ.

Divorce and Remarriage: Divorce is a devastating, personal experience. The Covenant seeks to help individuals reconstruct their lives through the grace and strength of God.

Government: Congregational Polity. Churches call their own pastors, set their own budgets, and own their buildings.[37]

Heaven/Hell: The Covenant affirms the biblical reality of an eternal destiny.

Homosexuality: God created people male and female and provided for the marriage relationship in which two become one. A publicly declared, legally binding marriage between one man and one woman is the appropriate place for sexual intercourse. Heterosexual marriage, faithfulness within marriage, and abstinence outside of marriage constitute the Christian standard. When people fall short, they are invited to repent, receive the forgiveness of God, and amend their lives.

Inspiration of Scripture: The Covenant believes the Holy Scriptures, the Old and New Testament, are the Word of God. The authority of the Bible is supreme in all matters of faith, doctrine, and conduct.[38]

Miracles: The Covenant believes God can and does perform miracles, but not that he does or must in any given personal circumstance.

Restrictions: None.

Security of Salvation: Justification, as an act of God through Christ's death on the cross, is complete and eternal. Sanctification, a process of growing in conformity to the image of Christ through the power of the Holy Spirit, is a process that lasts a lifetime.

Speaking in Tongues and Other Gifts of the Spirit: The Covenant affirms spiritual gifts which are given for the completion of the church body and not for personal stature. Such gifts are not a measure of spiritual maturity. Gifts of the Spirit, such as tongues, are not to be confused with the fruits of the Spirit, which are evidence of Christian character.[39] The Covenant demands none of the gifts for every individual, nor does it elevate any of the gifts above another.

Trinity: The Covenant affirms the triune God: Father, Son, and Holy Spirit.

Women in Ministry: The Covenant affirms the ministry gifts of all members of the body of Christ. Women have been ordained since 1976.

For more information contact: 5101 N. Francisco Ave., Chicago, IL 60625; Phone: (773) 784-3000; Fax: (773) 784-4366; E-mail: ecc-cge@aol.com; Web site: http://www.northpark.edu/cov/

Evangelical Free Church of America, The

The Evangelical Free Church of America has its roots in a Bible reading revival which swept the Scandinavian countries. The movement came to the United States through immigrants who established the Swedish ethnic church in 1884. During the same time period the Norwegian-Danish Association was formed. In 1950 the two merged at a conference in Medicine Lake, MN, and adopted the current name. In 1997, there were 1,217 churches with 124,000 members.

Abortion: Human life is a gift from God to be cherished from the time of conception until natural death. God has chosen to involve himself with human life at every age and to affirm its value under all conditions. It is imperative to maintain this same high regard for life. An unborn child has the right of a person from conception and these rights may not be properly abrogated by law.

Baptism: Baptism is an ordinance to be observed, but not regarded as a means of salvation. Believers are baptized, usually by immersion.

Birth Control: The decision to use birth control is a personal matter. However, methods which cause an abortion in the early days of pregnancy are inconsistent with the EFCA's position on abortion.

Capital Punishment: No position.

Christ's Return: The EFCA holds to a personal, premillennial, and imminent return of Christ.

Communion: Communion is an ordinance to be observed by the church. It is held as a symbol of Christ's death. It is not a means of salvation. It is for believers only and is usually observed monthly.

Creation vs. Evolution: The church believes in God's divine intentional act of creation of the universe and the world out of nothing.

Deity of Jesus: Jesus Christ is true God and true man, having been conceived of the Holy Spirit. He is now a high priest and advocate.

Divorce and Remarriage: Divorce is to be avoided if at all possible. Divorce is accepted on grounds of immorality or if the unbelieving spouse leaves a believing spouse. Remarriage is on the basis of individual review.

Government: Congregational. Congregations call their own pastors, elect and select their own leaders, set their own budget, decide on all major projects, and accept members.

Heaven/Hell: Heaven and hell are both literal places where people will live for eternity. Heaven is for those who have responded to the gift of salvation through Jesus Christ. Hell is for those who have not received Jesus Christ as Savior.

Homosexuality: Homosexuality is a practice which is totally contrary to the teachings of the Bible. The EFCA desires to love the individual, but cannot accept the act of homosexuality.

Inspiration of Scripture: The Bible, both Old and New Testaments, is the inspired, infallible and inerrant Word of God, without error in the original writings. It is the complete revelation of God's will and is the final authority for Christian faith and practice.

Miracles: The church believes all the miracles told of Jesus, Moses, and the prophets in the Bible.

Restrictions: None.

Security of Salvation: Some in the EFCA hold to eternal security, and some hold that a person can denounce his faith. However, the church does not believe that you can easily lose your faith.

Speaking in Tongues and Other Gifts of the Spirit: The gifts of the Spirit are given to believers as the Spirit determines. Every true believer has at least one gift of the Spirit. The EFCA is not charismatic in doctrine or practice but it is not anti-charismatic. Sign gifts are not the practice of EFCA churches in their worship.

Trinity: The Father, Son, and Holy Spirit are individual persons, yet one in essence and life. The EFCA does not believe in modalism.

Women in Ministry: Women have been given gifts of ministry and service. However, the EFCA holds that only men will be ordained for the preaching/teaching pastor of a local church.

For more information contact: 901 E. 78th St., Minneapolis, MN 55420; Phone: (800) 745-2202 or (612) 854-1300; Fax: (612) 853-8488; E-mail: 74453.2762@compuserve.com; Web site: http://www.halcyon.com/churches/efca/efca.html

---

Evangelical Friends Church, The

George Fox founded the Friends in England in 1648. Following its migration to the United States, the group was known as the Ohio Yearly Meeting of Friends from 1813 until 1971. The Evangelical Friends Church, whose motto is, "Great Commission Driven in the Spirit of the Great Commandment," was the branch most influenced by the Holiness Movement that swept the United States before and after the Civil War.[40] It is also one of the four branches of the Religious Society of Friends. However, Evangelical Friends are not the same as Quakers. In 1997, there were 93 churches with 8,700 members.

Abortion: Life is the gift of God. To take life from the unborn cheapens the value of life in all its facets and leads to despair.

Baptism: The baptism of the Holy Spirit comes to a believer as their life is yielded to the Lord. This is more important than water baptism.

Birth Control: No position.

Capital Punishment: It is not inconsistent to be pro-life and pro-capital punishment. If a person's actions are so heinous as to subject them to death, it should only be done with legal due process and without glorifying in that person's death.

Christ's Return: Jesus is returning as he promised. Most Friends believe this will be in a pre-tribulation rapture and a later 1,000-year reign of justice.

Communion: Communing with the Savior is pre-eminent. But the communion ceremony is valuable to the believer as a worship experience.

Creation vs. Evolution: Evangelical Friends are creationists. God is the creator, redeemer, sustainer, and coming King. His creation is accountable to him.

Deity of Jesus: Jesus is God's Son. He is in creation clear through to eternity. More than a good man or teacher, Jesus deserves worship and obedience.

Divorce and Remarriage: God hates divorce, but not divorced persons. Friends' pastors in various churches take different positions regarding remarriage.

Government: On a local basis, the EFC's government is congregational. On a denominational basis, its government is connectional.

Heaven/Hell: Heaven and hell exist as eternal destinies for people. Believers will be admitted to the glories of heaven by God's grace. Nonbelievers will not be admitted, and thus they will suffer in hell.

Homosexuality: Homosexual behavior is sinful. It is chosen, not inherited, and God's grace is any person's hope in changing behavior and eternal destiny.

Inspiration of Scripture: The historical canon is God's Word. It is God-breathed and still speaks reliably to mankind's need.

Miracles: Miracles happen in response to a believer's prayers and God's sovereignty.

Restrictions: None.

Security of Salvation: Evangelical Friends are sometimes called Calmenian, which means that they embrace both Calvinistic and Arminian theology. Historically, the church believes salvation can be lost, but they also recognize God's sovereignty and grace.

Speaking in Tongues and Other Gifts of the Spirit: Many Friends have the gift of speaking in tongues, but it is not commonly practiced in public worship.

Trinity: God is one being in three persons: Father, Son, and Holy Spirit.

Women in Ministry: Women have been valued in ministry and leadership since the 1600s with a biblical understanding that there is no ministerial difference between sexes.

For more information contact: 5350 Broadmoor Cir. NW, Canton,

OH 44709; Phone: (330) 493-1660; Fax: (330) 493-0852; E-mail: efcer@aol.com

---

Evangelical Lutheran Church in America

The Evangelical Lutheran Church in America was officially constituted on April 30, 1987. It united three predecessor church bodies: The American Lutheran Church, The Association of Evangelical Lutheran Churches, and the Lutheran Church in America. In this country, the Evangelical Lutheran Church in America traces its organizational roots to the Ministerium of Pennsylvania, which was founded in 1748 as the first Lutheran denomination in North America. It teaches that the church consists of those people who gather around the preaching of the Word of God and the celebration of the sacraments. Through these means God bestows saving grace to all who believe in Jesus Christ as Savior of the world. In 1997, there were 11,000 congregations with 5.2 million members.

Abortion: In a social statement approved in 1991, the church took the position that abortion is always a tragic option of last resort. From an ethical point of view, a therapeutic abortion may be obtained in the following three circumstances: when the life of the mother is threatened, when the condition of the fetus is incompatible with life, and when the pregnancy has resulted from rape or incest.

Baptism: Baptism is administered to adults, children, and infants in the name of the Father, and the Son, and the Holy Spirit. In baptism, the candidate is united with the death and resurrection of Christ and receives the promises of forgiveness and eternal life.

Birth Control: Various forms of contraception are recognized as legitimate means of birth control.

Capital Punishment: In a social statement adopted in 1991, the Evangelical Lutheran Church in America declared its opposition to the death penalty on the basis of justice, the need to minister to those affected by violent crime, and because of the death penalty's inconsistent record of use.

Christ's Return: In concert with the witness of the Holy Scriptures and the tradition of the church, the Evangelical Lutheran Church in America looks and prays for the return of Christ, who will judge both the just and sinners and will establish a new heaven and a new earth.

Communion: With Lutherans throughout the world, the Evangelical Lutheran Church in America confesses that the crucified and risen Christ is present in, with, and under the bread and wine of Holy Communion. It offers those who receive his body and blood the gifts of forgiveness, life, and salvation.

Creation vs. Evolution: As a matter of faith, the Evangelical Lutheran Church in America holds the position that God, through Christ the Word, has created the world and all that is in it, and continues to sustain this creation by grace. The means by which God accomplishes this creative activity is open to scientific investigation.

Deity of Jesus: The Evangelical Lutheran Church in America states in its confession of faith that Jesus Christ is the Word of God incarnate, through whom everything was made and through whose life, death, and resurrection God fashions a new creation.

Divorce and Remarriage: The Evangelical Lutheran Church in America recognizes that divorce is often a tragic necessity when, as a result of sin, a marriage is no longer viable. Those who obtain a divorce are encouraged to recognize their own contributions to the failure of the marriage. Divorced persons may remarry in the church.

Government: The Evangelical Lutheran Church in America recognizes three major expressions: congregations, synods, and the churchwide organization. Congregations normally are led by pastors together with a congregational council, which acts on behalf of all the members of the congregation. In most cases the congregation conducts an annual meeting for the purpose of deciding crucial issues. Congregations are gathered into one of 65 synods, whose chief pastor is a bishop elected to a six-year term. Together with the Synod Council, which meets several times a year, the bishop provides leadership to the Synod, which meets annually in assembly. The churchwide organization, based in Chicago, IL, is led by a presiding bishop who is elected to a six-year term by a biennial churchwide assembly, the highest legislative authority in the Evangelical Lutheran Church in America. Between meetings of the churchwide assembly, the Church Council, meeting semiannually, provides direction for the Evangelical Lutheran Church in America.

Heaven/Hell: Based upon the ancient creeds of the Christian church, the Evangelical Lutheran Church in America holds a belief in both heaven and hell. It confesses that heaven is the dwelling place of God, from which Christ descended when he became incarnate and to which he returned following his earthly ministry, death, and resurrection. Hell is conceived as the place of the dead and the lost who are separated from the presence of God.

Homosexuality: The Evangelical Lutheran Church in America, by action of the 1995 churchwide assembly and the Conference of Bishops, has issued a statement in which it urges gay and lesbian persons to become active members of the congregations of the church. The ELCA advocates on behalf of gay and lesbian persons in matters of justice and equal treatment under the law. The ELCA requires that gay and lesbian persons who are ordained ministers of the church remain celibate.

Inspiration of Scripture: In its confession of faith, the Evangelical Lutheran Church in America accepts the canonical Scriptures of the Old and New Testaments as the inspired Word of God and the authoritative source and norm of its proclamation, faith, and life.

Miracles: The ELCA recognizes that events that have no logical or scientific explanation, which are appropriately called miracles, have been attested to in Scripture. In the same way, there is evidence of healing in persons suffering from terminal diseases which also cannot be explained.

Restrictions: According to the constitution, bylaws, and continuing resolutions of the ELCA, after January 1, 1988, no ordained ministers of this church may seek membership in a non-church organization which claims to possess in its teaching and ceremonies that which the Lord has given solely to the church.

Security of Salvation: The ELCA teaches, with regard to Holy Baptism, that the baptized person enters a voluntary relationship with God, who promises always to offer grace and love. An individual may, however, choose to reject this covenant of forgiveness and grace.

Speaking in Tongues and Other Gifts of the Spirit: The Holy Spirit is active in the church, guiding its faith and life, and empowering the members of the church to engage in their ministries of love and service. These gifts may include speaking in tongues, prophecy, and interpretation of tongues, although not many members of the ELCA would claim to have received these gifts.

Trinity: The ELCA confesses the triune God: Father, Son, and Holy Spirit.

Women in Ministry: By action of its predecessor church bodies, the ELCA has welcomed women into the ministry since 1970.

For more information contact: 8765 W. Higgins Rd., Chicago, IL 60631-4198; Phone: (773) 380-2809; Fax: (773) 380-2977; E-mail: info@elca.org; Web site: http://www.elca.org/index.html

---

Evangelical Lutheran Synod

The Evangelical Lutheran Synod had its origins among the early settlers of Norwegian descent who came to America during the 19th century. As they settled in the wilderness of Wisconsin, Iowa, Minnesota, and other states, they had no churches, pastors, or leadership. In 1853, the first church body was organized. It was known as the Norwegian Synod. In July of 1872, the group joined the Wisconsin Synod, the Missouri Synod, and others in forming the Evangelical Lutheran Synod. In the 1880s a controversy over the doctrine of election divided the Synod, and in 1917 a merger brought together various groups of Norwegian churches into a new church body, which one year later adopted the original name. The name was later changed to the Evangelical Lutheran Synod. The Synod rejects unionism (church fellowship with adherents of false doctrine) and ecumenical endeavors which it feels compromise God's Word. In 1993, the group established a new alliance known as the Confessional Evangelical Lutheran Conference. There were 125 congregations in 1993.[41]

Abortion: Because abortion results in the death of an unborn human being, it is never justified except in those rare and tragic circumstances when continuation of the pregnancy would clearly threaten the life of the mother. Abortion for any other reason is a great sin in the eyes of God.[42]

Baptism: Holy Baptism has the power to work the new life of faith in the heart of sinners. This regenerative washing with water is intended for all people, since all—including infants and children—are members of a sinful human race and are in need of God's grace and forgiveness.[43]

Birth Control: No answer.

Capital Punishment: God has given the State the right to administer capital punishment.[44]

Christ's Return: The Evangelical Lutheran Synod rejects all forms of millennialism, that is, the teaching that Christ will reign visibly over an earthly kingdom for a thousand years before the day of resurrection and judgment.[45]

Communion: In the Lord's Supper, the true body and blood of Christ are distributed to the communicants. It is the Word of God connected with the earthly elements which makes the Lord's Supper an effective means through which forgiveness, life, and salvation are truly offered to those who receive these sacraments.[46]

Creation vs Evolution: God created all things in six days by the power of his Word, exactly as it is set forth in Genesis and elsewhere in Scripture. The church therefore rejects the theories of evolution including theistic evolution.[47]

Deity of Jesus: Jesus Christ is true God and true man in one person, conceived by the Holy Spirit and born of the Virgin Mary. He is the world's only Savior from sin, death, and the devil.[48]

Divorce and Remarriage: No answer.

Government: Congregational.

Heaven/Hell: At the time of physical death, a believer's soul goes to heaven and an unbeliever's soul goes to hell. On the last day, Christ will return visibly to the world and will raise the bodies of all the dead, both believers and unbelievers. At that time their bodies and souls will be reunited. Believers will enter into eternal life in the new heavens and the new earth, but unbelievers will be cast forever into the fiery lake of burning sulfur.[49]

Homosexuality: Scripture condemns homosexuality. Nevertheless, when an individual caught up in such sin truly repents, the forgiveness of the Gospel is to be fully applied.[50]

Inspiration of Scripture: The canonical books of the Old and New Testament, in their original form as written by prophets, apostles, and evangelists, were given by inspiration of God. God reveals himself through Holy Scriptures, his written Word. The true way of salvation is revealed only through God's Word and any claims for revelation of the way of salvation through other means must be rejected. The Scriptures not only contain the Word of God, but they are the very Word of God in their entirety.[51]

Miracles: The Scriptures are true and reliable in all that they report, including their accounts of Old and New Testament miracles. The Evangelical Lutheran Synod therefore regards the denial of these miracles as blasphemous and as setting up man's reason as a judge over God's Word.[52]

Restrictions: The church rejects participation or membership in religious organizations which have features that are in conflict with the Christian faith, such as the Masonic Lodge and similar organizations.[53]

Security of Salvation: Those in this life who, through the Gospel, have been called, enlightened, sanctified, and preserved in the true faith have from eternity been elected according to God's unmeritted love. They are adopted as his children and have been chosen in Christ before the creation of the world to be heirs of everlasting life. Therefore, Christians can and should be sure of their salvation, since God's promise is steadfast and his gracious election to salvation stands firm.[54]

Speaking in Tongues and Other Gifts of the Spirit: No answer.

Trinity: God is the triune God revealed in Scripture as the Father, the Son, and the Holy Spirit. There is only one divine essence.[55]

Women in Ministry: When God's Word says that women are not to teach or exercise authority over men in the church, this means that the pastoral office cannot be conferred upon women. It is God's will that only properly qualified men be called to this office.[56]

For more information contact: 6 Browns Ct., Mankato, MN 56001-6121; Phone: (507) 388-4868.

Evangelical Mennonite Church, Inc.

The Evangelical Mennonite Church was influenced early on by the Reformation, the Anabaptist movement, and the leadership of Menno Simons in Europe. After immigrants came to the United States, they severed their ties with the Amish and became known as Defenseless Mennonites. In 1948, that name was officially changed to Evangelical Mennonites.[57] There were 30 churches with 5,623 members in 1997.

Abortion: Human life, created in the image of God, is sacred. It begins at the moment of fertilization. Evangelical Mennonites abhor and decry any attempt to deliberately induce the extraction or expulsion of the human fetus with the intent of terminating life at any time between fertilization and birth.

Baptism: Water baptism symbolizes the experience of regeneration and union with Jesus Christ. Baptism is administered to believers in the name of the Father, Son, and Holy Spirit. The church encourages immersion, but recognizes other modes.

Birth Control: No statement.

Capital Punishment: No statement.

Christ's Return: Christ will return personally, visibly, and before the millennium. This will be accomplished in two phases. First, Christ will descend from heaven to claim his waiting bride—the living church—and departed believers. Then he will descend with his saints to establish the long-promised Kingdom and reign upon the earth for 1,000 years.

Communion: Communion is open to all believers who know themselves to be in a right relationship with God. It consists of partaking of the bread and the fruit of the vine which symbolize the broken body and shed blood of Christ for the remission of sins. It reaffirms a believer's continuing dependence on him. Its observance is to be preceded by honest self-examination.

Creation vs. Evolution: God is the creator and sustainer of all things both visible and invisible. He is both immanent in, and transcendent to, the creation.

Deity of Jesus: The Evangelical Mennonite Church believes in the deity of the Lord Jesus Christ, his virgin birth, his sinless life, his miracles, his vicarious and atoning death through his shed blood, his bodily resurrection, his ascension to the right hand of the Father, and his personal return in power and glory.[58] Ultimately every knee shall bow to him and every tongue will confess that he is Lord.

Divorce and Remarriage: Divorce is a basic violation of God's original intention for marriage. Divorce is permissible only for two reasons: when one partner has committed adultery, and when a non-believing partner chooses to desert a believer. Remarriage is permitted in the case of a partner's death.

Government: No answer.

Heaven/Hell: There are two eternal conscious destinies for man. Heaven is for the righteous and hell is for the unrighteous.

Homosexuality: Homosexual activity is condemned in Scripture. Homosexuality is not an inherited condition in the same category as race, gender, or national origin. It is a deviation from the creator's plan for human sexuality.

Inspiration of Scripture: The original texts of the 66 books of the Bible are God-breathed. The Scriptures are truth, written by holy men who were chosen and equipped by God for this special task.

Miracles: The Evangelical Mennonite Church believes in the miracles of Jesus Christ.

Restrictions: No answer.

Security of Salvation: Every Christian can have a valid sense of assurance concerning their salvation, their relationship with God, and their destiny. Through faith in Jesus Christ, a knowledge of the Scriptures, and the ministry of the Holy Spirit, such assurance becomes real and personal.

Speaking in Tongues and Other Gifts of the Spirit: No statement.

Trinity: God exists and reveals himself as three persons: Father, Son, and Holy Spirit.

Women in Ministry: God designated man to hold teaching authority and administrative heads in the local church for these reasons: the order of creation, woman's deception and resultant sin, and the orderly nature of God. While accepting and fulfilling delegated leadership positions, a woman should neither seize nor aspire to the highest positions of authority in the church.

For more information contact: 1420 Kerrway Ct., Fort Wayne, IN 46805; Phone: (219) 423-3649; Fax: (219) 420-1905.

Evangelical Methodist Conference

In 1946, Dr. W.W. Breckbill met with several other men in Memphis, TN to form a new organization which protested the liberal direction they saw the Methodist Church taking. In 1997, there were 33 churches with 5,000 members.

Abortion: Abortion is murder of the unborn.

Baptism: Baptism is for believers only.

Birth Control: No official position.

Capital Punishment: The Evangelical Methodist Conference believes in capital punishment.

Christ's Return: Christ's return will be premillennial and pretribulation.

Communion: Communion is for the believer. It has no saving power, but is a reminder of the atoning work of Christ.

Creation vs. Evolution: God created this universe according to the Scriptures. The church rejects evolution as man's explanation apart from God.

Deity of Jesus: The Evangelical Methodist Conference believes in the incarnation of Christ, that he truly was God in the flesh.

Divorce and Remarriage: Marriage, which is ordained by God, is a picture of Christ and the Church. Therefore divorce is wrong.

Government: Congregational.

Heaven/Hell: Heaven and hell are both literal places of abode. Hell is for the unsaved. Heaven is for all of God's redeemed.

Homosexuality: Homosexuality, a sin, is condemned by the Scriptures.

Inspiration of Scripture: God inspired his Word and he has preserved it throughout the ages.

Miracles: The Evangelical Methodist Conference affirms the accuracy of the scriptural account of miracles. However, it rejects the notion that men today are performing miracles.

Restrictions: None.

Security of Salvation: The genuinely saved are genuinely saved.

Speaking in Tongues and Other Gifts of the Spirit: Speaking in tongues and other sign gifts are not scriptural.

Trinity: The church believes in the triune Godhead.

Women in Ministry: Women are not ordained. Pastors do not conduct joint meetings with women.

For more information contact: P.O. Box 751, Kingsport, TN 37662; Phone: (423) 245-6341; Fax: (423) 245-9288.

Evangelical Presbyterian Church

The Evangelical Presbyterian Church was formed by several groups who were committed to the historic Presbyterian confessional position and who were convinced that mainline Presbyterian churches were no longer faithful to that position. It is the only conservative Presbyterian body which adheres to the Westminster Confession of Faith, permits the ordination of women, and allows charismatic expression in public and private worship. Officially chartered in 1981, the EPC had 180 churches with 57,000 members in 1997 whose motto is, "In essentials, unity; in non-essentials, liberty; in all things, charity."

Abortion: The Bible does not distinguish between prenatal and postnatal life. It attributes personhood to the unborn child. The EPC is opposed to abortion and encourages alternatives to abortion, including the support and care for all children who result from unwanted pregnancies. Abortion must never be used as a convenience or a means of birth control.[59]

Baptism: Baptism is a sacrament ordained by Jesus Christ which solemnly admits a person into the visible church. It is a sign of the covenant of grace. It is a mark of God's promise whether administered to an adult or an infant. Baptism is usually administered by pouring or sprinkling water.

Birth Control: No official position.

Capital Punishment: No official position.

Christ's Return: Jesus Christ will come again to the earth—personally, visibly, and bodily—to judge the living and the dead and to consummate history and the eternal plan of God.[60] No one knows when that day will be. Christians are to be alert and always ready for Christ's return.

Communion: The Lord's Supper is one of two sacraments ordained by Christ to be observed in the church until the end of the world. It is a perpetual remembrance of his sacrificial death. Participation in communion with Jesus and his body, the church, spiritually nourishes believers.

Creation vs. Evolution: The triune God created the world out of nothing. He made everything in the world, visible and invisible, in the space of six days, and it was very good.

Deity of Jesus: Jesus Christ, the living Word, became flesh through his miraculous conception by the Holy Spirit and his virgin birth. He who is truly the eternal God, of one substance and equal with the Father, became true man united in one person forever. He died on the cross as a sacrifice for sins according to the Scriptures. On the third day he arose bodily from the dead and ascended into heaven, where at the right hand of the Majesty on high, he now is high priest and mediator.[61]

Divorce and Remarriage: Marriage is for life. Scripture teaches that divorce is always an abnormality arising out of sinfulness. Divorce is accepted as permissible in cases of extreme unfaithfulness for which there is no repentance and which is beyond remedy. Remarriage of divorced persons is sanctioned when sufficient penitence for sin is evident.

Government: A Presbyterian church is governed by elders chosen by the congregation. This representational form of church government includes the courts of the local body (session), the regional (presbytery), and the national (General Assembly).

Heaven/Hell: Scripture teaches only two places for souls separated from their bodies: heaven, where believers behold the face of God and receive full redemption of their bodies, and hell, where the wicked remain in torment and complete darkness.

Homosexuality: Biblical teaching makes it clear that the practice of homosexuality is a sin. While God hates the sin, he loves the sinner.[62] Unrepentant homosexual behavior is incompatible with membership in the EPC and with its ordination vows. However, the church recognizes the need to reach out to persons struggling with homosexuality, offering them friendship, therapy, and intercession.

Inspiration of Scripture: The infallible Word of God, the 66 books of the Old and New Testaments, is a complete and unified witness to God's redemptive acts culminating in the incarnation of the living Word, Jesus Christ. The Bible, uniquely and fully inspired by the Holy Spirit, is the supreme and final authority on all matters on which it speaks. All Scripture is self-attesting and, being truth, requires an unreserved submission in all areas of life.[63]

Miracles: The Evangelical Presbyterian Church believes in the God of miracles and in the many miracles of salvation and healing by the divine healer as recorded in the Scriptures.

Restrictions: None.

Security of Salvation: Those whom God has accepted in his Son and has effectually called and sanctified by his Spirit can never completely or finally fall out of their state of grace. They shall continue in that state to the end and are eternally saved.

Speaking in Tongues and Other Gifts of the Spirit: The gifts of God's Spirit are biblically valid for today. They should be exercised under the guidance of God's Word and the authority of the local session. Since the Holy Spirit is the source of Christian unity, any use of the gifts which would lead to division within the church must be guarded against. The church also affirms the priority of the fruit of the Spirit over the gifts in the Christian life.[64] Speaking in tongues may be a form of worship, but it is not in any sense an extra-biblical revelation.

Trinity: The Evangelical Presbyterian Church believes in one God, the sovereign creator and sustainer of all things, infinitely perfect and eternally existing in three persons: Father, Son, and Holy Spirit.[65]

Women in Ministry: Local congregations are free to elect women as ruling elders and deacons, and presbyteries are free to ordain women as teaching elders if they so choose.

For more information contact: 29140 Buckingham Ave., Ste. 5, Livonia, MI 48154; Phone: (313) 261-2001; Fax: (313) 261-3282; E-mail: 76155.3570@compuserve.com; Web site: http://www.epc.org/index.html

---

Fellowship of Evangelical Bible Churches

In 1889, two Mennonite groups merged under the name United Mennonite Brethren of North America. Two men of Russian birth, Elder Aaron Wall and Elder Isaac Peters, provided leadership for the new conference. The group was founded over three distinguishing principles: the emphases on new birth and changed lives as a requirement for baptism and church membership, the emphasis on a separated walk as a result of the new birth, and the practice of church discipline.[1] The name was changed to Defenseless Mennonite Brethren of Christ in North America, then to Evangelical Mennonite Brethren[2] before the current name, Fellowship of Evangelical Bible Churches, and motto, "Proclaiming the Gospel of Jesus Christ at home and abroad for the salvation of the lost," were adopted in 1987. In 1997, there were 17 churches with 1,534 members in the United States.

Abortion: Abortion is opposed in all instances.

Baptism: Water baptism expresses the experience of regeneration and union with Christ. It is a public testimony of the inner experience preceding church membership. It is to be administered to believers only. It has no saving or cleansing merits, but is rather an act of obedience demonstrating the new relationship with Christ. Infant baptism cannot be recognized as valid according to the Scriptures. The Fellowship of Evangelical Bible Churches practices the immersion method, but other modes are valid providing salvation preceded baptism.[3]

Birth Control: No position.

Capital Punishment: No position.

Christ's Return: The FEBC believes in the personal, visible, imminent, and premillennial return of Christ. The second coming covers a period of events, such as the rapture, the great tribulation, the revelation of Christ at the end of the great tribulation period, and the Great White Throne Judgment. No one knows when he will return, but one can know when it is near at hand. This hope of the second coming is a purifying element in the life of the believer and a warning to the unbeliever.[4]

Communion: The Lord's Supper is an ordinance to be observed frequently (at least four times a year) by believers until he returns. The consecrated emblems consist of bread symbolizing Christ's broken body and the fruit of the vine as a symbol of his shed blood. The observance of this ordinance is to be preceded by honest self-examination. There is no salvation element in this ordinance, it rather serves as a reminder of Christ's vicarious atonement and a believer's continued dependence upon him. Communion is open to all believers who practice consistent Christian living.[5]

Creation vs. Evolution: By an immediate act of God, man was created in his image.[6]

Deity of Jesus: Jesus Christ is the eternal Son of God. The Son is from eternity the only begotten of the Father. Being conceived of the Holy Spirit, he was born man of the Virgin Mary in order to fulfill the purpose of God from the foundation of the world—to redeem us from eternal curse and bring about our eternal salvation by making full atonement for our sins through his vicarious suffering and death on the cross. He took upon himself the likeness of sinful flesh, being true God and also perfect man, being made in all things as humans are, yet without sin. He rose triumphantly from the grave the third day and ascended into heaven and is now at the right hand of God interceding on behalf of mankind.[7]

Divorce and Remarriage: Historically the FEBC has held the view that marriage is an indissoluble union of husband and wife. Therefore, divorce should not be considered by believers, and neither divorced party should marry another as long as both live. However, there are differences of opinion on this question. Some would grant a divorce on the ground of fornication or desertion by an unbelieving spouse and not stand in the way of remarriage while both partners live. Because of these differences of interpretation, pastors follow the constitution of their local church.[8]

Government: No answer.

Heaven/Hell: The wicked after death will be in torment until the judgment at the Great White Throne when they will be eternally separated from God and cast into the lake of fire (everlasting hell). The final state of the believer is far better than this present life in the body. The believer's final and eternal home is in heaven, the New Jerusalem.[9]

Homosexuality: Homosexuality is not an inherited condition in the same category as race, gender, or national origin, all of which are free from moral implication. Homosexuality is a sinful deviation from the creator's plan for human sexuality. While homosexuals as individuals are entitled to civil rights, including protection of the law, the FEBC opposes legislation which would extend special consideration to such individuals based upon their sexual orientation.[10]

Inspiration of Scripture: All Scripture, both the Old and New Testaments, is the only inerrant, inspired Word of God, written by holy men as they were moved by the Holy Spirit. It reveals the will of God to man. It is the truth. The gospel is the power of God unto salvation to everyone that believes, and all Scripture is profitable for doctrine, for reproof, for correction, and for instruction in righteousness: that the man of God may be perfect, thoroughly furnished unto all good works. It is the guide to eternal bliss.[11]

Miracles: Divine healing of the body can be realized by God's children on conditions as set forth in Scripture. However, the FEBC cautions against the obvious abuse of the spectacular in the modern day phenomena of mass faith healing.[12]

Restrictions: All secret orders are contrary to the teaching of Scripture. Therefore, under no circumstances should members be allowed to hold membership in any secret organization.[13]

Security of Salvation: Once a person has come to salvation it cannot be taken away.

Speaking in Tongues and Other Gifts of the Spirit: The New Testament use of tongues was an Apostolic sign to proclaim the mighty works of God to Jews of all nations in their own language. The Holy Spirit's purpose in causing tongues was to authenticate the apostles. Tongues were a sign of his presence and ministry for the purpose of validating the Apostolic message before it was made into Scripture. The purpose of biblical tongues limits them to the Apostolic age. The FEBC believes the gift of tongues is not a valid gift for the church today and should not be tolerated in the church.[14]

Trinity: The Trinity is made up of three distinct persons; God the Father, God the Son, and God the Holy Spirit. These three, though one in essence or equal in their divine perfection, yet individual in personality, perform different but harmonious offices in the great plan of redemption. God, who is one with respect to his essence, is three with respect to the modes or distinctions of his being.[15]

Women in Ministry: Women are not placed in pastoral positions.

For more information contact: 5800 S. 14th St., Omaha, NE 68107-3584; Phone: (402) 731-4780; Fax: (402) 731-1173; E-mail: febcoma@aol.com; Web site: http://www.rhesys.mb.ca/rhema/febc/

Fellowship of Grace Brethren Churches

The Fellowship has German roots that go back to 1708. In Germany, on the banks of the Eder River, Alexander Mack and a small group of Christians committed themselves to the Bible instead of the state church. They determined they would adopt no human creed, since such a creed would limit them in the search for scriptural truth. The church's motto, "The Bible, the Whole Bible, and Nothing But the Bible," reflects its position.[16]

Abortion: No answer.

Baptism: Jesus commands every believer to publicly declare his faith in Christ by being baptized in water. Baptism does not save. It is a testimony of conversion and obedience to the commands of the Savior, Jesus Christ. Three submersions under water communicates worship of the triune God. Children who have received Christ personally should, at their parents' discretion, be encouraged to obey the Lord in baptism.[17]

Birth Control: No answer.

Capital Punishment: No answer.

Christ's Return: No answer.

Communion: The Fellowship of Grace Brethren Churches practices a three-fold communion consisting of the washing of the feet, the Lord's Supper, and the bread and the cup. It is an observance commanded by the Lord as a symbolic teaching of great spiritual truths.[18]

Creation vs. Evolution: The one true God is the creator and sustainer of the universe.[19]

Deity of Christ: No answer.

Divorce and Remarriage: No answer.

Government: Each congregation is an autonomous organization, and is free to make its own decisions and govern itself. By being part of the larger fellowship, the churches voluntarily choose to be accountable to one another and to work together in fulfilling the great commission.[20]

Heaven/Hell: The future life of mankind will be a conscious existence of eternal life for the saved in Christ and eternal punishment for those who are lost in their sin.[21]

Homosexuality: No answer.

Inspiration of Scripture: The Bible is the infallible Word of God, supernaturally inspired and preserved by God to be the only authority and standard for doctrine and practice.[22]

Miracles: No answer.

Restrictions: None.

Security of Salvation: No answer.

Speaking in Tongues and Other Gifts of the Spirit: No answer.

Trinity: The one true God exists eternally in three persons: Father, Son, and Holy Spirit.[23]

Women in Ministry: No answer.

For more information contact: P.O. Box 386, Winona Lake, IN 46590; Phone: (219) 269-1269; Fax: (219) 267-4745; E-mail: graceb@netwalk.com; Web site: http://38.226.140.6/welcome2.htm

---

Free Gospel Church, Inc.

The Free Gospel Church, Inc. was established in the early 1900s and incorporated in 1916 as the United Free Gospel and Missionary Society. In 1957, a constitutional revision changed the name to the current one. There are ten churches whose property is owned by the Free Gospel Church, Inc., along with independent churches who fellowship with the group and support their Bible school and missions program. The church emphasizes holy living.

Abortion: The church is opposed to all abortion, with the possible exception of one needed to save the mother's life.

Baptism: Baptism by immersion follows conversion and personal faith in Christ. No infants are baptized.

Birth Control: No stated position. Birth control is a matter of personal conviction.

Capital Punishment: The Free Gospel Church favors capital punishment for murder, treason, and other serious crimes.

Christ's Return: The church believes in the imminent, literal, and personal return of Christ when the dead in Christ shall be raised and living believers caught away.

Communion: Communion is usually served once a month to remember Jesus' death at Calvary and to look forward to his coming. The elements are symbols of the actual body and blood of Jesus.

Creation vs. Evolution: The church believes the biblical record of creation.

Deity of Jesus: Jesus is divine, the pre-existent Son of the Father, with all the attributes of the Father.

Divorce and Remarriage: Ministers and congregational officials cannot be divorced and remarried. Persons who were divorced and remarried prior to conversion may be members and vote in the local church, but they cannot hold office.

Government: Each church governs its affairs within the limits of the constitution. Pastors are selected by local congregations with the advice and consent of the Board of Trustees of the Free Gospel Church, Inc.

Heaven/Hell: Heaven and hell, as stated in Scripture, are literal and eternal. Heaven is achieved by personal faith in Jesus Christ—the only Savior from sin.

Homosexuality: Homosexual behavior is sin, clearly stated by the Scriptures. However, Christ offers forgiveness and deliverance. No person involved in homosexuality may hold membership or an office.

Inspiration of Scripture: The Bible is the inspired Word of God, a revelation from God to man. It is the final authority in all matters.

Miracles: The Free Gospel Church fully accepts the biblical accounts of miracles and believes that God still performs miracles today. All power is his and he can set aside natural laws as he desires.

Restrictions: Although the constitution does not specify restrictions, the church discourages card playing, dancing, movies, gambling, mixed swimming, smoking, alcohol, immodest dress, tobacco, non-prescription drugs, gambling, and sex outside of marriage.

Security of Salvation: Salvation is dependent upon sincere, personal faith in the finished work of Christ at Calvary, and is secure so long as one continues in faith. If one deliberately turns to the beggarly elements of this world, their relationship with Christ may be broken.

Speaking in Tongues and Other Gifts of the Spirit: Those filled with the Holy Spirit in response to asking the Father for this endowment will speak with tongues as the initial sign of such infilling. Each should then seek earnestly the best gifts as indicated in I Corinthians.

Trinity: There is one God manifested in three persons: the Father, the Son, and the Holy Ghost, each of whom has the attributes of deity. The mystery of the Godhead is beyond full human comprehension.

Women in Ministry: Women are not barred from ministry, because in the Scriptures God sometimes used them. However, in most cases pastors and those excising authority over others are men. Women make valuable contributions in a variety of supporting roles.

For more information contact: P.O. Box 477, Export, PA 15632; Phone: (412) 373-0307; Fax: (412) 327-3419.

Free Methodist Church
of North America

Born at a time when representative government was being developed by free societies, the Free Methodist founders reaffirmed the principle of lay ministry. They spoke out against the institution of slavery and the class distinction inherent in the rental of pews to the wealthy. Influenced by the holiness movement, Rev. Benjamin T. Roberts and others involved with the Genessee Conference of the Methodist Church encouraged the return to primitive Methodism and the doctrine of entire sanctification. They were expelled from the Methodist Episcopal Church and were unable to join any other Methodist body. Therefore they began the Free Methodist Church on August 23, 1860.[24] In 1997, there were 1,077 churches, fellowships, and new church plants with 76,000 members in the United States.

Abortion: The intentional destruction of human life is murder if any degree of malice or selfishness accompanies the decision and act. Therefore, induced abortion is morally unjustifiable except when the act has been decided upon by responsible and competent persons, including Christian and professional counsel, for the purpose of saving the life of a pregnant woman. Abortion, when it serves the ends of population or birth control, personal preference or convenience, and social or economic security must be considered selfish and malicious.[25]

Baptism: Water baptism is a sacrament of the church, commanded by the Lord, signifying acceptance of the benefits of the atonement of Jesus Christ to be administered to believers, as declaration of their faith. Baptism is a symbol of the new covenant of grace, just as circumcision was the symbol of the old covenant. And, since infants are recognized as being included in the atonement, they may be baptized upon the request of parents or guardians who shall give assurance for them of necessary Christian training.[26]

Birth Control: No position.

Capital Punishment: No position.

Christ's Return: The return of Christ is certain and may occur at any moment, although no one knows the hour. At his return he will fulfill all prophecies concerning his final triumph over evil.[27]

Communion: The Lord's Supper is a sacrament of redemption by Christ's death. To those who rightly, worthily, and with faith receive it, the bread is a partaking of the body of Christ and the cup of blessing is a partaking of the blood of Christ. The supper is also a sign of love and unity among Christians. Christ is really present in the sacrament. But his body is given, taken, and eaten only after a heavenly and spiritual manner. No change is effected in the element; the bread and wine are not literally the body and blood of Christ. Nor is the body and blood of Christ literally present with the elements. The elements are never to be considered objects of worship.[28] The body of Christ is received and eaten in faith.

Creation vs. Evolution: The church is concerned that concepts of first origins shall have completely fair consideration in public schools. Instructional materials are available that permit a scientific treatment of the several concepts of origin, including special creation. Therefore, the church expects that the concept of special creation (that all basic life forms and life processes were created by a supernatural creator) will be presented in, or along with, all courses, textbooks, library materials, and teaching aids dealing in any way with the subject of first origins.[29]

Deity of Jesus: God was himself in Jesus Christ to reconcile man to God. Conceived by the Holy Spirit, born of the Virgin Mary, he joined together the deity of God and the humanity of man. Jesus was God in human flesh, truly God and truly man. He came to save sinners. The Son of God suffered, was crucified, dead and buried. He pored out his life as a blameless sacrifice for sin and transgressions. He rose victoriously from the dead. Then he ascended into heaven. There he sits as exalted Lord at the right hand of God the Father.[30]

Divorce and Remarriage: Regarding divorce, several scriptural principles apply. When one marriage partner is a Christian and the other a nonbeliever, the Christian may not for that reason divorce the unchristian mate. A person denies the faith who deserts a spouse deliberately and for an extended period of time. When the desertion leads subsequently to divorce, the deserted partner is no longer bound by the marriage. Even when a marriage is violated by sexual infidelity, the partners are encouraged to work for restoration. Where reconciliation is impossible, divorce may be unavoidable. Persons who have been involved in divorce while in a state of unbelief shall not be barred from becoming members, even though they remarry. Believers are not pro-hibited from marrying a person who was divorced while an unbeliev-er. A member of the church divorced from an adulterous spouse or de-serted by an unbelieving mate, after attempts at forgiveness and reconciliation have been rejected, may remarry.[31]

Government: The Free Methodist Church is a modified episcopacy with equal lay representation in all the major governing bodies of the church.

Heaven/Hell: For those who trust Jesus Christ and obediently follow him, there is a heaven of eternal glory and the blessedness of Christ's presence. But for the finally impenitent there is a hell of eternal suf-fering and of separation from God.[32]

Homosexuality: Homosexual behavior is a perversion of God's created order and is contrary to the will of God as clearly stated in Scripture. The forgiving and delivering grace of God in Christ is all-sufficient for the homosexual. The church has a personal and corporate responsibil-ity to be God's instrument of healing, restoring love to the homosexu-al seeking recovery. The Free Methodist Church opposed legislation which makes homosexual conduct or life-style legitimate.[33]

Inspiration of Scripture: The Bible is God's written Word, uniquely in-spired by the Holy Spirit. It bears unerring witness to Jesus Christ, the living Word. As attested by the early church and subsequent councils, it is the trustworthy record of God's revelation, completely faithful in all it affirms. It has been faithfully preserved and proves itself true in human experience. The Scriptures have come to us through human au-thors who wrote, as God moved them, in the languages and literary forms of their times. The Bible has authority over all human life. What-ever cannot be found in the Bible nor can be proved by it is not be re-quired as an article of belief or as necessary to salvation.[34]

Miracles: Free Methodists hold that all healing, whether of body, mind, or spirit, has its ultimate source in God who is above all and through all and in all. He may heal by the mediation of surgery, medication, change of environment, counseling, corrected attitudes, or through the restorative process of nature itself. He may heal through one or more of the above or in combination with prayer. Or he may heal by direct intervention in response to prayer.[35]

Restrictions: Members are expected to abstain from: the manufacture, sale, and use of alcohol, harmful drugs and tobacco; all forms of gambling; membership in secret societies; and involvement with pornography.[36]

Security of Salvation: God gives assurance of salvation and peace of heart to all who repent and put their faith in him. The Holy Spirit witnesses to their own spirits that they are forgiven of their sins and adopted into the family of God. The Christian has peace with God through Jesus Christ because guilt is taken away and fear of judgment is removed. God continues to give assurance to believers through the Scriptures, the conscious presence of the Holy Spirit, and love for and fellowship with other Christians.

Speaking in Tongues and Other Gifts of the Spirit: The believer is to seek as the evidence of the Holy Spirit's fullness, not the gifts themselves, but the giver. Speaking or teaching to speak unintelligible sounds is not consistent with the order brought about by the Holy Spirit. The language of worship is the language of the people. All communication in worship is to be experienced with understanding.[37]

Trinity: There is but one living and true God, the maker and preserver of all things. In the unity of this Godhead there are three persons: the Father, the Son, and the Holy Spirit. These are one in eternity, deity, and purpose, everlasting, and of infinite power, wisdom, and goodness.[38]

Women in Ministry: The Gospel of Jesus Christ, in the provisions which it makes and in the agencies which it employs for the salvation of humankind, knows no distinction of race, condition, or sex. With these beliefs, women should be encouraged to take their place in all areas of church leadership and ministry.[39]

For more information contact: P.O. Box 535002, Indianapolis, IN 46253-5002; Phone: (317) 244-3660; Fax: (317) 241-1247.

Friends General Conference

Friends had their beginnings in the spiritual quest of George Fox, an Englishman who lived during the 17th century. He began to minister publicly in 1652. His writings and journal continue to be the basic works of Friends. The first Quakers arrived in Boston in 1656. In 1682, William Penn began a "holy experiment" when he established the colony of Pennsylvania which based its government on Quaker principles and ideas.[40]

In the 1820s the Friends General Conference, one of four major branches of Friends, was formed because of a controversy surrounding the beliefs of Elias Hicks, a preacher who emphasized the "Inner Light" and unprogrammed worship, and rejected the divinity of Christ.[41] This branch of Friends worships in silence punctuated by attendees speaking as they feel led. There are no pastors and worship services are unprogrammed. The church believes in continuing revelation,[42] and that there is a spirit of God (the Inner Light) in every single person.[43] In 1997, the conference had approximately 30,000 adherents.

Abortion: Friends abhor violence of any kind.

Baptism: No outward sacraments are observed.[44]

Birth Control: This issue is left up to the individual.

Capital Punishment: Friends General Conference opposes capital punishment.

Christ's Return: No answer.

Communion: No outward sacraments are observed.[45]

Creation vs. Evolution: No answer.

Deity of Jesus: There is a variety of opinion on this topic, with some meetings leaning toward universalism and others toward a scriptural base.[46]

Divorce and Remarriage: No answer.

Government: The FGC is governed by a central committee composed of 170 Friends, 112 of whom are appointed by affiliated yearly and monthly meetings (or individual congregations).[47]

Heaven/Hell: No answer.

Homosexuality: Homosexuals are welcome to worship and some monthly meetings conduct same-sex marriage ceremonies.

Inspiration of Scripture: No answer.

Miracles: No answer.

Restrictions: Friends do not serve in the military and refrain from swearing oaths.[48]

Security of Salvation: No answer.

Speaking in Tongues and Other Gifts of the Spirit: No answer.

Trinity: No answer.

Women in Ministry: Women have been in ministry since the beginning.

For more information contact: 1216 Arch St., 2B, Philadelphia, PA 19107; Phone: (215) 561-1700; E-mail: www@fgc.quaker.org; Web site: http://www.quaker.org/fgc/index.html

Friends United Meeting

Friends United Meeting is another branch of the Religious Society of Friends or Quakers (see above entry or the section on Evangelical Friends for more information on the other branches). Formerly called the Five Years' Meeting, FUM grew out of the western migration of Quakers in the late 1800s. When meetings grew rapidly, pastors were hired to provide leadership.[49] Friends recognize the immediate presence of Jesus as Lord, teacher, and head of the church through silent worship. Pastors teach and equip all believers for ministry. The church emphasizes peace, equality, integrity, and simplicity of life. They do not practice outward rituals of baptism and communion. In 1997, there were approximately 43,000 members in the United States and Canada.

Abortion: Friends differ on the question of whether abortion should be legal.

Baptism: Friends believe that one essential baptism is spiritual and inward.

Birth Control: Friends allow freedom of conscience regarding birth control.

Capital Punishment: Friends oppose capital punishment.

Christ's Return: The church believes that Jesus will come again.

Communion: The essential communion is inward attention and obedience to God.

Creation vs. Evolution: God created and continues to care for the earth.

Deity of Jesus: Friends affirm the deity of Christ and seek to gather people into fellowship where Jesus Christ is known, loved, and obeyed as teacher and Lord.

Divorce and Remarriage: Friends affirm the sanctity of marriage, but recognize divorce and remarriage.

Government: The Friends United Meeting is made up of 20 yearly meetings, each of which is represented on the General Board which meets three times a year. As a body, the FUM meets every three years in triennial sessions. Friends' business is at every level conducted as worship decision reached in unity, not by vote.

Heaven/Hell: There is resurrection—some to eternal life and some to eternal separation from God.

Homosexuality: Marriage is between one man and one woman.

Inspiration of Scripture: Basic belief is that all Scripture is inspired by God and must be read through the same Spirit that inspired it.

Miracles: God still performs miracles today.

Restrictions: Friends believe that the way of love overcomes violence and are recognized as a peace church. However, service in the military is an issue of individual conscience. Friends do not swear on oaths, they affirm.

Security of Salvation: Salvation is a gift to be received by the grace of God. A person can backslide and, if repentant, receive forgiveness.

Speaking in Tongues and Other Gifts of the Spirit: The church recognizes gifts of the Spirit as described by Scripture. Individuals within congregations may speak in tongues or use their prayer language, but it is rarely done publicly. Understanding of spiritual gifts has led to controversy.

Trinity: The FUM believes in the triune God: Father, Son, and Holy Spirit

Women in Ministry: Men and women are equal in all roles in the church.

For more information contact: 101 Quaker Hill Dr., Richmond, IN 47374; Phone: (765) 962-7573; Fax (765) 966-1293.

Full Gospel Evangelistic Association

The Full Gospel Evangelistic Association was established by Rev. Clarence Robinson and was officially organized on June 1, 1982 in Lafayette, LA. The association uses only the King James Version of Scripture. In 1997, there were 90 members in the United States.

Abortion: The church is anti-abortion.

Baptism: Baptism is proof of a new life, but it is not necessary for salvation.

Birth Control: Birth control is the responsibility of married couples.

Capital Punishment: Individual members must decide for themselves.

Christ's Return: Christ will return before the beginning of the tribulation.

Communion: Communion is one of the sacraments for those of like faith. The church should be in one accordance before partaking.

Creation vs. Evolution: Everything was created by God. The Full Gospel Evangelistic Association is anti-evolution.

Deity of Jesus: The deity of Jesus is undeniable.

Divorce and Remarriage: Divorce is necessary in the case of adultery. Remarriage should be to a Christian.

Government: The Full Gospel Evangelistic Association is governed by the laws of the King James Version of the Bible. Changes to the by-laws are voted on by a two-thirds majority of the membership.

Heaven/Hell: Both heaven and hell are undeniable as described in the Holy Bible.

Homosexuality: Homosexuality is described in God's Word as an abomination.

Inspiration of Scripture: The Scriptures were inspired by the triune Godhead: Father, Son, and Holy Ghost.

Miracles: Miracles are still in existence today.

Restrictions: The church objects to membership in secret orders and membership in any other organization of ministerial credentials.

Security of Salvation: The Full Gospel Evangelistic Association believes in the security of salvation as outlined in the Holy Scriptures.

Speaking in Tongues and Other Gifts of the Spirit: The Association affirms the gifts of the Holy Spirit.

Trinity: The Trinity is undeniable.

Women in Ministry: Women are allowed to minister as called by God.

For more information contact: P.O. Box 1122, Cleveland, TX 77328-1122; Phone: (281) 593-0495; Fax: (281) 593-3223.

General Association of General Baptists

In 1801, Separate Baptists and Regular Baptists merged to become United Baptists. Benoni Stinson was originally a member of a United Baptist Church but, because of his Arminian views, Stinson left and formed an independent church. Other new congregations were started based on Stinson's teaching. In 1824, these organized into the Liberty Association of General Baptists and were renamed the General Association of General Baptists in 1870.[1]

Abortion: General Baptists acknowledge the sanctity of unborn human life and believe the act of deliberate abortion in the case of an unwanted pregnancy is an act of murder. The church feels equally bound to acknowledge the sacredness of the life and well-being of the mother. They oppose comprehensive legalized abortion, but are in sympathy with medical ethics and laws that permit therapeutic abortion when the mother's life and physical or mental health are clearly jeopardized as determined by authorized reliable physicians. State and federal laws relative to abortion should be strictly scrutinized and responded to by both parents and the medical profession. Victims of a disastrous pregnancy should in every case seek medical and pastoral counsel as they give prayer and thoughtful consideration concerning personal decisions on abortion.[2]

Baptism: Those believers of an accountable age who have come into a pardoned relationship with God through faith in Jesus Christ are baptized by immersion. Baptism is not essential to the pardon of past sins. It is an act of righteous obedience to the command and example of the Lord. Baptism serves as an open confession to the world that the subject has put away sin and put on Christ.[3]

Birth Control: Each potential set of parents must make decisions relative to birth control, whether it is right or wrong in their particular situation.[4]

Capital Punishment: No Statement.

Christ's Return: General Baptists believe in the personal return of Jesus Christ and in the bodily resurrection of the dead.[5]

Communion: The Lord's Supper, which is open to all believers, is a memorial instituted by Jesus Christ to perpetuate the memory of his atoning work. The emblems represent the broken body (unleavened bread) and the shed blood (sweet wine) of Christ. Only ordained ministers are allowed to preside at the table, and only ordained ministers or deacons are qualified to distribute the emblems.[6]

Creation vs. Evolution: God created the world and all things in it. Creation belongs to God. All mankind are his stewards.[7]

Deity of Jesus: The second person of the Trinity, Jesus, is God as Son.[8]

Divorce and Remarriage: God has planned that those who enter the marriage covenant should become inseparably united. Husband and wife are one flesh, a condition that continues under the ordinance of God until death parts them or until unfaithfulness destroys the marriage union. The Bible gives no other just cause for annulling and dissolving that which God has joined together. When sufficient penitence for sin and failure is evident, and a firm purpose and sincere effort for Christian marriage are manifested, the Christian church can accept remarriage as profitable unto the Lord.[9]

Government: The government of the church rests primarily in the whole body of its membership. All members are equal in voting privileges and responsibilities. The General Association is composed of local General Baptist Associations and churches. Representation to the General Association is by delegate.[10]

Heaven/Hell: God will judge all mankind by Jesus Christ and he will reward the righteous with eternal life in heaven. He will banish the unrighteous to everlasting punishment in hell.[11]

Homosexuality: General Baptist churches abhor the practice of homosexuality and consider this practice to be a growing deviance, incompatible with Christian teaching. The church must be diligent to keep this evil under control in society. The church must be prepared and ready to give guidance to the deviant persons who have fallen into immoral practices in their struggle for human fulfillment.[12]

Inspiration of Scripture: The Holy Scriptures are the Old and New Testaments, the only inspired and infallible Word of God. The Bible is the only reliable guide of Christian faith and conduct.[13]

Miracles: No answer.

Restrictions: Christians should demand the enforcement of laws against the production and sale of pornographic materials. Drugs should be used only as prescribed or directed by reliable physicians. The church also endorses a total abstinence from alcoholic beverages and opposes the sale and use of tobacco.[14]

Security of Salvation: Those who abide in Christ have the assurance of salvation. However, the Christian retains his freedom of choice. Therefore it is possible for him to turn away from God and be finally lost.[15]

Speaking in Tongues and Other Gifts of the Spirit: According to the Word of God and the practices of the early church, public worship and prayer should be in a language of the people. It is clear that the Apostle Paul placed the strongest emphasis upon rational and intelligible language in worship.[16]

Trinity: There is only one true, living, and eternal God and the Godhead is revealed as Father, Son, and Holy Spirit.[17]

Women in Ministry: No answer.

For more information contact: 100 Stinson Dr., Poplar Bluff, MO 63901; Phone: (573) 785-7746; Fax: (573) 785-0564; Web site: http://www.comsource.net/~knelson/webdoc7.htm

---

General Association of Regular Baptist Churches

In 1932, 22 churches affiliated with the American Baptist Convention left in protest. These churches were concerned with the liberal direction they saw the convention heading and desired to return to historic Baptist tenants such as the autonomy of the local church. They formed the General Association of Regular Baptist Churches and required that all member congregations separate themselves from any modernist groups.[18] In 1996, there were 1,440 churches with 115,950 members.

Abortion: No statement.

Baptism: Christian baptism is the single immersion of a believer in water. It shows, in a solemn and beautiful emblem, identification with the crucified, buried, and risen Savior.[19]

Birth Control: No statement.

Capital Punishment: No statement.

Christ's Return: The GARBC believes in the premillennial return of Christ.[20]

Communion: The Lord's Supper is the commemoration of his death until he comes again. It should always be preceded by solemn self-examination.[21]

Creation vs. Evolution: The biblical account of creation is a literal, historical account of the direct, immediate acts of God without any evolutionary process. Man was created by a direct work of God and not from previously existing forms of life. All men are descended from the historical Adam and Eve, first parents of the entire human race.[22]

Deity of Jesus: Jesus was begotten of the Holy Spirit in a miraculous manner, born of Mary, a virgin, as no other man was ever born or can be born of woman. He is both the Son of God and God the Son. He was bodily resurrected and ascended into heaven, where he sits at the right hand of the Father as a high priest and intercessor.[23]

Divorce and Remarriage: No answer.

Government: Churches are autonomous. There is an annual meeting where business is transacted and officers are elected. A missionary conference is also held annually at a date fixed by the Council. The Council is made up of 18 members of fellowshipping churches, nine of whom are elected annually for a period of two years.[24]

Heaven/Hell: The GARBC believes in the everlasting felicity of the saved and the everlasting conscious suffering of the lost in the lake of fire.[25]

Homosexuality: No answer.

Inspiration of Scripture: The GARBC believes in the authority and sufficiency of the Holy Bible. It was verbally and plenarily inspired and is the product of Spirit-controlled men. Therefore, it is infallible and inerrant in all matters of which it speaks. The Bible is the true center of Christian unity and the supreme standard by which all human conduct, creed, and opinions shall be tried.[26]

Miracles: No answer.

Restrictions: None.

Security of Salvation: All who are truly born again are kept by God the Father for Jesus Christ.[27]

Speaking in Tongues and Other Gifts of the Spirit: No answer.

Trinity: In the unity of the Godhead there are three persons: the Father, the Son, and the Holy Spirit. They are equal in every divine perfection and execute distinct but harmonious offices in the great work of redemption.[28]

Women in Ministry: No answer.

For more information contact: 1300 N. Meacham Rd., Schaumburg, IL 60173-4888; Phone: (888) 588-1600 or (847) 843-1600; Fax: (847) 843-3757; E-mail: garbc@garbc.org; Web site: http://www.garbc.org/index.html

---

General Association of Separate Baptists, The

Roots of Separate Baptist Churches go all the way back to the Separatist movement which took place in England in the 17th century. Throughout the late 1700s there were mergers of Separate Baptists with other Baptist churches, however this branch remained independent.[29] One of the earliest Separate Baptist groups, the South Kentucky Association, was organized and constituted in the late 1700s. In 1996, there were 78 churches with 6,000 members. The association's motto is, "The Bible is our guide, God our ruler, Christ our redeemer."

Abortion: The Bible teaches respect for the sanctity of human life, both of the born and unborn. Thus, all abortion and euthanasia or mercy killing are forbidden.

Baptism: Baptism is ordained of Christ and appointed in the church. None but true believers are proper subjects. Immersion is the Gospel mode of baptism.

Birth Control: No official stand.

Capital Punishment: No official stand.

Christ's Return: At Christ's coming in the clouds of heaven, all Christians will be gathered with him in the clouds and time shall be no more. Therefore there will be no time for a literal 1,000 year reign.

Communion: The Lord's Supper is ordained of Christ and appointed in the church. None but true believers are proper subjects. The General Association of Separate Baptists practices feet washing.

Creation vs. Evolution: No official stand.

Deity of Jesus: In the Godhead there are three divine personages: the Father, the Son, and the Holy Spirit. Jesus Christ, by the grace of God, tasted death for every man. None can partake of these benefits except by repentance toward God and faith in the Lord Jesus Christ.

Divorce and Remarriage: No official stand.

Government: No official stand.

Heaven/Hell: Separate Baptists believe in the resurrection of the body, the just and the unjust, every man in his own order. Those who have done good will be resurrected to eternal life. Those who have done evil will be resurrected to eternal damnation. God has appointed a day in which he will judge the world in righteousness by Jesus Christ.

Homosexuality: Christians must abstain from all sexual relationships outside the sanctity of marriage. Therefore, fornication, adultery, and homosexuality are sinful behavior.

Inspiration Scripture: The Scriptures of the Old and New Testament are the infallible Word of God, and the only safe rule of faith and practice. Separate Baptists use the King James Version of the Holy Bible.

Miracles: No official stand.

Restrictions: No official stand.

Security of Salvation: He who endures to the end shall be saved.

Speaking in Tongues and Other Gifts of the Spirit: No official stand.

Trinity: There is in the Godhead three divine personages: the Father, the Son, and the Holy Spirit.

Women in Ministry: No official stand.

For more information contact: 10102 N. Hickory Ln., Columbus, IN 47203; Phone: (812) 526-2540; Fax: (812) 372-6691.

General Conference Mennonite Church

The General Conference Mennonite Church has it roots in the Anabaptist movement which began in Europe in the 16th century. Followers of this movement sought more radical reform than the Protestant Reformation. Specifically they challenged the practice of infant baptism. In 1525, many of these reformers were rebaptized (thus the name Anabaptist). After years of persecution, German-speaking Mennonite immigrants came to the United States.[30] In 1995, the General Conference Mennonite Church and the Mennonite Church adopted a joint *Confession of Faith in a Mennonite Perspective.* In 1996, there were 271 General Conference Mennonite Churches in the U.S. with 36,685 members. General Conference Mennonites believe peace is the will of God and practice non-resistance even in the face of violence and warfare.[31]

Abortion: The official guidelines of the church state that it cannot and does not support the use of abortions as a means of birth control. The majority believe most abortions cannot be based on moral grounds, although they are unwilling to say that abortion is never justified.[32]

Baptism: Baptism of adult believers with water is a sign of their cleansing from sin. It is also a pledge before the church of their covenant with God to walk in the way of Jesus Christ through the power of the Holy Spirit. Believers are baptized into Christ and his body by the Spirit, water, and blood.[33]

Birth Control: The church takes no official stand other than to say that abortion as a means of birth control is against the will of God.

Capital Punishment: Since Christ through his redemptive work has fulfilled the requirement of the death penalty and has given the church a ministry of reconciliation, and (in view of the injustice and ineffectiveness of capital punishment as a means for the achievement of the purpose of government) the General Conference Mennonite Church expresses its conviction that the use of capital punishment should be discontinued.[34]

Christ's Return: Christ will come again in glory to judge the living and the dead. He will gather his church, which is already living under the reign of God. In God's final victory at the end of this present age of struggle, the dead will be resurrected, and there will be a new heaven and a new earth. There the people of God will reign with Christ in justice, righteousness, and peace for ever and ever.[35]

Communion: The Lord's Supper is a sign by which the church thankfully remembers the new covenant which Jesus established with his death. In this communion meal, the church renews its covenant with God and with each other, and participates in the life and death of Jesus Christ until he comes.[36]

Creation vs. Evolution: God created the heavens and the earth, and all that is in them. He preserves and renews what has been made. All creation has its source outside itself and belongs to the Creator. The world was created good because God is good and provides all that is needed for life. God created human beings in the divine image. God formed them from the dust of the earth and gave them a special dignity among all the works of creation. Human beings have been made for a relationship with God, to live in peace with each other, and to take care of the rest of creation.[37]

Deity of Jesus: Jesus Christ is the Word of God become flesh. He is the Savior of the world, who has delivered believers from the dominion of sin and reconciled them to God by his death on a cross. He was declared to be the Son of God by his resurrection from the dead. He is the head of the church, the exalted Lord—the lamb who was slain.[38]

Divorce and Remarriage: The Mennonite Church believes in chastity and the loving faithfulness to marriage vows.[39] God intends marriage to be a covenant between one man and one woman for life. However, the church is called to encourage reconciliation in times of conflict and to minister with truth and compassion to persons in difficult family relationships.[40]

Government: Churches, a seminary, and three departments called commissions carry out the work of the General Conference Mennonite Church. The commissions and seminary provide funds for the General Board to coordinate and help direct the work of the General Conference. The Conference general secretary, staff members, those with ministerial leadership services, and a higher education council make up the General Board. The division of general services does administrative, financial, and communications work.[41]

Heaven/Hell: The righteous will rise to eternal life with God, and the unrighteous to hell and separation from God.[42]

Homosexuality: In a resolution on human sexuality, the church confesses its fear and repents of its rejection of those with a different sexual orientation. It understands the Bible to teach that sexual intercourse is reserved for a man and a woman united in marriage and that violation of this teaching is a sin. This teaching also precludes premarital, extramarital, and homosexual sexual activity. The church covenants with each other to mutually bear the burden of remaining in loving dialogue with each other in the body of Christ.[43]

Inspiration of Scripture: All Scripture is inspired by God through the Holy Spirit for instruction in salvation and training in righteousness.

The Scriptures are the Word of God and are the fully reliable and trust-worthy standard for Christian faith and life.[44]

Miracles: Although there is no official stand, many members believe that expressions of God's grace on earth occur and are very real.

Restrictions: Members avoid the swearing of oaths and violence of any kind.[45]

Security of Salvation: Through the life, death, and resurrection of Jesus Christ, God offers salvation from sin and a new way of life to all people. Believers receive God's salvation when they repent of sin and accept Jesus Christ as Lord and Savior.[46]

Speaking in Tongues and Other Gifts of the Spirit: The denomination does not take an official stand on speaking in tongues. It does occur in few congregations. As for other gifts of the Spirit, the church believes by the gifts of the Holy Spirit, all Christians are called to carry out their particular ministries.[47]

Trinity: There is one holy and loving God who is Father, Son, and Holy Spirit eternally.[48]

Women in Ministry: The church calls, trains, and appoints gifted men and women to a variety of leadership ministries on its behalf. These may include such offices as pastor, deacon, and elder as well as evangelists, missionaries, teachers, conference ministers, and overseers.[49]

For more information contact: 722 Main St., P.O. Box 347, Newton, KS 67114-0347; Phone: (316) 283-5100; Fax: (316) 283-0454; E-mail: gcmc@gcmc.org; Web site: http://www2.southwind.net/~gcmc

---

General Conference of the Church of God (Seventh Day), The

The Sabbath-keeping churches of God were born in the 1850s, after the Millerite movement anticipating the return of Christ. The General Conference of the Church of God grew up alongside the Seventh Day Adventist Church, differing primarily in their refusal of the visions and prophecies of Ellen G. White. The General Conference was formed in 1884 and moved to its current location in Denver, CO in 1950. The church believes the seventh-day Sabbath (Saturday) is a memorial of both creation and redemption (rest from works). Members avoid military service, the eating of unclean meats, and the common celebrations of Christmas, Easter, and Halloween.

Abortion: The church opposes abortion, and views it as the wrongful taking of a human life.

Baptism: The conference practices baptism by immersion, not as a saving act, but as an act of obedience to the gospel for those who have exercised faith and repentance. They do not baptize infants.

Birth Control: Birth control is a matter of personal conviction.

Capital Punishment: Unofficially the church favors it.

Christ's Return: Jesus Christ will come again audibly, visibly, bodily, and suddenly to consummate the redemption of believers. No one can know when it will be, but many signs indicate that it may be near.

Communion: The Lord's Supper service is celebrated annually on the fourteenth of Niean. It consists of the partaking of unleavened bread and unfermented grape juice and the practice of footwashing.

Creation vs. Evolution: God created the universe in six days. The earth is still young.

Deity of Jesus: The Lord Jesus Christ existed before time began. He is of the same substance as the Father. He is deity.

Divorce and Remarriage: Marriage is permanent. Only continued fornication is sufficient cause for divorce. Remarriage is sanctioned only in that case.

Government: Modified congregationalism. All the elders are responsible to state the church's doctrine.

Heaven/Hell: The righteous will enjoy their eternal reward on a renewed earth. Therefore, the church prefers the terms Kingdom of Heaven or Kingdom of God instead of heaven. The Conference believes in conditional immortality—that humans have eternal life only by the regeneration of the Holy Spirit and faith in Christ. The unrighteous are not immortal and will be destroyed in the lake of fire—not tormented eternally in hell.

Homosexuality: Homosexuality is one of the many forms of immorality and sexual deviance.

Inspiration of Scripture: The Old and New Testaments together are the only infallible and authoritative Scriptures for the faith and practice of God's people.

Miracles: Biblical miracles are valid. God still interrupts the normal course of affairs in miraculous ways according to his own time and purpose.

Restrictions: None.

Security of Salvation: Nothing can separate us from the salvation of God, except our own willingness to depart from Christ through unbelief and continual, willful sin. Apostasy is possible.

Speaking in Tongues and Other Gifts of the Spirit: Spiritual gifts for service are valid and necessary. However, speaking in tongues is a unique sign gift of baptism with the Spirit. The churches do not practice tongues speaking in the congregations.

Trinity: The General Conference of the Church of God (Seventh Day) does not officially endorse the concept of the Trinity and does not believe it is the only way to express the truth about the Father, Son, and Holy Spirit.

Women in Ministry: Women are not ordained as elders or pastors.

For more information contact: P.O. Box 33677, Denver, CO 80233; Phone: (303) 452-7973; Fax: (303) 452-0657; E-mail: cofgsd@denver.net; Web site: http://www.denver.net/~cofgsd/

General Conference of Mennonite Brethren Churches, The

During the Protestant Reformation, Menno Simons experienced a spiritual renewal and became a leader in the movement. He identified with the Anabaptists, who emphasized new birth through faith in Christ, adult baptism, and freedom from governmental control. Those who followed Simons became known as Mennonites. Because of religious persecution, these followers fled first to Prussia, then to Russia. In Russia the group became known as Mennonite Brethren. In 1874, the first of this group immigrated to the United States. Five years later, the pioneers had organized an American conference of churches.[50] Mennonite Brethren churches are opposed to war and encourage their members to avoid any connection to waging war, including service in the military. There were 151 churches with 20,524 members in the U.S. in 1996.

Abortion: The Confession of Faith states opposition to all forms of violence.

Baptism: Baptism by water is a public sign that a person has repented of sins, received forgiveness of sins, died with Christ to sin, been raised to newness of life, and received the Holy Spirit. Baptism is a sign of the believer's incorporation into the body of Christ as expressed in the local church. Baptism is also a pledge to serve Christ according to the gifts given to each person.[51]

Birth Control: No position.

Capital Punishment: The church opposes violence of any kind.

Christ's Return: God who acts in history will bring his purposes to a final consummation. When the Lord returns, living believers will be raptured and the dead in Christ will be resurrected to be with him forever. Christ will judge all men. In the end, death will be destroyed, Antichrist will be defeated and Satan will be cast into the lake of fire. Christ will create a new heaven and a new earth in which righteousness reigns, and God shall be all in all. This is the blessed hope of the church.[52]

Communion: The Lord's Supper, instituted by Christ, points to him whose body was broken and whose blood was shed to assure salvation for believers and to establish the new covenant. In the Supper, the church identifies with the life of Christ given for the redemption of humanity and proclaims the Lord's death until he comes. The Supper expresses the fellowship and unity of all believers with Christ. It is a supper of remembrance, celebration and praise which strengthens believers for true discipleship and service.[53]

Creation vs. Evolution: The General Conference of Mennonite Brethren Churches traditionally holds a creationist viewpoint.

Deity of Jesus: Jesus Christ is the eternal Son of God whom the Father sent to reconcile sinners to himself and to redeem them from sin and eternal death. He was conceived by the Holy Spirit and born of the Virgin Mary. He is true God and true man according to the Scriptures. He lived a perfect holy and sinless life. In the redemptive purpose of God, he suffered crucifixion and death for the sins of mankind. He rose from the dead for mankind's justification and ascended into heaven where he now intercedes for all who believe.[54]

Divorce and Remarriage: God instituted marriage for the intimate companionship of husband and wife and for the procreation and nurture of children. A believer should not marry an unbeliever. Divorce constitutes a basic violation of God's intention for marriage.[55]

Government: Quasi-presbyterian.

Heaven/Hell: At death the righteous enter a state of rest in the presence of God, in fellowship with Christ. The unrighteous suffer the torment of separation from God while awaiting final judgment. When Christ returns, the righteous who were raptured will inherit the Kingdom of God and the unrighteous shall suffer the anguish of eternal hell.[56]

Homosexuality: There is no stated position, but the church is opposed to homosexual practice.

Inspiration of Scripture: All Scripture is inspired by God as men of God were moved by the Holy Spirit. The Old and New Testaments are the infallible Word of God and the authoritative guide for the faith and life of Christian discipleship. The old covenant was preparatory in nature, finding its fulfillment in the New Covenant. Christ is the key to understanding the Bible: the Old Testament bears witness to him, and he is the One whom the New Testament proclaims.[57]

Miracles: No position.

Restrictions: Mennonite Brethren encourage their members to have no part with war.[58]

Security of Salvation: Within the Mennonite Brethren church are those who believe that salvation can be lost and those who believe that salvation is assured.

Speaking in Tongues and Other Gifts of the Spirit: There is no stated position. However, the church is generally negative to speaking in tongues, except in personal worship.

Trinity: The Mennonite Brethren believe in God, the eternal spirit, infinite in holiness, power, wisdom, righteousness, goodness, love, and mercy. This one and only eternal God has revealed himself as Father, Son, and Holy Spirit.[59]

Women in Ministry: Women are encouraged in forms of service, except the senior pastor position.

For more information contact: 4812 E. Butler, Fresno, CA 93727; Phone: (209) 452-1713; Fax: (209) 452-1752; E-mail: 74577.334@ compuserve.com; Web site: http://www.mbconf.org/mbc/

General Council Churches of God (7th Day)

The General Council Churches of God (7th Day) was formed in 1950. Its stated purpose is to advance the Gospel message around the world and to promote the general welfare of the Churches of God, 7th Day as a whole. The church observes the Sabbath on the seventh day or Saturday.

Abortion: Abortion is murder.

Baptism: Full water baptism is the command of Christ.

Birth Control: Each person must decide for themselves.

Capital Punishment: No stand.

Christ's Return: Jesus will return soon.

Communion: Communion is observed once a year.

Creation vs. Evolution: Evolution is a lie. God created the heavens and the earth in six days.

Deity of Jesus: Jesus is deity.

Divorce and Remarriage: Divorce is wrong except in the case of adultery or other sexual sin.

Government: Congregational.

Heaven/Hell: No person will burn forever in hell but will simply be burned up and cease to exist.

Homosexuality: Homosexuality is a sin and a great perversion which results in one being destroyed by God unless they repent and believe in Jesus Christ.

Inspiration of Scripture: The Scriptures are God's Word.

Miracles: Miracles still occur today.

Restrictions: None.

Security of Salvation: Salvation can be lost by losing faith in God.

Speaking in Tongues and Other Gifts of the Spirit: No stand.

Trinity: Nowhere in Scripture is the word Trinity found, therefore the church does not teach the doctrine of the Trinity.

Women in Ministry: No stand.

For more information contact: 1827 W. 3rd St., Meridian, ID 83642, Phone and Fax: (208) 888-3380.

General Council of the Assemblies of God, The

The Assemblies of God was born in the fires of revival that swept the world at the beginning of the 20th century. Because participants in the revival were filled with the Holy Spirit in similar fashion to the followers of Jesus on the Jewish Feast of Pentecost, they were called Pentecostals. The church, founded in 1914 in Hot Springs, AR with 300 Pentecostals, met and formed a loosely knit fellowship of independent churches. In 1997, the Assemblies of God had 11,823 churches in the United States, and more than two and one half million members.

Abortion: The Assemblies of God is pro-life. The Bible teaches the prenatal phase of life is that of a child, not a meaningless product of conception. If a mother's life is endangered because of the pregnancy, the church leaves a decision on abortion as a matter between she, her husband, and God.

Baptism: The church teaches the ordinance of baptism by immersion in water.

Birth Control: No official position. However, the church officially opposes the use of chemically induced or surgical abortion as a means of birth control. Any birth control method that functions to destroy a fertilized egg rather than actually preventing conception is considered unacceptable.

Capital Punishment: No official position.

Christ's Return: All Christians who have died will one day rise from their graves and meet Jesus in the air. Christians who are alive will be raptured with them, to be with the Lord. Then Christians of all ages will live with God forever. Those who are not Christians will be left behind at the rapture and will experience indescribable suffering as God judges a rebellious and disobedient world.

Communion: One of two ordinances of the church. The Lord's Supper or communion, consisting of bread and the fruit of the vine, is a memorial of Christ's suffering and death. Communion is a periodic reminder that the believer has received his free salvation through the suffering, death, and resurrection of Jesus Christ.

Creation vs. Evolution: The Assemblies of God is committed to creationism—God is the author and creator of all life. God created everything out of nothing. The church teaches that the Genesis account of creation should be taken literally.

Deity of Jesus: The Lord Jesus Christ, the Son of God, has always existed. Like God, he is without beginning or end. The supernatural birth of Jesus, his sinless life, and his working of miracles all give proof that he is the divine Son of God who came to earth in human form to give himself as the ultimate sacrifice for sin.

Divorce and Remarriage: The church opposes divorce. They believe God's plan is for one man and one woman to covenant together in marriage until death parts them. The Bible permitted a Christian to initiate a divorce when adultery was involved. This is permission however, not a command. The Bible also makes an exception for divorce when a partner who is not a Christian leaves the Christian partner. These two exceptions permit remarriage. However, the church does not credential ministers who are divorced and remarried. Also, the offices of elder and deacon are not open to those who are remarried.

Government: The Assemblies of God has a combination of presbyterian and congregational type governments. On the national and district levels, presbyteries oversee the affairs of the church. However, at the local level each congregation has responsibility to elect its own pastor, own property, and determine the ministries and programs of the church.

Heaven/Hell: The church believes in a real heaven and a real hell. God will judge every person, but there will be a different judgment for those who have accepted Christ as Savior than for those who have rejected him. The heaven that awaits the faithful Christian is wonderful. It is not God's will for any person to go to hell. But those who willfully turn from his Son as their source of salvation will go to hell.

Homosexuality: The Assemblies of God opposes homosexuality as a sin against God. The church's concern about this problem is not a matter of discrimination against a minority group. It is a moral concern. The Bible says homosexuality is sin because it is contrary to the principles of sexuality which God established in the beginning. However, Scriptures also indicate the homosexuals can be saved through the regenerating power of the Holy Spirit.

Inspiration of Scripture: The Bible is the written Word of God. It is the revelation of the truths of God conveyed by inspiration to writers of old. God prompted the original thought in the mind of the writers. He then guided their choice of words to express such thoughts. He illuminates the mind of the reader in a way that they potentially can comprehend the same truth as was originally in the mind of the writer. The Scriptures are God's revelation of himself—they are infallible, and they are the divinely authoritative guide for faith, belief, and manner of living.

Miracles: God continues to perform miracles in the world today.

Restrictions: The church believes Christians should lead a life separated from sin and dedicated to God.

Security of Salvation: It is possible for a person who has been saved to turn away from God and be lost. The security of the believer depends on a living relationship with Christ.

Speaking in Tongues and Other Gifts of the Spirit: The baptism of Christians in the Holy Spirit is accompanied by the initial physical sign of speaking in other tongues as the Spirit of God gives audible expression. All the gifts of the Holy Spirit are for today and should be operating in the church.

Trinity: God exists in three persons—the Father, the Son, and the Holy Spirit. All three are alive and at work today. This God of three persons is the one and only true God.

Women in Ministry: Women have been ordained to the ministry since the church's inception in 1914. Credentialled women hold pastorates, missions appointments, teach in Bible schools, evangelize, and participate in every ministry role open in the church. Women who have met all the requirements of the credentials committees of the district councils are entitled to whatever grade of credentials their qualifications warrant. They have the right to administer the ordinances of the church.

For more information contact: 1445 Boonville Ave., Springfield, MO 65802; Phone: (417) 862-2781; Fax: (417) 862-5554; Web site: http://www.ag.org/

God's Missionary Church

Two traveling evangelists who had Wesleyan, Methodist, and Evangelical backgrounds held a tent meeting near Elizabethville, PA in the 1930s. Rev. William E. Straub and Rev. Daniel W. Dubendorf continued hold-

ing meetings in Beavertown, PA and other small towns until a denomination officially began in central Pennsylvania. In 1997, there were 52
congregations in the United States. The church emphasizes modesty, simplicity, and holy living.

Abortion: God's Missionary Church is pro-life. Life is the right of every
child, not a special privilege for the fortunate, the planned, and the perfect.

Baptism: Water baptism has no saving or cleansing efficacy. It is a visible or outward sign of an inward work of grace.

Birth Control: No official position.

Capital Punishment: No official position.

Christ's Return: God's Missionary Church believes in the literal bodily return of Christ.

Communion: Communion is observed to commemorate the death of
Christ. The Lord's Supper was instituted for the children of God only.

Creation vs. Evolution: Creation is a fact. The church opposes the evolution theory.

Deity of Jesus: Christ was eternally from the Father, conceived by the
Holy Ghost, born of the Virgin Mary, and crucified. He died and was
buried—a sacrifice for original sin and committed sin. He truly arose
from the dead, took again his body, and ascended into heaven.

Divorce and Remarriage: God's Missionary Church discourages divorce and opposes remarriage.

Government: The General Conference is composed of delegates from
each local church and ministers who hold a conference license or an
ordination certificate from God's Missionary Church. This Conference
is the ultimate authority for the organization.

Heaven/Hell: Heaven and hell are real places. Every soul of human race
will make his eternal abode in one or the other of the two places.

Homosexuality: Homosexuality is a sin.

Inspiration of Scripture: The 66 canonical books of the Old and New
Testaments are the Word of God, given by divine inspiration. They
contain all things necessary for salvation.

Miracles: God's Missionary Church believes in the literal miracles of
the Bible.

Restrictions: In the Wesleyan Methodist tradition, the church requires moderation in amusements, modesty in dress, commitment to the Sabbath, and diligence to maintain a holy life in every aspect of this modern culture.

Security of Salvation: Believers are secure in God's grace. However, it is possible to sin and forfeit salvation.

Speaking in Tongues and Other Gifts of the Spirit: The so-called gift of tongues, gibbering or the making of strange noises which cannot be understood or interrupted, is unscriptural and cannot be taken as a sign of the Holy Ghost.

Trinity: There is but one true and living God. In the unity of this Godhead there are three persons, equal in power and eternity: the Father, Son, and Holy Ghost.

Women in Ministry: God's Missionary Church licenses women ministers. However the church does not support the women's liberation movement sweeping the church world.

For more information contact: Penn View Bible Institute, P.O. Box 970, Penns Creek, PA 17862; Phone and Fax: (717) 837-1855.

Holiness

The Holiness Church, whose motto is, "It can be done," has pentecostal and apostolic roots. There were nine churches with 300 members in 1997.

Abortion: The Holiness Church does not believe in abortion.

Baptism: The church baptizes in the name of Jesus Christ.

Birth Control: The church has no official position on birth control.

Capital Punishment: Capital punishment is not supported by the church.

Christ's Return: Christ will return.

Communion: The church takes the Lord's body which was broken for sin.

Creation vs. Evolution: The Holiness Church holds a creationist viewpoint.

Deity of Christ: Jesus and God are one.

Divorce and Remarriage: Divorce is acceptable only in the case of fornication.

Government: Democratic.

Heaven/Hell: There is a literal heaven and hell.

Homosexuality: Homosexual activity is a sin.

Inspiration of Scripture: The Scriptures were written by men inspired by God.

Miracles: Miracles do occur.

Restrictions: The Holiness Church does not allow smoking, drinking, cursing, gambling, or swearing.

Security of Salvation: There is security in Christ.

Speaking in Tongues and Other Gifts of the Spirit: The Holiness Church practices speaking in tongues and other gifts of the Spirit.

Trinity: There is but one God.

Women in Ministry: Women minister the Word of God.

For more information contact: 432 W Street, NW, Washington, DC 20001; Phone: (202) 234-3940.

House of God Which is the Church of the Living God the Pillar and Ground of the Truth Without Controversy, Inc. Keith Dominion, The

Mary Magdalena L. Tate founded the House of God Church with her two sons, Walter Curtis and Felix Early Lewis, in 1903. The church was first incorporated under the name, The Church of the Living God, the Pillar and Ground of Truth in 1908. In 1924, the headquarters was established in Nashville, TN. Six years later Tate died[1] and three chief overseers were appointed. The church divided with these three overseeing different branches.[2] From 1931 to 1962, Dr. Mary F. L. Keith was the overseer of this particular branch. On August 1990, the fourth chief overseer, Bishop James C. Elliott, began his administration with the theme, "Continuous Progress Through Evangelism."[3] The church observes Lent and a Seven Day Fast at the beginning of every year. Lent begins on Ash Wednesday and continues through Palm Sunday. The Seven Days Fast begins January 1. The daily fasting period is from midnight to sundown. In 1997, this dominion had 200 churches in the United States.

Abortion: The church is opposed to abortion and believes life begins at conception.

Baptism: Baptism of water by immersion is a token of the real baptism of the Holy Ghost. Water points to salvation but it is not in itself salvation, nor can it wash away sin. It is a necessary ordinance to be observed by all. The baptism of the Holy Ghost of God puts believers into the name of Jesus and into Jesus himself. It is God's Spirit that saves from sin.

Birth Control: Except for natural means, the church is opposed to the use of birth control.

Capital Punishment: No stance.

Christ's Return: The Church of the Living God the Pillar and Ground of the Truth is the waiting and preparing bride of Christ. When she is sufficiently prepared and made glorious without spot or wrinkle, Christ will catch his bride away to the marriage supper of the lamb to live and reign with him for a period of a thousand years. At this time, the dead in Christ will rise at the sounding of the first trumpet.

Communion: The Lord's Supper, Holy Communion, or Passover is observed once a month by using unleavened bread as a token of Christ's body and by using pure unadulterated water as a token and agreement of his blood, as nothing except water will agree with his blood. The washing of one another's feet is performed after communion.

Creation vs. Evolution: God created man, male and female, in his own image and likeness. All things were made by him and without him was not anything made that was made. The church does not believe in evolution.

Deity of Jesus: Jesus Christ is the Son of the Living God and was born of the Virgin Mary by spiritual conception in the likeness of sinful flesh and for sin condemned sin in the flesh. His purpose was, and is, to save his people from their sins.

Divorce and Remarriage: Divorce and remarriage is permitted only in limited cases.

Government: The Constitution Government and General Decree Book contains the laws and rules that govern the church.

Heaven/Hell: There is a final judgment day in store for all, for both the good and the bad. In it sinners will be justly judged, condemned, and separated from the righteous and turned into the place called the lake of fire and brimstone, prepared for those that do evil and for the devil and his angels. In the judgment, the righteous shall be changed from their corruptible body and given a body fashioned like the glorious body of the Son of God. There is a place of inheritance, joy, and happiness beyond expression for those that long for the appearing of the Lord, and to those that keep his sayings and do his will. This place is eternal into heaven and is the heaven of heavens.

Homosexuality: The church is opposed to homosexuality.

Inspiration of Scripture: All Scripture is given by the inspiration of God and is profitable for doctrine, for reproof, for correction, and for instruction in righteousness.

Miracles: Miracles were performed in biblical times by God, Jesus, the apostles, prophets, and chosen men of God. God still performs miracles today.

Restrictions: Drinking alcoholic beverages, using illegal drugs, and practicing immoral and unethical behavior. Members must avoid all places that are prepared, or are being used, for evil pleasures.

Security of Salvation: People are justified and made clean through faith and by the words of Christ. Believers are glorified and made wholly sanctified by receiving the baptism and fire of the Holy Ghost with biblical evidence. There are two stages of sanctification. First, an individual's sanctification followed by whole sanctification—which is also the glorification of the body through the Spirit of the Living God.

Speaking in Tongues and Other Gifts of the Spirit: Biblical evidence of receiving the baptism and fire of the Holy Ghost is speaking with tongues as the Spirit of God gives utterance as on the day of Pentecost. The gifts of the Spirit are exercised in the church.

Trinity: God the Father, God the Son, and God the Holy Ghost are one in three in the holy estate of power and the Godhead.

Women in Ministry: Women shall lead, preach, or preside over the flock of God. According to the Bible, God has made no distinction in his Kingdom between men and women. They all have the same happy privileges.

For more information contact: 2714 Scovel St., Nashville, TN 37208 or P.O. Box 22675, Nashville, TN 37202-2675; Phone: (615) 329-1625; Fax: (615) 329-0354.

Hutterian Brethren Church (Lehrerleut)

The Hutterian Brethren date back to the mid-1500s, when a group who followed the Anabaptist philosophies and believed in communal living formed settlements in Miraria and then Hungary, Romania, and Russia. Named after leader Jacob Hutter, who was martyred, the group experienced a renewal in the 1850s. After this renewal, members were divided into leuts (colonies).[4] Hutterian Brethren practice the community of goods, where all things are in common. Hutterian Brethren migrated to the United States and Canada in 1874. The Lehrerleut had 29 colonies in the U.S. with approximately 2,900 members in 1997.

Abortion: The Lehrerleut are totally against abortion and class it as murder.

Baptism: Believers are baptized upon a confession of faith. Persons must ask to be baptized, which usually occurs between the ages 19-25.

Birth Control: The colonies do not believe in birth control.

Capital Punishment: Thou shalt not kill. Vengeance is mine says the Lord.

Christ's Return: Christ will return to judge the world. There will be no millennium or 1,000 year Kingdom.

Communion: Communion is observed only once a year, not for forgiveness of sin but as a remembrance of Christ's atonement for sin through his death on the cross.

Creation vs. Evolution: Evolution is a fickle and wishful product of man's mind to do away with God and obedience to him.

Deity of Jesus: Jesus is the Son of God and the redeemer of mankind.

Divorce and Remarriage: Divorce is not allowed. In more than 400 years of the Lehrerleut, only one divorce has occurred—when the father left the family and got a divorce without his wife's consent.

Government: The church is governed by elders and ministers under one bishop.

Heaven/Hell: There is a literal heaven and hell.

Homosexuality: Homosexuality is the absolute in loose morality and will be punished by God as explained in Romans 1.

Inspiration of Scripture: The Scriptures were inspired by God and the Holy Ghost. They are an absolute truth that will stand forever.

Miracles: Miracles do not occur in modern time as in the prophets' or Jesus' and the apostles' time. However, it is a miracle when one can live a godly and Christian life in a corrupt world.

Restrictions: Card playing and many other amusements are not allowed.

Security of Salvation: Salvation occurs by the grace of God through a life of self control over all vices and sins until the end of life. Baptism alone is not salvation.

Speaking in Tongues and Other Gifts of the Spirit: Hutterian Brethren do not practice speaking in tongues or sign gifts, but they do believe in other gifts of the Spirit.

Trinity: God the Father, Jesus the Son, and the Holy Ghost are one entity. Like the sun, light, and warmth, they are different in character but still emanate from one body. They are inseparable.

Women in Ministry: Jesus did not send out women as apostles. Paul plainly says women should keep silence in the church.

For more information contact: Box 210, Chateau, MT 59422; Phone: (406) 466-2232.

Hutterian Brethren of North America

The Hutterian Brethren of North America are another branch of the Hutterian Brethren (see previous entry) who were established in 1530 as part of the Anabaptist Reformation. The group, whose motto is, "Christianity Without Community is Flawed," has more than 400 colonies with 40,000 members. Like their sister organization, all assets are in common.

Abortion: The Hutterian Brethren of North America oppose abortion.

Baptism: Only believers are baptized.

Birth Control: Birth control is allowed for medical reasons only.

Capital Punishment: No official position.

Christ's Return: The church looks for the blessed hope of Christ's return.

Communion: Closed communion, for baptized members only, is celebrated.

Creation vs. Evolution: The Hutterian Brethren believe in creation as expounded by Scripture.

Deity of Jesus: Jesus is part of the Godhead. He is God.

Divorce and Remarriage: No divorce is allowed except in adulterous situations. No divorced person can remarry someone else unless their former spouse dies.

Government: Officials are elected by vote of the male members.

Heaven/Hell: Heaven is for believers in Christ. Hell is for the godless.

Homosexuality: The Hutterian Brethren of North America are opposed to homosexuality.

Inspiration of Scripture: The Scriptures were inspired by God.

Miracles: Miracles are possible. The church has no desire to limit God.

Restrictions: The colonies are opposed to all forms of worldliness, including fashion, arts, theater, cards or gambling, musical instruments in worship service, television, and radio.

Security of Salvation: Security of salvation is conditional on a believer's continuation on faith in Christ.

Speaking in Tongues and Other Gifts of the Spirit: Tongues are definite languages to substantiate the coming of the Holy Spirit. Other gifts of the Spirit are essential to the function of the full body of Christ.

Trinity: God the Father, God the Son, and God the Holy Spirit are all one and cannot be separated.

Women in Ministry: Women have no official position in spiritual ministries but serve as teachers, head cooks, and other service related positions.

For more information contact: 66 Byemoore, Alberta, Canada, T0J 0L0; Phone: (406) 353-2800; Fax: (406) 353-4746; E-mail: 7hope@3rivers.net

---

Independent Assemblies of God International

The Independent Assemblies of God was born in 1918 as the Scandinavian Assemblies of God in the United States of America, Canada, and Foreign Lands. It existed under this name from 1918 to 1935. In 1935, at an annual convention in Minneapolis, MN, the Scandinavian Assemblies of God merged with a group called the Independent Pentecostal Churches. At that time, the fellowship adopted the current name.[1] There were 400 congregations in the U.S. in 1997.

Abortion: Abortion is sin, although there may be situations where it can be acceptable. For example, when the life of the mother or child is in danger.

Baptism: Baptism is performed by water immersion after conversion.[2]

Birth Control: The Independent Assemblies of God are not against the use of birth control.

Capital Punishment: The church is not against capital punishment.

Christ's Return: Christ will return again. This return is imminent.[3]

Communion: The church celebrates the Lord's Supper, a fellowship and memorial of his death, with wine and bread. [4]

Creation vs. Evolution: The church is creationist.

Deity of Christ: The Independent Assemblies of God International believes in the virgin birth of Christ, his vicarious, atoning death, bodily resurrection, and ascension.[5]

Divorce and Remarriage: Though seen as sin, divorce can be forgiven. Divorced and remarried ministers can be ordained depending upon the circumstances.

Government: Local churches are sovereign. It is imperative that ministers and churches are able to follow through on the mandate given by God without interference from an ecclesiastical hierarchy.[6]

Heaven/Hell: There is a blessed hope resurrection and translation of those who have fallen asleep in Christ and those who are alive at his coming. There will be a final judgment of those who have not accepted Christ as Savior, with the devil and his angels in the lake of fire.[7]

Homosexuality: Homosexuality is wrong. It is a sin before God.

Inspiration of Scripture: The Bible is the inspired and infallible Word of God.[8]

Miracles: The church believes in divine healing through the redemptive work of Christ on the cross.[9]

Restrictions: None.

Security of Salvation: Man can lose his salvation when he chooses to sin and turn his back on God.

Speaking in Tongues and Other Gifts of the Spirit: With the baptism of the Holy Spirit comes the initial evidence of speaking in other tongues.[10]

Trinity: There is one God, eternally existent in three persons: Father, Son, and Holy Spirit.[11]

Women in Ministry: Women are allowed in ministry and can be ordained.

For more information contact: 24411 Ridge Route Dr., Ste. 120, Laguna Hills, CA 92653; Phone: (714) 859-6946; Fax: (714) 859-0683.

Independent Christian Churches, International

Independent Christian Churches, International was formed in 1973 by Dr. Donald Ned Hicks, former pastor of the Metroplex Bible Chapel in Dallas, TX.[12] Proclaiming the motto, "Contending for the faith once delivered," the group had 75 churches with approximately 1,000 members in 1997.

Abortion: Abortion, except in very limited cases, (for example: incest, rape, or threat to the life of the mother), is inexcusable and should be considered as murder.

Baptism: The ordinance of baptism by a burial with Christ should be observed as commanded in the Holy Writ by all who have truly repented and in their hearts have really believed in Christ as Savior and Lord. In so doing, they have the body washed in pure water as an outward sign or symbol of cleansing, while their hearts have already been sprinkled with the blood of Christ as an inner cleansing. Thus, they proclaim to the world that they have died with Christ to sin, and that they have also been raised with him to live and walk in newness of life.

Birth Control: The church takes no position on birth control.

Capital Punishment: Although no official stand is taken, the church notes that the Bible does not condemn the death penalty and capital punishment.

Christ's Return: The revelation of the Lord Jesus Christ from heaven, the salvation of mankind then completed, and the millennial reign of Christ is the scriptural promise of the world's hope.

Communion: The Lord's Supper, consisting of the elements, is the symbol which expresses a believer's sharing the divine nature of the Lord Jesus Christ. It is a memorial of his suffering and death and a prophecy of his second advent. It is commended to all believers as such a sign until he returns.

Creation vs. Evolution: Independent Christian Churches International believes in the creation of man by the direct act of Jehovah God as recorded in the first three chapters of the book of Genesis.

Deity of Christ: Independent Christian Churches believe in the incarnation and virgin birth of the blessed Lord and Savior Jesus Christ— the Son of God.

Divorce and Remarriage: No position.

Government: Each individual church is an independent, sovereign body, free to establish its local church government according to the desires of its congregation.

Heaven/Hell: The devil and his angels, the beast and the false prophet, and whosoever is not found written in the book of life shall be sentenced to everlasting punishment in the lake which burns with fire and brimstone, which is the second death. According to his promise, the church looks for new heavens and a new earth where righteousness dwells.

Homosexuality: The apostle Paul makes it extremely clear in Romans 1 that this is abnormal behavior and thus an abomination to God.

Inspiration of Scripture: Independent Christian Churches believe in the complete and total divine inspiration of the Bible (both the Old and New Testaments). It is the inspired Word of God, a revelation from God to man. It is the infallible rule of faith and conduct, and is superior to conscience and reason, while not being contrary to reason.

Miracles: Deliverance from sickness is provided for in the atonement, just as is salvation from sin.

Restrictions: None.

Security of Salvation: No official position.

Speaking in Tongues and Other Gifts of the Spirit: No official position.

Trinity: The one true God has revealed himself as the eternally self-existent, self-revealed "I Am." He has further revealed himself as embodying the principles of relationship and association as the Father, Son, and Holy Spirit.

Women in Ministry: God's call is without repentance and is extended without regard to race or gender.

For more information contact: P.O. Box 414, Spur, TX 79370-0414; Phone: (806) 271-3387; Fax: (806) 271-3634.

Independent Fundamental Churches of America

The Independent Fundamental Churches of America (IFCA) started in 1930 as an association of Bible believing churches, organizations, and men. It brought together several Congregational Churches and the American Conference of Undenominated Churches.[13]

Abortion: No answer.

Baptism: All believers are encouraged to follow the biblical teaching regarding water baptism.[14]

Birth Control: No answer.

Capital Punishment: No answer.

Christ's Return: The church believes in: the blessed hope of the personal, imminent, pretribulation, and premillennial coming of the Lord Jesus Christ for his redeemed ones; and in his subsequent return to earth, with his saints, to establish his millennial Kingdom.[15]

Communion: All who are truly born-again are invited to remember the Lord at the communion table regardless of church membership.[16]

Creation vs. Evolution: No answer.

Deity of Christ: The Lord Jesus Christ, the eternal Son of God, became man, without ceasing to be God, having been conceived by the Holy Spirit and born of the Virgin Mary, in order that he might reveal God and redeem sinful men. The Lord Jesus Christ died on the cross for all mankind as a representative, vicarious, and substitutionary sacrifice. The sufficiency of this atoning sacrifice to accomplish the redemption and justification of all who trust in him is assured by his literal, physical resurrection from the dead. The Lord Jesus Christ ascended into heaven and is now exalted at the right hand of God. There, as high priest, he fulfills the ministry of representative, intercessor, and advocate.[17]

Divorce and Remarriage: No answer.

Government: The Independent Fundamental Churches of America establishes an organizational structure to coordinate and encourage joint participation in mutual activities. This is provided while guaranteeing the autonomy of congregational government. The constitution and by-laws of the fellowship provide for voluntary membership of churches, organizations, and individuals. Membership is reaffirmed annually. An annual convention is held where delegates and members determine the course of the fellowship and elect its officers.[18]

Heaven/Hell: The church believes in the bodily resurrection of all men—the saved to eternal life, and the unsaved to judgment and everlasting punishment. The souls of the redeemed are, at death, absent from the body and present with the Lord, where in conscious bliss they await the first resurrection—when spirit, soul, and body are reunited to be glorified forever with the Lord. The souls of unbelievers remain, after death, in conscious misery until the second resurrection, when with soul and body reunited they shall appear at the Great White Throne Judgment, and shall be cast into the lake of fire, not to be annihilated, but to suffer everlasting conscious punishment.[19]

Homosexuality: No answer.

Inspiration of Scripture: The Holy Scriptures of the Old and New Testaments are the verbally inspired Word of God, the final authority for faith and life, inerrant in the original writings, infallible, and God-breathed.[20]

Miracles: God does hear and answer the prayer of faith, in accordance with his own will, for the sick and afflicted.[21]

Restrictions: No answer.

Security of Salvation: The redeemed, once saved, are kept by God's power and are thus secure in Christ forever. It is the privilege of believers to rejoice in the assurance of their salvation through the testimony of God's Word which, however, clearly forbids the use of Christian liberty as an occasion to the flesh.[22]

Speaking in Tongues and Other Gifts of the Spirit: God is sovereign in the bestowment of all his gifts; the gifts of evangelists, pastors, and teachers are sufficient for the perfecting of the saints today. Speaking in tongues and the working of sign miracles gradually ceased as the New Testament Scriptures were completed and their authority became established.[23]

Trinity: The church believes in one triune God, eternally existing in three persons—Father, Son, and Holy Spirit—co-eternal in being, co-identical in nature, co-equal in power and glory, and having the same attributes and perfections.[24]

Women in Ministry: No answer.

For more information contact: P.O. Box 810, Grandville, MI 49468; Phone: (800) 347-1840 or (616) 531-1840; Fax: (616) 531-1814; E-mail: gregory@ifca.org; Web site: http://www.ifca.org/

International Church of the Foursquare Gospel

On December 30, 1927, four years after the dedication of Angelus Temple by Aimee Semple McPherson and those who followed her ministry, the International Church of the Foursquare Gospel was incorporated and registered in California. Mrs. McPherson served as president of the church during her lifetime and oversaw the denomination's expansion together with a board of directors. Upon her death in 1944, her son, Rolf Kennedy McPherson, became president. Upon Dr. McPherson's retirement from the presidency on May 31, 1988, the position was filled by Dr. John R. Holland. In 1996, there were 1,742 churches with 224,374 members in the United States. The International Church of the Foursquare Gospel's motto is, "Jesus Christ is the Same Yesterday, Today and Forever."

Abortion: Acknowledging that abortion on demand is a moral and spiritual wrong which strikes at the very foundation of decency, human responsibility, and godliness, the church expresses its commitment to support the God-given right of each child to live out their full and natural life span from conception. The church also remains committed to its sacred call to minister to any and all who have been impacted by the events surrounding abortion.

Baptism: Water baptism is a blessed outward sign of an inward work—a beautiful and solemn emblem reminding believers that even as the Lord died upon the cross of Calvary so they reckon themselves dead indeed to sin. The Foursquare Gospel Church normally practices immersion and believes the act of baptism is for all who have confessed the Lord Jesus Christ as their Savior.

Birth Control: The means of birth control is left to the individual. Following conception, the church is opposed to the use of abortifacients.

Capital Punishment: The Bible authorizes the death penalty, but permits mercy. No one is beyond the redemptive grace of our Lord.

Christ's Return: The second coming of Christ is literal, personal, and imminent. He will descend from heaven and the dead in Christ shall rise, then the redeemed that are alive and remain shall be caught up together with them in the clouds. No man knows the time of his appearance, but must be busy in the work of spreading the Gospel until that day arrives.

Communion: Foursquare Gospel Churches commemorate and observe the Lord's Supper by the sacred use of the broken bread, a precious type of the bread of life, even Jesus Christ, and by the juice of the vine, a blessed type which should ever remind the participant of the shed blood of the Savior. This should be taken following self-examination, forgiveness, and love toward all men.

Creation vs. Evolution: There is no written stance on this. However, the vast majority of Foursquare churches teach creationism in some form. The church does believe in the uniqueness of God's creation of man from the other forms of creation.

Deity of Jesus: Jesus, the Son, is coexistent and co-eternal with the Father. Conceived by the Holy Spirit and born of the Virgin Mary, he took upon himself the form of man, bore our sins, carried our sorrows, and, by the shedding of his precious blood, purchased redemption for all who would believe upon him. He is fully God and fully man.

Divorce and Remarriage: Strong marital relationships are encouraged and divorce is discouraged, except in extreme cases—and then only as a last resort. Divorced and remarried persons are accepted in love and grace as members, provided they have received Christ as their Savior and demonstrate the Christian life. Healing for crumbling or broken marriages is possible.

Government: Business of the International Church of the Foursquare Gospel is conducted by a president, a board of directors, the Foursquare Cabinet and an executive council. The highest seat of authority is the Convention Body, which alone has the authority to make or amend the bylaws of the church. District supervisors are appointed for districts in the United States and are ratified by the pastors of the respective districts every four years. The ministry of each local congregation is cared for by a pastor and/or staff, a church council, deacons, deaconesses, and elders, and is expected to contribute monthly to home and foreign missionary work. Pastors of local churches are appointed by the board of directors upon recommendation of the district supervisor. Both men and women are allowed to minister on all levels of leadership within the church, including the Foursquare Cabinet and board of directors.

Heaven/Hell: Heaven is literal—the indescribably glorious habitation of the living God. The Lord has gone to prepare a place for his children where believers in Jesus Christ will be carried. There, the Lord Jesus Christ will present them to the Father without spot or wrinkle and there will be eternal joy in the everlasting Kingdom. Hell is a place of outer darkness and deepest sorrow. It is a place where the fire is not quenched; a place prepared for the devil and his angels. All unbelievers who have rejected and spurned the love and sacrifice of the redeemer will be cast into the lake of fire which burns with fire and brimstone forever.

Homosexuality: The church opposes homosexuality. Based on the teaching of the Holy Scripture, it is declared to be sin. However, it encourages those engaged in homosexual activity to cease such acts and to seek forgiveness and deliverance through Jesus Christ.

Inspiration of Scripture: The Holy Bible is the Word of the living God: true, immutable, steadfast, and unchangeable. It was written by holy men of old as they were inspired by the Holy Spirit.

Miracles: Miracles have occurred throughout biblical history. Much of Jesus' ministry was that of performing miracles. Such were done because of God's compassion for the hurts and need of humanity. And because Jesus Christ is the same yesterday, today, and forever, miracles will continue to happen through his church today.

Restrictions: There are no published guidelines. The church approves of good, clean, healthy recreation and entertainment.

Security of Salvation: As long as believers place their trust in Jesus Christ as Savior, their salvation is totally secure. However, people may apostatize after they have known the way of truth. But God's mercy is still extended to the apostate so that they might return to the Lord who gave himself for them.

Speaking in Tongues and Other Gifts of the Spirit: The Holy Spirit bestows gifts upon the believer such as wisdom, knowledge, faith, healing, miracles, prophecy, discernment, tongues, and the interpretation of tongues. These gifts are divided to every man as the Holy Spirit wills. The purpose of the gifts is to edify the church and evangelize the unbeliever. The baptism with the Holy Spirit is accompanied by the speaking in other tongues. The purpose is to glorify and exalt the Lord Jesus, to give inspired utterance in witnessing of him, and to equip the individual and the church for practical, efficient, and joyous soul-winning.

Trinity: There is but one true and living God, the maker of heaven and earth and all that is in them. In the unity of the Godhead there are three, equal in every divine perfection, executing distinct but harmonious offices in the great work of redemption. These are known as the Father, the Son, and the Holy Spirit.

Women in Ministry: A close study of the Word of God, both Old and New Testaments, indicates that God has seen fit to use women in his service in virtually every way he has employed men. Nothing should restrict the God-ordained and Spirit-filled ministry of women in any capacity in the church as long as they are submissive to the Word of God—a qualification which should guide men as well as women.

For more information contact: 1910 W. Sunset Blvd., Ste. 200, Los Angeles, CA 90026-0176; Phone: (213) 484-2400 Ext. 309; Fax: (213) 413-3824; E-mail: comm@foursquare.org; Web site: http:// www.foursquare.org

---

International Evangelical Church of the Soldiers of the Cross of Christ

The International Evangelical Church of the Soldiers of the Cross of Christ was founded in 1924 by Ernest Williams Sellers (1869–1953) of Wisconsin while he was on a missionary assignment in Cuba. The Day of the Lord for the church is the seventh day of the week, on which members rest from their daily activities and worship the Lord as a reckoning of their eternal repose in heaven and in the observance of all other commandments of God. In 1997, there were 50 churches in the United States who subscribed to the motto, "Jesus Christ is our all in all." There were approximately 2,000 members.

Abortion: Human life begins the instant a child is conceived in its mother's womb. Abortion, at any moment after conception, is the destruction of a human life and therefore is sin.

Baptism: The church practices baptism by immersion, as commanded by Jesus Christ in Mark 16:16, and the baptism of the Holy Spirit as the means of becoming a member of the body of Christ.

Birth Control: The Bible does not state that for every time a man cohabits with his wife it should be with the intention of conceiving a child. There were faithful married women in Bible times who were sterile. Therefore, natural birth control is safe for society and cannot be considered a sin.

Capital Punishment: Capital punishment is a civil action carried out by the state. Although the church should not interfere with the laws of any nation, the International Evangelical Church of the Soldiers of the Cross of Christ believes that any person serving any government as an executor of capital punishment is trespassing God's law.

Christ's Return: The church believes in the second coming of the Lord Jesus Christ, who will personally descend in all his glory, as promised by him, to take vengeance on the unjust and introduce his church into his Kingdom of glory, where believers shall live eternally with him.

Communion: Those admitted into the communion of the church should participate in all the ordinances set by Jesus Christ—as in the Lord's Supper, which is to be continued until his second coming, to commemorate his death and not his resurrection.

Creation vs. Evolution: According to the Holy Scriptures, man did not evolve but was created by the spoken Word of God.

Deity of Jesus: Jesus Christ is the eternal Son of God, conceived in the womb of the virgin by an act of the Holy Spirit in the fullness of time, to assume human nature in which nature he suffered and died, giving satisfaction for sins. He was resurrected on the third day, offering eternal life with him.

Divorce and Remarriage: Divorce is prohibited to all Christians. The Bible says the wife should not depart from her husband. But if she departs, she should remain unmarried. And a husband should not put away his wife.

Government: Government in the church is administered by the Holy Spirit. God has set first apostles, second prophets, and third teachers.

Heaven/Hell: There is eternal life in heaven for the redeemed in Jesus Christ. There is eternal punishment in hell for the wicked.

Homosexuality: The Holy Scriptures clearly state that those involved in the practices of homosexuality will not inherit the Kingdom of God.

Inspiration of Scripture: All Scripture is given by inspiration of God. Holy men of God spoke as they were moved by the Holy Ghost. The Old and New Testament are the only rule of faith and practice.

Miracles: Soldiers of the Cross of Christ believe in divine healing through fasting, prayer, and anointment with oil as well as in prophecies and revelations as acts of the Holy Spirit.

Restrictions: Restrictions are limited to those established in the Bible by the apostles, such as the modest apparel of women and the prohibition of all corrupt habits.

Security of Salvation: In Luke 10:20, the Lord tells his disciples to rejoice because their names were written in heaven. This passage reveals that every Christian should rejoice in the security of salvation.

Speaking in Tongues and Other Gifts of the Spirit: Speaking in tongues and all the gifts of the Spirit shall cease only when that which is perfect is come (i.e. the second coming of the Lord, when he will make all things perfect). Therefore, all manifestations of the Holy Ghost, as experienced in the church of biblical times, have remained and will remain until the Son of God comes for his church in the clouds of glory.

Trinity: There is only one living God and there are three persons consubstantial in one God: God the Father, God the Son, and God the Holy Spirit. All three are one and equal in divine perfection.

Women in Ministry: According to the Scriptures, women are also responsible for being involved in the ministry of the church. In Acts 21, Philip, the evangelist, had four daughters who prophesied.

For more information contact: 641 W. Flagler St., Miami, FL 33133; Phone: (305) 325-9653; Fax: (305) 324-1450; E-mail: mwingfield@aol.com; Web site: http://user.aol.com/soldiersof/

International Pentecostal Church of Christ

The IPCC is a result of the 1976 merger of the International Pentecostal Assemblies and the Pentecostal Church of Christ. The former originated with the founding of the Bridegroom's Messenger in 1907 and was officially organized in 1921. The Pentecostal Church was founded in 1917. In 1997, there were 73 churches in the United States.

Abortion: The International Pentecostal Church of Christ believes that all life is an expression of God's love and all forms of abortion are the taking of a human life. Neither the life of the unborn nor the mother may be taken lightly. The IPCC recognizes the rare need of therapeutic abortions to save the life of the mother. In cases of rape and incest, the church is encouraged to not censure a woman having an abortion providing there has been extensive medical, psychological, and religious counseling.

Baptism: The ordinance of baptism by immersion for believers in the name of the Father, the Son, and the Holy Ghost is commanded in the Scriptures. All who repent and believe on Christ as Savior and Lord are to be baptized. Thus they declare to the world that they have died with Christ and that they also have been raised with him to walk in newness of life.

Birth Control: Although the International Pentecostal Church of Christ takes no official stand on birth control, it is opposed to contraception methods that terminate a fertilized egg.

Capital Punishment: No official position.

Christ's Return: The IPCC believes in the personal return of Jesus Christ. The resurrection of those who have fallen asleep in Christ and their translation, together with those who are alive and remain unto the coming of the Lord, is the imminent and blessed hope of the church.

Communion: The Lord's Supper, consisting of the elements—bread and fruit of the vine—is the symbol expressing member's sharing in the divine nature of the Lord Jesus Christ. It is a memorial of his suffering and death, a prophecy of his second coming, and is enjoined on all believers until he comes.

Creation vs. Evolution: The triune God created the universe apart from pre-existing materials and without any evolutionary process. The church believes in the historicity of the first eleven chapters of Genesis.

Deity of Jesus: The International Pentecostal Church of Christ believes in the deity of the Lord Jesus Christ, his virgin birth, his sinless life, his miracles, his vicarious and atoning death through his shed blood, his resurrection, his ascension to the right hand of the Father, and his personal returning in power and glory.

Divorce and Remarriage: Low standards on marriage and divorce are very hurtful to individuals, the family, and the cause of Christ. Therefore, the IPCC discourages divorce. However, severely abusive marriages where the safety and well-being of family members is jeopardized would be grounds for exception. Membership is granted to applicants whose divorce and remarriage occurred prior to conversion. Ministerial applicants who have a living former spouse are not received.

Government: The government of the church is a blend of congregational and presbyterian structures. Churches select their own pastors and boards and conduct their own affairs. The denominational system is managed by a general board and a general overseer, elected by ministers, church delegates, and votes by an annual convention.

Heaven/Hell: There is an eternal heaven and a literal hell where residents will reside forever. There will be a final judgement in which the wicked dead will be raised and judged according to their works.

Homosexuality: The Scriptures explicitly pronounce judgement on sexual deviancy. Marriage was formed after the likeness of the Godhead and sexual sins defy the essence of God and beauty of marital unity. However, the love of all persons as God's creation is affirmed and the abuse of any person, for any reason, is an affront to the Christ who came to redeem all of humanity.

Inspiration of Scripture: The Bible is the inspired Word of God to man, infallible in its original form, and is the authoritative Word of God. The New Testament is the sole rule for discipline and government.

Miracles: The existence of God presupposes miracles that trescend all ages. The portrayal of miracles in Scripture is characteristic of an omnipotent and loving God. Divine healing is an integral part of the gospel and is provided for in the atonement and is the privilege of all believers.

Restrictions: The IPCC does not allow its members to indulge in activities that would defile or corrupt the mind or spirit, such as the use of alcoholic beverages, tobacco, illicit drugs, pornography, gambling, unbecoming speech, the breaking of laws, and sexual sins.

Security of Salvation: Mankind is saved by grace through faith and maintained by grace through faith. The security of salvation remains as long as believer's lives are an outgrowth of a continually internalized living faith.

Speaking in Tongues and Other Gifts of the Spirit: All believers are entitled to, and should ardently expect and earnestly seek, the promise of the Father—which is the baptism of the Holy Ghost and fire—according to the command of the Lord Jesus Christ. The Bible evidence of the baptism in the Holy Ghost is witnessed by the physical sign of speaking with other tongues as the Spirit of God gives utterance. With it comes the enduement of power for life and service, the bestowment of the gifts, and their uses in the work of the ministry. With the baptism in the Holy Ghost comes such experiences as an overflowing fullness of the Spirit, a deepened reverence for God, and a more active love for Christ, for his Word, and for the lost.

Trinity: The triune Godhead consists of one true God the Father, Jesus Christ his Son, and the Holy Ghost as the third person of the Godhead. The International Pentecostal Church of Christ opposes any effort to hold any person of the Trinity as greater than the others.

Women in Ministry: The Scriptures relate many instances where women were used of God as prophetesses, the bearers of good news, and many other forms of ministry. Therefore, the IPCC does not place restrictions on women in the ministry.

For more information contact: P.O. Box 439, London, OH 43140; Phone: (614) 852-4722; Fax: (614) 852-0348; E-mail: hqipcc@aol.com

---

International Pentecostal Holiness Church

The first congregation to bear the name Pentecostal Holiness was organized in 1898. In 1911, the Pentecostal Holiness Church and Fire-Baptized Holiness Churches merged to form what is now the International Pentecostal Holiness Church. There were 1,653 churches with 157,163 members in 1997.

Abortion: Every human life is sacred from conception by virtue of its being created by God in his own image. The International Pentecostal Holiness Church condemns the practice of abortion and supports legislation protecting the lives of the unborn.

Baptism: Water baptism is for the person who has repented of sin and believed on the Lord Jesus Christ as Savior. The church baptizes in the name of the Father, the Son, and the Holy Spirit. Immersion is preferable, but baptism by sprinkling or pouring is acceptable.

Birth Control: No stated policy.

Capital Punishment: No stated policy.

Christ's Return: The church believes in the imminent, personal, and premillenial second coming of Christ.

Communion: Holy communion commemorates a believer's redemption by Christ's death. The elements are symbolic of the blood and body of Christ. The International Pentecostal Holiness Church practices open communion, which means that all Christians present may partake.

Creation vs. Evolution: God created the heaven and the earth.

Deity of Jesus: Jesus Christ is the Son of God.

Divorce and Remarriage: Divorced and remarried persons are allowed to be licensed ministers and ordained ministers in the Pentecostal Holiness Church if the circumstances of their divorce meet certain criteria. Each case is considered on an individual basis. Divorced and remarried persons are allowed to hold offices in local churches.

Government: Connectional, with some elements of both episcopal and congregational forms of government.

Heaven/Hell: Eternal life with God in heaven is the reward of those who, by the grace of God, have received forgiveness for their sins. Hell is the place of everlasting banishment from the presence of God and is the wages of the persistently unrepentant wicked.

Homosexuality: The church maintains a strong position against premarital, extramarital, and deviant sex, including homosexual and lesbian relationships. It refuses to accept the loose moral standards of today's society. God's grace is sufficient to deliver those bound in this sin.

Inspiration of Scripture: The Bible is the inspired, inerrant, and authoritative Word of God.

Miracles: Jesus is the same yesterday, today, and tomorrow. He still performs miracles in this day and age.

Restrictions: The church is against gambling, the use of tobacco, illegal drugs or intoxicants, homosexual practices, and membership in organizations with objectives and activities not in harmony with Scriptures or which require oath-bound allegiance that infringes upon a member's allegiance to God.

Security of Salvation: A person is secure in their salvation unless they willfully reject the grace of God.

Speaking in Tongues and Other Gifts of the Spirit: Speaking in tongues is the initial evidence of being baptized in the Holy Spirit. Tongues is one of the nine manifestation gifts of the Spirit.

Trinity: There is one true and living God. There are three persons who make up the Godhead (the Trinity): God the Father, God the Son, and God the Holy Spirit.

Women in Ministry: All believers are given gifts of ministry. The International Pentecostal Holiness Church encourgages women to practice whatever ministry gifts they are given. It licenses and ordains women as ministers and has women pastors.

For more information contact: P.O. Box 12609 Oklahoma City, OK 73157; Phone: (405) 787-7110; Fax: (405) 789-3957; E-mail: www. iphc.org; Web site: http://www.iphc.org/info.html

---

Lutheran Churches of the Reformation

The Lutheran Churches of the Reformation was founded in 1964 after a separation from the Lutheran Church-Missouri Synod. The church has split twice more, but is currently seeking to reunite with others of sound doctrine. The group is also in fellowship with the Illinois Lutheran Conference. The Lutheran Churches of the Reformation emphasize atonement and justification by grace through faith. They distinguish between law and Gospel, reject fellowship with heretics, and recommend the King James Version of the Bible. In 1997, there were 20 churches with 2,000 members.

Abortion: Abortion is murder. The perpetrators must repent or they will perish.

Baptism: Baptism is God's means of regeneration. Baptism is gospel, not an ordinance.

Birth Control: Birth control is a sin against God's command to be fruitful and multiply.

Capital Punishment: The Lutheran Churches of the Reformation believe that capital punishment is ordained by God for the sake of order and discipline.

Christ's Return: Christ's return will be in glory at the end of the world. The church is amillennial.

Communion: Christ's body and blood are received by all communicants for forgiveness, faith, and fellowship. It is a means of grace.

Creation vs. Evolution: Evolution is unscriptural, unscientific, illogical, and a fraud.

Deity of Christ: Jesus is true God and true man in one undivided and indivisible person.

Divorce and Remarriage: Divorce and remarriage are permitted only for the innocent party in the case of fornication or desertion.

Government: Congregations are sovereign. The Bible alone rules.

Heaven/Hell: Both heaven and hell are quite real.

Homosexuality: The practice of homosexuality is sin.

Inspiration of Scripture: Every word of the Scriptures is God's Word. There are no errors.

Miracles: Miracles were rather frequent in Bible times for the Gospel's sake. Some miracles have occurred since that time. God does not promise further miracles, but may do them. Tongues and healings are not promised and are not to be prized.

Restrictions: The Lutheran Churches of the Reformation restrict church merchandising, unscriptural fellowship, and membership in lodges.

Security of Salvation: God promised salvation and preservation through the Gospel. There is no absolute certainty, but there is certainty of faith.

Speaking in Tongues and Other Gifts of the Spirit: Speaking in tongues and other sign gifts are not from the Holy Spirit but from the spirit or heart of man. Sometimes they are from evil spirits.

Trinity: God is one being in three persons.

Women in Ministry: The Bible forbids women ministers.

For more information contact: 4014 Wevonah Lane, Fort Wayne, IN 46809; Phone: (219) 747-5751.

Lutheran Church–Missouri Synod (LCMS), The

The LCMS was founded by German Saxon immigrants who came to America in 1838 and settled in Perry County, MO. Under the leadership of C. F. W. Walther, they formed The German Evangelical Lutheran Synod of Missouri, Ohio, and Other States. The first convention was held in April, 1847.[1] The LCMS adheres to the doctrines confessed in The Book of Concord, which includes the historic creeds of the church: the Apostles', Nicene, and Athanasian Creeds, the Augsburg Confession, and Luther's Large and Small Catechisms. There were 6,200 congregations with 2,600,000 baptized members in 1997.

Abortion: The living, but unborn, are persons in the sight of God from the time of conception. As persons, the unborn stand under the full protection of God's prohibition against murder. Since abortion takes a human life, abortion is not a moral option, except as a tragically unavoidable by-product of medical procedures necessary to prevent the death of another human being—the mother.

Baptism: Baptism is a sacrament, instituted by God. A valid baptism consists of the use of water together with God's Word. As a means of grace, it works forgiveness of sins, rescues from death and the devil, and gives eternal salvation to all who believe this. Infants are baptized according to Christ's command and promise.

Birth Control: In the absence of scriptural prohibition, there is no objection to contraception within a marital union which is, as a whole, fruitful.

Capital Punishment: Government has the God-given authority to exercise capital punishment, though government is not required by divine command to administer it. Christians should exert a positive influence on the government's exercise of punishment for wrongdoing and ensure that punishment is administered with utmost fairness.

Christ's Return: Jesus Christ will return on the last day for judgment and will raise up all the dead. On that day he will give eternal life and everlasting joy to believers and the elect, but will condemn unbelievers and the devil to hell and eternal punishment.

Communion: The Lord's Supper is a sacrament. It is the true body and blood of Jesus Christ under bread and wine, instituted by Christ for Christians to eat and to drink. As a means of grace, it gives the forgiveness of sins, life, and salvation to all who believe the words, "Given and shed for you for the forgiveness of sins." The LCMS practices closed communion, communing only with those individuals who share its confession of faith and doing so within the context of responsible pastoral care.

Creation vs. Evolution: The Lutheran Church-Missouri Synod believes that God, by the almighty power of his Word, created all things in six days. Adam, the first human being, was specially created in the image of God, that is, in a state of righteousness, innocence, and blessedness. Human beings did not come into being through a process of evolution from lower forms of life, but through the direct creative action of God.

Deity of Christ: Jesus Christ is true God, begotten of the Father from eternity and also true man, born of the Virgin Mary. As true God and true man, Jesus redeemed the world from sin. He had to be true God so that his fulfilling of the law and his life, suffering, and death might be a sufficient ransom for all people and so that he might be able to overcome death and the devil.

Divorce and Remarriage: When God instituted marriage, he intended that it be the lifelong union of one man and one woman. Divorce and remarriage, except in cases of sexual unfaithfulness and willful abandonment (malicious desertion), are contrary to the will of God.

Government: God instituted the office of pastor for the preaching of the Gospel and the administration of the sacraments. In order to carry out the mission of the church, the Synod is divided into 35 districts. Meetings of the members of the Synod take place in a three year cycle. The first year, convocations of circuit congregations are held. Conventions of districts, to which each congregation sends one voting lay and one pastoral delegate, are held in the second year. Districts elect their own officers. National assemblies, called synodical conventions, take place very third year. The Synodical Convention is the highest governing body in the Synod.[2]

Heaven/Hell: Holy Scriptures teach that heaven is the place where God dwells and where all true believers in his Son Jesus Christ will live with him forever. Hell is the place of eternal punishment and torment, where all unbelievers will dwell forever under the wrath of God.

Homosexuality: Homosexual behavior is intrinsically sinful. The LCMS urges that the law and the Gospel of the Scriptures be applied to all who engage in such behavior for the purpose of ministering the forgiveness of Christ to any and all sinners who are penitent.

Inspiration of Scripture: Holy Scripture is given by the inspiration of God the Holy Spirit. God is the true author of every word of Scripture. All Scripture, therefore, is without qualification God's very own Word and therefore without error.

Miracles: Since God is all-powerful, he can and does perform miracles as the New Testament testifies. Judgments regarding specific cases of miracles today must remain a matter of human opinion. Furthermore, Christians should place their trust in God's loving care, even if they must suffer.

Restrictions: No answer.

Security of Salvation: All those who place their trust in Jesus Christ and his saving work can be certain of their salvation and life forever with him in heaven. Their confidence rests not on their good works, nor anything within themselves, but only in the objective promises of the Gospel of Christ.

Speaking in Tongues and Other Gifts of the Spirit: God has not promised that all Christians will receive the gift of tongues referred to in the New Testament. Therefore, individual claims regarding the reception of this gift remain a matter of human judgment. God distributes the gifts of his Holy Spirit to Christians when and where he pleases, for the edification of his church and to his glory.

Trinity: The Holy Trinity, who is truly God, is three persons in one divine essence, equal in power and alike eternal: God the Father, God the Son, and God the Holy Spirit.

Women in Ministry: The Scripture prohibits women from holding the divinely instituted pastoral office or exercising any of the distinctive functions of this office. In all other areas of ministry, women are urged to serve and to use the gifts given to them by God.

For more information contact: 1333 S. Kirkwood Rd., St. Louis, MO 63112-7295; Phone: (888) 843-5267 or (314) 965-9917; Fax: (314) 822-8307; E-mail: infoctr@lcms.org; Web site: http://www. lcms.org/

Mennonite Church

The Mennonite Church and its sister denomination, The General Conference Mennonite Church, have a similar background (see entry on General Conference Mennonite Church, The). In 1995, the two adopted a joint *Confession of Faith in a Mennonite Perspective*. Mennonites believe peace is the will of God and practice non-resistance even in the face of violence and warfare.[1] The Mennonite Church had approximately 1,100 congregations with 110,000 members in 1997.

Abortion: The Mennonite Church does not excommunicate those who have had an abortion, but it clearly stands firmly on the side of life.

Baptism: Baptism of adult believers with water is a sign of their cleansing from sin. It is also a pledge before the church of their covenant with God to walk in the way of Jesus Christ through the power of the Holy Spirit. Believers are baptized into Christ and his body by the Spirit, water, and blood.[2]

Birth Control: Any form of birth control that involves abortion is unacceptable.

Capital Punishment: The church opposes capital punishment.

Christ's Return: Christ will come again in glory to judge the living and the dead. He will gather his church, which is already living under the reign of God. In God's final victory at the end of this present age of struggle, the dead will be resurrected and there will be a new heaven and a new earth. There the people of God will reign with Christ in justice, righteousness, and peace for ever and ever.[3]

Communion: The Lord's Supper is a sign by which the church thankfully remembers the new covenant which Jesus established with his death. In this communion meal, the church renews its covenant with God and with each other and participates in the life and death of Jesus Christ until he comes.[4]

Creation vs. Evolution: God created the heavens and the earth and all that is in them. He preserves and renews what has been made. All creation has its source outside itself and belongs to the creator. The world was created good because God is good and provides all that is needed for life. God created human beings in the divine image. God formed them from the dust of the earth and gave them a special dignity among

all the works of creation. Human beings have been made for a relationship with God, to live in peace with each other, and to take care of
the rest of creation.[5]

Deity of Jesus: Jesus Christ is the Word of God became flesh. He is the
Savior of the world, who has delivered believers from the dominion of
sin and reconciled them to God by his death on a cross. He was declared to be the Son of God by his resurrection from the dead. He is the
head of the church, the exalted Lord—the lamb who was slain.[6]

Divorce and Remarriage: The Mennonite Church believes in chastity
and the loving faithfulness to marriage vows.[7]

Government: Congregations have a great deal of autonomy, but each is
expected to relate to the Conference. The National Assembly meets
biannually.

Heaven/Hell: The righteous will rise to eternal life with God, and the
unrighteous to hell and separation from God.[8]

Homosexuality: Any practice of genital sexuality outside of the marriage covenant is unacceptable.

Inspiration of Scripture: All Scripture is inspired by God through the
Holy Spirit for instruction in salvation and training in righteousness.
The Scriptures are the Word of God and are the fully reliable and trust-
worthy standard for Christian faith and life.[9]

Miracles: Typical Mennonite churches accept the validity of continuing
miracles.

Restrictions: Members avoid the swearing of oaths and violence of any
kind.[10]

Security of Salvation: Through the life, death, and resurrection of Jesus Christ, God offers salvation from sin and a new way of life to all
people. Believers receive God's salvation when they repent of sin and
accept Jesus Christ as Lord and Savior.[11]

Speaking in Tongues and Other Gifts of the Spirit: The denomination
does not take an official stand on speaking in tongues. It does occur in
a few congregations. As for other gifts of the Spirit, the church believes
by the gifts of the Holy Spirit that all Christians are called to carry out
their particular ministries.[12]

Trinity: There is one holy and loving God who is Father, Son, and Holy
Spirit eternally.[13]

Women in Ministry: The church calls, trains, and appoints gifted men and women to a variety of leadership ministries on its behalf. These may include such offices as pastor, deacon, and elder as well as evangelists, missionaries, teachers, conference ministers, and overseers.[14]

For more information contact: 421 S. 2nd St., Ste. 600, Elkhart, IN 46516; Phone: (219) 294-7131; Fax: (219) 293-3977; E-mail: mcgb@ juno.com

---

Minnesota Baptist Association

The Minnesota Baptist State Association was formed in 1857 and has as its motto, "A Light in the Darkness." Because each church is independent, the following answers may vary with each congregation. In 1996, there were 61 churches who were members of the Association.

Abortion: The church is opposed to abortion, which is against biblical truth.

Baptism: Baptism is an act of obedience for all who are born again in Jesus Christ. Baptism by immersion is required for church membership.

Birth Control: The church has no official statement on birth control.

Capital Punishment: Capital punishment is a biblical principle.

Christ's Return: The church is premillennial and believes in the pre-tribulational rapture of believers. Christ will return to earth following the tribulation to establish his millennial Kingdom.

Communion: Communion is an act of obedience for born again believers only. Communion is open to members of other churches which have like faith and practice.

Creation vs. Evolution: The Association takes a literal view of Genesis 1–12.

Deity of Christ: Christ is fully God, yet fully man also.

Divorce and Remarriage: Divorce is contrary to God's design for marriage.

Government: There is a congregational form of government in the church with two biblical offices: pastors and deacons. Local churches are autonomous.

Heaven/Hell: There is a heaven and a hell. Both are eternal.

Homosexuality: Homosexuality is unbiblical and therefore opposed.

Inspiration of Scripture: The Scriptures are God-breathed and inerrant in the original autographs.

Miracles: Miracles are performed by the power of God according to the will of God as recorded in the Scriptures.

Restrictions: Any restrictions are placed by local church constitutions. To be a part of the Association, one must be in good standing in a recognized Baptist Church in the Association's fellowship.

Security of Salvation: There is security of salvation. Those who are truly born again are kept by God's power.

Speaking in Tongues and Other Gifts of the Spirit: Sign gifts are not for this age.

Trinity: There is one equal, yet distinct, Godhead consisting of God the Father, Jesus Christ the Son, and the Holy Spirit.

Women in Ministry: Women are not allowed in pastoral ministry, as that is contrary to the Scriptures.

For more information contact: 5000 Golden Valley Rd., Minneapolis, MN 55422; Phone: (612) 588-2755; E-mail: mbaexec@juno.com

---

Missionary Church, Inc.

The Missionary Church, Inc., is the result of a merger in 1969 between the Missionary Church Association and the United Missionary Church. The Missionary Church Association was formed in 1898, branching from the Defenseless Mennonites. The United Missionary Church had come into being as the Mennonite Brethren in Christ, after the Evangelical United Mennonites (a previous union of three smaller Mennonite groups) and the Brethren in Christ merged in 1883. The name was changed to United Missionary Church in 1947. World missions and church planting are top priorities. There were 320 churches with 29,500 members in the United States in 1997.

Abortion: All life is a gift of God. In Scripture, God himself has conferred divine blessing upon unborn infants and has provided penalties for actions which result in the death of the unborn. Therefore, the Missionary Church stands for the sanctity of human life and is against abortion, infanticide, euthanasia, and the general eradication of the unique God-given dignity and worth of all human beings. Except to save the very life of the mother, abortion is morally wrong and sinful.

Baptism: Baptism by water is the symbol of one's union by faith with Christ in death, burial, and resurrection. It constitutes the public confession of these spiritual realities. It is to be administered by immersion to those who have been born again by faith in the Lord Jesus Christ.

Birth Control: The Missionary Church has no official statement regarding birth control. There is no opposition to measures which prevent conception, but there is opposition to any means which ends life following conception.

Capital Punishment: The church has no official statement regarding capital punishment, and is divided among its leaders and constituents on the issue. The majority of leaders who do support it would favor capital punishment only in the case of premeditated murder.

Christ's Return: The second advent of Christ will be personal, bodily, visible, premillennial, and redemptive. Christ will first descend into the clouds where his church will be caught up to meet him. After the tribulation judgments, which will be poured out upon the earth, he will return with his church to judge the nations and to establish his Kingdom wherein he will rule upon the earth for a thousand years.

Communion: The Missionary Church believes in communion as a memorial of Christ's death, a center of communion and fellowship, a testimony to saving faith, and a visible seal of Christ's redemptive covenant. It is to be observed only by the children of God. While the Lord's Supper is open to all true believers regardless of denomination, each participant is strongly exhorted to examine himself.

Creation vs. Evolution: Man was created by an immediate act of God and not by a process of evolution. The Scripture is without error or fault in what it states about God's act of creation.

Deity of Christ: The church believes in the deity of the Lord Jesus Christ, in his eternal generation from the Father, and in his incarnation. He was conceived by the Holy Spirit and born of the Virgin Mary, thus uniting the divine and human natures in their completeness into one unique person of Jesus Christ.

Divorce and Remarriage: Christians are to seek by forbearance and forgiveness to preserve the marriage bond. Persons divorced and remarried, who give evidence of being genuinely born again, are eligible to be received into membership of the church. Ministers are to refrain from performing marriage ceremonies where one or both parties are divorced, except where adultery of the previous marriage partner is involved.

Government: The General Conference is the representative body through which the denomination acts to carry out its objectives and to which are delegated the highest supervisory legislative, judiciary, and policy-making powers. It meets biennially. Each district is governed by an annual district conference which functions in accord with authority delegated to it by the constitution and the General Conference. Local churches govern themselves within the guidelines and jurisdiction of the constitution of the denomination. Congregational rule in local churches is the accepted method of governance, though the use of elders is also accepted with final authority resting with the congregation.

Heaven/Hell: The Missionary Church believes there are two eternal destinies for mankind: heaven and hell—the one for the righteous and penitent, and the other for the unrighteous and impenitent. After the Great White Throne Judgment, and after all enemies of God are consigned to their place of eternal punishment in the lake of fire with Satan and his angels, the present order of things will be dissolved. Then the new heaven and the new earth, where righteousness dwells, shall be created as the final state in which the righteous shall dwell forever.

Homosexuality: Homosexual activity, like adulterous relationships, is clearly condemned in the Scriptures. The practice of homosexuality is an abomination in God's sight and is sin. If persisted in, it excludes one from the Kingdom of God. Christians, ministers, and congregations should compassionately proclaim the good news of forgiveness and encourage those involved in homosexual practices to cease those actions, accept forgiveness, and pray for deliverance. Nothing is impossible with God.

Inspiration of Scripture: The Bible, consisting of the 66 books of the Old and New Testaments, is the Word of God given by inspiration and is inerrant in the original manuscripts. It remains the unchanging authority in matters of faith and practice. It is true and reliable in all matters it addresses. The church affirms that inspiration, strictly speaking, applies only to the autographic texts of Scripture which, in the providence of God, can be ascertained from available manuscripts with great accuracy.

Miracles: God, through Christ, actively performs miracles today as he has throughout all of history.

Restrictions: Restrictions on the use of tobacco, intoxicating beverages, narcotics, and other harmful products are urged. However, there is not consensus on the issue of total abstinence. One must be willing to be baptized by immersion as the Spirit gives understanding and must not be a member of any secret oath-bound society. Believers shall not marry unbelievers and shall not compromise Christian principles in partnerships.

Security of Salvation: The New Testament teaches consistently that the keeping power of God becomes effective through the exercise of faith. The tense of the verb used in a number of sections implies not only an initial act of faith but a maintained attitude. God's sovereign provision is coupled with human responsibility. The security taught in the New Testament is conditional security. Security is for the one who keeps on believing. A lapse of vital, operative, obedient faith can result from persistent backsliding and will result in apostasy.

Speaking in Tongues and Other Gifts of the Spirit: All the gifts of the Spirit are available to the church today. Every Christian has at least one gift, but should not expect to receive or to exercise all the gifts. Gifts are always related to service and are not to be used as a measure of Christian experience. There is such a phenomenon as speaking in tongues. This is a valid gift of the Spirit which some Christians have today. However, every Christian does not have to speak in tongues and this gift is not necessarily the evidence of the baptism with the Spirit.

Trinity: The one and only true God is Spirit: self existent, infinite, personal, unchangeable, and eternal in his being. He is the creator and sustainer of all things visible and invisible, eternally existent in three persons, one in substance, and co-equal in power and glory—Father, Son, and Holy Spirit.

Women in Ministry: The important role of women in ministry is clearly affirmed in both the Old and New Testaments and is a vital part of the heritage of the Missionary Church. At the same time, there is a functional difference reflected in the New Testament which does not deny the essential equality of men and women. The New Testament references indicate that the elder, overseer, and pastor-teacher (which refer to the same office) should be filled by men. Therefore, other than in a situation of need, only men may serve as a pastor in a church with one pastor or as a senior pastor in a church with multiple staff. The president, vice-president, district superintendents, and vice-district superintendents shall be men.

For more information contact: 3811 Vanguard Dr., P.O. Box 9127, Fort Wayne, IN 46899-9127; Phone: (219) 747-2027; Fax: (219) 747-5331; E-mail: missionary.church@internetmci.com

---

Moravian Church in America

The Moravian Church was begun in 1457 in Bohemia and Moravia (which is now the Czech Republic) and was renewed in Saxony (now Germany) in 1727. Missionary zeal for Native Americans brought Moravians to America in 1735. Pennsylvania (1740) and North Carolina (1735) became the centers of the church in the United States. The church claims two mottos, "In essentials unity, in nonessentials liberty, in all things love," and "Christ and Him Crucified remain our confession of faith." It emphasizes heart religion as well as head religion. There were 172 congregations in the U.S. in 1997.

Abortion: Abortion should be a matter of responsible personal decision, with continuing qualified medical and spiritual counseling provided if desired. Alternatives to abortion should be given careful consideration in the perspective of possibly bringing mercy to a difficult situation. Those choosing these alternatives should be offered adequate counseling during pregnancy and after delivery. Abortion should be accepted as an option only where all other possible alternatives will lead to greater destruction of human life and spirit.[15]

Baptism: Baptism into the death of Jesus is administered in the name of the Father, Son, and the Holy Spirit in the presence of the congregation. The more commom practice is infant baptism. Baptized children are encouraged to later publicly confess their faith in the rite of confirmation. Adult baptism, when practiced, is not to be interpreted as a rejection of infant baptism.[16]

Birth Control: No statement.

Capital Punishment: No statement.

Christ's Return: The Moravian Church believes that Christ will return. However, they do not take a position on when that will occur.

Communion: In the celebration of the Lord's Supper, the congregations are united with the Lord, enjoy the fruits of his sufferings and death for the forgiveness of sins, unite with each other anew as members of his body, and rejoice in the hope of his return.[17]

Creation vs. Evolution: No statement.

Deity of Jesus: God has revealed himself once and for all in his Son Jesus Christ. The Lord has redeemed the whole of humanity by his death and resurrection. There is no salvation apart from him.[18]

Divorce and Remarriage: Christian marriage is an indissoluble union, which requires the lifelong loyalty of the man and the woman. Because any breaking of the marriage bond involves sin against God and causes human suffering, it is the duty of the husband and wife to persistently work for reconciliation. If stability of the marriage is threatened, the couple should seek counseling from their pastor or other spiritual leader before any other action is taken.[19]

Government: The government is neither congregational nor hierarchical, but conferential. Pastoral calls must have the concurrence of pastor, congregation, and denomination. There are two provinces in the U.S., each with a representative assembly called a Synod which meets every four years. The Worldwide Synod meets every seven years.

Heaven/Hell: No statement.

Homosexuality: The Moravian Church openly welcomes all people. It specifically recognizes that the homosexual is under God's care. The church is not agreed on the question of the acceptability of homosexual practice. However, congregations are urged to make support systems available for people whose lives are affected by homosexual issues. The church is committed to support basic human rights and civil liberties for homosexual persons. They condemn acts of violence and coercion against homosexuals and are developing educational materials on homosexuality for use in congregations in their quest for understanding on this issue.[20]

Inspiration of Scripture: The Scripture is the sole standard for doctrine and faith of the Unitas Fratum.

Miracles: No statement.

Restrictions: None.

Security of Salvation: No statement.

Speaking in Tongues and Other Gifts of the Spirit: No statement.

Trinity: The triune God as revealed in the Holy Scripture of the Old and New Testaments is the only source for life and salvation.

Women in Ministry: Women have been in the ministry since 1970.

For more information contact: Drawer O, Winston-Salem, NC 27108; Phone: (910) 725-5811; Fax: (910) 723-1029; or P.O. Box 1245, Bethlehem, PA 18016-1245; Phone: (610) 867-0594; Fax: (610) 866-9223; Web site: http://www.moravian.org

---

Mount Sinai Holy Church of America, Inc.

Mount Sinai Holy Church of America was founded in 1924 in Philadelphia, PA by Bishop Ida Robinson. The church, whose motto is, "Ye shall be unto me a kingdom of priests and an holy nation," had more than 100 churches in the United States in 1996.

Abortion: Abortion is a sin. It is considered murder and is forbidden and preached against.

Baptism: The church baptizes in the name of the Father, and the Son, and the Holy Ghost. Baptisms are done by total immersion.

Birth Control: Birth control by mechanical means is totally forbidden.

Capital Punishment: Capital punishment is the taking of life which usurps God's authority. It is murder by civil authority and is contrary to the commandment, "Thou shall not kill."

Christ's Return: Christ will come again. Christ will come back for the church during the period called the rapture. He will come to reign on the earth as recorded in the book of Revelation.

Communion: Communion is an ordinance of the church that is carried out once a month. The elements used to remember the death of Jesus are unfermented grape juice and unleavened bread. Each participant is served with an individual cup.

Creation vs. Evolution: God created the heavens, the earth, and all living creatures as described in Genesis 1.

Deity of Christ: The Mount Sinai Holy Church of America believes that Jesus is the second person in the Godhead and is part of the Trinity.

Divorce and Remarriage: The Word of God gives cause for divorce but there are no provisions for remarriage.

Government: The church is governed by corporate officers which include the president, vice-president, secretary, and treasurer. There is a board of directors made up of the bishops of the church and some elders. The president is the chairperson of the board of directors.

Heaven/Hell: There is a literal heaven and hell as explained in the Holy Scriptures.

Homosexuality: The Scripture specifically speaks against it. The church should love the homosexual, but not their lifestyle.

Inspiration of Scripture: The church believes according to 1 Timothy 3:16.

Miracles: Miracles are performed by God to prove his omnipotence.

Restrictions: No gambling, no movie attendance, and no violation of the commandments. A dress code requires modest apparel and no makeup.

Security of Salvation: There is security in Christ as long as one lives by the commandments and the Word of God. Once Christ is accepted as Savior, the person remains a child of God as long as he does not practice sin. A person falls from grace when he reverts to a life of sin.

Speaking in Tongues and Other Gifts of the Spirit: The Mount Sinai Holy Church of America believes that the experience that took place in the upper room on the day of Pentecost is just as alive and active in the life of the believer as it was on the day of Pentecost. The church believes that one speaks in unknown languages upon being baptized in the Holy Ghost. Those who totally surrender to God are endowed with gifts of the Spirit.

Trinity: There are three persons in the Godhead: God the Father, God the Son, and God the Holy Spirit. Each plays his own role in the plan of salvation. God the Father gave his son, God the Son gave his life, and the Holy Spirit indwells all believers.

Women in Ministry: In Christ there is neither male nor female. Women in the church have full rights and the senior bishop is a women. There are many women pastors.

For more information contact: 129 Van Buskirk Rd., Teaneck, NJ 07666; Phone: (201) 833-1299; Fax: (201) 833-0323.

National Association of Congregational Christian Churches

A congregation of Pilgrims who gathered as Scrooby Church in England fled persecution first to Holland and then to America. This small group composed the Mayflower Compact, the first democratic treatise in the new world.[1] Congregational Christian Churches preceded the National Association, which was founded in 1955 by members of the CCC who opted not to merge with the United Church of Christ.[2] The National Association of Congregational Christian Churches is not a denomination but an association of churches joined together in fellowship. Therefore, the national office cannot speak for individual churches on the topics listed. While the following answers are practiced by a majority of member churches, some may have entirely different answers. Check with your local church. There were 430 churches with approximately 70,000 members in 1997 in the United States.

Abortion: No statement. Check with your local church.

Baptism: The church observes the practice of infant baptism in which the Christian family dedicates itself to the nurture of its child, the church accepts responsibility for the provision of Christian nurture for the child, and God's presence is made known. Baptism for the mature is an outer and visible sign of a desire to seek cleansing of life sin. It is usually done as an accompaniment to joining the church. The method may be sprinkling, pouring, or immersion, whichever is most meaningful to the person being baptized.[3]

Birth Control: No statement. Check with your local church.

Capital Punishment: No statement.

Christ's Return: No statement. Check with your local church.

Communion: The Lord's Supper is observed every month or every other month. The reverent repetition of the acts and words serve as a reminder of Jesus' life, death, and resurrection. It offers assurance of his spiritual presence and unites the believer in fellowship with him and other church members. All believers are invited to participate.[4]

Creation vs. Evolution: No statement. Check with your local church.

Deity of Jesus: No statement. Check with your local church.

Divorce and Remarriage: While there is no statement regarding divorce, the church affirms the importance of Christian marriage.[5]

Government: The NACCC is a fellowship of self-governing congregations working together in area associations, state conferences, national council, and missions bodies. Control and authority is reserved for the local church.[6]

Heaven/Hell: No statement. Check with your local church.

Homosexuality: No position. Check with your local church.

Inspiration of Scripture: No statement. Check with your local church.

Miracles: No statement. Check with your local church.

Restrictions: There are no set rules and regulations.

Security of Salvation: No statement. Check with your local church.

Speaking in Tongues and Other Gifts of the Spirit: No statement. Check with your local church.

Trinity: No statement. Check with your local church.

Women in Ministry: Congregational ministers may be either a male or female who has prepared themselves with four years of college and three years of seminary, who has been invited to be a minister, and who has been ordained by their member church.[7] Congregational churches have had women ministers for more than 200 years.

For more information contact: 8473 S. Howell Ave., Milwaukee, WI 53154; Phone: (800) 262-1620 or (414) 764-1620; Fax: (414) 764-0319; E-mail: naccc1620@aol.com; Web site: http://www.arosnet.com/~fcc/web_page/naccc/index.html

---

National Association of Free Will Baptists, Inc.

With the influence of Arminian Baptists who came to the new world from England, two segments of Free Will Baptists began around the same time. The Palmer movement (or southern group) was started by Paul Palmer in Chowan, NC in 1727. Benjamin Randall started a northern congregation on June 30, 1780 in New Durham, NH.[8] In 1910–1911, the northern group of Free Will Baptists merged with the Northern Baptist denomination. Representatives from the remnants of the Randall movement and the Palmer movement met in Nashville, TN on Nov. 5, 1935 and organized the National Association of Free Will Baptists. The church practices the washing of feet as a sacred ordinance which teaches humility and reminds the believer of the necessity of a daily cleansing from all sin. In 1996, there were 2,485 congregations with 207,576 members in the United States.

Abortion: The church is pro-life and anti-abortion because they believe the Bible teaches that life begins at conception. They oppose the use of unborn babies, or any part thereof, for research and other purposes.[9]

Baptism: Christian baptism is the immersion of believers in water, in the name of the Father, the Son, and the Holy Spirit, in which are represented the burial and resurrection of Christ, the death of Christians to the world, the washing of their souls from the pollution of sin, their rising to newness of life, their engagement to serve God, and their resurrection at the last day.[10]

Birth Control: The church condemns and deplores any distribution of birth control devices that encourages and condones immoral behavior.[11]

Capital Punishment: The National Association of Free Will Baptists supports capital punishment as a deterrent to and a punishment for crime.[12]

Christ's Return: The Lord Jesus Christ, who ascended on high and sits at the right hand of God, will come again to close the Gospel dispensation, glorify his saints, and judge the world.[13]

Communion: The Lord's Supper is the commemoration of the death of Christ for sins in the use of bread, which he made the emblem of his broken body, and the cup, the emblem of his shed blood. By it the believer expresses his love for Christ, his faith and hope in him, and he pledges to him perpetual fidelity.[14]

Creation vs. Evolution: God created the world and all things that it contains for his own pleasure and glory and the enjoyment of his creatures.[15]

Deity of Jesus: Christ is God manifest in the flesh. In his divine nature, he is truly God. In his human nature, he is truly man. The mediator between God and man, he was once crucified. He is now risen and glorified and is the ever present Savior and Lord.[16]

Divorce and Remarriage: While the ideal of one husband and one wife is biblically insisted upon for elders, deacons, and ministers, it is an ideal for all believers. No one may serve in the capacity of elder, deacon, or minister if they have been divorced and remarried, regardless of the circumstances.[17]

Government: The local church is independent and self-governing. These churches form associations which organize and cooperate as Free Will Baptist. The associations are organized in either four or five circles, with the local church forming the first circle and the National Association forming the final circle.[18]

Heaven/Hell: All men will be resurrected on the last day. Those who have done good will be resurrected to life, while those who have done evil will be resurrected to damnation.[19]

Homosexuality: Homosexuality is sin, its participants are sinners, and the practice and the participant are condemned by God.[20]

Inspiration of Scripture: The Old and New Testaments were written by holy men inspired by the Holy Spirit. They are God's revealed Word to man. They are a sufficient and infallible rule and guide to salvation and all Christian worship and service. Since the Bible is the Word of God, it is without error in all matters upon which it speaks, whether history, geography, or matters relating to science or any other subject.[21]

Miracles: All the miracles recorded in the Bible are authentic.

Restrictions: Members are encouraged to avoid pornography and alcohol.[22] They are also encouraged to avoid secular labor on the Sabbath.[23]

Security of Salvation: A saved individual may, in freedom of will, cease to trust in Christ for salvation and once again be lost.[24]

Speaking in Tongues and Other Gifts of the Spirit: Speaking in tongues is not a valid gift for the church today because of the complete revelation of God given in the Bible. Speaking in tongues is not a visible sign of the baptism of the Holy Spirit.[25]

Trinity: There is one living and true God, revealed in nature as the creator, preserver, and righteous governor of the universe, and in the Scriptures as Father, Son, and Holy Ghost. Yet he is one God, infinitely wise and good.[26]

Women in Ministry: Free Will Baptist women have their own organization. The Women Nationally Active for Christ is a subsidiary organization of the National Association. It is authorized to organize at its own discretion and has power to create and adopt a constitution and by-laws. It maintains complete management of the work for which it is constituted.

For more information contact: P.O. Box 5002, Antioch, TN 37011-5002 or 5233 Mt. View Rd., Antioch, TN 37013-2306; Phone: (615) 731-6812; Fax (615) 731-0771; E-mail: mlw@nafwb.org; Web site: http://www.nafwb.org

---

National Association of Holiness Churches

At the Singing Hill Camp Ground, near Shoals, IN, an organizational meeting was held to form the National Association of Holiness Churches. This new organization was chartered under the laws of the state of Indiana on September 5, 1967. In 1996, there were 73 churches in the United States. The Association believes that the Bible teaches a second work of grace, subsequent to regeneration, whereby the believer is made perfect in love.

Abortion: The NAHC is opposed to abortion, except when the life of the mother is in danger.

Baptism: Baptism is an outward sign of an inward change of heart. The church does not believe in infant baptism.

Birth Control: No official statement.

Capital Punishment: While the association does not have an official statement, many of its members believe the Bible teaches capital punishment should be administered by civil authorities when it is necessary.

Christ's Return: The second coming of Christ will be premillennial and is imminent.

Communion: The taking of communion is a token of the symbolic act of sharing in Christ's redemptive plan of salvation.

Creation vs. Evolution: The Bible clearly teaches that man was created by God in his own image.

Deity of Jesus: The National Association of Holiness Churches believes in the deity of Jesus Christ as the Son of God.

Divorce and Remarriage: The Bible teaches that divorce and remarriage is evil. The marriage covenant is, "Until death do us part."

Government: Each member church, organization, or institution is regarded as autonomous and thus free to control its own finances, property, and ministry, to call its own pastor, and elect its own governing board and officers.

Heaven/Hell: There is a heaven prepared for those who have been made pure in heart, perfect in love, and continue steadfast in God's perfect fellowship. All others are doomed to a lake of fire and brimstone called hell.

Homosexuality: Homosexual practice is an abomination to God. The National Association of Holiness Churches therefore denounces it in the strongest way possible.

Inspiration of Scripture: All Scripture is given by inspiration of God. The Scriptures are inerrant.

Miracles: The NAHC believes in all the miracles that were performed in the Bible and further believes that God still performs miracles today in response to the faith and prayers of his true followers.

Restrictions: The church opposes card-playing, games of chance, wearing jewelry, television, movies, videos, drugs, alcohol, tobacco, and worldly places of amusement.

Security of Salvation: Salvation is conditional.

Speaking in Tongues and Other Gifts of the Spirit: The speaking in tongues is languages, or tongues wherein they were born.

Trinity: The Father, Son, and Holy Ghost are three distinct and separate personalities.

Women in Ministry: Women minister and are ordained.

For more information contact: 351 S. Park Dr., Griffith, IN 46319; Phone: (219) 924-3354.

Netherlands Reformed Congregations

The Netherlands Reformed Congregations are closely associated with a sister denomination in the Netherlands (Gereformeerde, Gemeenten) which formed under the leadership of Rev. G.H. Kersten in 1907. There were 23 congregations with 4,463 baptized members in 1995.

Abortion: The Netherlands Reformed Congregations are opposed to abortion unless the mother's life is endangered.

Baptism: The sacrament of baptism has come in the place of circumcision and therefore is also administered to infants of professing members.

Birth Control: Since marriage has been the means whereby the human race is to be continued, the receiving of children is a great gift of God. Therefore, the avoiding of pregnancy in order to enjoy the luxuries of life or to escape the burden of raising children is not justifiable. The husband and wife must act responsibly under the command of God to be fruitful.

Capital Punishment: Whoever sheds man's blood, by man shall his blood be shed.

Christ's Return: Christ shall return at the last day. Then he will appear to judge.

Communion: The sacraments are holy signs and seals appointed by God for the strengthening of the faith of his people. The Holy Ghost works faith in their hearts by the preaching of the gospel, and confirms and strengthens it by the sacraments.

Creation vs. Evolution: The creation as recorded in Genesis 1 and 2 is a record of historical facts, not a myth.

Deity of Jesus: Jesus Christ is the only begotten Son of God, begotten from eternity, co-essential, and co-eternal with the Father and the Holy Ghost.

Divorce and Remarriage: Divorce is only possible when adultery has taken place, since that which God has joined together may not be put asunder.

Government: Presbyterian.

Heaven/Hell: The future dwelling place of the righteous is heaven. Hell is the future abode of the wicked.

Homosexuality: Homosexuality is condemned by God's Word.

Inspiration of Scripture: The Word of God was not sent nor delivered by the will of man, but holy men of God spoke as they were moved by the Holy Ghost. The Three Forms of Unity, which consist of the Heidelberg Catechism, the Belgic Confession of Faith, and the Canons of Dordt, are subservient to the Word of God.

Miracles: The miracles which took place in the time of the Lord Jesus and the apostles were special for those days. However, the Lord continues to be active in providing his wonders in the lives of people, especially his people.

Restrictions: Members are warned against the entertainments of the world such as television, the theater, dancing, and fashions.

Security of Salvation: The assurance of salvation is possible.

Speaking in Tongues and Other Gifts of the Spirit: The extraordinary gifts of the Spirit at the time of the apostles no longer exist. However, the Lord bestows talents and gifts to men as it pleases him.

Trinity: There is only one God, who is one single essence, yet distinguished in three persons—the Trinity: the Father, the Son, and the Holy Ghost.

Women in Ministry: Scripture does not allow women in ministry.

For more information contact: 3211 Woodmont Dr., Portage, MI 49002; Phone: (616) 345-3475; Fax: (616) 383-2001.

New England Evangelical Baptist Fellowship

The New England Evangelical Baptist Fellowship is a small group that recently celebrated their 150th anniversary. In 1997, there were 25 churches associated with the Fellowship.

Abortion: Abortion is allowed only to preserve the mother's safety.

Baptism: Baptism is by immersion.

Birth Control: Couples must seek the Lord's will on the use of birth control.

Capital Punishment: The New England Evangelical Baptist Fellowship supports capital punishment.

Christ's Return: Christ will come again.

Communion: At least one Sunday a month is set aside to celebrate communion.

Creation vs. Evolution: As the Scripture says in Genesis, God created all things.

Deity of Jesus: Jesus is deity.

Divorce and Remarriage: Divorce and subsequent remarriage are determined according to circumstances. However, the Fellowship prefers
not to remarry divorced persons.

Government: Churches are autonomous.

Heaven/Hell: There is a literal heaven and hell.

Homosexuality: Homosexuality is not scriptural.

Inspiration of Scripture: The Scriptures were inspired by God and only
they can make man a new person in Christ.

Miracles: Miracles still happen. Christ sponsors them when a believer
is in him.

Restrictions: None.

Security of Salvation: The New England Evangelical Baptist Fellowship believes in eternal security as taught by the Lord in the Gospels.

Speaking in Tongues and Other Gifts of the Spirit: Speaking in
tongues is acceptable if it is truly a gift of the Spirit as taught by the
Lord.

Trinity: The Trinity is three persons: God the Father, Jesus the Son of
God, and the Holy Spirit.

Women in Ministry: Women are allowed to minister when they are truly called of God in their particular services.

For more information contact: 40 Bridge St., Newton, MA 02158;
Phone: (617) 527-0189.

North American Baptist Conference

While the roots of the Conference are not specifically German, early on
the church was influenced by immigrants and a sister church from that
country. When German pilgrims came to America, religious bodies
sprang up to meet their spiritual needs. Conferences were formed and divided over the years, resulting in a church that was less ethnically ori-
ented.[27] In 1995, there were more than 385 churches with a total membership of more than 62,500 in the United States and Canada.

Abortion: The church is pro-life.

Baptism: Baptism is the immersion of a believer in water in the name of the Father, Son, and Holy Spirit. It is an act of obedience symbolizing the believer's identification with the death, burial, and resurrection of Jesus Christ.[28]

Birth Control: No official position.

Capital Punishment: No statement.

Christ's Return: The North American Baptist Conference believes in the imminent, physical return of Christ.

Communion: The Lord's Supper is the partaking of the bread and the cup by believers together as a continuing memorial of the broken body and shed blood of Christ. It is an act of thankful dedication to him and serves to unite his people until he returns.[29]

Creation vs. Evolution: God created man in his own image to have fellowship with himself and to be stewards over his creation.[30]

Deity of Jesus: Jesus Christ was conceived of the Holy Spirit and born of the Virgin Mary. Being fully God and fully man, he revealed God through his sinless life, miracles, and teaching. He provided salvation through his atoning death and by his bodily resurrection. He ascended into heaven where he rules over all creation. He intercedes for believers and dwells in them as their ever-present Lord.[31]

Divorce and Remarriage: Divorce is sin. There is no official statement on remarriage.

Government: Congregational. Each local church is self-governing, however it is also voluntarily united with other congregations in associations. There is a triennial conference.[32]

Heaven/Hell: The unrighteous will be consigned to the everlasting punishment prepared for the devil and his angels. The righteous, in their resurrected and glorified bodies, will receive their reward and dwell forever with the Lord.[33]

Homosexuality: Homosexuality is a sinful, but forgivable, practice.

Inspiration of Scripture: The Bible is God's Word given by divine inspiration—the record of God's revelation of himself to humanity. It is trustworthy, sufficient, and without error. It is the supreme authority and guide for all doctrine and conduct. It is the truth by which God brings people into a saving relationship with himself and leads them to Christian maturity.[34]

Miracles: Miracles still happen today.

Restrictions: None.

Security of Salvation: The North American Baptist Conference believes in the security of true believers.

Speaking in Tongues and Other Gifts of the Spirit: No official stand.

Trinity: There is one living and true God, perfect in wisdom, sovereignty, holiness, justice, mercy, and love. He exists in three co-equal persons who act together in creation, providence, and redemption.[35]

Women in Ministry: No answer.

For more information contact: 1 S. 210 Summit Ave., Oakbrook Terrace, IL 60181-3994; Phone: (630) 495-2000; Fax: (630) 495-3301; Web site: http://www.midplains.net/~brandel/baptist.htm

---

Old German Baptist Brethren

The Old German Baptist Brethren date back to the ministries of Alexander Mack (see entry above). Organized in Germany in 1708,[1] and one of the larger branches that subsequently divided,[2] the church had 55 congregations and 5,500 members in 1997. It believes in nonconformity to the world in lifestyle and entertainment. Members wear plain clothes, practice nonresistance and feet washing, and sisters wear prayer coverings.

Abortion: Although there is no official statement, the church considers it a grave sin.

Baptism: Water baptism is by triune immersion with a forward action. Baptism of the Spirit accompanies water baptism when preceded by faith and repentance.

Birth Control: The matter of birth control is left to each family's discretion.

Capital Punishment: No official statement.

Christ's Return: Jesus Christ will return literally, and soon.

Communion: The bread and the cup are a sacred ordinance of the church.

Creation vs. Evolution: The church believes the Genesis account to be literal and true.

Deity of Jesus: Jesus Christ is God, the Son.

Divorce and Remarriage: Any person with one of two (or more) living spouses, would not be eligible for membership.

Government: The authority of the church lies in the Spirit-led body. Councils are held congregationally once a year at an annual brotherhood conference.

Heaven/Hell: Heaven and hell are literal realities.

Homosexuality: The practice of homosexuality is an abominable sin.

Inspiration of Scripture: All Scriptures are inspired of God.

Miracles: The miracle gifts expired with the Apostles. However, miracles still occur, especially in the spiritual realm.

Restrictions: Television, radio, attending theaters, and other worldly entertainments are prohibited.

Security of Salvation: There is no security for wicked believers. Security is in Christ.

Speaking in Tongues and Other Gifts of the Spirit: The sign gifts have ceased.

Trinity: The Old German Baptist Brethren believe in the deity of the Father, the Son, and the Holy Ghost.

Women in Ministry: Women have no preaching or teaching ministry in the church.

For more information contact: 701 State Rt. 571, Union City, OH 45390; Phone and Fax: (937) 968-3877.

Open Bible Standard Churches, Inc.

In 1935, two revival movements, Bible Standard Conference of Eugene, OR and Open Bible Evangelistic Association of Des Moines, IA, merged to form Open Bible Standard Churches.[3] The church has as its purpose statement, "Introducing." There were approximately 360 churches with 45,000 members in the United States in 1997.

Abortion: The moral issue of abortion is more than a question of the freedom of a woman to control the reproductive functions of her own body. It is rather a question of those circumstances under which a hu-

man being may be permitted to take the life of another. The church deplores in the strongest possible terms the decision of the U.S. Supreme
Court which has made it legal to terminate a pregnancy. In extreme cases, where the life of the unborn child threatens the life of the mother,
the doctor has two patients and should try to save both lives.[4]

Baptism: Water baptism, by immersion in the name of the Father, Son,
and Holy Ghost, is subsequent to conversion. It is not a saving ordinance, but an outward sign of an inward work.[5]

Birth Control: No statement.

Capital Punishment: No statement.

Christ's Return: The second coming of Christ is personal, imminent,
and premillennial. The Lord himself will descend from heaven and the
dead in Christ shall rise first. Then the redeemed which are alive and
remain shall be caught up together with them in the air. The coming of
Jesus Christ with his saints will end the great tribulation and establish
the millennial Kingdom on earth, when Christ shall rule and reign as
King of kings and Lord of lords.[6]

Communion: The commemoration of the Lord's Supper is: a type of the
broken body and shed blood of Jesus Christ; an ordinance showing
forth the death, burial, and resurrection; and a looking forward to the
marriage supper of the lamb. All Christian believers, regardless of
church affiliation, may partake.[7]

Creation vs. Evolution: God made the heavens and the earth and all that
is in them.[8]

Deity of Jesus: Jesus is coexistent and coeternal with the Father. He was
conceived by the Holy Spirit, born of the Virgin Mary, and took upon
himself the form of man. By his becoming obedient unto death, bearing the curse of sin, sickness, and sorrow, he redeemed believers back
to God. He arose the third day and ascended into heaven, where he sits
on the right hand of God, the Father. There he lives to make intercession.[9]

Divorce and Remarriage: Marriage was instituted by God, sanctioned
by Jesus Christ, and commended of Saint Paul to be honorable among
all men. A Christian man or woman should not marry an unsaved person. Having been united by God in holy matrimony, neither person, as
long as both shall live, shall be free to remarry, except in the case of
adultery.[10]

Government: Individual churches are congregationally governed, locally owned, and are affiliated by a charter with Open Bible Standard Churches. The highest governing body is the biennial national convention. Ministers and church delegates assume responsibility for oversight of the constitution, bylaws, and general direction. The national Board of Directors, consisting of national and regional representatives, approves policies for the movement.[11]

Heaven/Hell: Hell is a literal place of outer darkness, bitter sorrow, remorse, and woe. It was prepared by God for the devil and his angels. There, into a lake that burns with fire and brimstone, the unbelieving, the abominable, the murderers, sorcerers, idolaters, all liars, and those who have rejected the love of Jesus Christ shall be cast. Heaven is the habitation of the living God, where Christ has gone to prepare a place for all his children, where they shall dwell eternally in happiness and security with him.[12]

Homosexuality: The Holy Scriptures condemn practicing homosexuality and give no basis for approving this as an acceptable lifestyle. However, the church wants to extend the healing ministry of the entire Christian community to individuals who seek forgiveness and deliverance from the sin of homosexuality.[13]

Inspiration of Scripture: The Bible is the inspired Word of God and is the only infallible guide and rule for faith and practice.[14]

Miracles: The Holy Spirit has bestowed gifts upon the believer for the edification of the saints and the upbuilding of the church. These include gifts of healing, working of miracles, prophecy, discerning of spirits, diverse kinds of tongues, and the interpretation of tongues.[15]

Restrictions: Members are encouraged to abstain from alcohol, tobacco, substance abuse, and gambling.[16]

Security of Salvation: No statement.

Speaking in Tongues and Other Gifts of the Spirit: The baptism of the Holy Spirit is a definite experience, not identical with conversion. The initial evidence of this experience is the speaking in other tongues.[17]

Trinity: The Open Bible Standard Church believes in the eternal, omnipotent, omniscient, omnipresent, and immutable triune God. In the unity of the Godhead there are three persons, equal in every divine perfection and attribute, executing distinct but harmonious offices in the great work of redemption.[18]

Women in Ministry: Women are ordained.

For more information contact: 2020 Bell Ave., Des Moines, IA 50315; Phone: (515) 288-6761; Fax: (515) 288-2510.

Orthodox Presbyterian Church

In 1054, two churches of long-standing tradition and rivalry split over the issue of whether the Holy Spirit proceeds from the Father and Son (as the western or Catholic church believed) or from the Father only (as the eastern or Orthodox church professed). The Orthodox Presbyterian Church, despite its name, is a branch of the Western Church. The OPC was also strongly influenced by the Protestant Reformation of the 16th century and uses the Westminster Confession of Faith and Catechisms as its basis for doctrinal standards. Immigrants who came to America from Scotland, Ireland, and England established Presbyterian churches, which split geographically during the Civil War. The OPC came out of the northern Presbyterian church and was officially constituted on June 11, 1936 as the Presbyterian Church of America. After conflict with the Presbyterian Church in the USA, the group changed its name in 1939 to the current. There were 220 congregations in the U.S. and Canada in 1997.[19]

Abortion: The church denounces the practice of voluntary abortion except possibly for the purpose of saving the mother's life.[20]

Baptism: Baptism is to be administered to the children of believers, as well as to believers.[21]

Birth Control: No statement.

Capital Punishment: No statement.

Christ's Return: No statement.

Communion: The body and blood of Christ are spiritually present to the faith of believers.[22]

Creation vs. Evolution: God created the heavens and the earth and all they contain.[23]

Deity of Jesus: The Son of God took upon himself a human nature in the womb of the Virgin Mary so that in her son, Jesus, the divine and human natures were united in one person. Jesus Christ lived a sinless life and died on a cross, bearing the sins of, and receiving God's wrath for, all those who trust in him for salvation. He rose from the dead and ascended into heaven, where he sits as Lord and rules over his Kingdom.[24]

Divorce and Remarriage: No statement.

Government: The church is governed by elders, including ministers. Each congregation chooses its own elders, who are in turn responsible to regional and national assemblies of their peers.[25]

Heaven/Hell: No statement.

Homosexuality: The 1993 Assembly framed a petition urging the President of the United States to stand against the sin of homosexuality and specifically not to lift the ban on homosexuals in the military.[26]

Inspiration of Scripture: The Bible, having been inspired by God, is entirely trustworthy and without error. Therefore, its teachings should be believed and obeyed. The Bible is the only source of special revelation for the church today.[27]

Miracles: No statement.

Restrictions: Members are to avoid Freemasonry.[28]

Security of Salvation: Believers persevere to the end in communion with Christ, with assurance of their salvation.[29]

Speaking in Tongues and Other Gifts of the Spirit: The charismatic movement alleges that speaking in tongues, miraculous healings, and special revelations are present in the church today. The OPC rejects these claims, believing that these special gifts of the Holy Spirit ceased at the end of the Apostolic age, their purposes having been achieved.[30]

Trinity: In the unity of the Godhead there are three persons: the Father, the Son, and the Holy Spirit.[31]

Women in Ministry: All officers must be men, not women.[32]

For more information contact: 607 N. Easton Rd., Bldg. E, Willow Grove, PA 19090-0920; Phone: (215) 830-0900; Fax: (215) 830-0350; Web site: http://www.opc.org/

PDI

PDI, formerly People of Destiny International, traces its origins to relationships forged at Take and Give (TAG), a Washington, DC teaching ministry that held meetings from 1973–79. In 1977, approximately 40 adults associated with TAG began meeting. This group evolved into the 2,000 member Covenant Life Church in Gaithersburg, MD. Out of this congregation grew a vision for an association of churches. PDI's first church planting took place in 1981. The group holds to an essentially Reformed doctrinal perspective, while espousing a significant charismatic theology and dimension to their faith. In 1996, there were 30 churches in the United States with a membership totaling 11,000 that took the motto, "Proclaiming God's Grace, Developing Local Churches, Influencing Our World With the Gospel."

Abortion: Human life, both material (body) and immaterial (soul), begins at conception. Therefore, abortion is forbidden by God as the taking of an innocent human life. The only exception to this would be the rare case where the mother, and as a consequence the child, would die if the pregnancy were to continue. Even in this case everything possible should be done to preserve both lives. It is the church's responsibility to extend compassion and care to those who become pregnant out of wedlock and to promote adoption as an alternative to abortion.

Baptism: Baptism is an outward depiction symbolizing the inward reality of a believer's union with Christ in his death, burial, and resurrection to new life. Although it is not necessary for salvation, it is God's command for those who have responded to the Gospel with repentance and faith. Because such a response is not possible for an infant, infant baptism is excluded. In keeping with the only biblical example, and with the events which it symbolizes, baptism should be by immersion.

Birth Control: At no point does Scripture forbid non-abortive methods of birth control, and therefore there is no warrant for outright prohibition of every kind of family-planning practice. However, prospective parents should be extremely cautious regarding their motives behind limiting the size of their families. Because children are a gift from the Lord to be received with great joy and thanksgiving, each married couple should sincerely seek the Lord's will regarding family size and spacing, taking into account legitimate factors such as calling, capacity, age, and economic status, while being aware of temptations to materialism, fear, and selfishness.

Capital Punishment: Scripture teaches the principle of capital punishment for the shedding of innocent blood, since man is made in the image of God. It is part of the responsibility of the civil authority (which is ordained by God) to punish evildoers. Neglect of this responsibility on the part of the civil authority results in decreasing respect for human life.

Christ's Return: The consummation of all things includes: the visible, personal, and glorious return of Jesus Christ; the resurrection of the dead and the translation of those alive in Christ; the judgment of the just and the unjust; and the fulfillment of Christ's Kingdom in the new heavens and the new earth. Then shall the eager expectation of creation be fulfilled and the whole earth shall proclaim the glory of God who makes all things new. Although Christ's return and the fulfillment of all that is promised in Scripture is certain, no man knows or can know when this will take place.

Communion: Instituted by Jesus Christ, the Lord's Supper is regularly celebrated by Christians as a means of remembering his death, which was on their behalf as a punishment for their sins. The elements of bread and wine are symbolic of Jesus' body and blood poured out for the forgiveness of sins. The Lord's Supper is open to all who are believers in Jesus Christ. It is a solemn yet joyful expression of God's love for his people, keeping ever before them the centrality of the cross of Christ.

Creation vs. Evolution: The events of Genesis chapters 1 and 2 present an unambiguous account of God creating the universe and all that is in it out of nothing over a period of six, 24-hour days. Subsequently, God has and will continue sovereignly and providentially to uphold, govern, and care for his creation, in detail, for all eternity. Any theory of evolution—either that God did not create or that he created through evolutionary processes—is incompatible with the clear biblical revelation of special creation and providence. These truths establish an essential relationship to God as creator and Lord, and are thus vital to the Christian profession and walk.

Deity of Jesus: Jesus Christ is fully God and fully man, the image of the invisible God, who was always with God and is God, and in whom bodily dwells the fullness of the Godhead. He is the only begotten Son of God, the eternal Word made flesh, supernaturally conceived by the Holy Spirit, and born of the Virgin Mary. The first born of all creation, through him all things came into being and were created, for he was before all things and in him all things hold together by the power of his word. Following his vicarious death on Calvary's cross for all mankind, his burial and his resurrection, he ascended into heaven where, at God's right hand, he intercedes for his people and rules as Lord over all.

Divorce and Remarriage: God's intent from the beginning of time is that marriage should be honored by a life-long commitment between a man and a woman. However, Scripture does allow two exceptions to God's prohibitions: divorce and remarriage are allowed in the case of adultery, and remarriage is permitted in the case of desertion and divorce by an unbelieving spouse. Even in these cases divorce should be a last resort. A Christian couple should seek reconciliation rather than divorce, even in the case of adultery.

Government: The governmental leadership of churches in the New Testament is plural and male. Extra-local apostolic ministry is responsible for establishing churches. Locally, the terms elder, pastor, and bishop may be used to describe different aspects of the same individuals, who are leaders charged with the responsibility of overseeing the doctrine and practice of the church as well as the pastoral care of members. The standards for these leaders given in 1 Timothy and Titus 1 are high, and since they must give an account to God for their work, they must be called by God and demonstrate the gifts necessary to fulfill that call.

Heaven/Hell: In the consummation, Satan with his hosts and all those outside Christ are finally separated from the benevolent presence of God forever, enduring eternal punishment. The righteous in glorious bodies shall live and reign sinlessly with Christ forever in an actual and perfect physical universe—the new heavens and new earth. Married to Christ as his bride, the church will be in the presence of God forever, serving him and giving him unending praise and glory.

Homosexuality: In Scripture, homosexuality is forbidden both explicitly and implicitly (the only biblical context for sexual relations being marriage between a man and a woman). According to the New Testament, homosexuality is degrading, unnatural, indecent, and perverted, and no homosexual will inherit the Kingdom of God. Therefore, the Christian cannot treat homosexuality as an alternative lifestyle but only as a sin to be repented of and overcome. Like any other sin it can be conquered by God's regenerating and sanctifying power. The church's responsibility is to call such sinners to repentance and graciously help them in the process of overcoming their sins.

Inspiration of Scripture: The Bible—the 39 books of the Old Testament and the 27 books of the New Testament—is the written Word of God, an essential and infallible record of God's self-disclosure to mankind which leads them to salvation through faith in Jesus Christ.

It is the authoritative and normative rule and guide of all Christian life, practice, and doctrine. Being given by God, the Scriptures are both fully and verbally inspired by God, and therefore, as originally given, the Bible is free of error in all it teaches. Each book is to be interpreted according to its context and purpose and in reverent obedience to the Lord who speaks through it in living power. The Scriptures are not to be added to, superseded, or changed by later tradition or extra-biblical revelation. Every doctrinal formulation, whether of creed, confession, or theology, must be put to the test of the full counsel of God in Holy Scripture.

Miracles: A miracle is a uniquely powerful and unusual event in which God acts to bear witness to the message of the Gospel or help his people. Examples of biblical miracles are resurrections, healings, the parting of the Red Sea, extending the day, and the Incarnation. Such an event produces awe and wonder (or in the case of the hard-hearted, scoffing and unbelief) among those who see or hear of it. Because God is providentially in control of his creation, the possibility of miracles still exists. The motive for miracles still exists because God still desires to bear witness to the Gospel and to help his people. Therefore, Christians should pray for and believe in miracles today.

Restrictions: PDI believes the real issue of restrictions involves the believer's obligation to obey the moral law. Christ did away with the law as a means of obtaining righteousness, but not as a directive for holy living. Therefore, the believer is both obligated and graciously enabled to obey whatever God commands. Where there is no command, the believer is free to choose for himself based on the principles set forth in Scripture. Although there may be times when a believer willingly accepts certain restrictions out of love and respect for fellow believers, accepting tradition-based or legalistic restrictions that have no basis in Scripture is never needed.

Security of Salvation: No official position.

Speaking in Tongues and Other Gifts of the Spirit: All the gifts of the Holy Spirit at work in the church of the first century are available today and are to be earnestly desired and expected. This includes the gift of tongues, which can be received and used by all believers for personal edification. The purpose of these gifts is to edify the church and help individuals in their ministry to the world. The main emphasis of Scripture is not on possessing a gift but on using that gift to serve God and his people. The gifts of the Spirit are not optional extras but essentials in the mission of the church today.

Trinity: There is one God: infinite, eternal, almighty, and perfect in holiness, truth, and love. In the unity of the Godhead there are three persons: Father, Son, and Holy Spirit, who are co-existent, co-equal, and co-eternal. The Father is not the Son and the Son is not the Holy Spirit, yet each is truly deity. This one God—Father, Son, and Holy Spirit—is the foundation of Christian faith and life.

Women in Ministry: Both men and women are made in God's image and therefore have equal value in his sight. God places equally high value on the unique roles of both men and women—roles that are not concession to sin, but part of God's original intent. Scripture clearly prohibits women from exercising governmental authority over men in the church.

For more information contact: 7881 Beechcraft Ave., Ste. B, Gaithersburg, MD 20879; Phone: (301) 926-2200; Fax: (301) 948-7833; E-mail: pdi@pdinet.org; Web site: http://www.westol.com/~bassmstr/pdi

---

Pentecostal Church of God, Inc.

Modern Pentecostalism has its beginnings in the ministry of Charles Fox Parham, who opened Bethel Bible College as a "faith school," charging no tuition. At Bethel, the conclusion was first reached that speaking in tongues is the initial evidence of the infilling of the Holy Spirit. The Pentecostal message spread until on December 30, 1919, in Chicago, IL, the Pentecostal Assemblies of the USA was born. The church, whose motto is, "Proclaiming Bible Truth in Pentecostal Power," was reorganized and renamed the Pentecostal Church of God in 1922. General offices changed locations several times before settling in Joplin, MO.[1] In 1997, there were 1,264 congregations in the United States.

Abortion: The church is against abortion and is pro-life.

Baptism: Baptism is performed in water by immersion and is for believers only. The ordinance is a symbol of the Christian's identification with Christ in his death, burial, and resurrection.[2]

Birth Control: No official position.

Capital Punishment: No official position.

Christ's Return: The Pentecostal Church of God believes that the Bible presents the coming of Christ as personal imminent, pretribulational, and premillennial. This position alone admonishes watchfulness, incites holy living, prevents spiritual declension, and provides maximum incentive and motive for urgency and zeal in evangelizing the unsaved.[3]

Communion: The ordinance of the Lord's Supper is a commandment of the Savior. Being a memorial to his death and resurrection, it is strictly limited to Christians. The time and frequency of its observance is left to the discretion of each congregation.[4]

Creation vs. Evolution: Creation is as described in Genesis 1:1.

Deity of Christ: The Son is eternally begotten of the Father. He accepted earthly limitations for the purpose of incarnation, being true God and true man. He was conceived by the Holy Ghost and born of the Virgin Mary. He died upon the cross, the just for the unjust, as a substitutionary sacrifice. All who believe in him are justified on the grounds of his shed blood. He arose from the dead according to the Scriptures. He is now at the right hand of the Majesty on High as the great high priest. He will return again to establish his Kingdom of righteousness and justice.[5]

Divorce and Remarriage: The Pentecostal Church of God believes that no divorced and remarried Christian shall be granted credentials with the church except in the following cases: the divorce and remarriage occurred prior to the first experience of salvation, the divorce was for the cause of fornication, or that, although every effort was made personally and legally to save the marriage, the divorce occurred anyway against the will of the applicant.[6]

Government: No answer.

Heaven/Hell: The one who physically dies in his sins without Christ is hopelessly and eternally lost in the lake of fire, and therefore has no further opportunity of hearing the Gospel or repenting. The lake of fire is literal. The terms eternal and everlasting used in describing the duration of punishment in the lake of fire carry the same meaning of endless existence, as used in denoting the duration of joy and ecstasy of saints in the presence of God.[7]

Homosexuality: The church is opposed to homosexuality.

Inspiration of Scripture: The Scriptures of the Old and New Testaments are the inspired Word of God presenting the complete revelation of his will for the salvation of men. It constitutes the divine and only rule of Christian faith and practice.[8]

Miracles: Healing is for the physical ills of the human body and is wrought by the power of God through prayer and faith and by the laying on of hands. It is provided for in the atonement of Christ and is available to all who truly believe.[9]

Restrictions: None.

Security of Salvation: Man is a free moral agent and can at any time after the new birth experience turn away from God and die in a state of sin. He will then face the consequences of hell.[10]

Speaking in Tongues and Other Gifts of the Spirit: The baptism of the Holy Ghost and fire is a gift from God, as promised by the Lord Jesus Christ to all believers in this dispensation. It is received subsequent to the new birth. The baptism of the Holy Ghost is accompanied by the speaking in other tongues as the Holy Spirit gives utterance. This is the initial physical sign and evidence.[11]

Trinity: There is but one true and living God who is everlasting and infinite in power, wisdom, and goodness. He is the creator and preserver of all things, visible and invisible. In the unity of this Godhead there are three persons of one individual essence who are equal, co-existent, and co-eternal: namely, the Father, the Son, and the Holy Ghost. In the eternal relationship the Father is greater than all.[12]

Women in Ministry: When called of God and anointed by the Spirit, women may freely serve as helpers, pastors, and evangelists. But in order to fulfill the admonition of the Apostle Paul in 1 Timothy 2:12, all executive positions in the district and the national movement shall be occupied by men.[13]

For more information contact: 4901 Pennsylvania, P.O. Box 850, Joplin, MO 64802-0850; Phone: (417) 624-7050; Fax: (417) 624-7102; E-mail: pypa@pcg.org; Web site: http://member.aol.com/user257666/derek2.html

---

Pilgrim Holiness Church of NY, Inc.

The Pilgrim Holiness Church of NY, Inc., was first organized in 1897 as the Pentecostal Rescue Mission of Binghamton, NY. In 1922, the group affiliated with the International Holiness Church as an autonomous district. The following year the denomination and the conference adopted the name Pilgrim Holiness Church. In 1924, the New York district of the Pilgrim Holiness Church was incorporated under a charter designating it as the sole governing body of the Pilgrim Holiness Churches under its jurisdiction. In 1963, the New York conference, having withdrawn from the Pilgrim Holiness Church of America, became a fully independent organization and adopted the current name and the motto, "Holiness Unto the Lord." The church believes that sanctification is a second definite work of grace subsequent to regeneration that enables one to love the Lord God with all their heart. There were 54 congregations with approximately 800 members in 1997.

Abortion: The church is fully opposed to abortion. Abortion is murder.

Baptism: Baptism is an outward sign of an inward work of grace wrought by the Holy Ghost in the soul.

Birth Control: Birth control is an area where individuals should use wisdom and good sense to settle the issue before God.

Capital Punishment: The Scriptures advocate capital punishment. The church is in favor of that stand.

Christ's Return: Christ's return is imminent. It is to be personal and premillennial.

Communion: Communion is an ordinance whereby the body and blood of Christ are given, taken, and eaten after a heavenly and spiritual manner. The benefits accrue only to those who with a clear conscience partake in faith of the material elements of wine (juice) and bread. Those who receive them unworthily bring condemnation unto themselves.

Creation vs. Evolution: The Pilgrim Holiness Church believes only in the biblical account that teaches creation.

Deity of Christ: The Son, who is the Word of the Father, is the very eternal God, of one substance with the Father, who took man's nature, in the womb of the virgin, so that two whole and perfect natures, (the Godhead and manhood), were joined together in one person, never to be divided, who is one Christ, very God and very man.

Divorce and Remarriage: Beliefs regarding divorce and remarriage are consistent with the marriage vows and in harmony with the teaching of Scripture. The divorced person should not be allowed to remarry while their first partner is still alive.

Government: No answer.

Heaven/Hell: Everyone who has a saving knowledge of Jesus Christ, on departing from this life, goes to be in felicity with him. Then they will share the eternal glories of his everlasting Kingdom. While the saint goes from the judgment to enjoy eternal bliss, the impenitent sinner is turned away into everlasting condemnation, punishment, and misery.

Homosexuality: The Bible condemns homosexuality. God will punish this sin, as he never tolerated the perversion. The Pilgrim Holiness Church is opposed to homosexuality in any form or degree.

Inspiration of Scripture: The church believes in the inerrancy of Scripture and that the Holy Scriptures contain all things necessary to salvation.

Miracles: Christ performed miracles when he walked the earth as man and he still performs miracles today.

Restrictions: The Pilgrim Holiness Church is opposed to dancing, theaters, promiscuous bathing, horse races, gambling, secret societies, immodest attire, card playing, and alcohol. The church also discourages its members from having a television.

Security of Salvation: The church believes in the security of salvation but not in eternal security. This security is adequate, but there are conditions.

Speaking in Tongues and Other Gifts of the Spirit: The Pilgrim Holiness Church does not believe in the speaking in tongues as some do today. Speaking in tongues is not a sign of the inward dwelling of the Holy Spirit. It was a gift as any other gift that was given in the early church to propagate the Gospel in that day.

Trinity: The church believes in the Trinity: Father, Son, and Holy Ghost.

Women in Ministry: The church recognizes the gift given to women to perform in places in the ministry. However, it discourages women in the place of leadership based on Paul's teaching that women should not usurp authority.

For more information contact: 32 Cadillac Ave., Albany, NY 12205; Phone: (518) 456-3436.

Plymouth Brethren (Tunbridge Wells)

The Plymouth Brethren began in the mid-1800s in the British Isles. The group originally called themselves Brethren, but became known as Plymouth Brethren when a congregation in Plymouth, England, was recognized because if its missionary zeal.[14] The Tunbridge Wells got their name from a disciplinary action that took place in Tunbridge Wells, England, resulting in division of the Brethren. Tunbridge Wells Brethren in England have since reunited, but the group in North America chose to remain independent.[15] The Plymouth Brethren do not maintain a census of assemblies or individuals. However, there are assemblies worldwide and locations may be obtained through Bible Truth Publishers.

Abortion: The group believes from the Scriptures that God gives the soul of an individual at conception. Therefore, abortion is taking man's life.

Baptism: Baptism is by immersion since it figures being dead and risen with Christ. Baptism is not necessary for salvation and therefore is not considered a vital issue. There are none that practice infant baptism. Some practice household baptism and some practice Christian baptism.

Birth Control: Birth control is a matter of individual conscience before the Lord.

Capital Punishment: No statement.

Christ's Return: Christ's return is imminent. It will be premillennial, pretribulation, and will end the day of God's grace to man.

Communion: A remembrance of the Lord is celebrated weekly. It is a privilege for all believers in the body of Christ who are living in separation from evil practice and association.

Creation vs. Evolution: God is the sole creator through Jesus Christ, the Word. Everything that was made, he made. The church does not believe in evolution. God had an ordered plan. The creation and time did not necessarily begin with the creation of man.

Deity of Jesus: Jesus is the eternal Son of God. He always was and always will be. He is one of three in the Godhead.

Divorce and Remarriage: Marriage is a type of Christ and the church.

God does not expect it to be broken except by death. Remarriage is a matter of scriptural judgment for individual cases.

Government: There is no central headquarters. Christ leads his church as a body, but individual assemblies are local expressions of that body. The group believes that when Christ leads in a local expression of the body, he is leading for the whole body.

Heaven/Hell: Those that are saved will live in eternal bliss in the presence of Christ. Those that are not saved are eternally banned from his presence to suffer the punishment of hell.

Homosexuality: God created man and woman as a type of Christ and his church. Homosexuality makes a travesty of this type. It is expressly forbidden in God's Word.

Inspiration of Scripture: The Scriptures in their original language were verbally inspired by God and are inerrant.

Miracles: God performs miracles when and where he wants. The bodily resurrection of Jesus is a vital miracle of Christianity, which sets it apart from other religions.

Restrictions: Membership in secret societies is discouraged since these replace Christ and the fellowship of the church.

Security of Salvation: Since salvation is based solely on the work of Christ and gives eternal life, it is as sure as God's acceptance of Christ's work. This is assured by Christ's present position at God's right hand.

Speaking in Tongues and Other Gifts of the Spirit: God used these gifts in the early years of Christianity to show his approval of the Gospel since there was no written Word from him. God reveals himself now by the Holy Spirit through the Scriptures in understandable words.

Trinity: There is one God, fully revealed in Christ, and known through him as Father, Son, and Holy Ghost (Spirit). There are three persons in one God, or Trinity in unity.

Women in Ministry: There is no humanly ordained ministry for men or women. Christ gives servants to the church as it pleases him. Women are to keep silent in the church.

For more information contact: Bible Truth Publishers, 59 Industrial Rd., P.O. Box 649, Addison, IL 60101; Phone: (630) 543-1441; Fax: (630) 543-1476; Web site: http://www.storm.ca/%7esabigail/brethren.htm

Presbyterian Church in America, The

Organized at a constitutional assembly in December 1973, this church was first known as the National Presbyterian Church but changed its name in 1974 to Presbyterian Church in America (PCA). It separated from the Presbyterian Church in the United States because of its concerns about increasing liberalism which denied the deity of Jesus Christ and the inerrancy and authority of Scripture.[16] The PCA also objected to women in church office and the PCUS affiliation with the National Council of Churches and World Council of Churches. In 1982, the Reformed Presbyterian Church, Evangelical Synod joined the Presbyterian Church in America. The RPCES was formed in 1965 by a merger of the Evangelical Presbyterian Church and the Reformed Presbyterian Church in North America, General Synod. In 1997, there were 1,342 congregations with 279,581 members in the United States. The church believes in unconditional election and particular atonement whereby some are predestined for eternal life and others to everlasting death.

Abortion: The PCA is totally committed to a pro-life position, because persons are created in the image of God. Therefore, the PCA encourages adoption as a choice.

Baptism: Baptism is a sacrament of the New Testament, ordained by Jesus Christ, for the solemn admission of the party baptized into the visible church. It is also a sign and seal of the covenant of grace, of the baptized person's ingrafting into Christ, of regeneration, of remission of sins, and of the giving up unto God, through Jesus Christ, to walk in the newness of life. Baptism is performed in the name of the Father, and of the Son, and of the Holy Ghost. Dipping of the person into the water is not necessary. Baptism is rightly administered by pouring or sprinkling water upon the person. Infants of one or both believing parents are to be baptized.[17]

Birth Control: No statement.

Capital Punishment: The PCA's position is based on Genesis 9:6 which says that whoever sheds a man's blood, by man his blood shall be shed since God make man in his image.

Christ's Return: The PCA believes in the personal and bodily return of Jesus Christ.

Communion: The Lord Jesus instituted the sacrament of the Lord's Supper for: the perpetual remembrance of the sacrifice of himself in his death; the sealing all benefits thereof unto true believers, their spiritual nourishment, and growth in him; their further engagement in and to all duties which they owe unto him; and to be a bond and pledge of their communion with him, and with each other, as members of his mystical body. It is a commemoration of that one offering up of himself. In substance and nature, they still remain truly and only bread and wine, as they were before.[18]

Creation vs. Evolution: God, for the manifestation of the glory of his eternal power, wisdom, and goodness, in the beginning created (or made of nothing) all things visible and invisible in the space of six days. He created all things very good.[19]

Deity of Jesus: The Son of God, the second person of the Trinity, being very and eternal God, of one substance and equal with the Father, did, when the fullness of time was come, take upon him man's nature with all the essential properties and common infirmities thereof, yet without sin, being conceived by the power of the Holy Ghost, in the womb of the Virgin Mary, of her substance. So that two whole, perfect, and distinct natures, the Godhead and the manhood, were inseparably joined together in one person, without conversion, composition, or confusion. Which person is very God, and very man, yet one Christ, the only mediator between God and man.[20]

Divorce and Remarriage: Marriage is to be between one man and one woman. In the case of adultery, it is lawful for the innocent party to sue out a divorce and, after the divorce, to marry another, as if the offending party were dead. Nothing but adultery, or such willful desertion as can no way be remedied by the church or civil magistrate, is sufficient cause for dissolving the bond of marriage.[21]

Government: Presbyterian. The organization is ruled by presbyters (or elders) and the graded courts which are the session governing the local church, the Presbytery for regional matters, and the General Assembly at the national level.[22] Elders must meet the qualifications laid down in the pastoral epistles of the Bible. Ruling elders are elected by the people as their spiritual under-shepherds and teaching elders are the pastors of the church.[23] The PCA has taken a democratic position (rule from the grass roots up) on Presbyterian governance in contrast to a prelatical rule position (rule from the top assemblies down).

Heaven/Hell: The bodies of men, after death, return to dust, and see corruption. But their souls, which neither die nor sleep, having an immortal subsistence, immediately return to God who gave them. The souls of the righteous, being then made perfect in holiness, are received into the highest heavens where they behold the face of God in light and glory, waiting for the full redemption of their bodies. The souls of the wicked are cast into hell, where they remain in torments and utter darkness, reserved to the judgment of the great day.[24]

Homosexuality: The Bible condemns homosexual activity as sin and calls those involved in such a lifestyle to repentance.

Inspiration of Scripture: Inspiration is a special act of the Holy Spirit by which he guided the writers of the books of Scriptures (in their original autographs) so that their words should convey the thoughts he wished conveyed. The Bible is free from error of fact, doctrine, and judgment and is the infallible rule of faith and life.[25]

Miracles: The PCA believes that miracles occurred and are historically reported in the Old and New Testaments. Such miracles were signs by which God communicated divine truth. These miracles related to revelation have ceased, since revelation was completed with the closing of the canon in the New Testament era. Scripture uses the term miracle or wonder to describe the acts of God in all areas of creation and providence. The power of God, in response to believing prayer to work wonders and to heal the sick, cannot be limited. Such wonders certainly do continue to this day and are all for the glory of God, not man.

Restrictions: No statement.

Security of Salvation: The perseverance of the saints is that gracious work of God's sanctification whereby he enables a saved person to persevere to the end.[26] Even though not complete in this life, from God's perspective it is as good as accomplished.

Speaking in Tongues and Other Gifts of the Spirit: Spiritual gifts are granted to every believer by the Holy Spirit, who apportions to each Christian as he wills. Christians are to use these gifts to serve Christ in the work of his Kingdom and for the edification of the body of Christ. All true believers receive some spiritual gift or gifts. No spiritual gift is to be despised, nor is it to be misused to bring glory to any other than to Christ. Some spiritual gifts have ceased, such as the founding office of apostle. Others are obscure and cannot be clearly defined, such as the gift of helps. Others, such as giving and teaching, are seen today.

Any view of tongues which sees this phenomenon as an essential sign of the baptism of the Spirit is contrary to Scripture. Any practice of tongues which causes dissension and division in the body of Christ or diverts the church from its mission is contrary to the purpose of the Spirit's gifts.

Trinity: In the unity of the Godhead there are three persons of one substance, power, and eternity: God the Father, God the Son, and God the Holy Ghost. The Father is of none, neither begotten nor proceeding; the Son is eternally begotten of the Father; the Holy Ghost eternally proceeding from the Father and the Son.[27]

Women in Ministry: The PCA holds to the traditional position on the role of women in church offices.[28] The offices of teaching and ruling elders are reserved for qualified men in accordance with Scripture. Sessions are free to determine how women may exercise their gifts in all other functions.

For more information contact: 1852 Century Pl., Ste. 190, Atlanta, GA 30345; Phone: (404) 320-3366; Fax: (404) 329-1275. Web site: http://www.clark.net/pub/epchurch/pca.htm

---

Presbyterian Church, USA

The Presbyterian Church, USA was born out of the formal reuniting of two once-divided bodies: the United Presbyterian Church in the USA and the Presbyterian Church in the United States. Although they shared a rich history dating back to the first presbytery in the 1700s, they separated during the Civil War.[29] On June 10, 1983, the Presbyterian Church USA had their first communion together as a cooperative body.[30] In 1995, there were 11,361 congregations with 2,665,276 members.

Abortion: Abortion should not be restricted by law. The considered decision of a woman to terminate a pregnancy can be a morally acceptable, though certainly not the only or required, decision. However, the church does not accept abortion as a means of birth control, gender-selection, or as a means solely to obtain fetal parts for transplants.[31]

Baptism: Baptism is performed by the washing or sprinkling of an adult believer, or infant of one or both believing parents. Baptism is a one-time sacrament and is a perpetual sealing of the baptized.[32]

Birth Control: The PCUSA supports full and equal access to contraceptive methods.[33]

Captial Punishment: The church does not support capital punishment.

Christ's Return: Christ shall come again at the last day in great power and in the full manifestation of his own glory and of his Father's to judge the world in righteousness.[34]

Communion: The Lord's Supper is only for those who are believers and who can examine themselves in their faith and their duty to their neighbors. The doctrine which maintains a change of the substance of bread and wine into the substance of Christ's body and blood is not accepted in the PCUSA.[35]

Creation vs. Evolution: In sovereign love, God created the world good in the space of six days.[36]

Deity of Jesus: Jesus Christ was fully human and fully God.[37]

Divorce and Remarriage: The Presbyterian Church, USA prefers marriages to be healed through the ministry of the church. However, if divorce does occur, remarriage may take place in the church.

Government: Representative democracy. Elders are elected from the local congregation. Elders and pastors govern the church. Representatives from individual churches are elected to attend local presbytery meetings with pastors. Presbyteries elect representatives to Synod. Representatives are elected from the Presbytery to attend the annual General Assembly. The center of government is in the Presbytery, not the local church.

Heaven/Hell: The righteous go into everlasting life and receive that fullness of joy and refreshing which shall come from the presence of the Lord. The wicked, who do not know God and do not obey the Gospel of Jesus Christ, shall be cast into eternal torments. There they will be punished with everlasting destruction from the presence of the Lord and from the glory of his power.[38]

Homosexuality: Even where the homosexual orientation has not been consciously sought or chosen, it is neither a gift from God nor a state or a condition like race. It is a result of living in a fallen world. Although the church opposes homosexuality and refuses to ordain practicing homosexuals, it does not exclude homosexuals from membership. It urges an end to discriminatory legislation.[39]

Inspiration of Scripture: By the Holy Spirit the prophets were moved to speak the Word of God, and all the writers of the Holy Scriptures were inspired to record infallibly the mind and will of God.[40]

Miracles: Beliefs vary from church to church.

Restrictions: None.

Security of Salvation: Those that truly believe in the Lord Jesus may in this life be assured that they are in a state of grace. This is an infallible assurance of faith. They are sealed to the day of redemption.[41]

Speaking in Tongues and Other Gifts of the Spirit: The practice of sign gifts varies from church to church.

Trinity: The Presbyterian Church, USA trusts in the one triune God, who is one in substance and yet distinct in three persons: the Father, the Son, and the Holy Ghost.[42]

Women in Ministry: Women are ordained as elders and ministers.

For more information contact: 100 Witherspoon St., Louisville, KY 40202; Phone: (800) 872-3283 or (502) 569-5000; Fax: (502) 569-5018; E-mail: presbytel@pcusa.org; Web site: http://www.pcusa.org

---

Primitive Baptist

Primitive Baptists descended primarily from baptist churches in Wales and the Midlands of England.[43] The name Primitive Baptist became popular in the early 1800s when the term primitive conveyed the idea of originality rather than backwardness.[44] Primitive Baptists believe that all who are to possess spiritual life were individually chosen by God, that the saving benefits of Christ's death were intended for the elect only, and that his redemptive work was alone sufficient to secure salvation.[45] Primitive Baptists do not use musical instruments and have no Sunday Schools.[46]

Abortion: No statement.

Baptism: Those who profess faith in Christ and make the same appear by their fruits are the proper subjects of baptism. Baptism is performed by dipping the person in water—representing the death, burial, and resurrection of Christ.[47] Primitive Baptists rebaptize persons joining them from other orders.[48]

Birth Control: No statement.

Capital Punishment: No statement.

Christ's Return: No statement.

Communion: The Lord's Supper is a commemoration of, and thanksgiving for, the benefits received by his sufferings and death. It is to be received in faith and love after examination.[49] Primitive Baptists use real wine and unleavened bread in communion, wash feet during the service, and commune only with baptized believers of like faith and practice.[50]

Creation vs. Evolution: God, almighty, unbounded in wisdom and infinite in goodness, has made all things. He created Adam after his own image and likeness.[51]

Deity of Jesus: Jesus Christ was, in the fullness of time, manifested in the flesh. Being born of a woman and perfectly righteous, he gave himself for the elect to redeem them to God by his blood. Christ is the only true King, priest, and prophet of the church. Jesus of Nazareth, of whom the Scriptures of the Old Testament prophesied, is the true Messiah and Savior of men. He died on the cross, was buried, and rose again in the same body in which he suffered. He ascended to the right hand of the majesty on high and appeared in the presence of God, where he makes intercession for mankind.[52]

Divorce and Remarriage: Marriage was instituted of God. It is holy and honourable.[53]

Government: Primitive Baptist elders (ministers) are chosen from male members of the congregation.[54]

Heaven/Hell: At the time appointed of the Lord, the dead bodies of all men, just and unjust, shall rise again out of their graves that all may receive according to what they have done in their bodies, be it good or evil.[55] After this life, there are two places: one for those that are saved (paradise), the other for the damned (hell). The church denies the concept of purgatory, which it believes was invented in opposition to the truth.[56]

Homosexuality: No statement.

Inspiration of Scripture: Primitive Baptists believe the Holy Scriptures, the Old and New Testament, to be the Word and revealed mind of God which are able to make men wise unto salvation, through faith and love which is in Christ Jesus. They are given by inspiration of God, serving to furnish the man of God for every good work. By them, in the strength of Christ, all things are determined to be true or false.[57]

Miracles: Any true Christian should firmly believe in the possibility of miracles, and most prayerful Christians can witness to the fact that miracles do occur. However, miracles are elicited by the general prayers of God's people rather than the workings of someone possessing a miraculous spiritual gift. The practice of counterfeiting miracles in the name of Christ is to be condemned, not only because it is deceptive, but because it tends to discredit the true miracles recorded in the Bible and diminishes belief in the power of prayer.[58]

Restrictions: Primitive Baptists have historically not accepted for membership anyone who is currently a member of a secret order. Similarly, the church has withdrawn fellowship from any member who became a member of a secret order unless, after appropriate labor with the erring brother or sister, the secret order membership was renounced.[59] They also do not have crucifixes or pictures of Jesus in their churches and homes.[60]

Security of Salvation: The blood of Christ is sufficient both to procure and secure salvation of all for whom it was shed. Therefore, all of the elect will finally be saved.[61]

Speaking in Tongues and Other Gifts of the Spirit: The frequency of miraculous gifts tended to diminish toward the end of New Testament times. This was due to the expiration of the apostolic era and partly due to the Gospel being carried to the Gentiles. Paul said that it was the nature of a Jew to require signs but the nature of the Gentiles to demand wisdom. Accordingly, the experience of Scriptures indicates that the Lord is most apt to give signs when dealing with the Jewish people.[62]

Trinity: There is only one true God, who is eternal, almighty, unchangeable, infinite, and incomprehensible. He is a Spirit, having his being in himself, and giveth being to all creatures. He does what he will in heaven and earth, working all things according to the counsel of his own will.[63]

Women in Ministry: There is no scriptural precedent for female elders. Churches placing women in ministerial offices appear to regard the authority of the Scriptures to be subordinate to current social fashions.[64]

For more information contact: Primitve Baptist Library, 416 Main St., Carthage, IL 62321; Phone: (217) 357-3723

Primitive Methodist Church

Primitive Methodism had its beginnings when an American preacher, Lorenzo Dow, during a prolonged visit to England, emphasized the great value of the Methodist Camp meetings. Inspired by Dow, Hugh Bourne and William Clowes called an all-day prayer, song, and preaching event. This gathering on May 31, 1807 resulted in many conversions. Converts made that day were refused admittance into the Wesleyan Church and, because of their part in this meeting, Bourne and Clowes were reprimanded and later dismissed from the church. The new converts organized their own society and chose a name that signaled a return to the grassroots of the Methodist movement, The Society of Primitive Methodists. In 1829, a group of Primitive Methodist missionaries arrived in New York City, from England. On September 16, 1940, the American Primitive Methodist Church was established.[65] There were 77 congregations with 5,130 members in the United States in 1997.

Abortion: Scripture indicates that human personality begins at conception. Every human fetus is a true human being. Therefore, the church is opposed to the practice of abortion which denies the dignity, development, and destiny of human personality.[66]

Baptism: Baptism is an outward sacred rite which symbolizes an inward purity accomplished by Christ's atonement. Infant baptism is a requirement. Baptism does not produce salvation.

Birth Control: No statement.

Capital Punishment: No statement.

Christ's Return: The church believes in the second coming of Christ in power and glory.[67]

Communion: Communion is a memorial of redemption through the suffering and death of Jesus Christ. The bread is the body and the grape juice is the blood. Most churches serve communion once a month at the alter.

Creation vs. Evolution: The Primitive Methodist Church believes in the creation of man by a direct act of God.[68]

Deity of Jesus: The church believes in the deity of Jesus Christ, the Son, who was conceived by the Holy Spirit and born of the Virgin Mary.[69]

Divorce and Remarriage: Divorce is permitted for fornication, adultery, incest, etc. Remarriage is permitted where sexual infidelity has occurred.

Government: Congregational in structure. Local churches administer their own affairs under basic guidelines set by the conference in a manual called the Discipline. Each church elects its own leaders and pastor. Pastors are selected from a list of men approved by the Primitive Methodist Conference. The local church operates under the leadership of the Pastor. Working with him may be a group of elders. A station steward is elected annually by the church to assist the Pastor and to serve as coordinator of the church in his absence. A board of trustees takes care of the finances of the church and maintains its properties. The quarterly Conference is responsible for the spiritual well-being of the church and for maintaining vital spiritual programs. Churches in a given area form a district, under the supervision of a district superintendent. The district meets annually. The Conference meets annually to conduct the business of the denomination. It is presided over by a president. Each church elects a delegate to represent it at Conference. An executive director, elected by Conference, is charged with the responsibility of coordinating and promoting the work of the Conference and its various boards and committees.[70]

Heaven/Hell: There will be a future judgment of both the just and the unjust resulting in eternal rewards and punishments of all men.[71]

Homosexuality: A homosexual orientation is inconsistent with the Christian experience. Acknowledging that the homosexual constitutes a portion of the "whosoever" for whom Christ came to bring both redemption and reconciliation, the church affirms its desire to be open and responsive to the homosexual, as a person, while rejecting the sin of homosexuality, so that it might become agents of help, hope, and healing. Primitive Methodists desire to treat the homosexual with dignity, sensitivity, and Christian love, so as to help him realize his full potential in Christ. While a homosexual orientation may never be completely evaded within an individual, it can be controlled and overcome.[72]

Inspiration of Scripture: The Bible, both Old and New Testaments, is the only true rule of faith and practice. It is wholly and verbally given by God, and therefore is without error in all its teachings.[73]

Miracles: Miracles still occur today.

Restrictions: The portrayal of erotic behavior intended to cause sexual excitement is immoral and socially destructive. The use of alcohol is contrary to the teachings of the Lord. The use of tobacco in all its forms, illicit drugs, and all habit-forming narcotics is not recommended. Gambling is a perversion of the Lord's concept of stewardship and is inconsistent with a Christian lifestyle.[74]

Security of Salvation: The church is Wesleyan in doctrine and does not believe in eternal security.

Speaking in Tongues and Other Gifts of the Spirit: The Primitive Methodist Church does not believe in the Pentecostal position of speaking in tongues.

Trinity: One God exists in three persons: Father, Son, and Holy Spirit.[75]

Women in Ministry: The church does not have women pastors.

For more information contact: 1045 Laurel Run Rd., Wilkes-Barre, PA 18702; Phone: (717) 472-3436; Fax: (717) 472-9283.

Protestant Reformed Churches

Founded in 1924, the PRC stands in the tradition of the Protestant Reformation of the 16th century. It originated as a denomination when controversy arose over the doctrine of common grace within the Christian Reformed Church in the early 1920s. The result was that several ministers and their congregations were dismissed from the Christian Reformed Church. These men then established the Protestant Reformed Churches.[76] The PRC believes that God preaches to the elect alone ("particular grace"). During services, members sing only the Psalms and use the King James Version of Holy Scripture.[77] There were 25 churches with 6,115 members in the United States in 1997.

Abortion: Although there is no official position, the church opposes abortion.

Baptism: Dipping in, or sprinkling with, water signifies the impurity of the soul. The person being baptized is admonished to loathe and humble themselves before God and to seek their purification and salvation without themselves. Holy baptism witnesses and seals the washing away of sins through Jesus Christ. Therefore baptism is performed in the name of the Father, the Son, and the Holy Ghost. He makes an eternal covenant of grace with and adopts the baptized for His children and heirs. Baptism has taken the place of circumcision, therefore infants are to be baptized as heirs of the Kingdom of God and of his covenant.[78]

Birth Control: No official position.

Capital Punishment: The careful use of the death penalty is required of the State.

Christ's Return: He will come to judge the quick and the dead.[79]

Communion: Communicants are to examine themselves in order to remember him.[80]

Creation vs. Evolution: He has made heaven and earth and all that is in them.[81]

Deity of Jesus: Christ is the true and eternal God, and very man.[82]

Divorce and Remarriage: The church promotes and defends marriage, the earthly symbol of the covenant between Christ and the church, as a life-long unbreakable bond. On this basis, the church should, and can, oppose the evil of divorce and remarriage in her communion.[83]

Government: Presbyterian. The denomination is organized in two classis, east and west, which meet two or three times a year. Synod meets annually in June. Each congregation is self-governing by a body of elders chosen from the congregation.[84]

Heaven/Hell: Heaven and hell are both objective, everlasting realities.

Homosexuality: Although there is no official statement, the church opposes homosexuality.

Inspiration of Scripture: The PRC notes with alarm, if not horror, the widespread abandonment of the doctrine of the inerrant inspiration of Scripture by reformed churches both in the United States and in Europe.

Miracles: The special gifts such as faith healing ended with the apostolic age.

Restrictions: Membership in secret societies.

Security of Salvation: No statement.

Speaking in Tongues and Other Gifts of the Spirit: The PRC is concerned with the openness of reformed churches to the charismatic movement.[85]

Trinity: The PRC believes in only one true God, distinct in three persons: Father, Son, and Holy Ghost.[86]

Women in Ministry: No statement.

For more information contact: 4949 Ivanrest Ave., Grandville, MI 49418; Phone: (708) 596-3113; Fax: (708) 333-9205; E-mail: 74170.3215@compuserve.com; Web site: http://www.mtcnet.net/ ~revmo/

Reformed Baptist Church

Reformed Baptists affirm the 1689 Baptist Confession of Faith and are theological descendants of the Particular Baptists which framed and subscribed that confession, which became known as the Philadelphia Baptist Confession in the United States. Many Baptist churches in the U.S. at one time also subscribed to the confession, but eventually adopted other statements of belief. The modern Reformed Baptist movement arose in the 1960s and 1970s as an antithesis to evangelical and fundamental churches. In 1997 there were more than 100 churches in the U.S. who were affiliated with the Reformed Baptists. Reformed Baptists are five-point Calvinists and hold the Puritan view of the moral law and the Christian Sabbath.

Abortion: Unborn babies are human beings. As such, the deliberate taking of their lives is in all but the rarest cases murder. It is, therefore, a violation of the sixth commandment. Since the purpose of government is to protect human life and property, abortion (in all but cases where the mother's life is truly endangered) ought to be illegal.

Baptism: The Reformed Baptist church believes in and practices baptism by immersion.

Birth Control: Children are a blessing of the Lord. The creation mandate for married couples to bear children remains in effect. Because of the effects of the fall, however, the church believes that birth control is necessary in some cases and that parents have a procreative stewardship which must be exercised consistent with other biblical responsibilities. Abortifacients must be avoided.

Capital Punishment: The Bible mandates the death penalty for the crime of murder. This mandate should be obeyed by the government.

Christ's Return: The church believes in the bodily return of Christ in glory. It rejects classical dispensationalism but mandates no particular millennial view as a matter of fellowship.

Communion: Normally, Reformed Baptists reject both open and closed communion and practice some form of restricted communion in which the Lord's table is open only to those who are genuine Christians and members in good standing of evangelical churches. There are differences in the degree of restriction practiced.

Creation vs. Evolution: Reformed Baptists reject theistic evolution and the theory of evolution as inconsistent with the teaching of the Bible about the origin of the world, life, and mankind.

Deity of Christ: The church believes in the full and unqualified deity and Godhead of Jesus as the eternal Son of God.

Divorce and Remarriage: No position is taken on this issue. Normally, however, the view of the Westminster Confession of Faith is held on this issue. It allows divorce and remarriage on the grounds of adultery and desertion.

Government: The church is ruled by a plurality of elders. A common vote of the church is necessary for the election of officers, the enactment of corrective discipline, and a few other major issues of church life.

Heaven/Hell: Reformed Baptists believe in a literal heaven in this age and a literal new heavens and new earth in the age to come as the final inheritance of God's people. There is a literal hell now and literal place of eternal punishment in the age to come, which the Bible calls the lake of fire.

Homosexuality: Homosexuality, both in orientation and act, is a wicked abomination in the eyes of God. Homosexuals can be saved from this sin by the sovereign grace of God.

Inspiration of Scripture: The church believes in the inerrancy of the Scriptures in all that they affirm, not only about faith and practice, but also about history and science.

Miracles: God is able to work above and without the means he normally uses to accomplish his will. Such operations are commonly called miracles. Christ bodily and literally rose from the dead and he literally performed the miracles the Bible ascribes to him.

Restrictions: Many Reformed Baptists do not add restrictions for church membership beyond those taught in the Bible. For instance, the consumption of alcoholic beverages is not forbidden. However, disciplinary action could be taken for drunkenness.

Security of Salvation: Reformed Baptists believe in the preservation and the perseverance of the saints. All those who are truly saved will persevere in faith, repentance, and generally increasing holiness to eternal life. However, Reformed Baptists reject the doctrine usually called eternal security which means people will be saved irrespective of how they live after conversion.

Speaking in Tongues and Other Gifts of the Spirit: The church does not believe in, or practice, speaking in tongues or other extraordinary gifts of the Spirit. They believe these were signs for the apostolic age and ceased after the death of the apostles.

Trinity: The church affirms the orthodox, Nicene doctrine of the Trinity that there is one God who exists in three persons: Father, Son, and Holy Spirit.

Women in Ministry: Women should not lead in the assemblies of the church or hold the office of elder or deacon in the government of the church. The valuable and divinely appointed sphere of service for gifted women is to be found in other spheres.

For more information contact: 3181 Bradford NE, Grand Rapids, MI 49505; Phone: (616) 940-0972; Fax: (616) 940-0589; E-mail: 7653@compuserve.com; Web site: http://www.vor.org/truth/

Reformed Church in America

The Reformed Church in America was established on this continent 150 years before the Revolutionary War. The word reformed comes from the Protestant Reformation which swept across Europe in the 1500s under the leadership of Martin Luther and John Calvin. Calvin's reformation at Geneva spread to many countries, including Scotland (where it became the Presbyterian Church) and the Netherlands (where it became the RCA's predecessor, the Dutch Reformed Church). The Dutch Reformed Church established its first congregation in New Amsterdam in 1628.[1] There were 946 congregations with approximately 300,000 members in the United States in 1997.

Abortion: The Bible teaches the sanctity of human life. People are given the precious gift of life from God and are created in the image of God. Therefore the RCA believes, in principle, that abortion ought not to be practiced at all. Abortions performed for personal reasons to ensure individual convenience ought not to be permitted. However, in this complex society where many times one form of evil is pitted against another form of evil, there could be exceptions. The ability to make a decision regarding legal abortion is every person's right under Christian freedom.[2]

Baptism: Christ places baptism in the world as a seal of God's covenant to people, placing them in ministry and assuring them of forgiveness of sins.[3]

Birth Control: No statement.

Capital Punishment: The church is compelled to speak against the lovelessness and evil of capital punishment.[4]

Christ's Return: Jesus will come again to judge the living and the dead.[5]

Communion: Christ places the Lord's table in this world. Jesus takes up the bread and wine to represent his sacrifice, to bind his ministry to the communicant's daily work, and to unite them in his righteousness. Here Christ is present in his world proclaiming salvation until he comes, a symbol of hope for a troubled age.[6]

Creation vs. Evolution: The Father Almighty made the heavens and the earth—all that is, seen and unseen.[7]

Deity of Jesus: Jesus Christ was born of the Virgin Mary, sharing human genes and instincts, entering human culture, speaking the language, fulfilling the law of God. Jesus Christ is the hope of God's world. In his death, the justice of God is established and forgiveness of sin is proclaimed. On the day of the resurrection, the tomb was empty.[8]

Divorce and Remarriage: God's intention for marriage is that it is to be permanent. Divorce involves sin. Permissible grounds for divorce are only two: adultery, based on the exceptive clause in Matthew 19:9, and desertion of the believing spouse by the unbeliever, based upon the so-called "Pauline Privilege" in 1 Corinthians 7:15. A pastor may with good conscience officiate in the remarriage of divorced persons, if, in his judgment and the judgment of the congregation's board of elders, the persons have met the following requirements: they recognize their personal responsibility for the failure of the former marriage, they are penitent and have made an effort to overcome limitations and failures, they have forgiven the former partner, they have fulfilled their obligations involved in the former marriage, and they are willing to make the new marriage a Christian one by dependence upon Christ and participation in his church.[9]

Government: Each RCA congregation is governed by an elected consistory, made up of elders, deacons, and the pastor(s). Several RCA congregations in the same geographic region make up a classis. All ordained ministers are accountable to a classis, which supervises the churches within its region. The denomination is divided into eight regional synods, which are made up of the churches and classis within their geographical boundaries. The General Synod is the highest representative body of the church, meeting once a year to make decisions which affect the life and work of the entire RCA. This body, made up of elder and clergy delegates from each classis, sets overall policy and program direction for the denomination.[10]

Heaven/Hell: In the age to come, Christ is the judge, rejecting unrighteousness, isolating God's enemies to hell, and blessing the new creation in Christ.[11]

Homosexuality: Homosexual behavior is not God's intended expression of sexuality. Homosexuality is neither more nor less serious than other forms of human sinfulness. There are varied and complex causes of homosexual orientation and behavior; hence, simplistic analyses and solutions should be questioned. Any expectation for persons of homosexual orientation to experience wholeness should be shaped by both the hope and the realism of the Christian life. Homosexual persons should be accorded their full measure of human and civil rights.[12]

Inspiration of Scripture: The final authority in reformed faith is the Bible. The Bible is God's Word for every person, made understandable and alive through the Holy Spirit's ministry. It is more than a textbook; it is the living Word of God, the source of all revelation of God's will, and the norm by which all teaching must be checked.[13]

Miracles: No statement.

Restrictions: No statement.

Security of Salvation: Those who call on the name of Jesus will have eternal life.[14]

Speaking in Tongues and Other Gifts of the Spirit: No statement.

Trinity: The church believes in God the Father, Jesus Christ His only Son, and the Holy Spirit who proceeds from the Father and the Son.[15]

Women in Ministry: Women are ordained and serve in all offices of the church.

For more information contact: RCA Communications Dept., 475 Riverside Dr., New York, NY 10115; Phone: (212) 870-3020; Fax: (212) 870-2499; E-mail: rcamail@iserv.net; Web site: http://www.rca.org

---

Reformed Church in the United States

The Reformed Church in the United States is an immigrant church from Germany that originated out of the 16th century Reformation. The church's beginnings in the United States go back to 1725. The Reformed Church takes its theology from Calvinism, which was developed by the influential reformer, John Calvin (1509–1564). Doctrinal standards, also originating from the 16th century Reformation, are the Heidelberg Catechism (1563), the Canons of Dordt (1618–19), and the Belgic Confession. The Reformed Church in the United States prohibits the use of images, including pictures of Christ, in worship. There were 40 congregations with 4,250 members in the United States in 1997.

Abortion: The church is categorically opposed to abortion at any stage. Abortion is murder prohibited by the sixth commandment.

Baptism: Baptism is the sign and seal of God's covenant of grace established with Abraham, the spiritual father of all believers. It is to be administered to all who believe and their children, including infants.

Birth Control: Birth control is a matter to be decided by a husband and wife. It is permissible so long as it does not involve the destruction of an embryo (abortion) or is not an attempt to disobey the biblical mandate to be fruitful and multiply.

Capital Punishment: The Reformed Church in the United States believes in retributive justice. In other words, the punishment must fit the crime. A capital crime must receive a capital punishment.

Christ's Return: Christ will visibly return at the end of the world to judge the living and the dead. Of that day and hour no one knows, except God the Father.

Communion: The church believes in restricted or guarded communion, where the table is fenced—those who show themselves by their confession and life to be unbelieving and ungodly are refused admittance.

Creation vs. Evolution: Creation is as described in Genesis 1 with the chronological sequence of six normal days of light and darkness. On the sixth day God formed man from the dust of the ground, breathed into him the breath of life, and man became a living soul, created in the image of God. Evolution is a godless and false faith.

Deity of Christ: Jesus, in one person, is true God and also a true and righteous man.

Divorce and Remarriage: Reconciliation is always first and foremost. Divorce is permitted only on biblical grounds, which are adultery and desertion by an unbelieving spouse. Remarriage is permissible for the innocent party.

Government: The form of government held by the church is Presbyterian (rule by elders) and reformed. This form avoids both independentism (congregationalism) and synodicalism (hierarchism).

Heaven/Hell: Heaven and hell are real. Heaven is the place of eternal bliss. Hell is a place of eternal torment. At death and at the end of the world, people will go to one or the other.

Homosexuality: Homosexuality is an abomination to the Lord. However, change and forgiveness is possible.

Inspiration of Scripture: The Bible is the infallible, inerrant, plenarily and verbally inspired Word of God. The Lord God in his all wise providence has faithfully maintained the purity of his Word in its transmission unto this very day.

Miracles: Miracles in biblical times had the specific purpose of revelation: to show that Jesus was truly God and that the prophets and apostles were imbued with power from God. In this sense, miracles are no longer necessary nor do they occur. This does not mean that supernatural acts of God no longer occur.

Restrictions: None other than those imposed by the Bible.

Security of Salvation: Once God begins the work of salvation within an individual, he will complete it.

Speaking in Tongues and Other Gifts of the Spirit: Some gifts were given as signs and as revelation until the Word of God was inscripturated. Their purpose has been fulfilled and they have ceased.

Trinity: God has so revealed himself in his Word, that the three distinct persons: Father, Son, and Holy Spirit, are the one, true, eternal God.

Women in Ministry: Women are commanded to be in subjection, to keep silent in the churches, and not to teach or usurp authority over the man. They are not permitted to hold the office of elder or deacon, nor are they allowed to vote in congregational meetings.

For more information contact: 235 James St., Shafter, CA 93263; Phone: (805) 746-6907; Web site: http://www.geocities.com/heart-land/1136/rcus.htm

---

Reformed Episcopal Church in America

The Reformed Episcopal Church was founded by the Rt. Rev. George David Cummins after he wrote a letter of resignation to the bishop of the Protestant Episcopal Church in the diocese of Kentucky. The Nov. 10, 1873 letter expressed Cummin's desire to find union with other Christian churches. Although he resigned his position with the Protestant Episcopal Church, he made clear that he was transferring his office and work (as bishop) to another sphere. Cummins then called others of like mind and persuasion to meet on Dec. 2 for the purpose of organizing an, "Episcopal Church on the basis of the Prayer Book of 1785: a basis broad enough to embrace all who hold 'the faith once delivered to the saints,' as that faith is maintained by the Reformed Churches of Christendom."[16] Underlying this call was a protest against the growing Anglo-Catholic movement within the Protestant Episcopal Church. There were 153 churches with approximately 13,000 baptized members in the United States in 1997.

Abortion: The Reformed Episcopal Church vigorously affirms the biblical teaching of the sanctity of human life and deplores the practice of permitting abortions, with the possible exception of cases where it has been clearly established that the life of the mother is in danger.[17]

Baptism: Baptism as an outward sign of an inward grace such that regeneration should be understood as normally occurring at Holy Baptism, but not inseparable with baptism.[18] Baptismal regeneration is denied.[19]

Birth Control: This is left up to individual couples, provided birth control is utilized before conception, not afterwards.

Capital Punishment: There is no official statement. Individual beliefs on this issue are tolerated, although many believe this is a right given by God to the state to punish wrong and promote justice.

Christ's Return: The Scriptures as prime authority, the Apostles' and Nicene Creeds and the Thirty-Nine Articles of Religion all affirm that Christ will return in the same manner as he ascended—bodily, visibly, and as King and judge. Various millennial positions may be individually held, but are not required for church membership.

Communion: The Lord's table is a type of an altar since the "sacrifice of Praise and Thanksgiving" is offered.[20] Most understand that Christ is really but not corporeally present in the Holy Supper. Transubstantiation is denied.[21]

Creation vs. Evolution: Individual views are permitted as long as they do not deny the scriptural account. Most understand that Adam was a unique creation of God.

Deity of Jesus: The statements in the Nicene Creed are true. There is one Lord, Jesus Christ, the only Son of God, eternally begotten of the Father, God from God, light from light, true God from true God, begotten, not made. He is of one being with the Father. By the power of the Holy Spirit, he was incarnate of the Virgin Mary and was made man. He was crucified, suffered death, and was buried. He arose on the third day, ascended into heaven, and is seated at the right hand of the Father.

Divorce and Remarriage: Adultery and desertion are acknowledged as the two grounds for divorce. Depending on individual circumstances and reasons for the divorce, remarriage may be allowed.

Government: Episcopal.

Heaven/Hell: Creedal statements affirm the eternal blessedness of the righteous in Christ and the divine judgment and condemnation of those who have not received God's provision of redemption in Christ.

Homosexuality: Homosexual acts are sinful in all circumstances.[22] No person may be ordained into, or continue in the ministry of, the church who actively practices or advocates a homosexual lifestyle. Repentance, forgiveness, and renewal are always possible and are a pastoral objective of rectors.

Inspiration of Scripture: The Reformed Episcopal Church declares its belief in the Holy Scriptures of the Old and New Testaments as the Word of God. It recognizes Scripture as a primary authoritative document, but not exclusively so. Holy Scripture was not given in a vacuum apart from the church. Therefore, the ancient creeds, as interpreted by their English commentary and the Thirty-Nine Articles of Religion, are also authoritative.[23]

Miracles: Many feel that miracles ceased when the final Scriptures were written and in place in A.D. 100. Others feel that God may still work miracles, not limiting his sovereignty. However, these would not be everyday occurrences.

Restrictions: The church tries to avoid legalism by understanding that there are weak and strong Christians. Individual behavior must be reconciled with the standards of God's commandments and the witness of Christ's church to the world. Church discipline is pastorally handled by the individual rectors.

Security of Salvation: The Thirty-Nine Articles indicate that once God has worked genuinely in a person's life, his spiritual position cannot be altered.

Speaking in Tongues and Other Gifts of the Spirit: Most feel that sign gifts passed away with the apostolic age, but some would not limit God's use of sign gifts where special circumstances are needed to attest to his work in the church today.

Trinity: The ancient documents all affirm that there is one God in three persons: God is Father, Son, and Holy Spirit. There is no mixing of persons, but all are equally God in substance.

Women in Ministry: Women are not ordained in the church, although there is discussion about acknowledging women's roles in the Diaconate.

For more information contact: P.O. Box 20068, Charleston, SC 29413; Phone: (803) 723-5500; Fax: (803) 723-2500; Web site: http://www.recus.org/index.htm

---

Regular (Old Line) Primitive Baptists

The Old Line Primitive Baptists are a descendant of the ancient Waldenses, Anabaptists, ancient Baptists of England and Wales, and the Original Baptists of America (hence, the name Primitive). The Old Line separated from the Beebe Baptists (absoluters) around 1910. The denomination's motto is, "The Bible teaches us all that we need to know, believe, and practice in our efforts to serve God." There were approximately 1,700 congregations with 40,000 members in 1997. Some distinctive beliefs are that the earth is young, there is only one true church in the world, and the trichotomy of man.

Abortion: Primitive Baptists are opposed to abortion and consider it to be a form of murder, except in cases of rape or to save the mother's life.

Baptism: Baptism by immersion is performed only by duly ordained ministers of the same faith and order.

Birth Control: Contraception and preventive measures are acceptable, but only within the bonds of sacred marriage.

Capital Punishment: The church agrees with capital punishment, but recommends mercy in cases where the offender is irresponsible.

Christ's Return: Christ is sure to return back to the earth to redeem the bodies of the saints at the general resurrection and general judgment. No man knows the day, hour, or year of his return. The church is amillennial.

Communion: Communion is performed with pure, fermented grape wine and unleavened bread. It is open to all of same faith and order but is closed to all outside the fellowship of the church.

Creation vs. Evolution: All things were literally created in six days as given in Genesis. All forms of evolution are false theories that cannot be proven. However, evolution is possible in social, moral, and educational fields.

Deity of Jesus: The Regular Primitive Baptist Church believes in the deity of Christ and his impeccability.

Divorce and Remarriage: Fornication is the only biblical grounds for divorce. A faithful spouse may divorce and remarry, but only to one who is scripturally eligible or whose spouse is dead.

Government: Congregations are autonomous. They govern themselves and call their own pastors, who are amenable to the church for deportment, morality, and theology.

Heaven/Hell: Heaven and hell are eternal. The punishment of the wicked will last as long as the bliss of the saved in heaven.

Homosexuality: The church is opposed to all forms of homosexuality. Practicing persons are not admitted into the fellowship of the church.

Inspiration of Scripture: Old Line Primitive Baptists believe in the complete verbal inspiration of the original manuscripts. The Bible is the providential preservation of truth into many languages, including the King James Version, which is preferred above later translations into English.

Miracles: Miracles continue in this age through providential acts of God only; they are not given as gifts to any men since the apostolic age. God may heal in answer to sincere prayers of believers—but not like in the apostles' time.

Restrictions: Gambling, witchcraft, and all forms of sorcery are forbidden.

Security of Salvation: All believers will be saved who have true faith in God the Father and Christ the Son. Others, also of the elect family of God, will be securely saved who were given to Christ but never heard the gospel.

Speaking in Tongues and Other Gifts of the Spirit: Sign gifts are not given to believers in this age. They were to pass away following the apostolic age.

Trinity: God the Father, God the Son, and God the Holy Ghost are one God.

Women in Ministry: Women are forbidden to teach or preach.

For more information contact: Elder S.T. Tolley, P.O. Box 68, Atwood, TN 38220; Phone and Fax: (901) 662-7417.

Salvation and Deliverance Church

Rev. William Brown, who was raised Roman Catholic and served as vice-president of marketing for a major corporation, started the Salvation and Deliverance Church in 1975 with an emphasis on an interracial Holiness ministry. The church had more than 100 congregations worldwide, with approximately 500,000 members in 1997.

Abortion: The church does not believe in abortion. Only God holds life and death in his hands.

Baptism: Believers are baptized in water and in the Spirit for remission of sins.

Birth Control: God created man to be fruitful and multiply. It is a blessing to give birth.

Capital Punishment: The church does not believe in capital punishment.

Christ's Return: The Lord shall descend from heaven with a shout, with the voice of the archangel and with the trumpet of God, and the dead in Christ shall rise first. Those who are alive and remain shall be caught up together with them in the clouds to meet the Lord in the air. The dead in Christ are raised and living believers will be transfigured, putting on immortality. Christ shall return for his church, a holy church without spot or blemish, irrespective of denomination.

Communion: The church has been commissioned to observe communion often in remembrance of the Lord's body which was broken for sinners.

Creation vs. Evolution: The world did not evolve. God created all things and without him was not anything made that was made.

Deity of Jesus: The church believes in one God who is Jesus.

Divorce and Remarriage: The Salvation and Deliverance Church does not believe in divorce except for fornication. Remarriage is allowed only in the case of the death of a spouse.

Government: No answer.

Heaven/Hell: They both exist. Heaven is a prepared place for a prepared people: the saints of God. Hell was not designed for men, but for the devil and his angels.

Homosexuality: God loves the homosexual but not the act of homosexuality. It is immoral and is an abomination to God.

Inspiration of Scripture: All Scripture is given by inspiration of God. It is good for use as doctrine, in reproof and correction, and for instruction towards righteousness.

Miracles: Signs and wonders shall follow them that believe. Miracles are still happening today.

Restrictions: Anything that is harmful to the body, such as drugs, alcohol, fornication, and unmarried couples living together is prohibited. The body is to be presented as a living sacrifice, holy and acceptable unto God.

Security of Salvation: Salvation is free. It is the believer's blessed assurance.

Speaking in Tongues and Other Gifts of the Spirit: Speaking in tongues as the Spirit gives utterance builds up and sanctifies. It is a manifestation of the Spirit, the initial outward sign of baptism in the

Holy Spirit. The church also believes in the gifts of the Spirit as well as the fruits of the Spirit.

Trinity: God the Father, the Son, and the Holy Ghost are the triune God: three divine persons are the manifestations of the one.

Women in Ministry: There is neither male or female in Christ. Therefore women are permitted to preach the Gospel and to minister.

For more information contact: 37 W. 116th St., New York, NY 10026; Phone: (212) 722-5488; Fax: (212) 722-6563.

Salvation Army

In London, in 1865, many were suffering from hunger, homelessness, and illness. William Booth and his wife Catherine began the Salvation Army in response to the need they saw around them.[1] Booth, who had a Methodist background, first organized under the name East London Christian Mission. The Salvation Army emigrated to America in 1880.[2] The Salvation Army maintains a military-like structure. Its emphasis on evangelism is demonstrated through its social programs.

Abortion: The Salvation Army is opposed to abortion on demand or as a means of birth control. Termination of a pregnancy may be justified in those rare instances where, in the judgment of competent medical staff, the pregnancy poses a serious threat to the life of the mother, could result in irreversible physical injury to the mother, or is a case of proven rape or legally defined incest.[3]

Baptism: The Army does not use the sacraments. It believes that it is possible to live a holy life without the use of sacraments and that the sacraments should not be regarded as an essential part of becoming a Christian. The sacraments are an outward sign of inward experience and the inward experience is the most important.[4]

Birth Control: Many married couples will find it necessary to limit the number of their children for various reasons. Any such decision, including the contraceptive means to be used, should be taken responsibly and where necessary under medical advice.[5]

Capital Punishment: The opinions of Salvationists are divided on the moral acceptability of capital punishment and its effectiveness as a deterrent. However, to advocate in any way the continuance or restoration of capital punishment would be inconsistent with the Army's purposes and contrary to its belief that all human life is sacred and that each human being, however wretched, can become a new person in Christ.[6]

Christ's Return: No answer.

Communion: See note on baptism.

Creation vs. Evolution: God created, preserves, and governs all things.[7]

Deity of Jesus: In the person of Jesus Christ, the divine and human natures are united, so that he is truly and properly God, and truly and properly man.[8]

Divorce and Remarriage: The Salvation Army, while defending vigorously the ongoing relevance of God's will for men and women in relation to marriage, recognizes the reality that some marriages fail. It is therefore willing to offer counsel and practical help to couples so affected. The Army permits (but does not require) its officers to perform a marriage ceremony for a divorced person, following careful counseling, where it is considered that remarriage could lead to the healing of emotional wounds.[9]

Government: The United States is divided into four territories. Each territory has its own commander holding the rank of commissioner. The National Commander and National Chief Secretary serve in coordinating capacities at The Salvation Army National Headquarters. Each territory operates under the broad general policies established by the International Headquarters. National policies are made by the Commissioners Conference, comprised of the four territorial commanders and presided over by the National Commander.[10]

Heaven/Hell: The Army believes in the immortality of the soul, in the resurrection of the body, in the general judgment at the end of the world, in the eternal happiness of the righteous, and in the endless punishment of the wicked.[11]

Homosexuality: God's intention for mankind is that society should be ordered on the basis of lifelong, legally sanctioned, heterosexual unions. Such marriages lead to the formation of families, which are essential to human personal development and therefore to the stability of the community. Scripture opposes homosexual practice by direct comment and by clearly implied disapproval. The Bible treats such practices as self-evidently abnormal. Homosexual practice rejects both the obvious implications of human physiology and the potential for pro-

creation. Romans 1 sees homosexual acts as a symptom of a deeper refusal to accept the organizing scheme of God for the created order. Salvationists seek to understand and sensitively to accept and help those
of a homosexual disposition and those who express that disposition in
sexual acts. The Army is opposed to the victimization of persons on the
grounds of sexual orientation and recognizes the social and emotional
stress and loneliness borne by many who are homosexual. The Army
does not regard the homosexual disposition as blameworthy in itself or
rectifiable at will. Such practices, if unrenounced, render a person in-
eligible for Salvation Army soldiership in the same way that unrenounced heterosexual sin is a bar to soldiership. The Army firmly believes in the power of God's grace to enable the maintenance of a
lifestyle pleasing to him.[12]

Inspiration of Scripture: The Scriptures of the Old and New Testaments were given by inspiration of God. They constitute the divine rule
of Christian faith and practice.[13]

Miracles: No answer.

Restrictions: No answer.

Security of Salvation: Continuance in a state of salvation depends upon
continued obedient faith in Christ.[14]

Speaking in Tongues and Other Gifts of the Spirit: No answer.

Trinity: There is only one God, who is infinitely perfect, the creator, preserver, and governor of all things. He is the only proper object of religious worship. There are three persons in the Godhead the Father,
Son, and Holy Ghost, undivided in essence and co-equal in power and
glory.[15]

Women in Ministry: Women hold rank in the church.[16]

For more information contact: 615 Slaters Ln., Alexandria, VA 22313;
Phone: (703) 684-5500; Fax: (703) 684-3478; Web site: http://www.
salvationarmy.org/home.htm

Seventh-day Adventist Church

After the Great Disappointment of 1844, when Christ did not return as
predicted, some Adventists reinterpreted the promises in Daniel 8 while
others determined that on that date Christ instead changed his ministry in
heaven. The latter developed into the Seventh-day Adventists.[17] Seventh-

Day Adventists believe that Daniel 8:14 points to a heavenly judgment which began in 1844 and will conclude just prior to the second coming. They believe in the perpetuity of God's Ten Commandments and that they are still an obligation of Christians today as a fruit of faith, not righteousness by works. This includes the fourth commandment. The Sabbath is Saturday. In 1997, there were 42,119 churches with 9.3 million members worldwide.

Abortion: Abortion is accepted only in the cases of rape, incest, major congenital abnormality, or if the physical health of the mother is threatened.

Baptism: Adults are baptized by immersion upon request.

Birth Control: The Seventh-day Adventist church allows the use of birth control.

Capital Punishment: No position.

Christ's Return: Christ's return is strongly stressed and preached. It will occur in the near future.

Communion: Communion is seen as a symbolic reminder that is practiced on a quarterly basis along with footwashing.

Creation vs. Evolution: The church is a strong supporter of creationism.

Deity of Jesus: Jesus was fully divine and fully human in the incarnation. As a deity, Jesus was pre-existent prior to the incarnation.

Divorce and Remarriage: Divorce and remarriage is allowed on biblical grounds only.

Government: Modeled after the Methodist Church, with the flow of authority which begins at the local church, then moves from the local conference to the unions, then to divisions, and finally to the General Conference.

Heaven/Hell: The soul is not mortal. There will be separate resurrections for the righteous and the wicked. The wicked will be destroyed in the lake of fire rather than live on in an ever-burning hell.

Homosexuality: Homosexuality is considered immoral and unacceptable.

Inspiration of Scripture: All Scripture was given by inspiration of God. The Bible is the ultimate and final authority on what is truth.

Miracles: Seventh-day Adventists accept the full historicity of biblical miracles and allow for (but do not stress) their possible reoccurrence in modern times.

Restrictions: Tobacco, alcoholic beverages, and addictive drugs are prohibited. Movies, card-playing, and dancing are discouraged as subversive to spirituality.

Security of Salvation: Security rests upon Christ's atonement upon the cross, making him able to save to the uttermost any who come to him.

Speaking in Tongues and Other Gifts of the Spirit: Pentecostal speaking in tongues is not accepted. However, the translation into foreign languages to communicate the Gospel is acknowledged.

Trinity: The Father, Son, and Holy Spirit are all fully divine and fully cooperative within the work of the Trinity.

Women in Ministry: Women as elders and associate pastors are accepted on the local level in some parts of the world. The denomination does not sanction ordination. This matter is still under discussion, but was voted down again at the 1995 General Conference session.

For more information contact: 12501 Old Columbia Pike, Silver Spring, MD 20904-6600; Phone: (301) 680-6300; Fax: (301) 680-6312; Web site: http://www.adventist.org

---

Seventh Day Adventist Reform Movement

The Seventh Day Adventist Reform Movement was officially organized in 1925. The church's motto is, "To the Law and to the testimony." There were 17 churches and several groups assembling in the United States in 1997. The church focuses on obedience to God's moral law of the Ten Commandments through the power of Christ, the unconsciousness of the dead, and healthful living.

Abortion: Believing that human life begins in the womb, church members neither practice nor perform abortions.

Baptism: Baptism by immersion symbolizes death to the old man of sin and resurrection to new life in Christ.

Birth Control: Physical, mental, and spiritual health, as well as temperance, are scriptural principles which conflict with the excessive sexuality of this present generation. While the church does teach the importance of self-control even within the marriage relationship, it is also careful to avoid undue meddling into the sanctity of the family circle.

Capital Punishment: Jesus teaches not to kill, as human life and death are prerogatives of God. Prophecy warns also that those who seek to inflict the mark of the beast will be strongly pressuring the state to use capital punishment. In cases of serious crimes, capital punishment is a matter for the state and not for the church.

Christ's Return: Christ's coming in the clouds will be plainly visible, audible, literal, and personal. His feet will not touch the ground, for the saints from all ages who are resting in their graves will then resurrect to join the living faithful, and together meet the Lord in the air.

Communion: Communion is derived from the Passover, for a united people to symbolize the sacrifice of the lamb of God for redemption from sin. Christ performed it alone with his disciples, along with the preparatory service of foot washing. The Lord's Supper is the communion of the body of Christ.

Creation vs. Evolution: God created the world and its inhabitants in six literal days. The New Testament confirms the validity of the Genesis record through the words of Christ and in the epistles of Paul.

Deity of Jesus: Jesus existed from eternity as the creator and came to the planet veiled in human flesh. His victory over death and his ascension to minister from heaven on behalf of his followers further confirm his deity.

Divorce and Remarriage: Marriage was established from the beginning of mankind in Eden, and Jesus confirmed that it is a commitment for life, until the death of either of the two parties. While separation may occasionally be necessary, remarriage while both partners are alive is unscriptural.

Government: The church is organized for service with a representative type of government.

Heaven/Hell: Heaven refers to the Kingdom of glory to be established by Christ at his coming. A fiery hell will be the destiny of the wicked who are resurrected after the earth is desolate for 1,000 years. At that time, there will be a hell—a lake of fire—which will consume the wicked to ashes and purify the earth to become the new home of the redeemed saints.

Homosexuality: This lifestyle practice is not in harmony with God's will. Therefore, church members do not participate in it nor endorse it.

Inspiration of Scripture: The Holy Scriptures constitute the Word of the living God—his plans, desires, and thoughts are made available for the reader's information, that all may be restored to his image, as he originally made man and women in Eden.

Miracles: Miracles are indeed possible through God, for nothing is impossible for him. But not all miracles are from God. Many supernatural phenomena are from the powers of darkness, especially nowadays. Therefore, everyone should be on guard to ensure that the miracle-workers harmonize with all that God has stated in Scripture. None can simply rely on their feelings, or on what they see and hear. Miracles, therefore, are not a basis for belief.

Restrictions: Any defiling, degrading practice, or amusement which undermines the high calling of the Christian life is not in harmony with faith.

Security of Salvation: Believers are secure in Christ through eternity as long as they continually choose to abide in him.

Speaking in Tongues and Other Gifts of the Spirit: By miraculous power, the disciples were given ability to share the Gospel in the appropriate foreign languages needed after the day of Pentecost. The gift of tongues was the ability to speak languages of different nationalities. However, now that the Bible is already written in nearly all languages, some other gifts of the Spirit are more important. The apostle bids believers to be more eager to understand prophecy.

Trinity: Because the trinitarian concept is easily misinterpreted and misunderstood, Seventh-Day Adventist Reform churches prefer to recognize the scriptural term, Godhead.

Women in Ministry: While women can be effective Bible workers and teachers, the scriptural qualifications for elders and bishops apply specifically to men as overseers of the Lord's flock.

For more information contact: P.O. Box 7240, Roanoke, VA 24019; Phone: (540) 362-1800; Fax: (540) 366-2814; E-mail: sdarm@worldnet.att.net; Web site: http://www.sdarm.org

Southern Baptist Convention

Baptists came into being in the early 17th century, when religious reform was sweeping England. Immigration to escape persecution brought the first group of Baptists to America around the same time. In 1707, five churches in Pennsylvania established the Philadelphia Baptist Association, the first in the new world. A century later, the first national organization was formed. During the Civil War, the question of slavery divided Baptists, resulting in the formation of a southern group in 1845.[18] There were 40,613 congregations with 15,694,050 members associated with those churches in 1996.

Abortion: God created human beings in his own image. Therefore, human life is sacred. The Convention affirms the biblical prohibition against the taking of unborn human life except to save the life of the mother.

Baptism: Baptism is performed by immersing a believer in water in the name of the Father, Son, and Holy Spirit. It is a prerequisite to the privileges of church membership and to communion.[19]

Birth Control: The Convention opposes the distribution of birth control devices to minors.

Capital Punishment: No official position.

Christ's Return: Jesus Christ will return personally and visibly in glory to the earth. The dead will be raised and Christ will judge all men in righteousness.[20]

Communion: Communion is a symbolic act of obedience open to members of the church.[21]

Creation vs. Evolution: God is the creator, redeemer, preserver, and ruler of the universe.[22]

Deity of Jesus: Christ is the eternal Son of God. In his incarnation, he was conceived of the Holy Spirit and born of the Virgin Mary. He was raised from the dead and ascended into heaven. He is now exalted at the right hand of God.[23]

Divorce and Remarriage: God established marriage, and Jesus declared it to be a sacred, monogamous, and life-long institution joining one man and one woman. It is a holy covenant of trust and commitment and is to be kept in purity and faithfulness. The conditions permitting divorce are limited. When marriage relations are strained or damaged, reconciliation is God's ideal.

Government: Congregational. Each member has a voice and vote in the decisions of the church. The District Association is geographically the closest unit to the churches. There are 39 state conventions which exist to help the churches. The Southern Baptist Convention, which meets once a year, is composed of messengers from the churches.[24]

Heaven/Hell: The unrighteous will be consigned to hell, the place of everlasting punishment. The righteous in their resurrected and glorified bodies will receive their reward and will dwell forever in heaven with the Lord.[25]

Homosexuality: Homosexuality is a perversion of divine standards, a violation of nature and natural affections. It is an abomination in the eyes of God. Though homosexual practice is not a normal lifestyle, God loves the homosexual and offers salvation. Homosexuals, like all sinners, can receive forgiveness and victory through repentance and personal faith in Jesus Christ.

Inspiration of Scripture: The Holy Bible was written by men divinely inspired and is the record of God's revelation of himself to mankind. It is a perfect treasure of divine instruction. It has God for its author, salvation for its end, and truth, without any mixture of error, for its matter. It is the supreme standard by which all human conduct, creeds, and all religious opinion should be tried.[26]

Miracles: No answer.

Restrictions: None.

Security of Salvation: All true believers endure to the end. Those who God has accepted in Christ and sanctified in the Holy Spirit, will never fall away from the state of grace, but shall persevere to the end.[27]

Speaking in Tongues and Other Gifts of the Spirit: No answer.

Trinity: The Southern Baptist Convention is trinitarian and believes in God the Father, Christ the eternal Son, and the Holy Spirit. The eternal God reveals himself as Father, Son, and Holy Spirit without distinct attribute, but without division of nature, essence, or being.[28]

Women in Ministry: Women are not ordained.

For more information contact: 127 Ninth Ave. N, Nashville, TN 37234; Phone: (800) 458-2772 or (615) 244-2495; Fax: (615) 242-0065; Web site: http://www.sbcnet.org/index.htm

Southern Methodist Church, The

The Southern Methodist Church began in 1940, following the unification of the Methodist Church (north), the Methodist Episcopal Church (south), and the Protestant Methodist Church. The SMC withdrew from this merger over issues of theology, central control, and denominational ownership of all churches. The church claims the motto, "Keeping our eyes on Jesus, our feet firmly planted on the Word of God, and our hearts knit together in the love and unity of the Holy Spirit, we are more than conquerors." In 1997, there were 126 congregations with 7,835 members.

Abortion: Infant life begins at the moment of conception. To destroy that conceived embryo, wherein life has begun, is murder and is wrong.

Baptism: Baptism is a symbolic sign of regeneration. It is the outward testimony of the inward cleansing through faith in Christ.

Birth Control: Such contraceptive means that interferes with the fertilization of the egg are acceptable birth control means. Abortion is not acceptable.

Capital Punishment: Murder should be punishable by death, thus, endorsing the dignity of man's creation in the image of God.

Christ's Return: Southern Methodists believe in the future literal, bodily, personal, visible, imminent, and premillennial return of Christ.

Communion: The bread and grape juice remain their created substance. Each symbolizes the crucified body and shed blood of Jesus Christ. The receiving and partaking of the same by the communicant of faith focuses on Christ in a heavenly and spiritual manner only.

Creation vs. Evolution: The Genesis account of creation teaches that all things were created by God according to each living kind and that the entire creation was accomplished in six literal days.

Deity of Jesus: Jesus Christ is the virgin-born, eternal, and divine only begotten Son of God.

Divorce and Remarriage: The church does not recognize divorce and remarriage for simply any cause. The Scriptures allow divorce and remarriage for one just cause: infidelity.

Government: Connectional-congregational form. Churches are connectional in name, doctrine, and program. They are congregational in ownership of property, calling of pastors, and in the implementation of conference programs. There is a president for the entire denomination, with lay and clergy delegates attending conferences.

Heaven/Hell: There is a literal eternal place called hell, where there is eternal punishment and separation from God. There is an eternal heaven of joy for the saved.

Homosexuality: Homosexuality is a chosen lifestyle. According to Romans 1, it is a sin. Like any other sinful behavior, it must be abandoned by the help of God through the inspiration of the Holy Spirit.

Inspiration of Scripture: The Bible is the inerrant, verbally inspired, infallible, and absolute Word of God, given to men of old through the inspiration of the Holy Spirit.

Miracles: Every miracle mentioned in the Word of God was a literal, supernatural performance. Today the greatest continuing miracle is a sinner becoming saved.

Restrictions: Gambling in any form is not permitted. Clergy are not allowed to smoke or drink alcoholic beverages. The laity are strongly admonished to refrain from the same. Lay leadership is expected to comply with the same restrictions as a minister. Partaking of any form of contraband drugs is prohibited.

Security of Salvation: The Southern Methodist Church affirms the security of the believing believer. God will never take salvation away. However, individuals, through sin or complacency, can recant their faith and be eternally lost. This security is not based on holding on or good works. It is simply based on remaining in the continuing saving relationship with Christ.

Speaking in Tongues and Other Gifts of the Spirit: The gifts of the Spirit are for ministry, not manifestation. Therefore, the Holy Spirit gives gifts to people according to the ministry need. This being true, where all speak the same language, the gift of tongues is not needed, just as the gift of healing is not needed where there are no sick.

Trinity: The SMC believes in the triune Godhead: the Father, the Son, and the Holy Spirit.

Women in Ministry: Women are not ordained into the ministry role. However, they are commissioned to unordained ministry roles, such as prison ministries, Child Evangelism Fellowship ministry, and nursing home ministries.

For more information contact: P.O. Box 39, Orangeburg, SC 29116-0039; Phone: (803) 536-1378; Fax: (803) 535-3881; E-mail: smchq@juno.com

---

Sovereign Grace Believers

Sovereign Grace Believers have much in common with the Reformed Baptist movement that began in the mid-1950s. The impetus for this reformation focused on the desire of some Baptist churches to return to a Calvinistic theology. The first Sovereign Grace Conference was held in Ashland, KY in 1954. Sovereign Grace is not a denomination, but a fellowship of churches who share common doctrine and methods.[29] Views on cultural issues are held by some but not all churches. There were approximately 300 Sovereign Grace fellowships in 1997.

Abortion: Abortion is wrong ninety-nine percent of the time.

Baptism: The person baptized, regardless of age, must be a believer in Christ.

Birth Control: Birth control is a matter of liberty for each couple.

Capital Punishment: The state has the right to take life under certain circumstances.

Christ's Return: Christ will return at the end of the age in glory, receiving believers to himself and judging unbelievers.

Communion: The Lord's Supper is for believers to remember the Lord's death until he returns.

Creation vs. Evolution: Macroevolution is false and unproven. Microevolution (within a species) is observable. Creation by God, not evolution by chance, is the Bible's teaching.

Deity of Jesus: Jesus is Immanuel, God with us.

Divorce and Remarriage: The grounds for divorce are sexual unfaithfulness and desertion. Divorces under such circumstances allow the parties to remarry. Each case must be examined separately. No blanket statements can be made.

Government: Congregations are governed by elders and deacons. Individual churches are autonomous.

Heaven/Hell: Heaven is for believers. Unbelievers will be eternally separated from God.

Homosexuality: The practice of homosexuality is sinful, just like adultery and gossip.

Inspiration of Scripture: The Scriptures of the Old and New Testaments are the result of God's will, not the will of man.

Miracles: God works special miracles on behalf of his people in all ages.

Restrictions: None.

Security of Salvation: Jesus stated, "All that the Father has given me will come to me and I will raise them upon the last day. I will lose none of them."

Speaking in Tongues and Other Gifts of the Spirit: The church believes the gifts of the Spirit are for this age. There is no New Testament evidence that certain gifts ceased.

Trinity: The fellowship believes God is manifested in three persons: Father, Son, and Spirit.

Women in Ministry: The church does not allow women as elders in the body, but otherwise they can function fully, including prophesying and teaching.

For more information contact: P.O. Box 548, St. Croix Falls, WI 54024; Phone: (715) 755-3560; Fax: (612) 465-5101; E-mail: heitmant@ bucky.win.bright.net

---

Traditional Episcopal Church

The Traditional Episcopal Church, whose motto is, "Deum Colere (To Serve God)," is an outgrowth of division in the Episcopal church. It was founded in 1992 by Right Reverend Richard G. Melli. The church believes they are the one, holy, catholic, and apostolic church.

Abortion: The Traditional Episcopal Church opposes the practice of abortion.

Baptism: There is one baptism by water for infants, children, and adults.

Birth Control: Birth control is a personal decision.

Capital Punishment: The church is against capital punishment.

Christ's Return: Christians should live every day as if Christ's return were to be tomorrow.

Communion: The Traditional Episcopal Church is a sacramental church and considers the Holy Eucharist to be the central act of the church. Communion should be availed of as often as possible.

Creation vs. Evolution: Evolution and creation are not in conflict with each other. Both are a tool of God.

Deity of Jesus: The church believes that Jesus is the only begotten Son of God.

Divorce and Remarriage: Marriage cannot be dissolved. The church will consider decrees of nullity in qualified cases.

Government: Synodical and tricameral.

Heaven/Hell: The ancient teachings of the church are followed concerning heaven and hell. Heaven is unity with God, while hell is separation from God.

Homosexuality: To be a homosexual is not a sin. However, to practice homosexuality is a sin.

Inspiration of Scripture: The Scriptures were inspired by God and written by man.

Miracles: Miracles are part of the works of God in and through his church.

Restrictions: The Traditional Episcopal Church allows only male priests, bishops, and deacons.

Security of Salvation: Salvation is the stated goal of every Christian and needs to be worked on every day of their life.

Speaking in Tongues and Other Gifts of the Spirit: The church recognizes the seven gifts of the Holy Spirit.

Trinity: The Traditional Episcopal Church is trinitarian.

Women in Ministry: Women are restricted to the Ancient Order of Deconesses, who are set apart but not ordained.

For more information contact: 20253 Twin Oaks Rd., Springhill, FL 34610; Phone and Fax: (352) 799-7465; E-mail: tec@innet.com

Unamended Christadelphians
(Brethren In Christ)

Christadelphians trace their modern history to the pre-Civil War era. In the mid-19th century, Dr. John Thomas left England to emigrate to America. During his Atlantic crossing, a terrible storm almost sunk the ship that carried Thomas to his new home. As he faced his mortality, Thomas realized he knew nothing of life after death. He vowed that if he survived the storm, he would not rest until he found the answer. He devoted the rest of his life to studying the Bible.[1] Because Christadelphians have no central organization, accurate membership figures are unavailable, but it is estimated there are 15,000 members in 250 ecclesias. Christadelphians believe in the Hope of Israel, the representative (not substitutionary) sacrifice of Christ, the resurrection of the responsible dead, and conditional immortality in God's Kingdom on earth.

Abortion: Most members are firmly opposed to abortion, but there is no official stance.

Baptism: Baptism by immersion, as practiced in the first century church, is the means of coming into Christ. Infants are not baptized.

Birth Control: No official stance.

Capital Punishment: No official stance.

Christ's Return: Christ's return and the setting up of God's millennial Kingdom on earth is eagerly awaited and expected sometime in the near future. Faithful believers will be rewarded with immortality and will reign with Christ on earth.

Communion: Communion is practiced weekly among validly baptized members, including visitors from affiliated congregations.

Creation vs. Evolution: Evolution is vigorously opposed as an unproven hypothesis. All of the design and order of nature speaks eloquently of creation.

Deity of Jesus: Jesus was a man—divine in origin, but human in nature, of the same nature as all other men.

Divorce and Remarriage: Some churches strongly oppose divorce and remarriage, but there is no official stance.

Government: There is no central hierarchy. Each congregation (ecclesia) is autonomous. Church functions are handled by a board of arranging brothers. There are no ordained clergy. Lay ministers carry out pastoral duties.

Heaven/Hell: Heaven is declared to be God's abode and possession—the earth has been given to man. Hell is the grave, the abode of the dead.

Homosexuality: Homosexuality is condemned, as in Scripture.

Inspiration of Scripture: The Bible is the inspired Word of God.

Miracles: Miracles have always been used by God to validate the messages he was communicating to mankind. Today, the most obvious miracle is his preservation of the Bible, his Holy Word.

Restrictions: No official restrictions.

Security of Salvation: Salvation is ultimately dependent upon faithful endurance after commitment to God and Christ.

Speaking in Tongues and Other Gifts of the Spirit: Like other miracles, these manifestations of Holy Spirit power were always needed to validate and confirm the message of the Gospel. It is preaching the gospel that builds up the church, not gifts.

Trinity: The Trinity was an invention of the church in the 4th century and following. Neither the word nor the concept are stated in Scripture.

Women in Ministry: Although women perform many functions in Sunday school teaching, study groups, writing, and certain pastoral duties, most churches do not have women in leadership roles.

For more information contact: Christadelphian Action Society, 1000 Mohawk Dr., Elgin, IL 60120-3148; Phone: (847) 888-3334 or (847) 741-5253; Fax: (847) 888-3334; E-mail: nz-cas@juno.com; Web site: http://www2.bath.ac.uk/~ensjmpf/delph/home.html

---

United Church of Christ

The United Church of Christ came into being in 1957 with the union of two Protestant denominations: the Evangelical and Reformed Church, and the Congregational Christian Churches. Each of these was, in turn, the result of a union of two earlier denominations. The Congregational Churches were organized when the Pilgrims of Plymouth Plantation and the Puritans of the Massachusetts Bay Colony acknowledged their essential unity in the Cambridge Platform. The Reformed Church in the United States traces its beginnings to congregations of German settlers in Pennsylvania founded from 1725. The Christian Churches sprang up in the late 1700s and early 1800s in reaction to the theological and organizational rigidity of the Methodist, Presbyterian, and Baptist churches of the time. The Evangelical Synod of North America traces its beginnings to an association of German Evangelical pastors in Missouri. This association, founded in 1841, reflected the 1817 union of Lutheran and Reformed churches in Germany. Churches are autonomous and most issues are decided on the local level.[2] In 1995, there were 6,145 churches with 1,472,213 members.

Abortion: The General Synod since 1975 has adopted a pro-choice position.

Baptism: Baptism is one of two sacraments practiced in the church. The church practices both infant and believer's baptism.[3]

Birth Control: No official position. However, the church has no opposition to birth control.

Capital Punishment: General Synod opposes capital punishment.

Christ's Return: Christ will come again to judge all mankind.[4] There is no formal position on when he will return.

Communion: Holy Communion is the second sacrament practiced in the United Church of Christ.[5] Communion is open to all baptized Christians.

Creation vs. Evolution: God called the worlds into being, created man in his own image, and set before man the ways of life and death.[6]

Deity of Jesus: Jesus Christ, the man of Nazareth, the crucified and risen Lord, has come and shared mankind's common lot, conquering sin and death and reconciling the world to himself.[7]

Divorce and Remarriage: Divorced and remarried persons are welcome to participate fully in the life of the church.

Government: The basic unit of the United Church of Christ is the congregation. These congregations exist in covenantal relationships with one another.[8]

Heaven/Hell: Views vary. Check with your local church.

Homosexuality: General Synod has approved open policy toward gay and lesbian persons and permits ordination of gay and lesbian persons.

Inspiration of Scripture: The United Church of Christ affirms the primacy of the Scriptures as a source for understanding the good news and as a foundation for all statements of faith.[9]

Miracles: Beliefs vary. Check with your local church.

Restrictions: None.

Security of Salvation: Believes in justification by grace through faith.

Speaking in Tongues and Other Gifts of the Spirit: The use of sign gifts is not common in the UCC, but would not be prohibited.

Trinity: The Nicene and other creeds affirm the doctrine of the Trinity.

Women in Ministry: UCC has ordained women since the 19th century and women are welcome as leaders at all levels of church life.

For more information contact: 700 Prospect Ave. E, Cleveland, OH 44115-1100; Phone: (216) 736-2100; Fax: (216) 736-2120; E-mail: langa@ucc.org; Web site: http://www.ucc.org/ucchp.htm

---

United Methodist Church

The United Methodist Church was created in 1968, when the Methodist Church and the Evangelical United Brethren Church merged.[19] Methodism, whose theological parents were John and Charles Wesley, began in the late 1700s when the Wesleys formed an alternative to the Church of England.[20] In 1997, there were 36,559 congregations with 8,600,000 members in the United States.

Abortion: The UMC believes in the sanctity of unborn human life, which makes it reluctant to approve abortion. But it is equally bound to respect the sacredness of the life and well-being of the mother, for whom devastating damage may result from an unacceptable pregnancy. Therefore, the church supports the legal option of abortion under proper medical procedures. The church cannot affirm abortion as an acceptable means of birth control and unconditionally rejects it as a means of gender selection.[21]

Baptism: Baptism is not only a sign of profession and mark of difference whereby Christians are distinguished from others that are not baptized, but it is also a sign of regeneration or new birth. The baptism of young children is performed in the church. Baptism, by sprinkling, is required for membership.[22]

Birth Control: People have the duty to consider the impact on the total world community of their decisions regarding childbearing. They should have access to information and appropriate means to limit their fertility, including voluntary sterilization.[23]

Capital Punishment: No statement.

Christ's Return: Christ will return again in glory to judge the righteous and the unrighteous.[24]

Communion: Communion is a sacrament of redemption by Christ's death. For those who rightly, worthily, and with faith receive it, the bread is the partaking of the body of Christ and the cup of blessing is partaking of the blood of Christ. Transubstantiation cannot be proved by Holy Writ and is repugnant to the plain words of Scripture. The body of Christ is given, taken, and eaten in the Supper, only after a heavenly and spiritual manner.[25] Open communion is performed monthly.

Creation vs. Evolution: No statement.

Deity of Jesus: The Son, who is the Word of the Father, the very and eternal God, of one substance with the Father, took man's nature in the womb of the blessed virgin so that two whole and perfect natures, the Godhead and manhood, were joined together in one person, never to be divided. Christ is very God and very man, who truly suffered, was crucified, dead, and buried to reconcile his Father to mankind. He was a sacrifice, not only for original guilt, but also for actual sins of men.[26]

Divorce and Remarriage: The UMC affirms the sanctity of the marriage covenant which is expressed in love, mutual support, personal commitment, and shared fidelity between a man and a woman. When marriage partners are estranged beyond reconciliation, the church recognizes divorce as regrettable, but also recognizes the right of divorced persons to remarry.[27]

Government: Episcopal democracy. Superintendents preside over districts made up of local congregations. Bishops supervise districts through annual conferences. There are five geographic jurisdictions formed by conferences. These meet quadrennially. The General Conference, made up of delegates from the annual conferences, meets every four years.[28]

Heaven/Hell: The UMC believes in the resurrection of the dead: the righteous to life eternal, and the wicked to endless condemnation.[29]

Homosexuality: The church does not condone the practice of homosexuality and considers it incompatible with Christian teaching. However, the UMC also affirms that God's grace is available to all. Homosexual persons are individuals of sacred worth and the church supports basic human rights and civil liberties for homosexual persons.[30]

Inspiration of Scripture: The Holy Bible, Old and New Testaments, reveals the Word of God so far as it is necessary for salvation.[31]

Miracles: The UMC accepts the biblical accounts of miracles.

Restrictions: The church supports abstinence from alcohol, illegal drugs, and tobacco. Christians should refrain from gambling.[32]

Security of Salvation: After a believer has received the Holy Ghost, they may depart from grace given and fall into sin, and, by the grace of God, rise again and amend their life.[33]

Speaking in Tongues and Other Gifts of the Spirit: It is repugnant to the Word of God and the custom of the primitive church to have public prayer in the church or to minister the Sacraments in a tongue not understood by the people.[34]

Trinity: There is but one living and true God, everlasting, without body or parts, of infinite power, wisdom, and goodness. He is the maker and preserver of all things, both visible and invisible. And in unity of the Godhead there are three persons, of one substance, power and eternity—the Father, the Son, and the Holy Ghost.[35]

Women in Ministry: The UMC affirms the importance of women in decision-making positions at all levels of church life, including pastoral positions. It urges churches to guarantee their presence through policies of employment and recruitment.[36]

For more information contact: 601 W. Riverside Ave., Dayton, OH 45406; Phone: (800) 672-1789; Fax: (615) 742-5469; Web site: http://www.umc.org

---

United Pentecostal Church International

The modern Pentecostal movement developed beginning in 1901 from a Bible school in Topeka, KS led by Charles Parham.[37] The basic and fundamental doctrine of this organization is the standard of full salvation, which is repentance, baptism in water by immersion in the name of the Lord Jesus Christ for the remission of sins, and the baptism of the Holy Ghost with the initial sign of speaking with other tongues as the Spirit give utterance.[38] The United Pentecostal Church International has more than 3,800 churches and 8,000 ministers in the United States and Canada.

Abortion: The church is on record as being opposed to abortion on demand and partial birth abortion. However, it expresses a strong compassion of forgiveness and assistance for those who have abortions.

Baptism: Repentant believers are baptized in water by immersion in the name of Jesus Christ.[39]

Birth Control: No statement.

Capital Punishment: No statement.

Christ's Return: Christ will return to earth to rapture the saved, judge the nations, and rule the earth for 1,000 years.

Communion: The UPCI follows this ordinance in recognition of the sacrificial atoning death of Jesus Christ and with the hope in his return.

Creation vs. Evolution: God is a Spirit, the eternal one, the creator of all things—including mankind—thus making him their Father (through creation).[40]

Deity of Jesus: Jesus Christ is the one God incarnate, the manifestation of God himself in the flesh. He is the union of absolute deity and sinless humanity. Jesus is Savior; his name is the only name given for salvation.[41]

Divorce and Remarriage: The church allows divorce and remarriage only on the grounds of adultery on the part of either spouse.

Government: The headquarters of the United Pentecostal Church International is the World Evangelism Center in the St. Louis suburb of Hazelwood, MO. The work is organized into administration, editorial, education, foreign missions, Harvestime Radio, home missions (North America), ladies auxiliary, Sunday school, youth, and publishing. The basic form of church government is congregational. The local assembly is autonomous, controlling its own affairs—the pastor being the leader under Christ. The UPCI has a modified presbyterian form of organization for the sake of ministerial standards, fellowship, and evangelism.[42]

Heaven/Hell: Both heaven and hell are viewed as real and the final abode for mankind.

Homosexuality: Homosexuality is viewed as sin, but as with all other sins, God forgives those who through faith repent.

Inspiration of Scripture: The Bible is the inspired and infallible Word of God, the sole authority for faith, doctrine, and instruction in Christian living.[43]

Miracles: The church seeks and looks for miracles, including divine healing, answered prayer, and the provision of need.[44]

Restrictions: The UPCI expects its members to maintain a standard of living that separates them from sinful behavior and activities.

Security of Salvation: The believer is secure in Jesus Christ as long as he maintains faith and commitment to God and strives to obey the Word of God.

Speaking in Tongues and Other Gifts of the Spirit: Speaking in other tongues is an external, outward evidence of one's receiving the Holy Ghost.[45]

Trinity: God is absolutely one, with no distinction of persons. In order to save sinful humanity, God provided a sinless man as a sacrifice of atonement—Jesus Christ, the Son of God. In begetting the Son and in relating to humanity, God is the Father. In working to transform and empower human lives, God is the Holy Spirit. Thus, for salvation, God has revealed himself as Father (in parental relationship to humanity), as his Son (in human flesh), and as the Holy Spirit (in spiritual action).[46]

Women in Ministry: Women may hold all levels of ministerial license, including ordination, and may engage in all areas of ministry including the position of pastor.

For more information contact: 8855 Dunn Rd., Hazelwood, MO 63042-2299; Phone: (314) 837-7300; Fax: (314) 837-4503; E-mail: higher-fire@prairienet.org; Web site: http://www.upci.org

---

Wesleyan Church, The

Two branches of the holiness movement, The Pilgrim Holiness Church and the Wesleyan Methodist Church of North America, joined hands on June 26, 1968 to form The Wesleyan Church. The Pilgrim Holiness Church had its beginnings with the formation of the International Holiness Union and Prayer League in 1897. It became an official denomination in 1922. The Wesleyan Methodist Church has roots that reach back to the ministry of John Wesley. It was first named in 1841 and experienced a period of waning interest before a holiness revival swept the United States.[1] The church's motto is, "Pursuing and Proclaiming Holiness." There were 1,580 congregations with 118,021 members in 1997.

Abortion: Except in the case of risk to the life of the mother, the Wesleyan Church stands firm against the evil of abortion—both the personal evil of abortion by any individual and the worldwide social evil of abortion. However, the church rejects the use of violence to force a change in abortion practice.[2]

Baptism: Water baptism is a sacrament of the church, commanded by the Lord, and administered to believers. It is a symbol of the new covenant of grace and signifies acceptance of the benefits of the atonement of Jesus Christ. By means of this sacrament, believers declare their faith in Jesus Christ as Savior.[3]

Birth Control: No statement.

Capital Punishment: Capital punishment should be reserved for those crimes committed in serious circumstances which are clearly defined by law and administered by justice.[4]

Christ's Return: The certainty of the personal and imminent return of Christ inspires holy living and zeal for the evangelization of the world. At his return, he will fulfill all prophecies made concerning his final and complete triumph over evil.[5]

Communion: The Lord's Supper is a sacrament of redemption by Christ's death and of hope in his victorious return, as well as a sign of the love that Christians have for each other. To such as receive it humbly, with a proper spirit and by faith, the Lord's Supper is made a means through which God communicates grace to the heart.[6]

Creation vs. Evolution: God is the creator.[7]

Deity of Jesus: Jesus Christ is the only begotten Son of God, conceived by the Holy Spirit, and born of the Virgin Mary, truly God and truly man. He died on the cross and was buried, to be a sacrifice both for original sin and for all human transgressions, and to reconcile believers to God. Christ rose bodily from the dead and ascended into heaven, where he intercedes for mankind at the Father's right hand until returning to judge all humanity at the last day.[8]

Divorce and Remarriage: Divorce is a sin. In a day of easy divorce, Wesleyans continue to stand firm on the Bible's teaching that God's plan for marriage is that one man and one woman stay together for their entire lives. Sexual immorality is the only possible reason for divorce, and only then after serious spiritual counsel. Divorce is not reversible. The divorced status can be changed only by a new marriage to the same person or another person. Divorce is not unpardonable. A redeemed sinner or reclaimed backslider is free to marry in the Lord or to remain unmarried. The one exception to this freedom is a believer who disobeys the commandment of God and puts away a believing spouse. That person must remain unmarried to leave room for reconciliation to the spouse.[9]

Government: Modified congregational form of government.

Heaven/Hell: There is a conscious, personal existence after death. Heaven with its eternal glory and the blessedness of Christ's presence is the final abode of those who choose the salvation which God provides through Jesus Christ. Hell, with its everlasting misery and separation from God, is the final abode of those who neglect this great salvation.[10]

Homosexuality: Homosexuality is immoral and sinful. However, the grace of God is sufficient to redeem and restore the homosexual.[11]

Inspiration of Scripture: The books of the Old and New Testaments constitute the Holy Scriptures. They are the inspired and infallibly written Word of God, fully inerrant in their original manuscripts and superior to all human authority. The Scriptures have been transmitted to the present without corruption of any essential doctrine. They contain all things necessary to salvation. Whatever is not in the Bible nor may be proved thereby is not to be required as an article of faith or be thought requisite or necessary to salvation.[12]

Miracles: Miracles still occur within God's sovereign plan and are witnessed from time to time.

Restrictions: The Wesleyan Church is opposed to the production, sale, purchase, and use of alcoholic beverages. Tobacco, narcotics, and other harmful drugs are not to be used unless for mechanical, chemical, or medicinal purpose. The church also opposes the legalization of merchandising on the Lord's day.[13]

Security of Salvation: When one repents of personal sin and believes on the Lord Jesus Christ, he is justified, regenerated, adopted into the family of God, and assured of personal salvation through the witness of the Holy Spirit.[14]

Speaking in Tongues and Other Gifts of the Spirit: The gift of the

Spirit is the Holy Spirit himself. He is to be desired more than the gifts of the Spirit which he in his wise counsel bestows upon individual members of the church to enable them to fulfill their function as members of the body of Christ. The Wesleyan Church believes in the miraculous use of languages and the interpretation of languages in its biblical and historical setting. But it is contrary to the Word of God to teach that speaking in an unknown tongue or the gift of tongues is the evidence of the baptism of the Holy Spirit or of that entire sanctification which the baptism accomplishes. Therefore, only a language readily understood by the congregation is to be used in public worship. The Wesleyan Church believes that the use of an ecstatic prayer language has no clear scriptural sanction or any pattern of established historical usage in the church. Therefore, the use of such a prayer language shall not be promoted.[15]

Trinity: There is one living and true God, both holy and loving, eternal, unlimited in power, wisdom, and goodness. He is the creator and preserver of all things. Within this unity there are three persons of one essential nature, power, and eternity: the Father, the Son, and the Holy Spirit.[16]

Women in Ministry: For the past 100 years, the Wesleyan Church has ordained women.

For more information contact: P.O. Box 50434, Indianapolis, IN 46250-0434; Phone: (317) 570-5154; Fax: (317) 570-5280; E-mail: gensecoff@aol.com

---

Wisconsin Evangelical Lutheran Synod

German Lutherans began coming to the new world to start new lives, often settling among the various communities that were most familiar to them. In the course of American Lutheranism, groups of churches often came to be known by the state in which they lived. The Wisconsin Evangelical Lutheran Synod held its constituting convention on May 26, 1850 in Granville, WI. This Synod has no official ties to the modern Evangelical movement. The church believes that in eternity God chose those individuals whom he would in time convert through the Gospel and preserve in the faith to eternal life.[17] In 1997, there were 1,235 churches with 412,942 members in the United States.

Abortion: Human life is the gift of a gracious God. Life is a time of grace during which humans have the opportunity to learn the way of salvation through faith in Jesus Christ. Only God has the right to take the life he has given. Life begins at conception and ends when the soul leaves the body.[18]

Baptism: Baptism is a sacred act, instituted by God, using water and God's Word, that offers and gives the forgiveness of sins, spiritual life, and eternal salvation. It is meant for young and old, including children. Infants also are sinful and therefore need the rebirth effected through baptism.[19]

Birth Control: No statement.

Capital Punishment: No statement.

Christ's Return: Jesus will come from heaven on the last day to judge all the living and the dead. On that day all who have died without faith in Jesus Christ will also be condemned to hell. Hell is a place of eternal torment and separation from God. On judgment day, when all the dead shall rise, the souls of all believers will be reunited with a glorified body and live forever in heaven. This is a place of eternal joy, for there will be no more tears or sorrow.[20] The WELS rejects every form of millennialism, since it has no valid scriptural basis and leads Christians to set their hopes upon the Kingdom of Christ as an earthly kingdom. It likewise rejects as unscriptural any hopes that the Jews will all be converted in those final days or that all people will ultimately enjoy eternal bliss.[21]

Communion: Holy Communion is a sacred act instituted by Christ. In, with, and under the bread and wine communicants receive Jesus' true body and blood. In this meal Jesus gives the forgiveness of sins, strengthens faith, and gives eternal salvation to all who believe. Only penitent sinners who have received proper instruction in the Christian faith should be admitted to this sacrament.[22]

Creation vs. Evolution: At the beginning of time God created the universe, heaven, earth, and all creatures. He did this in six natural days using his almighty Word. He made everything out of nothing. Man and woman are God's special creation.[23]

Deity of Jesus: Jesus Christ, the Savior of mankind, is the Son of God, equal to the Father and the Holy Spirit. He is also the Son of the Virgin Mary and became man to redeem mankind. He is God and man in one person. As a substitute, he lived a perfect life keeping the law for all. He died a perfect death on the cross to pay a sufficient price for mankind's sin. After rising from the dead, he ascended into heaven.[24]

Divorce and Remarriage: Marriage is a loving relationship in which the man is the head and the woman is the helper. A married person sins if he or she divorces without biblical reason. Since marriage is established by God, it is a holy relationship not to be broken. Before God, no divorce is valid except in cases of fornication or desertion.[25]

Government: Lutheran.

Heaven/Hell: When people die, their bodies remain on this earth but their souls are sent by God either to heaven or to hell, depending on the condition of their souls at death. On the last day, all who have died without faith in Jesus Christ will be condemned to hell. Hell is a place of eternal torment and separation from God. On judgment day, when all the dead shall rise, the souls of all believers will be reunited with a glorified body and live forever in heaven. This is a place of eternal joy, for there will be no more tears or sorrow.[26]

Homosexuality: Scripture condemns homosexual conduct as a sin, as it does adultery, murder, and drunkenness. The homosexual needs to repent of that sin and receive forgiveness through faith in Christ.

Inspiration of Scripture: The Bible is the very Word of God. It was inspired by the Holy Spirit. God breathed into the writers the very thoughts and words they were to write. As a result, every statement in the Bible is true; it is without error. The Bible interprets itself. It is the only guide for faith and life.[27]

Miracles: No statement.

Restrictions: No statement.

Security of Salvation: Faith is a penitent sinner's acceptance of Jesus Christ as his only Savior and full reliance on Jesus' merits for forgiveness of sins and salvation. Whoever remains in this faith to the end of life will be saved eternally.[28]

Speaking in Tongues and Other Gifts of the Spirit: No statement.

Trinity: There is only one true God. This God is invisible, holy, eternal, and possesses infinite power and wisdom. God reveals himself as three persons: Father, Son, and Holy Spirit. These three persons in one God are of one essence, equal in power, glory, and in every other quality. To deny or ignore one person is to disavow all of them.[29]

Women in Ministry: No statement.

For more information contact: 2929 N. Mayfair Rd., Milwaukee, WI 53222; Phone: (414) 256-3888; Fax: (414) 256-3899; Web site: http://www.wels.net

---

Worldwide Church of God

In 1931, Herbert Armstrong began a radio ministry, a magazine, and a church that eventually became The World Tomorrow, *The Plain Truth,* and the Worldwide Church of God. After Armstrong died in 1986, church leaders began to believe that many of Armstrong's doctrines were not biblical. These doctrines were rejected, and today the church and The Plain Truth are in agreement with the statement of faith of the National Association of Evangelicals. When the church changed its views, some members continued to hold Armstrong-era doctrines. Many of these left the Worldwide Church of God to form other denominations. Most congregations meet for worship on Saturdays. Church tradition also includes observances for the Festival of Unleavened Bread, Pentecost, the Feast of Trumpets, the Day of Atonement, and the Festival of Tabernacles. Although attendance at these festivals was once required of all members, they are now optional. In 1997, there were approximately 420 churches with 50,000 members in the United States.

Abortion: Under ordinary circumstances, abortion is not a legitimate biblical or ethical choice. When a mother's life is at stake, however, abortion is considered to be a legitimate choice. Members' choices about abortion in other extraordinary circumstances, such as rape or incest, are not considered a test of fellowship.

Baptism: Baptism signifies a believers's repentance and acceptance of Jesus Christ as Lord and Savior. The Worldwide Church of God does not baptize infants and practices baptism by immersion.

Birth Control: The church permits most forms of birth control.

Capital Punishment: God has placed responsibility for human government and justice into human hands, under his sovereign authority. Capital punishment may or may not be appropriate, depending on its administration. All human government is ultimately responsible to God and will answer to God for all injustice.

Christ's Return: Jesus Christ, as he promised, will return to earth to judge and reign over all nations in the Kingdom of God. His second coming will be visible, and in power and glory. This event inaugurates the resurrection of the dead and the reward of the saints. The church makes no predictions as to when this will be.

Communion: At the Lord's Supper, baptized members participate in the new covenant as they partake of bread and wine in remembrance of the Savior. Members of other denominations may participate if they have faith in Jesus Christ as Lord and Savior. Once each year the ceremony includes the washing of feet.

Creation vs. Evolution: God is the creator of heaven and earth and of all life. The church sees no biblical reason to reject the conclusions of scientists that the earth is billions of years old and that life has been on earth for billions of years. Similarly, the church sees no biblical reason to reject evidence that life forms have been changing for billions of years.

Deity of Jesus: Jesus is the Word, by whom and for whom God created all things. As God was manifest in the flesh for the salvation of man, he was begotten of the Holy Spirit and born of the Virgin Mary, fully God and fully human, two natures in one person. Jesus is the Son of God and Lord of all, worthy of worship, honor, and reverence.

Divorce and Remarriage: The church upholds the sanctity of marriage but also recognizes that humans have hardened their hearts. The church discourages divorce, but in most cases permits divorced persons to re-marry.

Government: The Worldwide Church of God has an episcopalian form of government. The decision-making process involves councils of ministers who report to the Pastor General, which is the chief admin-istrative office in the church.

Heaven/Hell: The church has traditionally taught that souls of both be-lievers and unbelievers are unconscious until the resurrection. Those who deliberately reject salvation will eventually be thrown into the fires of hell and will perish; their souls will be destroyed and they will return to eternal unconsciousness. The church recognizes that these doctrines are not essential to salvation and does not make them a test of fellowship or a point of contention with other Christians.

Homosexuality: Homosexual behavior, like all sexual relations outside of marriage, is a sin. However, a homosexual orientation is not a sin in itself. The church does not sanction discrimination against homosexuals in the workplace.

Inspiration of Scripture: The 66 canonical books of the Old and New Testaments are the inspired Word of God, the foundation of truth, and the accurate record of God's revelation to humanity. The Holy Scriptures constitute ultimate authority in all matters of doctrine and embody the infallible principles that govern all facets of Christian living.

Miracles: The church believes in the supernatural—including angels, demons, miracles, and answers to prayers. God still works miracles, such as instantaneous healings and intervention in physical circumstances.

Restrictions: The church permits card-playing, dancing, and alcoholic beverages in moderation. The use of tobacco is strongly discouraged, and smoking is not permitted at church gatherings. Illegal drugs are forbidden.

Security of Salvation: The church is traditionally Arminian. Believers are assured of salvation by the inward witness of the Holy Spirit. Their salvation is secure in Jesus Christ.

Speaking in Tongues and Other Gifts of the Spirit: The Holy Spirit distributes gifts to believers, gifts that are to be used to serve others. The church neither forbids nor encourages members to speak in tongues.

Trinity: Scripture teaches that there is one God. It also teaches the divinity of the Father, Son, and Holy Spirit. Based on the biblical revelation, the church believes in the doctine of the Trinity: that God is one divine being in three eternal, co-essential, yet distinct persons.

Women in Ministry: The church encourages women to contribute in leadership roles of every kind. However, based on the teachings of the Apostle Paul, the church does not ordain women as pastoral overseers of local congregations.

For more information contact: 300 W. Green St., Pasadena, CA 91129; Phone: (626) 304-6181; Fax: (626) 304-8172; E-mail: greg_albrecht@ wcg.org; Web site: http://www.wcg.org

Appendix: Additional Denominations

We were unable to include the following groups due to lack of response and space constraints. Many of these denominations are small, having only a handful of congregations across the country. If you would like information on these, please write to the addresses provided or call the phone numbers listed. All addresses, phone numbers, and web sites are subject to change.

African Methodist Episcopal Zion
Box 23843, Charlotte, NC 28232; (704) 332-8979

African Universal and African Universal, Inc.
2336 S.W. 48th St., Hollywood, FL 33023; (954) 964-2270

Assembly of Yahvah
Box 89, Winfield, AL 35594

Assembly of YHWHHOSHUA
1998 58th Ln., Boone, CO 81025; (719) 947-3847

Associated Churches of Christ (Holiness)
1302 E. Adams Blvd., Los Angeles, CA 90011

Association of Fundamental Gospel Churches
9189 Grubb Ct., Canton, OH 44721

Bethel Fellowship, International
(206) 443-9752

Bible Church of Christ
1358 Morris Ave., Bronx, NY 10456

Bible Methodist Connection of Tennessee
Rt. 5, Box 324-A, Salisbury, NC 28146

Bible Presbyterian Church
756 Haddon Ave, Collingswood, NJ 08108

Bible Way of Our Lord Jesus Christ Worldwide
4949 Two-Notch Rd., Columbia, SC 29204; (800) 432-5612 or (803) 691-0622

Body of Christ Movement
Attn.: Foundational Teachings, Box 6598, Silver Springs, MD 20906

Christian Apostolic Church
205 South 16th St., Sabetha, KS 66534; (913) 284-2885

Christian Congregation
2877 W. Valley Blvd., Alhambra, CA 91803

Christian Nation Church, USA
11245 State Rt. 669 NE, Roseville, OH 43777

Christ's Holy Sanctified Church of America
5204 Willie St., Ft. Worth, TX 76105

Christ's Sanctified Holy Church (GA)
Attn.: CSHC Campgrounds and Home for the Aged, Box 1376, Perry GA
   31068

Churches of God Holiness
170 Ashby St., NW, Atlanta, GA 30314

Church of Christ Holiness Unto the Lord
1650 Smart St., P.O. Box 1642, Savannah, GA 31401

Church of Christ Holiness USA
329 E. Monument St., Jackson, MS 39202

Church of Christian Liberty
502 W. Euclid Ave., Arlington Heights, IL 60004; (847) 259-8736

Church of Daniel's Band
2960 Croll Rd., Beaverton, MI 48612; (517) 435-3649

Church of God by Faith, Inc.
3220 Haines St., Jacksonville, FL 32206

Church of God (Holiness)
7415 Metcalf, Overland Park, KS 66204

Church of God in Christ, Mennonite
420 N. Wedel, Moundridge, KS 67107; (316) 345-2532

Church of God, Mountain Assembly
110 S. Florence Ave., P.O. Box 157, Jellico, TN 37762

Church of God (Sanctified Church)
1037 Jefferson St., Nashville, TN 37208

Church of God Which He has Purchased With His Own Blood
1907 N.E. Grand Blvd., Oklahoma City, OK 73111; (405) 427-2166 or (405) 427-9643

Church of Our Lord Jesus Christ of the Apostolic Faith, Inc.
1421 5th Ave., New York, NY 10035; (919) 693-9449

Church of the Bible Covenant
Rt. 8, Box 214, 450 N. Fortville Pike, Greenfield, IN 46140

Church of the Living God
430 Forest Ave., Cincinnati, OH 45229

Church of the Living God the Pillar and Ground of Truth, Inc.
4520 Hydes Ferry Pike, Box 80735, Nashville, TN 37208

Church of the Living Word
P.O. Box 3429, Iowa City, IA 52244-3429; (888) 292-9673 or (319) 656-4492

Deer Spring Bruderhof
207 West Side Rd., Norfolk, CT 06058-1225; (860) 542-5545

Deliverance Evangelistic Church
4732 Broad St., Philadelphia, PA 19141; (215) 226-7600

Dunkard Brethren Church
801 Main St., Quinter, KS 67752

Emmanuel Holiness Church
6217 Burt Rd., Fuquay-Varina, NC 27526

Emmanuel Tabernacle Baptist Church Apostolic Faith
329 N. Garfield Ave., Columbus, OH 43203

Evangelical Bible Church
2436-44 Washington Blvd., P.O. Box 7476, Baltimore, MD 21227;
   (410) 644-3185

Evangelical Christian Church
Box 277, Birdsboro, PA 19508; (610) 582-4352

Evangelical Church Alliance
205 W. Broadway St., P.O. Box 9, Bradley, IL 60915-2235; (815) 937-0720

Evangelical Wesleyan Church
Rt. 1, Box 87, Cooperstown, PA 16317

Faith Tabernacle Council of Churches, Intl.
7015 N.E. 23rd Ave., Portland, OR 97211; (503) 282-8071

Fellowship of Lutheran Congregations
300 N. Ridgeland Ave., Oak Park, IL 60302; (708) 386-6773

Free Christian Zion Church of Christ
1315 Hutchinson Ave., Nashville, AR 71852; (501) 845-4933

Free Gospel Church, Inc.
(412) 327-3419

Free Reformed Churches of North America
Attn: Rev. P. Vandermeyden, 950 Ball Ave. N.E., Grand Rapids, MI 49503;
(616) 456-5910; http://www.rim.org/frcpage.htm

Full Gospel Assemblies, Intl.
P. O. Box 1230, Coatesville, PA 19320

Full Gospel Church Association
Box 265, Amarillo, TX 79105

Full Gospel Truth, Inc.
304 3rd St., P.O. Box Q, East Jordan, MI 49727

Fundamental Methodist
1034 N. Broadway, Springfield, MO 65802

General Assembly of the Korean Presbyterian Church in America
P.O. Box 457, Morganville, NJ 07951; (908) 591-2771

Gospel Assemblies (Sowders/Goodwin)
7135 Meredith Dr., Des Moines, IA 50322; (515) 276-9047

Grace Gospel Fellowship
2125 Martindale SW, P.O. Box 9432, Grand Rapids, MI 49509; (616) 245-0100

Hall Deliverance Foundation
Box 9910, Phoenix, AZ 85068; (602) 944-5711

Healing Temple Church
660 Williams St., Macon, GA 31201

Heritage Netherlands Reformed Congregations
2919 Leonard St. N.E., Grand Rapids, MI 49505; (616) 977-0599; http://www.
heritagebooks.org

Highway Christian Church of Christ
436 W. St., NW, Washington, DC 20001; (202) 234-3940

House of God, Holy Church of the Living God, The Pillar and Ground of Truth, the House of Prayer for all People
548 Georgetown St., Lexington, KY 40508

House of God, Which is the Church of the Living God, The Pillar and Ground of Truth, Inc.,
58 Thompson St., Philadelphia, PA 19131

House of Yahweh (Abilene)
Box 242, Abilene, TX 79604; (915) 670-9492

House of Yahweh (Odessa)
Box 4938, Odessa, TX 79760

Hungarian Reformed Church in America
P.O. Box D, Hopatcong, NY 07843; (201) 398-2764

Hutterian Brethren of New York, Inc.
P.O. Woodcrest, Rte. 213, Rifton, NY 12471; (914) 658-8351

Independent Churches of the Latter-Rain Revival
Attn.: Faith Temple, 672 N. Trezevant, Memphis, TN 38112; (901) 324-3335

International Council of Community Churches
21116 Washington Parkway, Frankfort, IL 60423; (815) 464-5692;
http://www.akcache.com/communitychurch/iccc-nat.html

International Evangelical Church
610 Rhode Island Ave., NE, Washington, DC 20002

International Evangelism Crusades
14617 Victory Blvd., Van Nuys, CA 91411

International Lutheran Fellowship, Incorporated
387 E. Brandon Dr., Bismarck, ND 58501-0440; (701) 255-0519

Kentucky Mountain Holiness Association
P.O. Box 2, Vancleve, KY 41385; (606) 666-5008

Latin American Council of the Pentecostal Church of God of New York
115 E. 125th St., New York, NY 10035; (212) 427-2447

Methodist Protestant Church
S. Hwy. 27, Monticello, MS 39654

Methodist Union Episcopal Church
1136 Brody Ave., Charleston, SC 20407

Metropolitan Church Association
P.O. Box 156, Dundee, IL 60118; (847) 428-1207

Missionary Methodist Church of America
401 W. Ballard St., Cherryville, NC 28021

Molokan Spiritual Christians (Postojannye)
841 Carolina St., San Francisco, CA 94107

Mount Hebron Apostolic Temple of Our Lord Jesus Christ of the Apostolic Faith
27 Vineyard Ave., Yonkers, NY 10703

National Baptist Convention of America
7145 Centennial Blvd., Nashville, TN 37209; (615) 256-2480

National Baptist Convention of the USA, Inc.
915 Spain St., Baton Rouge, LA 70802; (205) 228-6292;
http://www.nbcusa.org/nbcusa.html

National Missionary Baptist Convention of America
6717 Centennial Blvd., Nashville, TN 37209; (615) 350-8000

National Primitive Baptist Convention
(704) 596-3153; http://blackhistory.eb.com/micro/417/21.html

New Apostolic Church of North America
3753 N. Troy St., Chicago, IL 60618; (312) 539-3652;
http://wwwagse.informatik.uni-kl.de/~ruf/nak/nakwas-e.html

New Testament Association of Independent Baptist Churches
1079 Westview Dr., Rochelle, IL 61068

New Testament Church of God
Box 611, Mountain Home, AR 72653

Old Brethren Church
19201 Cherokee Rd., Tuolumme, CA 95379; (209) 928-4664

Old Order River Brethren
701 State Rt. 571, Union City, OH 45390; (937) 968-3877

Old Order Amish
Attn.: Raber's Book Store, 2467 CR 600, Baltic, OH 43804; (216) 893-2883

Old Order Amish Mennonite Church
Attn.: Pathway Publishers, Rte. 4, Aylmer, ON, Canada N5H 2R3

Old Order Mennonite Church (Wisler)
376 N. Muddy Creek Rd., Denver, PA 17517; (717) 484-4849

Oriental Missionary Society Holiness Church of America
3660 S. Gramercy Pl., Los Angeles, CA 90018

(Original) Church of God
Box 592, Wytheville, VA 24382; (800) 827-9234 or (423) 629-4505

Original Free Will Baptists, NC State Convention
Box 39, Ayden, NC 28315

Pentecostal Assemblies of the World
Attn.: James A. Johnson, 3939 Meadows Dr., Indianapolis, IN 46205;
(317) 547-9541

Pentecostal Free Will Baptist, Inc.
Box 1568, Dunn, NC 28334; (910) 892-4161

People of the Living God
Rt. 2, Box 423, McMinnville, TN 37110-9512; (615) 692-3236

Pillar of Fire, Western Headquarters
(303) 427-5462

Plymouth Brethren (Ames)
Attn.: Christian Literature, Inc., Box 1052, Anoka, MN 55303-1052

Plymouth Brethren (Reunited)
Attn.: Grace and Truth, 210 Chestnut St., Danville, IL 61832

Primitive Advent Christian Church
395 Frame Rd., Elkview, WV 25071; (304) 965-1550

Redeemed Assembly of Jesus Christ Apostolic
734 1st St., SW, Washington, DC 20024; (804) 230-0974

Reformed Mennonite Church
1036 Lincoln Heights Ave., Ephrata, PA 17522; (717) 697-4623

Reformed Presbyterian Church of North America
7408 Penn Avenue, Pittsburgh, PA 15208; Phone: (412) 731-1177;
Fax: (412) 731-8861; E-mail: rpcnalou@aol.com; Web site:
http://www.reformed.com/rpcna

Reformed Zion Union Apostolic Church
Box 207, South Hill, VA 23970; (804) 676-8509

Separate Baptists in Christ
10102 N. Hickory Ln., Columbus, IN 47201; (812) 372-5900

Seventh Day Baptist General Conference
3120 Kennedy Rd., Janesville, WI 53547; Phone: (608) 752-5055;
Fax: (608) 752-7711; Web site: http://www.seventhdaybaptist.org/

Schwenkfelder Church in America
1 Seminary St., Pennsburg, PA 18073; (215) 679-3103;
http://sable.ox.ac.uk~rpcinfo/sfld/s_guide.htm

Shiloh Apostolic Temple
1516 W. Master, Philadelphia, PA 19121; (215) 763-7335

Smith Venner
470 Edison Ave., Winnipeg, Manitoba, Canada R2G 0M4;
  Phone: (204) 663-5269; Fax: (204) 667-1647

Tabernacle of Prayer for all People
90-07 Merrick Blvd., Jamaica, NY 11432; (718) 657-4210

Tioga River Christian Conference
RD 1, Box 134, Cherry Valley, NY 13320

Triumph the Church and Kingdom of God in Christ
213 Farrington Ave., SE, Atlanta, GA 30315-1922

Triumph the Church in Righteousness
P.O. Box 1572, Fort Lauderdale, FL 33302

True Grace Memorial House of Prayer
205 V. St., NW, Washington, DC 20001

True Vine Pentecostal Holiness Church
929 Bethel Ln., Martinsville, VA 24112

Ukrainian Evangelical Baptist Convention
6751 Riverside Dr., Berwyn, IL 60402

United Christian
523 W. Walnut St., Cleona, PA 17042; (717) 273-9629

United Christian Church and Ministerial Association
Box 700, Cleveland, TN 37311; (423) 479-6381

United Church of Jesus Christ (Apostolic)
5150 Baltimore National Pike, Baltimore, MD 21229

United Church of Jesus Christ Apostolic
2226 Park Ave., Baltimore, MD 21217

United Church of the Living God, the Pillar and Ground of Truth
601 Kentucky Ave., Fulton, KY 42021

United Evangelical Churches
(800) 228-2289 or (408) 757-2006

United Holy Church of America, Inc.
5104 Dunston Rd., Greensboro, NC 27405; (312) 849-2525

United Wesleyan Methodist Church of America
270 W. 126th St., New York, NY 10027

United Zion Church
270 Clay School Rd., Ephrata, PA 17522; (717) 733-3932

Way of the Cross Church of Christ
322 Ninth St. NE, Washington, DC 20002; Phone: (202) 543-0500;
Fax: (202) 543-4890.

Wesleyan Tabernacle Association
Attn.: Rev. Kent Kesecker, 1225 Laurel St., Indianapolis, IN 46203;
(317) 631-2748 or (317) 489-4320

Yahweh's Assembly in Messiah
Rt. 1, Box 364, Rocheport, MO 65279

Yahweh's Assembly in Messiah
401 N. Roby Farm Rd., Rocheport, MO 65279; Phone: (573) 698-4335;
Fax: (573) 698-3700.

Yahweh's Temple
Box 652, Cleveland, TN 37311

Endnotes

Notes to Pages 1–34

1. David A. Dean, *Resurrection Hope* (Advent Christian General Conference, 1992), 9.
2. Frank S. Mead, *Handbook of Denominations in the United States, Ninth Edition* (Nashville: Abingdon Press, 1990), 21.
3. Dean, 103.
4. Dean, 102.
5. Dean, 59.
6. Dean, 102.
7. Dean, 81.
8. Dean, 32.
9. Edgar L. Mack, *Our Beginning: Introduction to the African Methodist Episcopal Church* (n.p., n.d.), 1–2.
10. "The African Methodist Episcopal Church." 1997. Available from World Wide Web site @ http://www.voicenet.com/~jfisher/ame.html; INTERNET.
11. Mack, 3.
12. Mack, 3.
13. Mack, 2.
14. Mack, 3–4.
15. J. Gordon Melton, *Encyclopedia of American Religions, Fourth Edition* (Detroit: Gale Research Inc., 1993), 395.
16. The Christadelphians, *Christadelphians: Who are they? What do they stand for?* (n.p., n.d.), 1.
17. Melton, 531.
18. Christadelphians, 2.
19. Christadelphians, 2.
20. Christadelphians, 2.
21. Christadelphians, 2.
22. Christadelphians, 2.
23. Christadelphians, 2.
24. Christadelphians, 2.
25. Mead, 37–38.
26. American Baptist Association, *Doctrinal Statement* (n.p., n.d.).
27. ABA.
28. ABA.
29. ABA.
30. ABA.
31. ABA.
32. ABA.
33. ABA.
34. ABA.
35. ABA.
36. ABA.
37. ABA.
38. Office of Communication *We Are American Baptists: A People of Faith, A People in Mission* (n.p., n.d.), 2.
39. Office of Comm., 3.
40. Office of Comm., 3.
41. Office of Comm., 29.

Endnotes

42. Office of Comm., 5–8.
43. Office of Comm., 2.
44. Office of Comm., 2.
45. Melton, 543.
46. "The AECC Information Sheet," 1997. Available from World Wide Web site @ http:// www.rhesys.mb.ca/rhema/aecc/; INTERNET, 1.
47. "The AECC Information Sheet," 3.
48. "The AECC Information Sheet," 2.
49. "The AECC Information Sheet," 2.
50. The Most Rev. Dr. Robert J. Godfrey, *The Anglican Orthodox Church: The True Reformed Apostolic Church* (The Anglican Orthodox Church, n.d.).
51. Mead, 281.
52. Apostolic Lutheran Book Concern, *Principles of the Doctrine of Christ: As Taught in the Apostolic Lutheran Church of America* (n.p., 1996), 15–17.
53. ALBC, 26.
54. ALBC, 40–42.
55. ALBC, 13.
56. "The ARP Church Home Page," 1997. Available from World Wide Web site @ http:// www.arpsynod.org; INTERNET.
57. Associate Reformed Presbyterian Church, *Abortion*, minutes of Synod, 1981, 402–403.
58. Associate Reformed Presbyterian Church, *Homosexuality*, minutes of the General Synod, 1977, 444.
59. Associate Reformed Presbyterian Church, *Scripture*, minutes of the General Synod, 1979, 23.
60. Melton, 317.
61. "The Apostles' Creed," 1997. Available from World Wide Web site @ http://www.ai.mit.edu/ people/mib/anglican/intro/lr-apostles-creed. html; INTERNET.
62. "The Apostles' Creed."
63. Association of Seventh Day Pentecostal Assemblies, *Association of Seventh Day Pentecostal Assemblies Clarify Position* (n.p., n.d.).
64. Assoc. of SDPA.
65. Assoc. of SDPA.
66. Assoc. of SDPA.
67. Melton, 416.
68. Association of Vineyard Churches, *Association of Vineyard Churches: Theological and Philosophical Statements* (n.p., 1995), 26.
69. Assoc. of Vineyard, 20.
70. Assoc. of Vineyard, 21–23.
71. Assoc. of Vineyard, 20.
72. Assoc. of Vineyard, 4.
73. Assoc. of Vineyard, 11–13.
74. Melton, 416.
75. Assoc. of Vineyard, 17–18.
76. Assoc. of Vineyard, 25.
77. Assoc. of Vineyard, 16–17, 32.
78. Assoc. of Vineyard, 2–3.

Notes to Pages 35–52

1. Baptist Bible Fellowship, *Articles of Faith* (n.p., n.d.), 7.
2. BBF, 8–9.
3. BBF, 7.
4. BBF, 3.
5. BBF, 4.
6. BBF, 8.
7. BBF, 1.

Endnotes

8. BBF, 4–5.

9. BBF, 2.

10. Baptist General Conference *1989 Annual* (Arlington Heights: Baptist General Conference, 1989), 151–153.

11. Baptist General Conference, *An Affirmation of Our Faith: adopted 1951 and reaffirmed 1990* (n.p., 1990).

12. Baptist General Conference, *Statement on Marriage* (BGC Resolutions, 1977), 6.

13. BGC, *An Affirmation.*

14. Baptist General Conference, *Beliefs about Homosexual Behavior and Ministering to Homosexual Persons* (BGC Resolutions, 1992), 11.

15. BGC, *An Affirmation.*

16. BGC, *An Affirmation.*

17. *Baptist News Service: Directory and Handbook* (Baptist News Service, 1996–1997), 8.

18. *Yearbook of the Baptist Missionary Association of America, 1996* (Baptist Missionary Association of America, 1996), 204–205.

19. *Baptist News Service*, 20.

20. *Baptist News Service*, 20.

21. *Baptist News Service*, 20.

22. *Baptist News Service*, 19.

23. *Baptist News Service*, 19.

24. *Baptist News Service*, 20.

25. *Baptist News Service*, 20–21.

26. *Yearbook*, 204.

27. *Baptist News Service*, 19.

28. *Yearbook*, 203.

29. *Baptist News Service*, 20.

30. *Baptist News Service*, 19.

31. Frank S. Mead, *Handbook of Denominations in the United States, Ninth Edition* (Nashville: Abingdon Press, 1990), 58.

32. J. Gordon Melton, *Encyclopedia of American Religions, Fourth Edition* (Detroit: Gale Research Inc., 1993), 545.

33. Berean Fundamental Church, *Berean Constitution* (n.p., n.d.).

34. BFC.

35. BFC.

36. BFC.

37. BFC.

38. BFC.

39. BFC.

40. BFC.

41. BFC.

42. Alabama Conference Bible Methodist Connection of Churches, *Alabama Annual Conference Minutes*, minutes from the Annual Conference, 1996, 50.

43. The General Conference, *Bible Methodist Discipline 1990* (n.p., 1991), 12.

44. General Conference, 13.

45. General Conference, 13.

46. General Conference, 8.

47. General Conference, 30.

48. General Conference, 48.

49. General Conference, 14.

50. Alabama Conference, 50.

51. General Conference, 9.

52. General Conference, 14–16.

53. General Conference, 7–8.

54. Rev. Albert T. Ronk, *The Brethren Church: A brief treatise on the teachings, beliefs and practices of the Brethren* (The Brethren Book and Pamphlet Commission, n.d.), 3–7.

55. The Brethren Church, *Brethren Positions on Social Issues, Compiled by: The Social Responsibilities Commission, The Brethren Church, 1991* (n.p., 1991), 8.

56. Ronk, 8.

57. *The Brethren Church: A Centennial Statement* (Brethren Publishing Company, 1984), 4–5.

58. Ronk, 11.

59. *Centennial Statement*, 2.

60. Ronk, 15.

61. *Centennial Statement*, 5.

62. Brethren Church, *Social Issues*, 3–4.

63. The Brethren Church, *The Brethren Church: How Brethren Understand God's Word* (n.p., 1993), 2–3.

64. *Centennial Statement*, 9.

65. *Centennial Statement*, 3.

66. *Centennial Statement*, 1.

Notes to Pages 58–129

1. "Charismatic Episcopal Church: An Unofficial Page," 1997. Available from World Wide Web site @ http://www.intercom.net/user/vader/trinity2.html; INTERNET, 3–4.

2. "International Communion of the Charismatic Episcopal Church," 1997. Available from World Wide Web site @ http://www.iccec.org; INTERNET, 1–2.

3. "The Apostles' Creed," 1997. Available from World Wide Web site @ http://www.ai.mit.edu/people/mib/anglican/intro/lr-apostles-creed.html; INTERNET.

4. "Apostles' Creed."

5. "Charismatic Episcopal Church," 3.

6. "Apostles' Creed."

7. "The Nicene Creed," 1997. Available from World Wide Web site @ http:// www.ai.mit.edu/people/mib/anglican/intro-nicene-creed.html; INTERNET.

8. "International Communion," 2.

9. "International Communion," 1.

10. "International Communion," 1.

11. "The Nicene Creed."

12. The Christian and Missionary Alliance, *What is the Christian and Missionary Alliance?* (n.p., n.d.), 5.

13. C & MA, 3.

14. C & MA, 2.

15. C & MA, 6.

16. C & MA, 2–3.

17. C & MA, 2.

18. C & MA, 3.

19. C & MA, 2–3.

20. C & MA, 2.

21. Christian Churches and churches of Christ, *What Kind of Church is This?* (The Standard Publishing Company, 1993), 1–8.

22. Christian Churches, 3.

23. Christian Churches, 5.

24. Christian Churches, 3.

25. Christian Churches, 5.

26. Christian Churches, 3.

27. Christian Churches, 5.

28. Christian Churches, 5.

29. Christian Churches, 5.

30. Rev. Alfred Palma, *The Articles of Faith* (Christian Church of North America, 1987), v.

31. Palma, 29.

32. Palma, 57–60.

Endnotes

33. Palma, 10.

34. Palma, 15–19.

35. Palma, 21–23, 55–60.

36. Palma, 1.

37. Palma, 47–50.

38. Palma, 33–38.

39. Palma, 7.

40. J. Gordon Melton, *Encyclopedia of American Religions, Fourth Edition* (Detroit: Gale Research Inc., 1993), 388.

41. Melton, 327.

42. Christian Reformed Church, *Synodical Decisions on Doctrinal and Ethical Matters* (Grand Rapids: Board of Publications of the Christian Reformed Church, 1976), 33.

43. CRC, 31.

44. CRC, 33–35.

45. "Athanasian Creed," 1997. Available from World Wide Web site @ http://www.crcna.org/creeds/creeds.html; INTERNET.

46. "Heidelberg Catechism," 1997. Available from World Wide Web site @ http://www.crcna.org/creeds/crcheidelbergcatechism.html; INTERNET.

47. CRC, 20.

48. CRC, 3.

49. CRC, 60–64n.

50. CRC, 53–54.

51. CRC, 13.

52. CRC, 30.

53. CRC, 27–28.

54. Melton, 533.

55. Joe R. Barnett, *Churches of Christ: Who Are These People?* (Pathway Publishing House, 1984), 6–9.

56. Barnett, 14–15.

57. Barnett, 11.

58. Barnett, 7.

59. Melton, 376.

60. Melton, 376.

61. Melton, 376.

62. Melton, 376.

63. Melton, 376.

64. Melton, 376.

65. Melton, 376.

66. Melton, 376.

67. Melton, 403.

68. Church of God General Assembly, *Resolutions: Celebrating Our Heritage, A Century of Holy Spirit Revival* (n.p., 1996), 15–17.

69. Church of God GA, 23.

70. Church of God GA, 14–15.

71. Church of God GA, 53.

72. Church of God of Prophecy, *An Introduction to the Church of God of Prophecy* (n.p., 1996), 4–11.

73. Church of God, *Introduction*, 14.

74. Church of God, *Introduction*, 12–13, 15.

75. Church of God, *Introduction*, 14.

76. Church of God, *Introduction*, 12–13.

77. Church of God, *Introduction*, 16, 30.

78. Church of God, *Introduction*, 17–20.

79. Church of God, *Introduction*, 15.

80. Church of God, *Introduction*, 12.

81. Church of God, *Introduction*, 14.

82. Church of God, *Introduction*, 30.

83. Church of God, *Introduction*, 14.

84. Church of God, *Introduction*, 12.

85. Church of God (7th Day), *Doctrinal Points as Presented in the Bible, God's Holy Word* (Church of God Publishing House, n.d.), 1–22.

86. Church of God, *Doctrinal Points*, 9–10.

87. Church of God, *Doctrinal Points*, 17–18.

88. Church of God, *Doctrinal Points*, 10–11.

89. Church of God, *Doctrinal Points*, 4.

90. Church of God, *Doctrinal Points*, 4–5.

91. Church of God, *Doctrinal Points*, 21.

92. Church of God, *Doctrinal Points*, 8.

93. Church of God, *Doctrinal Points*, 15–20, 22.

94. Church of God, *Doctrinal Points*, 4.

95. Church of God, *Doctrinal Points*, 10.

96. Church of God, *Doctrinal Points*, 11–12.

97. Church of God (7th Day), *What the "Church of God" Believes, And Why* (Church of God Publishing House, n.d.), 11.

98. Church of God, *Doctrinal Points*, 6.

99. Church of God, *Doctrinal Points*, 4–6.

100. *The Brethren Encyclopedia, Volume 1* (Philadelphia: The Brethren Encyclopedia Inc., 1983), 253.

101. Church of the Brethren, *There Am I In The Midst of Them: Ordinances of the Church of the Brethren* (n.p., n.d.).

102. *Brethren Encyclopedia*, 591, 595.

103. The Church of the Brethren, *1983 Annual Conference Minutes*, minutes of the Annual Conference, 1983, 579–581.

104. *Brethren Encyclopedia*, 1275.

105. "CLC History and Differences," 1997. Available from World Wide Web site @ http://www.primenet.com/~mpkelly/clc/clc.html; INTERNET, 1.

106. Mark J. Gullerud, *Scripture Speaks for the Unborn* (Grace Lutheran Church, n.d.), 1–5.

107. The Church of the Lutheran Confession Fiscal Office, *"Here I Stand": Statement of Faith and Purpose of the Church of the Lutheran Confession* (n.p., 1990), 14.

108. Church of the Lutheran, 14.

109. Church of the Lutheran, 5.

110. Church of the Lutheran, 7.

111. Grace Lutheran Church, *The Shepherd Kindly Calls* (n.p., n.d.), 1.

112. Church of the Lutheran, 4.

113. Church of the Lutheran, 6.

114. *Manual: Church of the Nazarene, 1993–97* (Kansas City: Nazarene Publishing House, 1993), 49–50.

115. *Manual*, 32–33.

116. *Manual*, 33.

117. *Manual*, 47–49.

118. *Manual*, 34.

119. *Manual*, 50–51.

120. *Manual*, 27.

121. *Manual*, 33.

122. *Manual*, 45–47.

123. *Manual*, 326.

124. *Manual*, 26.

125. *Church of the United Brethren in Christ: Discipline, 1993–1997* (Huntington: Department of Church Services, 1993), 8–15.

126. *Discipline*, 29.

127. *Discipline*, 17.

128. *Discipline*, 29.
129. *Discipline*, 16.
130. *Discipline*, 17.
131. *Discipline*, 16.
132. *Discipline*, 28–29.
133. *UB: Getting Acquainted with the Church of the United Brethren in Christ* (Huntington: Department of Church Services, 1994), 18–22.
134. *Discipline*, 28.
135. *UB*, 37.
136. *Discipline*, 25, 31–34.
137. *UB*, 35.
138. *Discipline*, 46–47.
139. *Congregational Methodist Book of Discipline, 15th Edition* (Florence: Congregational Methodist Church, 1990), V–VII.
140. *Congregational Methodist*, 93.
141. Emma Bond, *What Congregational Methodists Believe* (Florence: Division of Church Ministries, n.d.), 14–15.
142. Bond, 7.
143. Bond, 5.
144. *Congregational Methodist*, 93.
145. Bond, 6.
146. Bond, 16–17.
147. Bond, 19, 23.
148. *Congregational Methodist*, 93.
149. *Congregational Methodist*, 93.
150. Bond, 12.
151. Bond, 21.
152. Bond, 5.
153. Melton, 343.
154. *1996 Yearbook: Conservative Congregational Christian Conference* (St. Paul: Conservative Congregational Christian Conference, 1996) 113–114.
155. *Yearbook*, i.
156. *Yearbook*, i.
157. *Yearbook*, 107–111.
158. *Yearbook*, i.
159. *Yearbook*, 112–113.
160. *Yearbook*, i.
161. *Yearbook*, 115–117.
162. *Yearbook*, 106.
163. *Yearbook*, i.
164. *Yearbook*, 118.
165. Melton, 333.
166. *Confession of Faith for Cumberland Presbyterians* (Memphis: The Office of the General Assembly, 1996), 15.
167. *Confession of Faith*, 24.
168. *Confession of Faith*, 16.
169. *Confession of Faith*, 3.
170. *Confession of Faith*, 6–7.
171. *Confession of Faith*, 20–21.
172. *Confession of Faith*, 17–18.
173. *Confession of Faith*, 24.
174. *Confession of Faith*, 1.
175. *Confession of Faith*, 11–12.
176. *Confession of Faith*, 1.
177. *Confession of Faith*, 33–34, 49.

Endnotes

Notes to Pages 132–156

1. "Elim Fellowship on the World Wide Web," 1997. Available from World Wide Web site @ http://www.frontiernet.net/~elim/efexec.htm; INTERNET, 1.
2. Elim Fellowship, Inc. *Elim Fellowship, Inc., Statement of Faith* (n.p., n.d.).
3. Elim Fellowship.
4. Elim Fellowship.
5. Elim Fellowship.
6. Elim Fellowship.
7. Elim Fellowship.
8. "What is the Episcopal Church?," 1997. Available from World Wide Web site @ http://www.ai.mit.edu/people/mib/anglican/anglican.html; INTERNET, 1.
9. "What is the Episcopal Church?," 1.
10. "The Nicene Creed," 1997. Available from World Wide Web site @ http://www.ai.mit.edu/people/mib/anglican/intro/lr-nicene-creed.html; INTERNET.
11. "What is the Episcopal Church?," 1.
12. "Nicene Creed."
13. "Nicene Creed."
14. "The Blue Book: Standing Commission on Human Affairs," 1997. Available from World Wide Web site @ http://newark.rutgers.edu/~lcrew/humanaff.html; INTERNET, 19–26.
15. "What is the Episcopal Church?," 1.
16. "Nicene Creed."
17. "What is the Episcopal Church?," 1.
18. *Abridged Discipline: Evangelical Congregational Church* (Myerstown: E.C. Church Center, 1992), 1–5, 10.
19. *Abridged Discipline*, 30.
20. *Abridged Discipline*, 12.
21. *Abridged Discipline*, 22–23.
22. *Abridged Discipline*, 12.
23. *Abridged Discipline*, 7.
24. *Abridged Discipline*, 7.
25. *Abridged Discipline*, 27, 29.
26. *Abridged Discipline*, 67–72.
27. *Abridged Discipline*, 29.
28. *Abridged Discipline*, 8.
29. *Abridged Discipline*, 26, 37.
30. *Abridged Discipline*, 10.
31. *Abridged Discipline*, 7.
32. Evangelical Covenant Church, *Covenant Distinctives: What does it mean to be Covenant?* (Covenant Publications, 1988).
33. Evangelical Covenant Church, *Resolution on Abortion*, (presented at the 109th Covenant Annual Meeting, n.d.).
34. Evangelical Covenant Church, *Baptism/One Wonderful Message* (Covenant Press, n.d.).
35. "The Apostles' Creed," 1997. Available from World Wide Web site @ http://www.ai.mit.edu/people/mib/anglican/intro/lr-apostles-creed.html; INTERNET.
36. *Covenant Affirmations* (Covenant Publications, n.d.), 17.
37. *Covenant Distinctives* (Covenant Publications, n.d.).
38. *Covenant Affirmations*, 5.
39. *Covenant Affirmations*, 21.
40. J. Gordon Melton, *Encyclopedia of American Religions, Fourth Edition* (Detroit: Gale Research Inc., 1993), 494.
41. Evangelical Lutheran Synod, *We Believe Teach and Confess: A Concise Doctrinal Statement of the Evangelical Lutheran Synod* (n.p., n.d.), 15–16.
42. Evangelical Lutheran Synod, 13.
43. Evangelical Lutheran Synod, 6–7.

Endnotes

44. Evangelical Lutheran Synod, 13.
45. Evangelical Lutheran Synod, 11.
46. Evangelical Lutheran Synod, 6–7.
47. Evangelical Lutheran Synod, 4.
48. Evangelical Lutheran Synod, 6.
49. Evangelical Lutheran Synod, 11.
50. Evangelical Lutheran Synod, 13.
51. Evangelical Lutheran Synod, 3–4.
52. Evangelical Lutheran Synod, 4.
53. Evangelical Lutheran Synod, 11.
54. Evangelical Lutheran Synod, 9.
55. Evangelical Lutheran Synod, 3.
56. Evangelical Lutheran Synod, 10.
57. Evangelical Mennonite Church, *Manual of Faith, Practice and Organization* (Evangelical Mennonite Church, 1990), 1–5.
58. National Association of Evangelicals, *Upon these NAE is united* (n.p., n.d.).
59. "Position Paper on Abortion," 1997. Available from World Wide Web site @ http://www.epc.org/index.html; INTERNET, 1–2.
60. "The Essentials," 1997. Available from World Wide Web site @ http://www.epc.org/index/html; INTERNET, 2.
61. "Essentials," 1.
62. "Position Paper on Homosexuality," 1997. Available from World Wide Web site @ http://www.epc.org/index/html; INTERNET, 1–4.
63. "Essentials," 1.
64. "Position Paper on the Holy Spirit," 1997. Available from World Wide Web site @ http://www.epc.org/index.html; INTERNET, 1–3.
65. "Essentials," 1.

Notes to Pages 156–168

1. Randy Smart, "A History of the Fellowship of Evangelical Bible Churches," (paper presented at the 100th Convention, n.p., July 13–17, 1994.)
2. J. Gordon Melton, *Encyclopedia of American Religions, Fourth Edition* (Detroit: Gale Research Inc., 1993), 484–485.
3. Fellowship of Evangelical Bible Churches, *Constitution of the Fellowship of Evangelical Bible Churches* (n.p., 1995), 6.
4. Fellowship of EBC, *Constitution*, 5.
5. Fellowship of EBC, *Constitution*, 6.
6. Fellowship of EBC, *Constitution*, 3.
7. Fellowship of EBC, *Constitution*, 1.
8. Fellowship of EBC, *Constitution*, 7.
9. Fellowship of EBC, *Constitution*, 5.
10. Fellowship of Evangelical Bible Churches, *Policy Statement: Homosexuality* (n.p., 1995), 1–2.
11. Fellowship of EBC, *Constitution*, 1.
12. Fellowship of EBC, *Constitution*, 8.
13. Fellowship of EBC, *Constitution*, 9.
14. Fellowship of EBC, *Constitution*, 8.
15. Fellowship of EBC, *Constitution*, 2.
16. "Welcome to Grace Brethren Church!," 1997. Available from World Wide Web site @ http://38.226.140.6/welcome2.htm; INTERNET, 1–2.
17. "What We Believe," Available from World Wide Web site @ http://38.226.140.6/welcome2.htm; INTERNET, 2.
18. "What We Believe," 2.
19. "What We Believe," 1.
20. "Welcome," 1.

21. "What We Believe," 2.

22. "What We Believe," 1.

23. "What We Believe," 1.

24. *The Free Methodist Church of North America: The Book of Discipline 1995* (Indianapolis: The Free Methodist Publishing House, 1995), 4.

25. *Book of Discipline*, 45.

26. *Book of Discipline*, 14.

27. *Book of Discipline*, 15.

28. *Book of Discipline*, 14–15.

29. *Book of Discipline*, 47.

30. *Book of Discipline*, 9.

31. *Book of Discipline*, 52–54.

32. *Book of Discipline*, 15–16.

33. *Book of Discipline*, 55.

34. *Book of Discipline*, 10.

35. *Book of Discipline*, 42.

36. *Book of Discipline*, 21, 43, 49, 50.

37. *Book of Discipline*, 42.

38. *Book of Discipline*, 9.

39. Free Methodist Church of North America, *Women in Ministry: Statement Adopted by the 1995 General Conference of the Free Methodist Church of North America* (n.p., n.d.), 2–10.

40. Gordon Browne, "Introducing Quakers," (adapted from a Pendle Hill-On-The-Road presentation, Nov. 2–3, 1990.)

41. Melton, 494.

42. Quaker Information Center, *What do Quakers believe?* (n.p., n.d.), 1–4.

43. Quaker Information Center, *Dear Friend* (n.p., 1996), 1.

44. Quaker Info. Ctr, *What do Quakers believe?*, 2.

45. Quaker Info. Ctr, *What do Quakers believe?*, 2.

46. Quaker Information Center, *Branches of the Religious Society of Friends in the Americas* (FWCC, 1995), 1.

47. "Friends General Conference—What is FGC?," 1997. Available from World Wide Web site @ http://www.quaker.org/fgc/index.html; INTERNET, 1.

48. Quaker Info. Ctr, *What do Quakers believe?*, 2, 4.

49. Quaker Info. Ctr, *Branches*, 1.

Notes to Pages 171–183

1. J. Gordon Melton, *Encyclopedia of American Religions, Fourth Edition* (Detroit: Gale Research Inc., 1993), 528.

2. *The Social Principles of General Baptists* (Stinson Press, n.d.) 7.

3. *General Baptist Doctrine and Usage* (Poplar Bluff: Stinson Press, 1990), 10.

4. *Social Principles*, 7.

5. *Doctrine and Usage*, 11.

6. *Doctrine and Usage*, 56–57.

7. *Social Principles*, 1.

8. *Doctrine and Usage*, 7.

9. *Social Principles*, 3–4.

10. *Doctrine and Usage*, 16, 29.

11. *Doctrine and Usage*, 11.

12. *Social Principles*, 6.

13. *Doctrine and Usage*, 7.

14. *Social Principles*, 8–10.

15. *Doctrine and Usage*, 8–9.

16. *Doctrine and Usage*, 58.

17. *Doctrine and Usage*, 7.

18. Frank S. Mead, *Handbook of Denominations in the United States, Ninth Edition* (Nashville: Abingdon Press, 1990), 47–48.

19. *General Association of Regular Baptist Churches 1997 Church Directory* (Schaumburg: General Association of Regular Baptist Churches, 1997) 18.

20. *General Association*, 19.

21. *General Association*, 18.

22. *General Association*, 16.

23. *General Association*, 17.

24. *General Association*, 13, 18.

25. *General Association*, 19.

26. *General Association*, 16.

27. *General Association*, 18

28. *General Association*, 16.

29. Mead, 53.

30. General Conference Mennonite Church, *General Conference Mennonite Church, congregations serving Christ together: An Introduction* (n.p., n.d.), 1.

31. *Confession of Faith in a Mennonite Perspective: Summary Statement* (Scottdale: Mennonite Publishing House, 1996), 6.

32. General Conference Mennonite Church, *Guidelines on Abortion* (n.p., 1980).

33. *Confession of Faith in*, 4–5.

34. General Conference Mennonite Church, *A Christian Declaration on Capital Punishment* (n.p., 1965).

35. *Confession of Faith in*, 7.

36. *Confession of Faith in*, 5.

37. *Confession of Faith in*, 3–4.

38. *Confession of Faith in*, 3.

39. *Confession of Faith in*, 11.

40. "Mennonite Confession of Faith: Article 19," Available from World Wide Web site @ http://www.mennolink.org/doc/cof/index.html; INTERNET.

41. General Conference Mennonite Church, *An Introduction* (n.p., n.d.), 2–3.

42. "Mennonite Confession of Faith: Article 24," Available from World Wide Web site @ http://www.mennolink.org/doc/cof/index.html; INTERNET.

43. "Mennonite Confession of Faith: Article 19."

44. *Confession of Faith in*, 3.

45. *Confession of Faith in*, 6.

46. "Mennonite Confession of Faith: Article 8," Available from World Wide Web site @ http://www.mennolink.org/doc/cof/index.html; INTERNET.

47. "Mennonite Confession of Faith: Article 3," Available from World Wide Web site @ http://www.mennolink.org/doc/cof/index.html; INTERNET.

48. *Confession of Faith in*, 3.

49. "Mennonite Confession of Faith: Article 15," Available from World Wide Web site @ http://www.mennolink.org/doc/cof/index.html; INTERNET.

50. The United States Conference of Mennonite Brethren Churches and Mennonite Brethren Foundation, *People on the Way!: The Story of the Mennonite Brethren Church, Its Faith, History and Mission* (n.p., n.d.).

51. *Confession of Faith of the General Conference of Mennonite Brethren Churches* (Winnipeg: The Christian Press, 1995), 16–17.

52. *Confession of Faith of*, 23.

53. *Confession of Faith of*, 17–18.

54. *Confession of Faith of*, 9.

55. *Confession of Faith of*, 19.

56. *Confession of Faith of*, 23

57. *Confession of Faith of*, 10–11.

58. *Confession of Faith of*, 21.

59. *Confession of Faith of*, 9.

Notes to Pages 190–193

1. The House of God Which is the Church of the Living God the Pillar and Ground of Truth Without Controversy, Inc. Keith Dominion, *Church History* (n.p., n.d.).
2. J. Gordon Melton, *Encyclopedia of American Religions, Fourth Edition* (Detroit: Gale Research Inc., 1993), 451.
3. House of God.
4. Melton, 647–649.

Notes to Pages 196–201

1. Independent Assemblies of God International, *Independent Assemblies of God International* (n.p., n.d.), 2.
2. Independent Assemblies, 1.
3. Independent Assemblies, 1.
4. Independent Assemblies, 1.
5. Independent Assemblies, 1.
6. Independent Assemblies, 2.
7. Independent Assemblies, 1.
8. Independent Assemblies, 1.
9. Independent Assemblies, 1.
10. Independent Assemblies, 1.
11. Independent Assemblies, 1.
12. J. Gordon Melton, *Encyclopedia of American Religions, Fourth Edition* (Detroit: Gale Research Inc., 1993), 547–548.
13. "IFCA Doctrine, Vision and Goals," 1997. Available from World Wide Web site @ http://www.ifca.org/; INTERNET, 1.
14. "IFCA Doctrine," 5.
15. "IFCA Doctrine," 8.
16. "IFCA Doctrine," 5.
17. "IFCA Doctrine," 6.
18. "IFCA Doctrine," 2.
19. "IFCA Doctrine," 9.
20. "IFCA Doctrine," 6.
21. "IFCA Doctrine," 8.
22. "IFCA Doctrine," 7.
23. "IFCA Doctrine," 8.
24. "IFCA Doctrine," 6.

Notes to Pages 213–214

1. Dr. Samuel H. Nafzger, *An Introduction to The Lutheran Church—Missouri Synod* (Concordia Publishing House, 1994), 4.
2. Nafzger, 14.

Notes to Pages 216–224

1. *Confession of Faith in a Mennonite Perspective* (Scottdale: Herald Press, 1996), 97.
2. *Confession of Faith in*, 46–49.
3. *Confession of Faith in*, 97–99.
4. *Confession of Faith in*, 50.
5. *Confession of Faith in*, 25.
6. *Confession of Faith in*, 13.
7. *Confession of Faith in*, 97.
8. *Confession of Faith in*, 90.

Endnotes

9. *Confession of Faith in*, 21.

10. *Confession of Faith in*, 75, 82.

11. *Confession of Faith in*, 35.

12. *Confession of Faith in*, 17.

13. *Confession of Faith in*, 10.

14. *Confession of Faith in*, 59.

15. *Resolutions and Elections of the Provincial Synod of the Northern Province of the Moravian Church, 1994* (Bethlehem: Moravian Church Northern Province, 1994), 47.

16. Unity Synod of the Unitas Fratum, *The Ground of the Unity* (a doctrinal statement adopted by the Unity Synod of the Unitas Fratum, or Moravian Church, held at Dar es Salaam, Tanzania, August 13 to 25, 1996), 9.

17. Unity Synod, 9.

18. Unity Synod, 3.

19. The Moravian Church in America, Northern and Southern Province, *The Moravian Covenant For Christian Living, formerly known as The Brotherly Agreement* (n.p., n.d.), 6.

20. *Resolutions and Elections of the Provincial Synod of the Northern Province of the Moravian Church, 1994* (Bethlehem: Moravian Church Northern Province, 1994), 49–50.

Notes to Pages 227–237

1. National Association of Congregational Christian Churches, *What About Our History* (n.p., n.d.).

2. National Association of Congregational Christian Churches, *Questions and Answers* (n.p., n.d.).

3. Henry David Gray, *What It Means to be a Member of a Congregational Christian Church* (Congregational Christian Churches National Association, 1995), 9.

4. Gray, 9.

5. Gray, 10.

6. NACC, *Questions*.

7. Gray, 8.

8. *Treatise: Of the Faith and Practices of the National Association of Free Will Baptists, Inc.* (Executive Office of the National Association of Free Will Baptists, Inc., 1996), Preface.

9. *Reports: Temperance Committee Resolutions Committee 1935–1992* (Antioch: The Executive Office National Association of Free Will Baptists, Inc., 1993), 79, 105.

10. *Treatise*, 15.

11. *Reports*, 96.

12. *Reports*, 64.

13. *Treatise*, 16.

14. *Treatise*, 15.

15. *Treatise*, 5.

16. *Treatise*, 35.

17. *Reports*, 74.

18. *Treatise*, 37–38.

19. *Treatise*, 36.

20. *Reports*, 76.

21. *Treatise*, 3.

22. *Reports*, 106.

23. *Treatise*, 13.

24. *Treatise*, 17.

25. *Reports*, 68–69.

26. *Treatise*, 35.

27. Stanley J. Grenz, *The Baptist Congregation: A Guide to Baptist Belief and Practice NAB Edition* (Valley Forge: Judson Press, 1985), 97.

28. North American Baptist Conference, *Statement of Beliefs*, North American Baptist Conference (n.p., n.d.), 4.

29. NABC, 4.

30. NABC, 3.

31. NABC, 2.
32. Grenz, 97, 112–113.
33. NABC, 5.
34. NABC, 1.
35. NABC, 2.

Notes to Pages 237–242

1. Old German Baptist Brethren *The Vindicator: A Brief Summary of the Old German Baptist Brethren Faith* (n.p., n.d.).

2. J. Gordon Melton, *Encyclopedia of American Religions, Fourth Edition* (Detroit: Gale Research Inc., 1993), 492.

3. Open Bible Churches, *Introducing Open Bible Churches* (n.p., n.d.).

4. *Policies and Principles of Open Bible Standard Churches* (Des Moines: Open Bible Publishers, 1995), 62.

5. Open Bible Churches, *We Believe: Articles of Faith* (n.p., n.d.), 3.

6. OBC, *We Believe*, 5.

7. OBC, *We Believe*, 3.

8. *Policies and Principles*, 66.

9. OBC, *We Believe*, 1.

10. OBC, *We Believe*, 3.

11. OBC, *Introducing*.

12. OBC, *We Believe*, 6–7.

13. *Policies and Principles*, 69.

14. OBC, *We Believe*, 1.

15. OBC, *We Believe*, 5.

16. *Policies and Principles*, 65, 68, 73–74.

17. OBC, *We Believe*, 3.

18. OBC, *We Believe*, 1.

19. "What is the OPC? Where We Came From," 1997. Available from World Wide Web site @ http://www.opc.org/what_is/the_opc.html; INTERNET, 1–4.

20. "What is the OPC? Where We Are Today," 1997. Available from World Wide Web site @ http://www.opc.org/what_is/the_opc.html; INTERNET, 5.

21. "Where We Are Today," 2.

22. "Where We Are Today," 2.

23. "Where We Are Today," 2.

24. "Where We Are Today," 2.

25. "Where We Are Today," 2–3.

26. "Where We Are Today," 6.

27. "Where We Are Today," 1.

28. "Where We Are Today," 4.

29. "Where We Are Today," 2.

30. "Where We Came From," 2.

31. "Where We Are Today," 2.

32. "Where We Are Today," 3.

Notes to Pages 247–265

1. *Pentecostal Church of God General Constitution and By-laws,* (Joplin: Messenger Publishing House, 1996), 101–105.

2. *Pentecostal Church of God*, 31.

3. *Pentecostal Church of God*, 32.

4. *Pentecostal Church of God*, 31–32.

5. *Pentecostal Church of God*, 30.

6. *Pentecostal Church of God*, 52.

7. *Pentecostal Church of God*, 32.

Endnotes

8. *Pentecostal Church of God*, 30.

9. *Pentecostal Church of God*, 32.

10. *Pentecostal Church of God*, 30.

11. *Pentecostal Church of God*, 31.

12. *Pentecostal Church of God*, 30.

13. *Pentecostal Church of God*, 46.

14. Frank S. Mead, *Handbook of Denominations in the United States, Ninth Edition* (Nashville: Abingdon Press, 1990), 194–196.

15. J. Gordon Melton, *Encyclopedia of American Religions, Fourth Edition* (Detroit: Gale Research Inc., 1993), 543.

16. "PCA History," 1997. Available from World Wide Web site @ http://www. clark.net/pub/epchurch/pca.htm; INTERNET, 1.

17. "Westminster Confession of Faith, Chapter XXVIII," 1997. Available from World Wide Web site @ http://www.ilinks.net/~faithpca/creeds/westmins.html; INTERNET, 1.

18. "Westminster Confession of Faith, Chapter XXIX," 1997. Available from World Wide Web site @ http://www.ilinks.net/~faithpca/creeds/westmins.html; INTERNET, 1.

19. "Westminster Confession of Faith, Chapter IV," 1997. Available from World Wide Web site @ http://www.ilinks.net/~faithpca/creeds/westmins.html; INTERNET, 1.

20. "Westminster Confession of Faith, Chapter VIII," 1997. Available from World Wide Web site @ http://www.ilinks.net/~faithpca/creeds/westmins.html; INTERNET, 1.

21. "Westminster Confession of Faith, Chapter XXIV," 1997. Available from World Wide Web site @ http://www.ilinks.net/~faithpca/creeds/westmins.html; INTERNET, 1.

22. "Doctrines of Grace," 1997. Available from World Wide Web site @ http://www.clark.net/pub/epchurch/pca.htm; INTERNET, 1.

23. "PCA History," 3.

24. "Westminster Confession of Faith, Chapter XXXII," 1997. Available from World Wide Web site @ http://www.ilinks.net/~faithpca/creeds/westmins.html; INTERNET, 1.

25. "PCA History," 2.

26. "PCA History," 2.

27. "Westminster Confession of Faith, Chapter II," 1997. Available from World Wide Web site @ http://www.ilinks.net/~faithpca/creeds/westmins.html; INTERNET, 1.

28. "PCA History," 1.

29. Melton, 335–336.

30. Mead, 203.

31. Presbyterian Church (USA), *Problem Pregnancies and Abortion: The 204ᵗʰ General Assembly (1992) Response to the Report of the Special Committee on Problem Pregnancies and Abortion, (Majority Report)* (Louisville: Office of the General Assembly, 1992), 11.

32. *The Book of Confessions: Presbyterian Church (USA)* (Louisville: Office of the General Assembly, 1996), 103, 230.

33. PCUSA, 13.

34. *Book of Confessions*, 209.

35. *Book of Confessions*, 24.

36. *Book of Confessions*, 130.

37. *Book of Confessions*, 275.

38. *Book of Confessions*, 163.

39. *The Church and Homosexuality: The United Presbyterian Church in the United States of America* (Louisville: Office of the General Assembly, 1978), 58–60.

40. *Book of Confessions*, 135.

41. *Book of Confessions*, 144.

42. *Book of Confessions*, 32, 58.

43. "Primitive Baptist Creeds," 1997. Available from World Wide Web site @ http://www.pb.org/; INTERNET, 1.

44. "Primitive Baptist FAQ," 1997. Available from World Wide Web site @ http://www.pb.org/; INTERNET, 1.

45. "Doctrinal Abstract," 1997. Available from World Wide Web site @ http://www.pb.org/; INTERNET, 2.

46. "Primitive Baptist FAQ," 8–9.

47. "Midland Confession of Faith," 1997. Available from World Wide Web site @ http://www.pb.org/; INTERNET, 2.

48. "Rebaptism and Acts 19," 1997. Available from World Wide Web site @ http://www.pb.org/; INTERNET, 1.

49. "Waldensian Confessions," 1997. Available from World Wide Web site @ http://www.pb.org/; INTERNET, 3.

50. "Primitive Baptist FAQ," 6–7.

51. "Waldensian Confessions," 1.

52. "Midland Confession of Faith," 1–2.

53. "Waldensian Confessions," 3.

54. "Primitive Baptist FAQ," 5.

55. "Midland Confession of Faith," 2.

56. "Waldensian Confessions," 1.

57. "Midland Confession of Faith," 1.

58. "Primitive Baptist FAQ," 10–11.

59. "Secret Orders and the Church," 1997. Available from World Wide Web site @ http://www.pb.org/; INTERNET, 1.

60. "Primitive Baptist FAQ," 10.

61. "Doctrinal Abstract," 4.

62. "Primitive Baptist FAQ," 11.

63. "Midland Confession of Faith," 1.

64. "Primitive Baptist FAQ," 5.

65. Board of Christian Ministries Primitive Methodist Church, *Let Me Tell You About the Primitive Methodist Church* (n.p., n.d.), 1.

66. Board of Christian Ministries Primitive Methodist Church, *The Primitive Methodist Perspective: Contemporary Social Issues* (n.p., n.d.), 1.

67. PMC, *Let Me Tell You*, 4.

68. PMC, *Let Me Tell You*, 4.

69. PMC, *Let Me Tell You*, 4.

70. PMC, *Let Me Tell You*, 3.

71. PMC, *Let Me Tell You*, 4.

72. PMC, *Contemporary Social Issues*, 2.

73. PMC, *Let Me Tell You*, 4.

74. PMC, *Contemporary Social Issues*, 2–3.

75. PMC, *Let Me Tell You*, 4.

76. "The Protestant Reformed Churches," 1997. Available from World Wide Web site @ http://www.mtcnet.net/~revmo/; INTERNET, 1.

77. "Protestant Reformed Churches," 3.

78. "Administration of Baptism," 1997. Available from World Wide Web site @ http://www.mtcnet.net/~revmo/; INTERNET, 1.

79. "Administration of the Lord's Supper," 1997. Available from World Wide Web site @ http://www.mtcnet.net/~revmo/; INTERNET, 4.

80. "Administration of the Lord's Supper," 1.

81. "Administration of Baptism," 4.

82. "Administration of Baptism," 4.

83. "Protestant Reformed Churches," 3.

84. "Protestant Reformed Churches," 2.

85. "Protestant Reformed Churches," 4.

86. "Administration of Baptism," 4.

Notes to Pages 268–275

1. "RCA History," 1997. Available from World Wide Web site @ http://www. rca.org; INTERNET, 1.

2. "Abortion Statements," 1997. Available from World Wide Web site @ http://www.rca.org; INTERNET, 1.

3. "Our Song of Hope," 1997. Available from World Wide Web site @ http://www.rca.org; INTERNET, 4.

4. "Capital Punishment Statements," 1997. Available from World Wide Web site @ http://www.rca.org; INTERNET, 1.

5. "Apostles' Creed, (contemporary language version)," 1997. Available from World Wide Web site @ http://www.rca.org; INTERNET, 1.

6. "Our Song of Hope," 4.

7. "Nicene Creed," 1997. Available from World Wide Web site @ http://www. rca.org; INTERNET, 1.

8. "Our Song of Hope," 1–2.

9. "Divorce Statements," 1997. Available from World Wide Web site @ http://www.rca.org; INTERNET, 1.

10. "RCA Government," 1997. Available from World Wide Web site @ http://www.rca.org; INTERNET, 1.

11. "Our Song of Hope," 2.

12. "Homosexuality," 1997. Available from World Wide Web site @ http:/ www.rca.org; INTERNET, 2.

13. "RCA Beliefs," 1997. Available from World Wide Web site @ http://www. rca.org; INTERNET, 1.

14. "Our Song of Hope," 5.

15. "Nicene Creed," 1.

16. "REC History," 1997. Available from World Wide Web site @ http://www. recus.org/index.htm; INTERNET, 1–4.

17. "Sanctity of Life," Available from World Wide Web site @ http://www.recus.org/index.htm; INTERNET, 1.

18. "Declaration of Principles," 1997. Available from World Wide Web site @ http://www.recus.org/index.htm; INTERNET, 2.

19. "REC History," 7.

20. "REC History," 7.

21. "Declaration of Principles," 2.

22. "REC Resolution," 1997. Available from World Wide Web site @ http://www.recus.org/index.htm; INTERNET, 1.

23. "Declaration of Principles," 2.

Notes to Pages 279–290

1. "War Cry!—The Salvation Army," 1997. Available from World Wide Web site @ http://www.salvationarmy.org/home.htm; INTERNET, 1–3.

2. J. Gordon Melton, *Encyclopedia of American Religions, Fourth Edition* (Detroit: Gale Research Inc., 1993), 385.

3. The Salvation Army, *What is the Salvation Army?* (n.p., 1991), 15.

4. "The Salvation Army: Frequently Asked Questions (FAQ)," 1997. Available from World Wide Web site @ http://www.salvationarmy.org/home.htm; INTERNET, 2.

5. "The Salvation Army: Positional Statement on Family Planning," 1997. Available from World Wide Web site @ http://www.salvationarmy.org/home. htm; INTERNET, 1.

6. "The Salvation Army: Positional Statement on Capital Punishment," 1997. Available from World Wide Web site @ http://www.salvationarmy.org/home. htm; INTERNET, 1.

7. "Doctrines of the Salvation Army," 1997. Available from World Wide Web site @ http://www.salvationarmy.org/home.htm; INTERNET, 1.

8. "Doctrines of the Salvation Army," 1.

9. "The Salvation Army: Positional Statement on Marriage and Divorce," 1997. Available from World Wide Web site @ http://www.salvationarmy.org/ home.htm; INTERNET, 1–2.

10. "What is the Salvation Army?," 9.

11. "Doctrines of the Salvation Army," 1.

12. "The Salvation Army: Positional Statement on Homosexuality," 1997. Available from World Wide Web site @ http://www.salvationarmy.org/home. htm; INTERNET, 1–2.

13. "Doctrines of the Salvation Army," 1.

14. "Doctrines of the Salvation Army," 1.

15. "Doctrines of the Salvation Army," 1.

16. "What is the Salvation Army?," 12.

17. Frank S. Mead, *Handbook of Denominations in the United States, Ninth Edition* (Nashville: Abingdon Press, 1990), 22–23.

18 "Southern Baptists Beginnings," 1997. Available from World Wide Web site @ http://www.sbcnet.org/index.htm; INTERNET, 1–3.

19. The Sunday School Board of the Southern Baptist Convention, *The Baptist Faith and Message: A Statement Adopted by the Southern Baptist Convention* (n.p., 1963), 13.

20. Southern Baptist Convention, 15.

21. Southern Baptist Convention, 13.

22. Southern Baptist Convention, 7.

23. Southern Baptist Convention, 8–9.

24. "Southern Baptists Working Together," 1997. Available from World Wide Web site @ http://www.sbcnet.org/index.htm; INTERNET, 1–2.

25. Southern Baptist Convention, 15.

26. Southern Baptist Convention, 7.

27. Southern Baptist Convention, 12.

28. Southern Baptist Convention, 7–9.

29 John Zens, *Reformed and Sovereign Grace Baptists* (Searching Together, 1985).

Notes to Pages 293–300

1. Christadelphian Action Society, *The Christadelphians: Who are They? What Do They Believe?* (n.p., n.d.), 2.

2. "The United Church of Christ," 1997. Available from World Wide Web site @ http://www.ucc.org/ucchp.htm; INTERNET, 1–2, 4.

3. "Preamble to the UCC Constitution," 1997. Available from World Wide Web site @ http://www.ucc.org/ucchp.htm; INTERNET, 1.

4. "The Apostles' Creed," 1997. Available from World Wide Web site @ http://www.ai.mit.edu/people/mib/anglican/intro/lr-apostles-creed.html; INTERNET, 1.

5. "Preamble," 1.

6. "UCC Statement of Faith," 1997. Available from World Wide Web site @ http://www.ucc.org/ucchp.htm; INTERNET, 1.

7. "UCC Statement of Faith," 1.

8. "The United Church of Christ," 2.

9. "The United Church of Christ," 3.

10. "Cult Awareness & Information Centre - Australia," 1997. Available from World Wide Web site @ http://student.uq.edu.au/~py101663/zentryl.htm; INTERNET.

11. "Fundamental Beliefs of the United Church of God," Available from World Wide Web site @ http://www.ucg.org/about.htm; INTERNET, 3.

12. "Fundamental Beliefs," 2.

13. "Fundamental Beliefs," 3.

14. "Fundamental Beliefs," 1.

15. "Fundamental Beliefs," 1.

16. "file://Untitled (Constitution of the United Church of God, an International Association)," 1997. Available from World Wide Web site @ http://www. ucg.org/about.htm; INTERNET, 5.

17. "Fundamental Beliefs," 1.

18. "Fundamental Beliefs," 2.

19. *Microsoft Encarta: Multimedia Encyclopedia*, 1994 ed., s.v. "United Methodist Church."

20. Frank S. Mead, *Handbook of Denominations in the United States, Ninth Edition* (Nashville: Abingdon Press, 1990), 154.

21. The General Board of Church and Society, *Social Principles: The United Methodist Church* (n.p., 1992), 10.

22. *The Book of Discipline of the United Methodist Church, 1992* (Nashville: The United Methodist Publishing House, 1992), 63.

23. The General Board, 15.

24. *Book of Discipline*, 66, 69.

25. *Book of Discipline*, 63.

26. *Book of Discipline*, 59.

27. The General Board, 7–8.

28. *Microsoft Encarta*, 1.

29. *Book of Discipline*, 69.

30. The General Board, 9–10.

31. *Book of Discipline*, 59.

32. The General Board, 15–16, 23.

33. *Book of Discipline*, 61.

34. *Book of Discipline*, 62.

35. *Book of Discipline*, 58–59.

36. The General Board, 14.

37. "Meet the United Pentecostal Church," 1997. Available from World Wide Web site @ http://www.upci.org; INTERNET, 1.

38. "Meet the United Pentecostal Church," 2.

39. "Meet the United Pentecostal Church," 2.

40. "Apostolic Doctrine—The New Birth, The Oneness of the Godhead," 1997. Available from World Wide Web site @ http://www.upci.org; INTERNET, 2.

41. "Meet the United Pentecostal Church," 2.

42. "Meet the United Pentecostal Church," 1.

43. "Meet the United Pentecostal Church," 1.

44. "A Handbook of Basic Doctrines," 1997. Available from World Wide Web site @ http://www.upci.org; INTERNET, 2.

45. "Apostolic Doctrine—Speaking in Tongues," 1997. Available from World Wide Web site @ http://www.upci.org; INTERNET, 1.

46. "Meet the United Pentecostal Church," 1.

Notes to Pages 301–305

1. Office of the General Secretary, The Wesleyan Church, *A History of The Wesleyan Church* (n.p., 1993), 3–12.

2. The Wesleyan Church, *Standing Firm: The Wesleyan Church Speaks on Contemporary Issues* (Wesleyan Publishing House, 1996), 28.

3. The Wesleyan Church, *This We Believe* (Wesleyan Publishing House, 1996), 10.

4 Wesleyan Church, *Standing Firm*, 31.

5. Wesleyan Church, *This We Believe*, 11.

6. Wesleyan Church, *This We Believe*, 11.

7. Wesleyan Church, *This We Believe*, 4.

8. Wesleyan Church, *This We Believe*, 4.

9. Wesleyan Church, *Standing Firm*, 21–23.

10. Wesleyan Church, *This We Believe*, 12.

11. Wesleyan Church, *Standing Firm*, 37.

12. Wesleyan Church, *This We Believe*, 4–5.

13. Wesleyan Church, *This We Believe*, 20–21.

14. Wesleyan Church, *This We Believe*, 8.

15. Wesleyan Church, *This We Believe*, 9, 15.

16. Wesleyan Church, *This We Believe*, 3.

17. "What is the WELS," 1997. Available from World Wide Web site @ http://www.wels.net; INTERNET, 1.

18. Harold A. Essmann, *What the Bible and Lutherans Teach* (WELS-BWM, 1996), 29.

19. Essmann, 21.

20. Essmann, 10, 23–24.

21. "This We Believe: IX. Jesus' Return and the Judgment," 1997. Available from World Wide Web site @ http://www.wels.net; INTERNET, 1.

22. Essmann, 22.

23. Essmann, 6.

24. Essmann, 10.

25. Essmann, 30.

26. Essmann, 23–24.

27. Essmann, 2.

28. Essmann, 16.

29. Essmann, 3.